the Best of the Best

MUTUAL FUNDS & BLUE-CHIP STOCKS for CANADIANS

2001

Wilfred Vos / Bruce McDougall

Prentice Hall Canada

A Pearson Company

Toronto

Canadian Cataloguing in Publication Data

Vos, Wilfred, 1972-
    The best of the best mutual funds & blue-chip stocks

Annual.
[1999]-
Tables.
Issues for 2000-   have title: Best of the best mutual funds & blue chip stocks for Canadians
ISSN 1490-8433
ISBN 0-13-089451-6 (2001)

1. Mutual funds-Canada. 2. Blue-chip stocks-Canada. 3. Investments-Canada. I. Title. II. Title: Mutual funds & blue chip stocks. III. Title: Mutual funds & blue chip stocks for Canadians.

HG5154.5.V67   332.63'27   C99-901063-8

ISBN 0-13-089451-6 (2001)

Editorial Director, Trade Division: Andrea Crozier
Acquisitions Editor: Andrea Crozier
Copy Editor: Catharine Haggert
Production Editor: Lori McLellan
Art Direction: Mary Opper
Cover Design: Sarah Battersby
Production Manager: Kathrine Pummell
Page Layout: B.J. Weckerle

1 2 3 4 5 WC 04 03 02 01 00

Printed and bound in Canada.

This publication contains the opinions and ideas of its authors and is designed to provide useful advice in regard to the subject matter covered. The authors and publisher are not engaged in rendering legal, accounting, or other professional services in this publication. This publication is not intended to provide a basis for action in particular circumstances without consideration by a competent professional. The authors, their employees and the publisher expressly disclaim any responsibility for any liability, loss, or risk, personal or otherwise, which is incurred as a consequence, directly or indirectly, of the use and application of any of the contents of this book.

Visit the Prentice Hall Canada Web site! Send us your comments, browse our catalogues, and more. www.phcanada.com.

Prentice
Hall
Canada

A Pearson Company

To our daughter, the most courageous little girl in the world,
Taylor Nicole.

Love, Daddy
W.V.

To Susan

B. McD.

The royalties of this book will be donated to the Canadian Diabetes Association
on behalf of Taylor.

For more information regarding diabetes, contact 1-800-BANTING
www.diabetes.ca

the Best of the Best

of the Best

MUTUAL FUNDS & BLUE-CHIP STOCKS for CANADIANS

2001

Contents

Preface

With over 3,000 different mutual funds, it's no wonder that investors may feel intimidated by the number of available choices. Many investors also have difficulty understanding the underlying characteristics of their investments. What is the upside potential of a fund? What are the risks involved?

At the other end of the spectrum, an increasing number of investors have decided to invest directly in stocks, doing for themselves what they've formerly left to a mutual-fund manager: select and invest in a blue-chip company that will enhance their net worth.

For these reasons, we decided to produce an expanded version of our easy-to-read but comprehensive guide to investing in Canada. It's still called *The Best of the Best: Mutual Funds and Blue-Chip Stocks for Canadians*. And we still believe that this book is truly unique and that it will enable you to make better and more informed investment decisions.

Acknowledgements

First I would like to thank Bruce McDougall, whose co-authorship has made a material difference. Bruce, your help is greatly appreciated. Thank you!

I would also like to take this opportunity to thank the many people who have helped bring this book to fruition for its third year.

I would also like to thank Tim McGowan at Datastream, who provided the historical stock price information for the stock charts. Without Tim's help we would not be able to provide any information on the stocks' performance in our stock ATP charts. Datastream International, Inc. is a unit of Primark Corporation's Financial Information Division. Primark is a global information services company that collects, integrates, and delivers financial, economic, and market research information for financial, corporate, and government decision-makers around the globe. Visit **www.primark.com**.

I would also like to thank all the unnamed individuals at all the mutual fund companies and Canadian corporations who helped me gather data on the underlying investments.

Thank you to all the people at Prentice Hall, especially Andrea Crozier, Michael Kelley, Lori McLellan, and Martin Litkowski, just to name a few. I would also like to thank Cat Haggert for her valuable contribution.

To my family, friends, and colleagues, thank you for your patience and understanding. And I thank God for giving me the ability and skill to complete this project.

Wilfred Vos

Introduction

This is the third edition of *The Best of the Best: Mutual Funds & Blue-Chip Stocks for Canadians*. With this edition, we continued to meet our initial objective: to publish value-added information from which investors can profit.

Two years ago there were more than 2000 mutual funds. Today there are more than 3000, and investors need a way to reduce the list to a more manageable number. Our solution was to write this book, which is intended to provide investors with 100, not 3000, different investment options. Our selections should provide investors with higher returns and less risk. In this book, you'll find lots of good investment ideas, whether you want conservative or highly aggressive investments, investments that provide income and stability, or investments that provide huge upside potential.

Before we unveil all our investment opinions in the following 250 pages, let's take a moment to review the opinions and recommendations of last year's book. Last year, the mutual-fund section contained 100 mutual funds, including 30 funds to watch. The previous year turned out to be a great one for capital markets, and in turn, for most of the investments in the book. The average fund posted a gain of 25 per cent. Of the 100 mutual funds we recommended, 49 generated first-quartile performance. Funds that fell into the first quartile outperformed 75 per cent of similar funds. Thirteen of the funds that we recommended generated second-quartile performance, outperforming 50 per cent of similar funds but underperforming 25 per cent of similar funds. What an excellent result! Twenty-two of the funds that we recommended generated third-quartile performance, where they outperformed 25 per cent of similar funds but underperformed 50 per cent. Finally, 16 of the funds that we recommended generated fourth-quartile performance, underperforming 75 per cent of similar funds.

In this year's edition, we've again included 100 mutual funds, but we've given a full two-page write-up to only 60, primarily because we increased the number of stocks we covered and didn't have enough space in the book to cover all of the mutual funds. Of the total of 100 funds, 35 are new. There are many reasons why we did not include some of the funds from last year's edition in this year's. They include:

- a portfolio manager left the fund to join another firm or retire;
- the investment strategy of the fund changed;
- we identified a better mutual fund;
- a material piece of information came to our attention;
- performance declined and we didn't know why;
- we continue to change and develop our process; and
- we learn from our mistakes.

In the stock section of this book, we have increased the number of stocks to 30 from 20. Like the mutual funds, the stocks generated some very impressive results over the last year. The Toronto Stock Exchange 300 Index generated a return of 47.4 per cent, but a portfolio of blue-chip stocks recommended in last year's book generated a gain in excess of 60 per cent higher than the index (limiting the Nortel Networks investment to 15 per cent).

Here are the stocks that we included in last year's book with their respective one-year returns:

COMPANY	ONE-YEAR RETURN
Abitibi-Consolidated	-18.6%
Barrick Gold	-5.8%
Alcan Aluminum	0.01%
ATI Technologies	-47.6%
Bombardier	78.7%
BCE*	102.0%
Canadian National Railway	-12.8%
Canadian Tire	-48.1%
Loblaw	13.5%
Magna International	-16.6%
Nortel Networks	224.0%
Power Corporation of Canada	7.8%
Rogers Communications	77.4%
Royal Bank of Canada	16.5%
Suncor Energy	13.3%
Toronto-Dominion Bank	7.9%
Thomson	13.8%
TransCanada Pipelines	-45.5%
Trizec Hahn	-11.4%
Seagram Company	18.6%

(*adjusted for the butterfly restructuring of Nortel)

Nortel Networks was clearly the big winner, but it was also a bigger weight in the index. With 10 new names, investors will have lots of interesting companies to choose from.

The following five companies were included in the prior edition but not in this one: Abitibi-Consolidated wasn't included this year because the paper and forest industry has encountered some difficult times. ATI Technologies provides a lot of upside and downside volatility, and you could have either made or lost a bundle on this stock during the year. The worst is likely over, but it still ended down on the year. Canadian Tire is looking for a new leader, TransCanada Pipelines disappointed, and Seagram was purchased.

Next Steps

There are three important steps to follow in achieving your investment goals. First, you need to develop an investment plan. Second, you have to diversify your investment portfolio. And third, you have to take the necessary time to allow your plan to work. More often than not, investors who jump from one fast-rising investment to another meet with disappointment.

The key to any investment plan is not selecting the particular investment that's right for your personal needs, but rather determining which investments in combination can help you to achieve your investment objectives. In other words, the key is diversification.

Diversification allows your portfolio to add value over the short and long term. Some investments will appreciate and some will depreciate in value, but your portfolio as a whole, properly diversified, will grow over time to meet your investment objectives. (We'll discuss this in more detail in the section on portfolio building, where you'll also find a summary of the performance of various portfolios.)

It's also critical to give your investments time to grow. From year to year your investment choices will underperform or outperform similar funds. In some years, the difference between a top-performing fund and an underperforming fund may seem significant. Yet over time the difference becomes less pronounced.

Table 1 illustrates this concept. During the previous year the top-performing balanced fund earned a return of 65.7 per cent, and an underperforming balanced fund posted a gain of 0.5 per cent. The difference between the two funds was 65.2 per cent. However, during the previous 10 years, the difference between the funds diminishes to only 8.5 per cent. In the long term, similar funds tend to post similar returns, and the variance between their performance can frequently be attributed to one exceptional year.

TABLE 1

	1 year	10 years
High	65.7%	16.2%
Low	0.5%	7.7%
Difference	65.2%	8.5%

Investors who jump from an underperforming fund to a top-performing fund may actually do themselves more harm than good. The key to investment success is to develop a good investment plan and stick to it. Many investors who aim to buy low and sell high end up buying high and selling low. The result is lower returns.

In Canada over the past 10 years, the best-performing funds have generated returns in excess of 20 per cent per year. But after closely reviewing cash flowing in and out of these funds, we determined that investors were not so fortunate. The difference can be attributed to timing. Most investors do not invest in the same mutual fund for 10 years; they tend to invest in flavour-of-the-month funds, jumping from one fast-rising investment to another and missing out on a large portion of the gains. However, funds often post big gains in very short periods, so missing 2, 3, or 4 of the best days or months can have a significant impact on the performance of a particular investment.

One Canadian mutual fund, for example, has a 10-year annualized rate of return of 21.1 per cent, but investors who failed to invest during the best 5 months during the previous 10 years earned a return of only 10.7 per cent. Thus, investors who missed the 5 best months or who did not invest during 4 per cent of the months during the last 10 years missed out on 50 per cent of the gains.

Another important step is to ensure that your investment portfolio does not appear at the bottom end of the range after 10 years. You can ensure that this doesn't happen by diversifying your investments over several investment categories, such as cash, bonds, and various equity or stock investments.

Table 2 illustrates the long-term performance of several optimal portfolios that have added value through proper diversification. (We feature these portfolios in the portfolio-building section of the book.) It shows how you can generate a very good rate of return over the long term without taking excessive risks by using a well-diversified portfolio of mutual funds. As you can see, the Moderate portfolio generates the same long-term return, after fees, as a balanced index, and with less risk. It pays to get properly diversified before you select individual investments for your portfolio.

TABLE 2

Portfolio Name	1 year	3 years	5 years	10 years
Conservative	8.3%	6.5%	7.8%	8.3%
Moderate	11.5%	9.1%	11.3%	10.6%
Aggressive	12.8%	10.2%	12.3%	11.1%
Very Aggressive	15.0%	11.7%	13.7%	11.7%

Mutual funds are a value-added investment for investors; that is, they allow investors to earn a higher rate of return than traditional investments, at a given level of risk. However, investors still have difficulty in selecting the investments that are right for them.

In the past, sophisticated investors have relied on such exotic statistical tools as time-weighted rates of return (the returns investors see in newspapers), standard deviation (a risk measure), Beta, Sharpe ratio, coefficient variation, variance, and Alpha (to name just a few) to measure the quality of an investment. Not all of these measures provide useful information, and some can actually mislead an investor.

Alternatively, many investors take a flavour-of-the-month approach to selecting mutual funds. Like fair-weather baseball fans, who go to the park only when the home team starts winning, these investors buy mutual funds only when they start to perform well. In fact, when we compare sales with performance of a mutual fund, we find that funds that perform well generate more sales, on average, than funds that do not perform well over a given period. Unfortunately, when funds falter, these investors walk away from the ball game instead of waiting patiently or even acquiring more shares in the fund at a temporarily low price.

A 1997 analysis of investor behaviour by Dalbar Financial Services concluded that most mutual-fund investors who do not invest for the long term do not fully benefit from the upside potential of mutual funds. In this book, we clearly identify investments with long-term growth potential and show how you can utilize these investments for your own financial gain.

When we calculate the weighted-average rate of return for the basket of mutual funds within our study using our evaluation techniques, we conclude that investors can do better using these techniques than they could using the traditional tools to select a mutual fund. It is very important to build a diversified portfolio to achieve your investment goals. *Proper diversification is far more important than the individual investments you select.* Unfortunately, this message hasn't reached most investors. Canadians still invest more money in first-quartile funds than in funds from the other three quartiles combined, even though historical quartile performance indicates an inverse relationship between historical and future performance.

That's not to say information about a fund's historical performance isn't useful. You can use it to inform yourself about the risk and return characteristics associated with an investment and how to diversify your portfolio to minimize such risks. A diversified portfolio that incurs an acceptable level of risk will eventually meet your return requirements, because you'll stick to your plan and not bail out before you reach your objectives.

The information we provide in *The Best of the Best* on a particular investment is both thorough and easy to read. All mutual funds included in the book have been analyzed using the All Time Periods (ATP) methodology. Each fund receives a Vos Value Rating (VVR), which considers 14 different factors—seven related to reward and seven related to risk—when comparing one fund to another. A summary of each mutual fund includes a fund profile and sections on performance and risk. We also include information on a mutual fund's future prospects, and you can evaluate a fund's historical performance using an easy-to-read ATP chart.

For investors seeking more diversification by investing internationally, the chart indicates how much of a fund is invested outside Canada. The ATP chart also provides the best, average, and worst rates of return for a fund, ending in June 2000. You can update this information yourself and quickly assess the upside and downside potential for each fund over different periods. You can see how often the fund made or lost money and assess the fund's downside risk.

The relative performance graph (Quartile Ranking) allows you to assess a fund's performance relative to similar funds over any 12-month period. With the Rolling 12-Month Period graph, you can assess the performance of a fund from one year to the next. Some mutual funds perform well consistently; while others perform well sporadically. The ATP chart highlights the performance of a fund in an easy-to-read format for quick reference.

You can use the Vos Value Rating to help you move in the right direction while building your portfolio. Table 3 illustrates the performance of funds receiving each of the five Vos Value Ratings for reward during the past 10 years (the results assume annual rebalancing each June).

TABLE 3

Portfolio rating	1 year	3 years	5 years	10 years
Five-star	13.26%	9.63%	12.56%	11.06%
Four-star	17.77%	9.44%	11.69%	10.91%
Three-star	15.39%	8.50%	11.08%	10.30%
Two-star	13.31%	7.64%	10.35%	9.51%
One-star	9.59%	7.13%	10.08%	9.61%

Table 3 illustrates that, over the long term, the average five-star Canadian balanced fund outperformed the average four-star fund; the average four-star fund outperformed the average three-star fund, and so on. Of course, if you manipulate data with enough determination you can make it confess to anything. But no one, not even us, can predict future performance with any certainty. We can say, however, that active investment management does add value over the long term.

During the previous 10 years a balanced index outperformed the majority of Canadian balanced mutual funds with a 10-year track record (without adjusting for fees). At first glance, this might encourage you to invest in a balanced index fund. But you should also note that a balanced index exhibited more risk than almost all the Canadian balanced mutual funds. By investing in one of these funds instead of an index fund, you can actually reduce risk and still earn a very respectable rate of return, especially on a risk-adjusted basis.

Finally, even if you don't buy individual equities, the section on stocks will help you to understand your mutual fund investments better. We've provided information on 30 large Canadian corporations from a variety of sectors, including each company's background, financial health, and historical stock performance. These companies shape and change the country we live in. They include retailing giant Sears Canada, fibre optics and networking king Nortel Networks, and TD, Canada's largest chartered bank, which has aggressively pursued electronic distribution channels.

We hope that you enjoy this book and put it to good use. May every investment be a successful one! Check out our Web site at **www.bestofbaystreet.com**.

Part A

Mutual Funds

Introduction to Mutual Funds

Mutual funds offer investors many benefits, such as diversification, professional management, low initial investments, and relatively high returns. As investors embrace these benefits, the mutual fund industry has expanded steadily while proceeding through the economic growth of the 1990s and into the new millennium. Interest rates have fallen and governments have wrestled inflation into submission, at least for the present time. The interest earned on investments such as guaranteed investment certificates (GICs), bonds, and term deposits is adequate but low; the only investments that promise higher returns are equities. But all equities are not created equal, and the average investor isn't always prepared or equipped to distinguish one stock from another. Leaving the selection of stocks and other investments to professional money managers, but still seeking the higher returns promised by equities, bonds, and treasury bills, investors have turned to mutual funds.

In addition to higher returns, mutual funds offer a number of potential advantages over other types of investment:

- Mutual funds are run by professional investment managers.
- Mutual funds reduce volatility and temper risk by spreading investments over a diversified portfolio.
- The average investor, making even a small contribution, gains direct access to a broad range of investments.
- An investor can also choose from a multitude of funds, which offer various risk and reward characteristics to meet a specific investment objective.
- Mutual funds can be easily bought and sold.

On the other side of the coin, mutual funds bring a few disadvantages:

- The fees charged by fund managers reduce a fund's total return, although these fees are usually reasonable.
- The individual investor has no influence on the specific investments selected by a fund manager.
- One investment held in a fund may perform well, but another may perform poorly, so the investor never enjoys the full benefit of a good investment. (Of course, the mutual-fund investor never suffers the full impact of a single bad investment, either.)
- Mutual funds are not guaranteed, and investors can lose money if they buy when the fund price is high and sell when it is low.

Probably the most attractive aspect of a mutual fund is the opportunity it affords the average investor to diversify his or her investment portfolio. Few individuals can afford to buy even one share of each of 100 companies. As investors in a mutual fund, however, people can reap the benefits of diversification while sharing the costs. The mutual fund pools an individual's money together with money from many other investors. With a pool of money at hand, the mutual fund manager can invest in a broad range of stocks, bonds, or other instruments.

In fact, diversification is one of the cardinal investment strategies for limiting stock-market risk. If you buy just one stock, such as IBM, and it goes down—or way down, as IBM did in the early 1990s—you'll lose money. If you buy shares in 100 companies, there's a good chance that some of the stocks in the portfolio will lose money, while the others will make money. At the end of the day, week, month, quarter, or year, a single stock may have gone up or down. But the diversified portfolio of a well-managed mutual fund will usually make a profit. That's the power of diversification. And that's what you get with a mutual fund.

In the 1990s, mutual funds have offered investors a chance to reap some of the benefits of an expanding economy without incurring excessive risk. In fact, mutual funds have historically been low-risk investments, although some are extremely volatile. Even if a mutual fund invests in risky securities—gold-mining shares, for example, whose value may rise and fall considerably—the fund itself remains stable. In fact, since the first open-end mutual fund was introduced in Canada in 1932, no one has ever lost money as a result of a fund company going out of business.

Canadians have now invested more than $420 billion in mutual funds, and there are more than 3,100 funds currently operating in Canada. Not only have more people than ever invested in mutual funds, but they also have more mutual-fund products and investment alternatives to choose from.

In addition, each year the mutual fund industry continues to offer investors new and innovative mutual funds based on a new idea or investment technique. Segregated and protected funds, for example, guarantee the individual's original investment. More recently, mutual funds have been developed that enable individuals to invest globally while retaining their eligibility for retirement savings plans (RSPs). Many of these new RSP mutual funds attempt to duplicate the performance of top-performing U.S., global, or international mutual funds. They provide a way for investors to put more of their pension savings to work in foreign markets, above the 25 per cent limit currently imposed by the federal government (foreign content will increase to 30 per cent in 2001). All these developments provide investors with more choice while improving their risk-and-reward profile.

Despite the proliferation of funds, only a relative handful of mutual funds attract most of the money. Of the total amount invested in Canadian mutual funds, approximately half has been placed with just 80 funds. The rest is divided among the remaining 3,020.

There are a number of reasons why the largest funds attract the most investors. Even seasoned investors are cautious. Understandably, they don't want to put their money into a risky investment. They assume that other investors know at least as much as they do, and they don't feel confident enough to defy conventional wisdom. If one mutual fund attracts the lion's share of investments, then it must be doing something right, and that's the fund that most conventional investors will choose.

In addition, investors base their decisions on a variety of factors, from catchy marketing to the recommendations of their next-door neighbour or associates at work. Their decisions are not necessarily wrong, but they could make better and more informed decisions if they relied on other sources of advice.

Our research shows that most Canadians could benefit from applying more rigorous criteria to their investment decisions. That's why we've developed the All Time Periods (ATP) methodology. (The ATP methodology is explained in the second chapter in this book.)

Buying and selling mutual funds

This book will help you to identify some of the better-performing funds available in Canada. Once you've identified them, you should then determine your investment objectives and tolerance for risk. After selecting the funds that correspond to your objective and risk factors, you should then gather as much information about these funds as you can.

You can find a lot of information in daily newspapers, magazines, and business journals. You can find more information using the World Wide Web. Finally, you should obtain prospectuses for funds of interest to you.

The prospectus describes a mutual fund's investment objectives, the fees that it charges, and the risks associated with purchasing the mutual fund. The prospectus also includes the fund's most recent financial statements. You can order a copy of a fund's prospectus directly from the mutual fund company. You may also get a copy from a financial advisor.

Investing in a mutual fund

You can buy and sell mutual funds through a number of channels, including:

- **Financial planners:** Financial planners cannot sell all mutual funds. Although they might be able to sell a variety of mutual funds, a planner may work for just one particular fund company and restrict recommendations to that company's funds. You should ask at the outset about the limitations on a planner's access to funds.

- **Stockbrokers:** Employed by investment dealers, stockbrokers sell a wide range of mutual funds. They usually charge a commission for each transaction they conduct on your behalf. They can provide you with a wealth of information and guidance on investing.

- **Discount brokers:** These organizations charge lower fees than conventional stockbrokers, but provide little or no guidance or information about particular investments.

- **Banks, trust companies, credit unions, and caisses populaires:** Your local financial institution sells a variety of mutual funds, including its own.

- **Insurance salespersons:** Your insurance representative usually sells mutual funds on behalf of his or her employer.

- **Buying direct:** Many mutual fund companies sell directly to the public. These companies are typically no-load companies.

You can sell your mutual fund investments within two or three business days through the outlet where you purchased them. You can sell your entire investment, or you can sell units in smaller amounts. One popular method is to redeem your units through regular withdrawal plans that allow weekly, monthly, or quarterly withdrawals.

Of course, nothing is free in the world of investing. Mutual fund companies make money on your investment, in at least one of several ways. First, many mutual fund companies charge a sales commission, either when investors purchase shares or when investors sell shares in the fund. These are called load funds. A mutual fund manager also receives a fee for managing the fund and for supervising its day-to-day administration and operations. This is called a management fee, which is deducted from the fund's total income. The management fee can range from 0.2 per cent to 3 per cent of the fund's income. These fees are explained in the fund's annual report.

Load, no-load, and so on

Fund companies commonly charge a commission on the shares they sell. This commission is also called a load. It compensates the fund company, financial planner, or stockbroker for providing you with a service.

Today, more than ever, competition among mutual funds is fierce. Every fund company wants you to invest your money with it. Fund companies have come up with innovative products and innovative ways of charging you for them, so you can get started at the lowest possible cost. These include:

- **Front-end-load funds:** If you choose a front-end-load fund, you pay a commission of 2 per cent to 9 per cent every time you buy shares.

- **Back-end-load funds:** With a back-end-load fund, your entire initial investment goes into the mutual fund. You pay no direct sales commission up front. But you have to leave your money in the fund for a minimum period; otherwise you have to pay a commission when you remove it, called a back-end load. The typical back-end-load fund charges a 6 per cent commission in the first year, based on the value of your portfolio when you sell your shares, 5 per cent in the second year, 4 per cent after three years, and so on. Long-term investors usually keep their money in a fund for at least five years.

- **No-load fund:** With no-load funds, you don't have to pay a commission to buy or sell your shares.

However, all mutual funds, including no-loads, pay their investment advisory team an annual management fee of between 0.2 per cent and 3 per cent of the fund's assets. This compensates them for making all the fund's investment decisions. Mutual funds also have to pay operating expenses. These additional charges are deducted from the assets in the fund's portfolio and are explained in the fund's prospectus.

Although many investors decide to develop their own investment strategies and execute their own buying and selling decisions, a good advisor can provide support and guidance to investors who need such reassurance. If you are looking for a good discount broker, you should read the following section. If you are looking for a good financial planner, skip the following section and go to the one after it.

Finding a discount broker

According to the Toronto consulting firm Investor Economics Inc., Canadians have invested more than $62 billion in discount brokerage accounts. This do-it-yourself crowd is gaining converts on a daily basis, and many discount brokerage firms are having difficulty dealing with the increased trading volume. At some discount brokerage houses, clients wait during some peak periods for up to an hour before they can speak with a representative. While these companies are continuing to train new staff, adapting to this new popularity takes time.

Last year, *Canadian Business* magazine conducted a review of the major discount brokerage houses and rated their services. Here is a summary of their results:

FIRM	CANADIAN BUSINESS RATING
TD Waterhouse	A–
Royal Bank Action Direct	B+
Bank of Montreal InvestorLine	B+
Charles Schwab Canada	B
E*Trade Canada	C+
HSBC InvestDirect	C
CIBC Investor's Edge	C
Sun Life Securities	C–
National Bank InvesTel	D+
Scotia Discount Brokerage	D

Firms were rated on cost, online trading availability, touch-tone trading, product selection, mutual funds, response time, user experience, and extra services available. Interestingly, while overall ratings varied widely, most of these discount firms charged the same cost per trade. If you invested $10,000 in an average-priced stock, most firms would charge you between $25 and $30—a big difference from a full-service broker, who would charge at least $100. To connect with these firms contact:

FIRM	INTERNET ADDRESS	TELEPHONE
TD Waterhouse	www.tdwaterhouse.ca	1-800-659-7553
Royal Bank Action Direct	www.actiondirect.com	1-800-ROYAL83
Bank of Montreal InvestorLine	www.investorline.com	1-800-387-7800
Charles Schwab Canada	www.schwabcanada.com	1-888-597-9999
E*Trade Canada	www.canada.etrade.com	1-888-TRADE88
HSBC InvestDirect	www.hsbcinvestdirect.com	1-800-398-1180
CIBC Investor's Edge	www.cibc.com	1-800-567-3343
Sun Life Securities	www.sunsecurities.com	1-800-835-0812
National Bank InvesTel	www.investnet.com	1-800-363-3511
Scotia Discount Brokerage	www.sdbi.com	1-877-536-7493

Finding a financial planner

During the past decade the financial planning industry has earned a reputation as a product-based industry: individuals who called themselves financial planners spent little time planning and a lot of time pushing a product to investors. Financial planners were not solely to blame. The mutual fund industry was growing at an annual rate of 30 per cent per year, and investors were demanding product and product information fast. Investors judged their financial planner's performance based on his or her investment advice, not on the implementation of a comprehensive financial plan. Yet a comprehensive financial plan is actually more important than the investments that you make. Therefore you should find a good planner who can develop a comprehensive financial plan and ensure that you meet your financial objectives.

Recently the financial planning industry has made several dramatic changes. The industry has transformed itself into a profession that provides total wealth management, which includes comprehensive planning and advice services. Financial planners now focus less on investment advice and more on the big picture to improve a client's current financial well-being and achieve his or her long-term financial objectives.

In short, a good financial planner can make or save you hundreds or thousands of dollars a year. However, most investors find it difficult to find a good financial planner, and sometimes they find out that the financial planner they're dealing with isn't right for them only after it's too late. So what should investors look for in a good financial planner?

First, don't hire the first person you talk to. You may choose the person in the end, but don't make a decision before talking with at least a couple of other individuals. This is the most important thing that you can do. To get such a list of potential candidates, you can ask for referrals from friends and relatives. You can also talk to a mutual fund company, your local bank or credit union, insurance agent, attorney, or tax preparer.

You should prepare a list of interview questions, much as you would to interview a potential employee, doctor, or nanny. You can also ask your financial planner for client referrals, and you should follow up with these past or current clients. You want to see if the candidate has a good personal fit with your own character, and you also want to assess whether the individual is up to the job. Has the person been in the industry for more than a couple of months, for example? Most importantly, does the individual have the qualifications to do the job right?

Anyone can call himself a financial planner, so make sure the person has an actual designation behind him. The standard is a CFP (Certified Financial Planner), but there is also the RFP (Registered Financial Planner), granted by the Canadian Association of Financial Planners, the CFC (Chartered Financial Consultant), and the CIM (Canadian Investment Manager). These are just a few, and there are also other designations that relate to investment management or insurance.

In short, make sure the planner you work with understands investments, estate planning, and tax planning. Don't expect a fortune teller who can propel you into instant riches. Instead, expect a competent individual who can help you achieve your financial goals by developing a comprehensive financial plan.

Open-end and closed-end funds

Most mutual funds currently traded in Canada are open-end. If a fund is open-end, there's no limit on the number of shares it can issue. The mutual fund company can always sell you more shares, at the current net asset value (NAV), or buy back the shares that you hold. (We'll explain NAV in more detail in the next section, when we discuss how to evaluate your portfolio.) The most popular mutual funds, listed in the mutual-fund section of your daily newspaper, are open-end, such as those offered by AGF, CIBC, Fidelity, Mackenzie, Trimark, Talvest, Royal Bank, and so forth.

Although we don't deal with them in this book, a few closed-end mutual funds operate in Canada as well. These funds issue a limited number of shares when they're first set up. Once they sell all the shares and there are none left to sell, the fund becomes closed. At that point, the fund stops issuing new shares, and the mutual fund company will no longer redeem your shares. Instead, you have to trade your shares in the closed-end fund on a stock exchange, just like shares in other public companies. The price of your shares will fluctuate. Sometimes the price per share will be higher than the NAV—commanding a premium. Sometimes it will be lower-offering a discount.

Monitoring your mutual funds

Fund companies issue shares in return for your investment. The price of a mutual fund's shares varies from day to day. Some days it's a little higher; other days it's a little lower. Over the long term, however, the share price usually goes up. Some prices go up more than others and some go down more than others.

You can determine the value of your mutual-fund holdings by examining the net asset value (NAV) of each fund in your portfolio. You calculate the NAV by dividing the mutual fund's total net assets by the total number of shares outstanding. (This information is included in the daily investment tables published in newspapers.) The resulting figure is the price that you have to pay for one share in the mutual fund. The NAV fluctuates daily. Some days it may be up 5 cents; other days it may be down 10 cents. That's called volatility. Some funds will fluctuate more than others. Small fluctuations indicate a fund has low risk and high fluctuations indicate a fund with high risk.

The share price for an individual company fluctuates in relation to the company's future prospects. When prospects are good, there are more buyers than sellers, and the share price rises. When prospects are bad, there are more sellers than buyers, and the share price falls. When the stocks that make up the mutual fund rise in price, so too will the mutual fund's share price. When the stock prices fall, so will the fund's share price.

Mutual Fund Performance Measurement

Using the All Time Periods (ATP) methodology, investors can make decisions based on something more substantial than a whim, a hunch, marketing hype, or misleading data. In preparing this book, for example, we've used the ATP methodology to select 100 of the best-performing funds in Canada. They're not the only funds available, and they may not perform better than all the other funds at all times. But we know from our research that investors can invest in these funds with confidence that their wealth will grow over time at a faster rate than it would if they had selected a fixed-income investment such as a GIC. Unfortunately, we prefer to rate only funds that have at least a three-year track record, but the most important factor is the fund's future potential.

Wilfred Vos developed the ATP methodology while he was still in university. Vos devised a graphical depiction of risk that would help the average investor understand how mutual funds perform. Unlike other methods of evaluating performance, the ATP methodology would be transparent and readily accessible. The investor would not have to conduct any complex calculations, apply obscure formulae, or take a fund's marketing campaign at face value to reach a conclusion about the fund. All the investor had to do was look at a graph that presented the fund's performance over the course of its entire existence and interpret its message. With some refinements, Vos made it even easier for an investor to distinguish one fund's performance from another's, to evaluate the risks involved in a particular fund, and to make an investment decision based on a fund's long-term potential performance.

Vos continued refining the ATP methodology to provide even more benefits to investors. For the last three years, he has applied it to selecting and evaluating funds for Gordon Pape, whose annual *Buyer's Guide to Mutual Funds* relies on the ATP methodology for its recommendations. *The Best of the Best* takes the methodology one step further, enabling investors to see for themselves some of the underlying data without overwhelming the reader with background information and calculations. Although readers see only the conclusions drawn from the methodology, they can feel confident that ATP is a unique and proven approach to selecting the best-performing mutual funds on the market. Investors can use the information in this book to confirm or adjust their own evaluations, confident that it is based on all the available data about a particular mutual fund.

In the course of his research, Vos proved categorically that diversification and time are an investor's two most powerful allies. Both work to reduce risk. Diversification works as a benefit by spreading an investor's money over a number of investments whose performance is affected by different factors at different times. Time works to an investor's benefit because the longer an investor leaves his or her money in a particular fund and the more regularly an investment is made, the better the chances of harvesting a superior return.

To reap the benefits of time in their portfolios, investors do not have to time the market or apply any other theory to their investment approach. All they have to do is invest regularly in good mutual funds such as the ones we've selected in this book.

Time: the investor's ally

The most important element in investing is time in the market not timing the market. Consider the following scenario. An investor decides to invest $1,000 per calendar year, and he has determined three options:

Invest at the yearly high.

Invest at the yearly low.

Invest 12 times a year (monthly).

If the investor is a perfect market timer, she will invest the yearly contribution at the yearly low; if she was the worst market timer she will make an annual contribution at the yearly high. Assume, for example, that, in January 1962, instead of timing the market perfectly, she initiated a systematic plan by investing $83.33 per month in the stock market through a pension plan, RRSP, or other investment plan. The table below illustrates the growth of a portfolio invested in the TSE 300 from January 1962 to June 2000.

As of June 2000, if she made her annual contributions at the market low she would have had a portfolio valued at $715,268; if she had made her contribution at the market high she would have a portfolio valued at $605,573. If she had decided to invest monthly she would have had a portfolio valued at $666,735. Finally, if she had put all her money in treasury bills (T-bills) she would have generated a portfolio valued at $246,945, significantly less than the portfolio of a poor market timer. Thus, even an investor who has poor market-timing skills can improve performance by investing systematically in equities and holding for the long term. Systematic investing in equities over time brings superior results to any fixed-income investment held over the same period.

MARKET TIMING STRATEGIES COMPARED

Strategy	Return
T-bills	$246,945
Market high	$605,573
Monthly plan	$666,735
Market low	$715,268

Investors who consider risk an enemy should find an ally in time. Thus, time in the market is more important than timing the market. Increase your time horizon, invest systematically, don't worry about timing stock markets, and you should outperform T-bills. Develop a plan, implement it, and let the benefits of investing in mutual funds come to fruition.

An investor will certainly benefit from choosing the best-performing funds, but such choices are not necessary to obtaining superior performance. An investor can obtain superior returns simply by getting onto a plan, diversifying his or her investments over a range of funds, and sticking to the plan over a long period.

Evaluating a mutual fund

Mutual fund investors tend to evaluate their investments by looking in the newspaper once a week or once a month to see how their selections have performed over a particular period. Based on a fund's performance over the previous month, year, or three-year period, the investor makes a decision. Usually, if the fund has performed well over the particular period, the investor will leave his or her money where it is or even invest more in the fund.

This is a good start to disciplined investing. In the process, an investor can see how funds perform and gain a better appreciation of volatility and fluctuations in performance. But the statistics published in Canadian newspapers show only a mutual fund's historical performance ending at one particular point. So a fund's performance becomes end-date sensitive. For example, a fund may show no growth at all over an 11-month period; in the twelfth month, it may suddenly gain 20 per cent in value. Based on this performance, at the end of the twelfth month the fund would show a one-month return of 20 per cent; it would also show a 20 per cent return over the previous year. The data would not necessarily indicate the inconsistency of the fund's performance.

It is very difficult to evaluate the consistent performance of a mutual fund by looking at only one period. By applying the ATP methodology, however, inconsistency and its implications become readily apparent. With the ATP methodology, an investor can distinguish the consistently good performers from the funds that perform well only sporadically.

The following table illustrates the performance of one fund for two consecutive months. For each time period, the return and quartile rating are given for the applicable month, three-month, one-year, three-year, and five-year periods. The quartile rating shows the fund's ranking compared to similar funds: 1 means the fund was in the top 25 per cent of comparable funds. As the table indicates, the performance shown for the two months can be drastically different. Thus, someone who invested in the fund during the first month would have invested in what appeared to be a good fund only to realize the following month that the fund wasn't that good after all. This is an example of end-date sensitivity.

FUND A ANALYZED IN TWO CONSECUTIVE MONTHS					
Time period	**1 month**	**3 months**	**1 year**	**3 years**	**5 years**
Fund A return in month 1	3.1%	6.7%	23.0%	13.7%	24.1%
Fund A quartile in month 1	1	2	1	1	1
Fund A return in month 2	−5.9%	−0.5%	14.0%	8.8%	22.9%
Fund A quartile in month 2	4	4	2	3	1

Unlike other methods that assess a fund's performance over an established and arbitrary period, the ATP methodology is based on a fund's performance over a variety of periods, with lengths from one month to 10 years. Using the ATP methodology, we review a fund's history, gather all the figures ever printed about its performance, and summarize them.

As the ATP methodology has gained in popularity, many fund companies and newspapers have adopted it with changes to suit their own purposes, for instance disclosing only calendar-year returns as opposed to rolling 12-month periods. This does not eliminate end-date sensitivity. Over a particular quarter, a fund's performance may place it within the first quartile of funds in the same category, but over a longer period, the fund may rank only in the second or third quartile.

The funds we have selected for this book have recorded superior performance over time. We have included funds from all categories, including equity funds, sector funds, and regional funds. As you will see from the data that accompany each fund, none performs well in every quarter or even in every year. However, the funds we've selected have performed over time better than comparable funds in the same category. If a fund has a bad period, investors can feel quite confident that, over time, this fund will turn its performance around.

Measuring risk

In developing our system of measuring risk and reward, Wilfred Vos evaluated all the current methodologies used by financial analysts. The following discussion is somewhat technical, but it provides detailed background to the development of the Vos Value Rating used in this book. (You may wish to skip to the section, "The ATP Methodology," on page 14.)

Risk analysis has been an intrinsic element of investing since the 1950s, when Harry Markowitz showed mathematically exactly how diversification reduces volatility. Risk is important. How we measure risk affects every investment decision, from evaluating a mutual fund to selecting the assets and investments for building a portfolio. Measuring risk correctly can help us make the best investment decisions.

All measures of risk attempt to show how the risk of a particular choice compares with risk levels associated with other options—in other words, how the uncertainty of returns from a particular fund compares with the uncertainty of returns from other funds. The uncertainty of returns is calculated by measuring the degree to which an investment can either outperform or underperform its average rate of return. A risky investment has a higher chance of earning a return either below or above its average rate of return; hence, investors will feel uncertain about its future performance. All single-number measurements of risk, such as standard deviation, value at risk (VAR), mean absolute deviation (MAD), downside risk, and shortfall probability attempt to summarize the historical returns and distinguish between more risky and less risky investments. "Hence all the definitions of risk will attempt to capture in a single number the essentials of risk more fully described in the complete distribution," observes Ronald N. Kahn in an article on mutual fund risk in a newsletter called *BARRA Research Insights*. "Each definition of risk will have at least some shortcomings, due to this simplification." Of these measures, standard deviation has reigned for almost four decades as the measurement of choice to measure risk.

Standard deviation is one measure of the risk level of a fund. It measures a fund's historical risk by indicating the volatility of the fund's historical monthly performance. The standard deviation of a fund is based on an analysis of the deviations of the fund's monthly returns from its average monthly return (over a specified period). The greater the monthly deviations, either above or below the average, the higher the standard deviation of the fund; the higher the fund's standard deviation, the higher the risk that the fund will not earn the average rate of return.

The standard deviation of a fund is compared with the standard deviations of other funds to determine the riskiest fund. However, standard deviation assumes that returns are symmetric; that is, that historically there have been as many monthly returns above as below the average monthly rate of return. In statistical terminology, standard deviation assumes that historical returns are accurately represented by the normal distribution, also known as the bell curve. However, the treatment of upside and downside surprises as equivalent presents a serious flaw in the theory of standard deviation as it relates to evaluating a fund's risk. Risk-averse investors appreciate that the utility from gains and losses of similar size is not equivalent. The erratic gains that are so critical to investing (especially in equities) become warning flags to investors using variance-based risk measures.

Recent work by Brian Rom introduced an excellent concept called downside risk, which recognizes that investors have diminishing marginal utility curves. Rom argues that investors are concerned about losing money; they are not concerned about risk when their investments are increasing in value. Thus, having an accurate measure of downside risk is very important. According to Rom, standard deviation relies on three assumptions:

1. Risk must be measured only in relation to the average return.

2. Above average and below average returns are equally likely to occur.

3. Returns closer to the average are more likely than extreme returns.

Unfortunately, these assumptions are not applicable to mutual fund investments, and an alternative risk measurement system has to be utilized.

Time-weighting problems

The Association for Investment Management and Research (AIMR) requires money managers to disclose the time-weighted rates of return (average annual compounded rates of return) of their portfolios. However, the fatal flaw in time-weighted rates of return is that they are end-date sensitive. A particular fund could go from the first quartile over three years down to the third quartile over three years by moving the valuation period one month ahead or back. The beauty of time-weighted rates of return is simplicity. But what they gain in simplicity they lose in accuracy. The 1-, 3-, 5-, and 10-year rates of return published by newspapers and mutual fund companies are all tied to one single ending date. Yet as we've seen, funds may register abnormal gains just prior to the evaluation date, distorting their true performance. To get a more accurate picture, we must measure the performance of a mutual fund by another method to supplement existing data.

The ATP methodology: A new approach

Given the asymmetry of investment returns, which can affect investment decisions, we need to find the best way to measure a mutual fund's performance.

The All Time Periods (ATP) methodology is a new way to evaluate and select investment options. In this book, mutual funds with very favourable ATP charts are distinguished with a high Vos Value Rating (VVR). The VVR compares a fund with others in the same narrowly defined category. Once you've selected a fund with a high VVR Rating, you can then examine its historical performance by reading its All Time Periods (ATP) chart, explained in detail in the next chapter.

The whole procedure of evaluating funds and reviewing their ATP charts is referred to as the ATP methodology. The ratings identify favourable funds; the charts plot the funds' historical performance.

The Vos Value Rating (VVR)

The Vos Value Rating (VVR) consists of three different modules. They include the VVR reward module (VVR P), which measures the performance of the mutual fund; the VVR risk module (VVR R), which measures the underlying risk of the mutual fund; and the VVR best balance between risk and reward module (VVR B), which identifies the funds that score highest on a combination of the VVR reward and the VVR risk modules (i.e., that deliver the best trade-off between risk and reward).

The funds included in this book that score the highest receive a five-star (★★★★★) rating, and the funds that score the lowest receive a one-star (★) rating. The top 20 per cent of all funds within the same VVR category receive a five-star rating; the next 20 per cent receive a four-star rating; and so on.

Reward module (VVR P)

The VVR reward module (VVR P) considers seven variables that measure the historical performance of a particular fund relative to its peers:

1. **Maximum** is the best one-month rate of return posted by the fund.

2. **First quartile** is the one-month rate of return that is lower than 25 per cent of all this fund's other monthly rates of return but higher than 75 per cent of all this fund's other monthly rates of return.

3. **Median** is the monthly rate of return that is lower than 50 per cent of all this fund's other monthly rates of return but higher than 50 per cent of all this fund's other monthly rates of return.

4. **Third quartile** is the one-month rate of return that is lower than 75 per cent of all this fund's other monthly rates of return but higher than 25 per cent of all this fund's other monthly rates of return.

5. **Average** is the average monthly rate of return posted by the fund.

6. **Average percentile rank (APR)** is the average of the fund's monthly percentile ranks when compared with other funds. For example, if the fund posted the fifteenth-highest rate of return out of 30 funds, the fund would have an APR of 0.5 or the fiftieth percentile for that particular month. After calculating each month's percentile rank, the module takes their average. Therefore, if the fund placed consistently in the first quartile month after month, it would have a very high APR. The higher the APR, the more often the fund does well from month to month compared with other funds within the mutual fund's peer group.

7. **Sum of all gains** is simply the addition of all the positive monthly rates of return. The cardinal rating increases with the number and size of positive rates of return.

After determining each variable's cardinal (numeric) rating, we give the fund an ordinal position within its peer group. The fund with the highest average ordinal position of all seven variables is the best performer. Such a fund would receive a five-star rating, since it would be in the top 20 per cent of all funds compared. This measure is more complex than a time-weighted rate of return, but it takes into consideration several measures of dispersion that influence upside potential and consistency.

Risk module (VVR R)

The VVR risk (VVR R) module considers seven variables when measuring the historical risk of a particular fund relative to its peers. It enhances the current information available and aids in the initial screening of the fund. The underlying investments made by the fund provide the best information for screening a fund, but an initial screening using the VVR R module reduces the workload.

The seven variables are:

1. **Frequency up:** the historical probability that the fund will earn a positive rate of return after one month.

2. **Minimum:** the worst one-month rate of return historically posted by the fund.

3. **Value at risk at 90 per cent:** the worst monthly loss or gain that investors can expect 10 per cent of the time. The higher the number the better, because the fund has incurred less downside risk.

4. **Sum of all losses:** the addition of all this fund's negative monthly rates of return. The sum of all losses increases with the number and size of the negative rates of return.

5. **Volatility of average percentile rank:** calculated by first determining the average percentile rank (APR) of each of the monthly rates of return. For example, if a fund placed fifteenth out of 30 funds, it would have an APR of 0.5 or be positioned at the fiftieth percentile for that one month. Then the standard deviation of each month's percentile rank is calculated. If the fund ranked consistently in the first quartile month after month, it would have a very low standard deviation of its monthly percentile ranks. The lower the standard deviation of the monthly percentile rank, the more consistent the fund from month to month relative to similar funds.

6. **Excess returns at 90 per cent:** a two-step process that begins with excess return, calculated by subtracting the average fund's return from this particular fund's return, then determining the largest positive variance between the fund's return and the average fund's return, 10 per cent of the time. This factor penalizes funds that provide big upside surprises, because they must be taking above-average risk to generate such high returns compared to similar funds.

7. **Excess returns at 10 per cent:** another two-step process that begins by taking a fund's excess return as calculated above and determining the largest negative variance between the fund's return and the average fund's return 10 per cent of the time. This factor penalizes funds that provide big downside surprises, because they must be taking above-average risk in order to generate such low returns compared to similar funds.

After determining the cardinal (numeric) rating for each variable, we give the fund an ordinal, assigning it a position within its peer group. The fund with the highest average ordinal position of all seven variables is the least risky. This measure is more complex than standard deviation, but it considers several measures of dispersion that influence upside potential and downside risk. Thus the fund that scores highest on the VVR risk measure will be less risky than others, because the value of the fund declines less often and with less severity. In addition, the fund would also be more consistent from month to month. Therefore, this fund would not likely appear at the bottom of its peer group. Such a fund would receive a five-star rating since it would be in the top 20 per cent of the funds being compared.

Best balance between risk and reward module (VVR B)

The fund with the highest risk-adjusted performance receives the highest rating (five-star) on the VVR best balance between risk and reward module. A fund that scores high on the VVR best balance module must score high on either risk or reward. For example, a fund that receives the highest reward rating but does not score the lowest risk rating will receive a good best balance between risk and reward rating. The higher the return for a given level of risk, the higher the best balance between risk and reward rating.

The VVR summarized

The VVR summarizes historical performance but does not predict the future. It is a historical profile. It is not an opinion of a fund's future potential; it is simply a first-stage screen that summarizes how well each fund has historically balanced risk and return.

The VVR illuminates and eliminates weaknesses displayed by existing tools used to measure performance. It also provides more information to aid investors in making decisions. Considering different risk variables can lead to different allocations of assets when creating portfolios. As a result, an investor can use this information to construct a better portfolio.

The Vos Value Rating assesses the performance of a fund measured against other funds in the same category. It is based on the fund's monthly performance during the previous three years. To determine a fund's VVR, Wilfred Vos has assessed the performance of all the funds in this book in every single month for three years. A fund will receive a high VVR if it historically adds value within the scope of its investment objectives compared with other funds in its category. The VVR compares funds in 30 narrowly defined investment categories, which are defined in the next chapter.

Various Investment Categories

The entire universe of mutual funds in Canada is broken down into a large number of investment categories (or peer groups or asset classes) for VVR analysis. Each peer group tends to perform differently under different economic conditions. Investors can select an above-average fund that has outperformed funds in its own narrowly defined category by identifying a fund with a high Vos Value Rating.

Different investment categories exhibit different risk and reward characteristics. Emerging markets, for example, have exhibited high reward and high risk, while the Canadian money market has exhibited low risk and low return.

Investment categories also perform differently during different stages of the business and economic cycle. Thus, an investor could invest in the right mutual fund in its category, but in the wrong overall investment category and achieve inferior returns during the short term. On the other hand, an investor could invest in the wrong fund in a category but still enjoy excellent performance because of the superior performance of the entire category.

Over the long term, investors will achieve their greatest success if they invest in a diversified portfolio of mutual funds in several investment categories, all of which meet their overall risk-and-return requirements.

The VVR compares funds in the following 30 narrowly defined investment categories. The categories appear in order from least risky to most risky.

Canadian Money Market

Canadian money market mutual funds invest primarily in treasury bills and some commercial paper. The money market mutual fund's net asset value per share (NAVPS) remains constant and does not change from month to month. This is the safest kind of mutual fund for investors who require the highest level of capital protection. Unfortunately, this protection comes at the cost of higher returns. In a volatile economy, many investors consider a successful investment to be one that doesn't lose money. In the long term, though, some investors want more than safety. Recently, many money market funds have generated returns between 4 to 5 per cent, and investors can expect these funds to post marginally but not significantly higher returns in the future. Meanwhile, investors should keep in mind the negative implications of inflation and taxes. People focused on conservative income-producing vehicles should keep some of their money in these funds, but they should also utilize more aggressive mutual funds such as dividend or short-term bond funds as a complement to money market funds.

Foreign Money Market

Foreign money market mutual funds invest primarily in short-term, liquid securities backed by the Canadian government or by a foreign government. Unlike Canadian money market mutual funds, their foreign counterparts carry a currency risk—the risk that the value of the Canadian dollar will rise in relation to the currency of the foreign government. (Most foreign money market mutual funds are denominated in U.S. dollars.) If a fund buys foreign securities worth C$500, for example, and then sells the securities later, after the Canadian dollar has risen in value, the investor will get less than C$500 back. On the other hand, if the Canadian dollar depreciates, domestic investors get more for their money. These funds are ideally suited for conservative investors who want to diversify their investments and protect themselves against a decline in the Canadian dollar. Investors who travel frequently outside of Canada may also find these funds useful. For the short term, you should keep in mind that the Canadian dollar should remain strong and could appreciate in value as more foreign investors buy Canadian goods, services, and securities, increasing demand for the Canadian dollar.

Canadian Short-Term Bond

Canadian short-term bond funds invest in Canadian government and corporate bonds and debentures with an average term to maturity of three to five years. Governments, provinces, or corporations that issue bonds have a legal obligation to pay principal and interest to investors. The value of short-term bonds fluctuates with interest rates. However, because they have a very short term to maturity, these bond funds fluctuate in value significantly less than a general Canadian bond fund. Recently, Canadian short-term bond funds have fared well as interest rates have risen, earning positive rates of return. Investors should expect similar returns in the future, although long-term bonds will likely perform better, because they incur additional risk. Investors should not expect much more than 5.5 per cent a year from this type of investment, but they won't incur any significant setbacks in the short term either.

Canadian Mortgage

Canadian mortgage mutual funds invest primarily in Canadian industrial, commercial, and/or residential mortgages and mortgage-backed securities. In the midst of recent capital market volatility, mortgage funds held their ground. Mortgage funds deliver consistent performance and tend to appreciate in value slowly with very little volatility. This makes them ideal for investors seeking a constant and steady stream of income, although they need more than a mortgage fund to produce income in their portfolio, since these funds are still susceptible to unfavourable changes in interest rates. However, mortgage funds do not decline in value to the same extent as bond funds. In future, investors can expect consistent, low single-digit returns.

Canadian Bond

Canadian bond mutual funds invest primarily in Canadian government and corporate bonds, debentures, and short-term notes. Governments, provinces, or corporations that issue bonds have a legal obligation to pay principal and interest to investors. This makes bond funds less risky than equity funds, although they're not without risk. Bond values rise and fall with changes in interest rates. If interest rates increase, bond values decline, and vice versa. The further in the future a bond has to repay its principal, the more susceptible its value becomes to changes in interest rates. With the recent increase in interest rates, Canadian bonds have incurred some setbacks. The Canadian currency should remain stable or appreciate in value, and inflation should remain in check in the near future. Under these circumstances, bond funds should generate consistent returns of between 6 and 7 per cent. However, bond funds can decline in value during the short term, as they did in early 2000, as interest rates inched upward.

Foreign Bond

Foreign bond mutual funds invest primarily in bonds denominated in foreign currencies and in other foreign debt instruments. Many foreign bond funds hedge at least a portion of their currency exposure to minimize currency risk. However, such a fund will not participate in any gains if the Canadian dollar declines in value relative to other major international currencies. Foreign bond funds provide investors with a steady income stream, opportunities for diversification, and international growth. They tend to go up when everything else goes down and vice versa.

High Yield Bonds—Canadian

High-yield Canadian bond mutual funds invest primarily in Canadian corporate bonds, debentures, and short-term notes that are below investment-grade, although some funds invest a portion of their investments in government bonds or higher-credit bonds as well. Corporations that receive a low credit rating from one of the major rating agencies such as Standard & Poor's issue below-grade bonds. These companies usually exhibit higher risk and have less financial flexibility. In turn, they must make higher interest payments on the bonds they issue. Investors benefit from the higher coupon payments and the possible capital gains associated with credit upgrades. Recently, high-yield bonds have been out of favour as credit spreads widened and interest rates inched upward. However, over the long term, corporate bonds provide higher returns for investors to compensate them for the additional risk, and high-yield bond funds should fare better in the future, especially if interest rates stabilize.

High Yield Bond—International

High-yield international bond mutual funds invest in international high-yield corporate debentures and short-term notes that are below investment grade. Investors benefit from the higher coupon payments and possible capital gains associated with credit upgrades. Recently, international high-yield bonds have been out of favour as credit spreads widened and interest rates inched upward. However, over the long term, corporate and emerging market bonds provide higher returns for investors to compensate them for incurring additional risk. International high-yield bond funds should fare better over the long term relative to domestic bonds, especially if interest rates stabilize.

Canadian Balanced

Canadian balanced mutual funds invest primarily in a combination of Canadian and foreign stocks and bonds. These funds have traditionally been popular with conservative investors because they offer both upside potential and diversification through a large combination of asset classes and securities. In the past, Canadian equity markets generated excellent performance, and these mutual funds provided investors with excellent returns. Recently Canadian equity markets have done well because of the price appreciation of Nortel during the past year, and many investors have made money with their Canadian balanced funds. Things should get even better. Canadian companies are growing, interest rates have inched upward but should remain stable, and inflation should remain in check. These factors should provide investors with higher returns in the short term and generate further gains over the long term.

Global Balanced

Conservative investors looking for one good mutual fund should consider a good global balanced mutual fund. Global balanced funds invest primarily in foreign stocks, bonds, and cash. They have been under-rated in the past, but they offer excellent upside potential for their given level of risk, because they invest in combinations of stocks, bonds, and cash from a variety of economic regions throughout the world. In turn, they provide investors with significantly more diversification than their domestic counterparts. These funds have recently fared worse than Canadian balanced funds because of the strength of Canadian equity markets. Over the long term you should expect a slightly higher return from these funds. But you should select a good fund. Global balanced funds invest in foreign bonds, and investors incur currency risk if the Canadian dollar appreciates in value. A domestic balanced fund could easily outperform in the short term. Over the long term, global funds will generate very acceptable rates of return for investors. Some global balanced funds are RSP-eligible, which means you can take full advantage of the performance of investments outside of Canada within your RRSP.

Canadian Dividend

Canadian dividend funds invest primarily in dividend-paying securities of Canadian corporations. The objective of these mutual funds is to provide a regular and tax-advantaged stream of income. Many of these funds have invested in Canadian banks, which have generated sensational returns during the previous 10 years. In the last two years, performance has been less spectacular, but still good. Most Canadian dividend funds encountered a setback in 2000, but astute investors may want to take this opportunity to invest now at more reasonable prices. In the meantime, these funds still generate a respectable level of income for investors, and taxable investors enjoy a dividend tax credit each April when their taxes come due. Canadian dividend funds have generated a positive return during the last year, but it was lower than Canadian equity funds. They should generate even better returns when economic conditions within Canada improve and there is a broader advance in the stock market.

Canadian Equity

Canadian equity funds invest in the shares of companies listed on Canadian stock exchanges. Most of these companies began in Canada, but many of them now operate internationally, with potential for international growth. During the last year, Canadian equities have generated exceptional returns. In particular, the share price of Nortel Networks tripled in value. Unfortunately, many mutual fund investors avoided Canadian equity funds. Canadian equities should fare even better in the future, especially when Canadian companies display their ability to compete globally and the depth of the market improves. The economy is still growing, some commodity prices have hit historic highs, and corporate profits are still healthy. Investors should not ignore Canadian equities in their portfolio, although they should have other equity exposure for diversification. In addition, investors should realize that Canada's largest stock, Nortel Networks, comprises more than 30 per cent of the value of the Canadian stock market. This could increase your risk if you invest a large portion of your money in a Canadian equity fund or in Nortel directly.

Canadian Small- to Mid-Cap Equity

Canadian small- to mid-cap equity mutual funds invest primarily in the stock of smaller, sometimes new companies listed on Canadian stock exchanges. These small companies have a market capitalization of around $500 million. Smaller companies can grow faster than their larger counterparts, but they also incur more risk. They have generated above-average returns over the long term, but haven't done so well lately if they didn't focus on growth stocks. (Funds that focused on growth stocks generated some very health gains with above-average volatility recently.) Some smaller companies are currently trading at very reasonable valuations, and many experienced investors expect Canada's smaller companies to outperform larger ones in the future. Aggressive investors might consider placing a small portion of their portfolio in this investment category.

Global Equity

Global equity mutual funds are a one-stop investment, in that they invest in different proportions in countries all over the world including the United States, Japan, the United Kingdom, Finland, Germany, France, Mexico, Brazil, Canada, Hong Kong, and China just to name a few. Equity investors should consider investing in a good global equity mutual fund for growth and diversification. Investing in global stock markets around the world, these funds can participate in the growth of any region or country to provide investors with reasonable rates of return from year to year. In addition, some funds offer RSP-eligible versions so your pension plan can take advantage of global growth. Capital markets will continue to display volatility in the future, but global equity funds can generate an average return of 12 to 14 per cent over the long term. A higher return would be difficult to achieve without incurring an excessive amount of risk.

U.S. Equity

U.S. equity mutual funds invest primarily in U.S. stocks. The U.S. stock market has generated exceptional returns for investors during the last 10 years. Last year, capital markets recovered from the volatility generated by Russia's debt crisis, and the U.S. economy has grown at a tremendous pace. Many investors fear that inflation and interest rates will inch higher, causing short-term capital-market corrections. But corporate profits and growth are still strong, and Asia and the Pacific Rim economies are recovering. These two factors should reduce the potential impact of higher inflation and interest rates. Nevertheless, after such an exceptional run in the U.S. stock market, investors should expect more downside risk. Investors should still have some investments in the U.S. stock market, especially if they prefer technology or Internet investments. They should note, however, that growth of 30 per cent per year is not sustainable, although normal rates of return are achievable.

U.S. Small- to Mid-Cap Equity

U.S. small- to mid-cap equity mutual funds invest primarily in the stock of smaller (and often newer) companies listed on American stock exchanges with a market capitalization of less than US$6 billion. U.S. small-cap stocks have recently outperformed their large-cap counterparts because of their bias towards technology stocks, which have performed very well during a very favourable capital market. Investors should realize that small-cap stocks will exhibit more risk, but over the long term they will also offer higher rates of return. During the previous year, some small American companies have grown at exceptional rates, particularly in the technology sector. Many mutual funds have made large investments in these companies, and the companies will likely continue to grow at above average rates.

International Equity

International equity mutual funds invest primarily in the stocks of companies outside Canada and the United States to participate in the growth of European, Asian, and Pacific Rim economies. Since these funds haven't benefited from U.S. stock market growth, their short-term performance hasn't been outstanding. But over the long term, international equity funds have generated similar rates of return to their North American counterparts. International equity funds also provide excellent diversification, and investors should seriously consider a strong international equity fund for a portion of their portfolio. With economic reform in Japan, Asia, and the Pacific Rim, international equity funds should provide competitive rates of return for their investors. With signs of life reappearing, the average international fund has the potential to generate sensational returns for investors. In fact, these funds have recently outperformed their U.S. counterparts.

European Equity

European equity mutual funds invest primarily in the stock of companies in developed European countries. These funds generated exceptional rates of return for investors during 1998. Last year was more difficult, and 2000 started as a difficult year as well. However, telecommunication stocks have driven the market up, and some European stock funds have posted gains of 50 per cent or more. The transition to economic monetary union (EMU) in January 1999 went relatively smoothly, but the Euro currency is still encountering some difficulty. The Canadian dollar has appreciated in value relative to most major European currencies, which was not a positive factor for Canadian investors. Investors may also obtain sufficient exposure to European equity markets through a good global or international equity fund, although a lot of European funds have merit over the short and long term and should be considered by the astute investors.

Japanese Equity

Japanese equity mutual funds invest primarily in Japanese common stock. The Japanese economy was the envy of the world in the late 1980s and early 1990s, while the U.S. economy went through a difficult period. But in the last seven years matters have reversed, and the U.S. economy has become the envy of the world while Japan flounders. In recent months, the Japanese economy has stabilized through bank reform and improved fiscal and monetary policies. The Japanese stock markets have displayed above-average downside risk, but opportunistic equity investors should consider these mutual funds for a portion of their mutual fund portfolio. During the previous 18 months some of them have appreciated in value by more than 100 per cent.

Asia Ex-Japan Equity

Asia ex-Japan equity mutual funds invest primarily in the common stock of Asian, Australian, and New Zealand companies, excluding Japan. These funds are an excellent complement for investors seeking higher returns and diversification. With economic and banking reform in this region and improved government monetary and fiscal policies, Asia ex-Japan equity funds have done very well recently. Capital markets in these regions exhibited above-average downside risk during the previous three to five years, so these funds now offer investors an excellent buying opportunity, and most have regained some of their value since hitting their lows. During the last year, this investment category generated double-digit returns, although there is still a substantial amount of bearish sentiment about these markets. Investors should not ignore these funds, but should not allocate a large portion of their investments here either. Invest cautiously and prudently and you should make money over the long term.

Asia/Pacific Rim Equity

Asia/Pacific Rim equity mutual funds invest primarily in the common stock of Asian, Australian, and New Zealand companies, including Japan. This investment category is broader and more diversified than Asia ex-Japan, since a good portfolio manager can add value by investing appropriately in the Japanese market. Capital markets in this region have experienced difficult times during the previous three years, but with bank reform, International Monetary Fund intervention, and corporate restructuring, the future looks brighter, especially for growth investors. During the previous 18 months these markets generated very acceptable double-digit gains for investors, and they still offer additional growth opportunities and diversification at reasonable prices. Although this region has not fully resolved its troubles, systematic investors should be able to generate some reasonable rates of return.

Latin American Equity

Latin American equity mutual funds invest primarily in the stocks of Latin American companies. Capital markets in Latin America are notoriously volatile. Last year, the Brazilian stock market continued to go up and down like a yo-yo, 10 to 15 per cent per day. Countering this volatility, Latin American stock markets can also grow at a faster rate than their developed counterparts. These markets frequently fulfill their downside risk, only to salvage their reputation by posting exceptional returns over very short periods. The International Monetary Fund (IMF) has intervened in these capital markets in the past to provide some stability, which should be conducive to investment. However, all the issues are not resolved, and investors should allot only a small portion of their portfolio to this region. Recently these funds have held their ground, which could indicate that better times are ahead, although investors may have to be patient.

Emerging Markets Equity

Emerging market equity mutual funds invest primarily in companies located in emerging markets around the world. Any country that is not considered a developed country is considered an emerging market. The developed markets are: Australia, Austria, Belgium, Canada, Denmark, Finland, France, Germany, Hong Kong, Ireland, Italy, Japan, the Netherlands, New Zealand, Singapore, Spain, Sweden, Switzerland, the United Kingdom, and the United States. Emerging market countries have potentially high economic growth rates but volatile economies. Recently they have been plagued by the global debt crisis, but with help from international advisors, many of the larger emerging markets have resolved their short-term problems and posted some good absolute rates of return. These countries frequently incur high rates of inflation and currency devaluation, and the funds that invest in these regions are also highly volatile, with significant downside risk. Only aggressive investors should consider them. In recent years, these funds have generated good double-digit returns, which could continue in the midst of higher short-term volatility.

Specialty Financial Services

These mutual funds invest in companies involved in banking, investment, and insurance—primarily major Canadian chartered banks, mutual fund companies, and insurance companies. Due to higher interest rates and cost cutting in the wake of the failed bank mergers, these funds have not outperformed during the previous year. They should do better because of the de-mutualization of insurance companies and stable interest rates. Over the long term, Canadian and global financial service companies have generated above-average returns for investors. Although these funds suffered severe setbacks of 20 per cent or more during 2000, there appears to be a good comeback on the horizon.

Specialty Natural Resources

These mutual funds invest in companies involved in finding, extracting, and processing natural resources. Commodity prices have rebounded recently from their historic lows, and some commodities are even starting to hit record highs. Stock prices of commodity companies have also appreciated in anticipation of better times ahead, although most stocks have not appreciated in value to the same extent as the commodities themselves. Improved macro-economic conditions, a threat of inflation, and supply control of oil by OPEC have contributed to the increase in commodity prices. If this continues, mutual funds that invest in natural resource companies could fare well. In the short term, oil and gas has been one of the best performing sectors. However, there is still a lot of excess capacity in the industry, and these companies remain susceptible to commodity price fluctuations.

Specialty Precious Metals

Precious metal mutual funds invest in precious metals, such as gold and silver, and in companies that find, produce, and extract these metals. The price of gold bullion continues to hit record lows as more central banks sell their reserves. In turn, gold companies have incurred difficult economic environments, some declaring bankruptcy, some restructuring, some merging, some selling assets, and some leaving the industry altogether. With consolidation, removal of excess capacity, and improved operational efficiency, and if the price of gold bullion improves, these companies could fare very well. Inflation is inching higher, which raises the price of gold. Unfortunately, gold tends to do well only when everything else is doing badly. A scenario of economic turmoil, war, and an end to central bank sell-offs will improve the prospects for gold, although these conditions seem unlikely in the short term. The worst is likely over for gold, but it has not yet regained its shine. Proceed with caution.

Specialty Science and Technology

These mutual funds invest primarily in companies involved in science and technology, restricting their focus to three or four specific industries. During the last three years, they have generated sensational returns, attributable to an extended bull market in the United States. This bull market has been fuelled by growth in the computer and Internet industry and particularly by companies like America Online and Yahoo. This sector will continue to exhibit high growth with above-average volatility. A move of 5 to 10 per cent on a daily basis in either direction is not unusual. Investors should invest a portion of their portfolio in this sector but should not go overboard, since most broad-based mutual fund managers like a global or U.S. equity manager will also invest in this segment of the capital market. The key will be to invest in a good-quality fund that invests in good-quality companies.

Specialty Telecommunications

These funds invest in companies that provide communications equipment, including cable, satellite, cellular equipment, and communication technology. Focusing on two or three very specific industries, these funds can be highly volatile. They've performed very well recently due to deregulation in the industry. Consolidation will likely continue in the industry as companies reposition themselves for increased competition. Have you ever walked through a mall and seen all the teenagers walking around with cell phones? The demand for these products will only increase when this segment of the population ages and the rest of the population attempts to catch up. (Almost 100 per cent of all 18 year olds in Finland have a cell phone.)

Specialty Health and Pharmaceutical

These mutual funds invest in health-care and pharmaceutical companies and exhibit above-average risk depending on the state of the industry. Over the longer term, this sector has delivered above-average performance, fuelled by new drugs and an aging population. Investors should expect some volatility, as large pharmaceutical companies search for new growth.

Labour-Sponsored Venture Capital

Labour-sponsored venture-capital mutual funds invest primarily in startup or expanding small- and medium-sized businesses. The majority are privately owned, although some may trade publicly. Defined by provincial and federal statutes, these funds offer investors a 30 per cent tax credit. This credit, in combination with additional foreign content in self-directed RSPs and an RSP deduction, has made these funds a popular investment. However, investors must hold these funds for eight years or repay their original tax credit upon redemption. And the funds themselves have performed sporadically. Some have generated excellent short-term returns, but others have delivered dismal short-term results. Aggressive investors with a long time horizon may consider such a fund for their portfolios. But they should remember that these mutual funds invest in high-risk start-up companies, tend to hold large cash balances, and generally charge high management fees. The tax credit makes these funds attractive and significantly increases the investor's after-tax rate of return, but investors should consider the fund's investment potential, not the tax credit. Investors should also avoid funds with large cash balances. Because of their investment objectives, these funds have difficulty investing large amounts of money effectively, so it's difficult to figure out which fund will perform well. However, don't ignore the merits of such a fund—some have doubled in value. See Appendix on page 255 for more details.

How to Read an All Time Periods (ATP) Chart

Each fund included in this book has been analyzed using the ATP methodology and has shown itself to be a worthwhile investment. The two-page spread for each fund provides general information about the fund and its performance and includes an evaluation chart that gives Vos Value Ratings for reward, risk, and the best balance between risk and reward. The ratings are explained in detail in the chapter entitled Mutual Fund Performance Measurement, on pages 14 to 17. Each right-hand page is an ATP chart, explained below.

The All Time Periods (ATP) chart presents a combination of tables that illustrate the historical performance of a mutual fund. There's an ATP chart for each mutual fund analyzed in this book. The six tables included in a one-page ATP chart are illustrated and explained below. First, a breakdown of the Fund Details table.

FUND DETAILS

Fund name	**Trimark Advantage Bond**	Fund size (in $ millions)	$618
Fund family	Trimark Investment Management Inc.	Percentage in foreign holdings	20.00%
Mutual fund investment category	High Yield Bond	RRSP eligible	100%
Start date for data shown	January 1995	Sales charge	Optional
Number of funds in investment category	18	Redemption charge	Optional
Dividend frequency	Monthly	Management expense ratio	1.30%

Fund name: This line discloses the name of the fund being analyzed.

Fund family: This discloses the name of the mutual fund company that sells the fund.

Mutual fund investment category: This line indicates the investment objective of the mutual fund. In this example, the mutual fund classification is global equity. Therefore, this mutual fund invests in leading companies around the world, and the fund is compared with other mutual funds that also utilize a similar investment strategy (see pp. 18–26 for a complete description of each fund category).

Start date for data shown: This is the date at which the analysis for the fund began. This date is usually the inception date, but there are some exceptions.

Number of mutual funds in investment category: This shows the number of mutual funds that are included in the investment category for analysis.

Dividend frequency: This discloses the timing of the dividends that the mutual fund pays out. The frequency may be monthly, quarterly (every three months), or annually.

Fund size: This is the total amount of money currently invested in the mutual fund.

Percentage in foreign holdings: This shows the portion of the assets held in the mutual fund that are invested outside Canada.

RRSP eligible: If the mutual fund is RRSP-eligible, it can be held in an RRSP without affecting the foreign content limit. (Canadians are allowed to hold up to 25 per cent of their RRSP investments in foreign securities, 30 per cent in 2001.) If the fund's RRSP eligibility is designated as foreign, then if it's held within an RRSP it will count as foreign content.

Sales charge: This line indicates whether or not investors in this mutual fund are charged a fee for buying shares in the fund.

Redemption charge: This indicates whether investors in this mutual fund are charged a fee for cashing in their investment.

Management expense ratio: This measures the total expenses charged to the mutual fund against the fund's assets. The fee includes the management fee, as well as fees for accounting, legal, and trading costs associated with the operation of the fund.

FUND PERFORMANCE

	1 month	6 months	1 year	3 years	5 years	10 years
Returns ending June 2000	1.3%	2.2%	2.7%	4.8%	8.1%	
Best historical return	4.3%	13.2%	23.6%	15.7%	10.2%	
Average historical return	0.8%	4.5%	9.1%	9.3%	9.0%	
Worst historical return	-3.1%	-1.4%	-0.5%	4.8%	8.0%	
Value at risk of $1,000	$984	$994	$1,012	$1,152	$1,474	

Returns ending June 2000: These are the returns earned by the fund for the periods ending June 2000. For example, the one-month rate of return for the Trimark Advantage Bond Fund was a gain of 1.3 per cent. The one-year rate of return from July 1, 1999 to June 30, 2000 was 2.7 per cent; the three-year rate of return for the fund from July 1, 1997 to June 30, 2000 was 4.8 per cent annualized. In short, the fund's average rate of return for the period July 1, 1997 to June 30, 2000 was 4.8 per cent per year for three years. The five-year rate of return from July 1, 1995 to June 30, 2000 was 8.1 per cent annualized. This format is the same as what investors receive from their mutual fund companies, or what major newspapers publish in their monthly mutual fund reviews.

The rest of the Fund Performance table summarizes the information you would accumulate if you gathered every single mutual fund review published by the *Globe and Mail*, the *Toronto Star*, or the *Financial Post* and looked at the historical performance of each fund. It discloses a range of results based on analysis of all this data.

Best historical return: The best historical return discloses the very best performance that the fund has ever achieved. The best one-month return for the Trimark Advantage Bond Fund was a gain of 4.3 per cent. Someone who invested in this global equity fund prior to its best one-month period would have gained 4.3 per cent. The best one-year rate of return was a gain of 23.6 per cent. Someone who invested in this fund and held the investment over the course of its best year would have gained 23.6 per cent. The best three-year rate of return was a gain of 15.7 per cent annualized. The best five-year rate of return was a gain of 10.2 per cent annualized. Here investors can determine whether recent performance—the performance of the mutual fund ending June 2000—is the fund's best, or if it falls short of this. Investors can update this information by following the fund's current performance. Note: all numbers are calculated using average annual compounded rates of return.

Average historical return: The average historical rate of return shows how well the mutual fund has performed historically on average.

Worst historical return: The worst historical return indicates the downside risk associated with a particular fund; that is, how an investor would fare if he or she invested in a fund at the worst possible time, and the fund subsequently declined in value. The worst historical return indicates the losses posted by the fund over different periods. The worst setback incurred by the fund within a month was a loss of 3.1 per cent. The worst loss posted by the fund after 12 months was a decline of 0.5 per cent. The worst rate of return posted by the fund after three years was a gain of 4.8 per cent annualized. Thus, those who invested in this fund for a minimum of three years have never lost money historically. The worst five-year rate of return for the fund was a gain of 8 per cent. So investors who invested for the long term always made money. If risk is your enemy, time is your ally.

Value at risk: Value at risk (VAR) of $1,000 shows investors the minimum value that their $1,000 investment would have reached after each period, with 95 per cent certainty. For example, $1,000 would have been worth more than $984 after the following month at least 95 per cent of the time. After 12 months it would also have been worth at least $1,012 at least 95 per cent of the time. After five years the $1,000 investment would have been worth at least $1,152 at least 95 per cent of the time. The higher the number, the better the downside protection for investors; the lower the VAR, the higher the implied risk for a particular investment. Investments with a high VAR over the short term have done an excellent job of preserving investors' wealth.

	RETURNS GREATER THAN					
	1 month	**6 months**	**1 year**	**3 years**	**5 years**	**10 years**
10 per cent	0%	39%	55%	32%	14%	
Zero	73%	90%	98%	100%	100%	
Percentage of time fund lost $	27%	10%	2%	0%	0%	
Number of periods evaluated	66	61	55	31	7	

The Returns Greater Than table illustrates the frequency with which a particular mutual fund achieves or fails to meet an investor's goals. The table discloses how often a fund achieved the most common objectives:

1. The frequency with which the fund achieved a return greater than 10 per cent over different periods

2. The frequency with which the fund achieved a return greater than zero

3. The frequency with which the fund achieved a return of less than zero (or lost money)

In this example, the Trimark Advantage Bond Fund achieved a return greater than zero after one month 73 per cent of the time. Its return was greater than zero after one year 98 per cent of the time, which means that the person who invested in this fund for one year made money 98 per cent of the time. It achieved a return greater than 10 per cent after one year 55 per cent of the time. After three, five, and ten years, the fund has always posted a return greater than zero. The last line in the table—Number of periods evaluated—indicates that the ATP chart looked at 66 one-month returns to calculate the best, average, and worst returns and their frequency. The more periods evaluated, the longer the fund has been available to investors and the more information is available to them for making a decision. There were 55 one-year periods evaluated for the Trimark

Advantage Bond Fund. When a fund has posted a one-month return, the ATP chart will evaluate one month of performance; if a fund has posted two monthly rates of return, the ATP chart will evaluate two months of performance; when a fund has posted 12 monthly returns, the ATP chart will evaluate 12 monthly returns and one one-year rate of return. When a fund has posted 13 monthly returns the ATP chart will evaluate 13 monthly returns and two one-year rates of returns (the first 12 months equal one year and the second month plus the remaining 11 months provide another one-year rate of return).

DOWNSIDE RISK

	Worst setback since start date	In bear 1987	In bear 1990	In bear 1994	In bear 1998
Setback for mutual fund	-3.1%				-3.1%
Setback for peer group	-3.5%				-4.2%
Setback ended in	Aug. 1998				Aug. 1998
Months to recover from loss	5				5

A change in economic conditions is characterized by changes in the growth of the economy, changes in interest rates, and changes in investors' outlook on the future. The downside risk table evaluates the performance of the mutual fund during different periods when capital markets have displayed significant declines in value as the result of changing economic conditions. Periods when investments decline in value are referred to as bear markets. During these periods different investments will react differently to changing economic conditions.

It's useful for investors to evaluate the performance of their investments during more difficult economic times. Some investments will decline significantly during a bear market; others will not. Investors can read the downside risk table and get a good idea of how a fund has reacted during such difficult times.

The Downside Risk table provides data on the fund's worst setback since it was established and on its performance during four bear-market periods (1987, 1990, 1994, and 1998). The Worst setback column measures the worst decline an investor could have experienced since the start date of the fund. The figure indicates the worst setback experienced by a person who invested in a fund at the top of the market before the fund declined to its lowest value. In other words, it discloses the largest drop from high to low the fund has posted since its start date.

The columns that indicate the fund's performance during the four bear markets evaluate the performance of the fund only during those particular periods. The worst setback since the start date may be different from a fund's loss during a bear market. The columns headed "In bear 1987, 1990, 1994, and 1998" highlight the downside risk displayed by the fund during those particular periods, respectively.

The Quartile Ranking table is a relative performance graph that shows how the fund's total return for a 12-month period (one year) compares with the returns for all the other funds with similar investment objectives or investment category. These are the same funds used to calculate the Vos Value Rating. The range of relative performance is expressed from the top of the graph to the bottom. The graph is also broken down into quartiles. The first quartile is represented by 1, the second quartile by 2, the third by 3, and the fourth by 4. The fund's relative performance is plotted within the range over time. If the fund is continuously number one within its peer group it will, of course, always be in the first quartile and its relative performance line will be plotted at the top of the graph at all times.

QUARTILE RANKING OF MUTUAL FUND PERFORMANCE AFTER 12 MONTHS OVER TIME

Global equity*

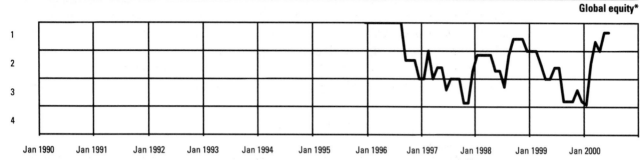

Jan 1990 Jan 1991 Jan 1992 Jan 1993 Jan 1994 Jan 1995 Jan 1996 Jan 1997 Jan 1998 Jan 1999 Jan 2000

1 is first quartile; 2 is second quartile; 3 is third quartile; 4 is fourth quartile. First quartile means that the fund outperformed 75 per cent of other similar funds after 12 months.
*This subheading refers to the Mutual fund investment category further clarified on pages 18–28.

Funds in quartile 1 performed best; funds in quartile 4 performed worst. If a fund's returns lie in the first quartile—quartile 1—its return was within the top 25 per cent of all the funds in its category, and the fund performed better than at least 75 per cent of all the other funds with similar investment objectives. While many mutual funds try to achieve first-quartile performance consistently, very few can actually achieve this. Most mutual funds aim to be in the first or second quartile at all times. If there are 10 mutual funds in a category, and one fund outperforms eight others after 12 months (one year) but underperforms one fund, then it would be in the first quartile. If a mutual fund underperformed eight funds and outperformed one fund, it would be a fourth-quartile performer.

For example, the Trimark Advantage Bond Fund for the period January 1, 1995, to December 31, 1996, posted a return that placed it in the first quartile, indicating that the fund did do better than the majority of other Canadian high-yield bond funds. Rolling ahead by one month, the investor can determine the relative performance of the Trimark Advantage Bond Fund for the period February 1, 1995, to January 31, 1996. As investors read the graph from left to right, they can appreciate the fund's relative performance from 1990 (if applicable) to the present. A fund that is consistently first quartile has generated better historical returns than other similar funds.

The Rolling 12-month Total Rate of Return table illustrates the fund's 12-month performance over time. If a fund posts a one-year rate of return from January 1, 1995, to December 31, 1996, this one-year rate of return will be disclosed on the left side of the graph. The next bar illustrates performance for the period February 1, 1995, to January 31, 1996. The ATP chart will keep rolling forward one month at a time until all the combinations of returns that have been posted by the fund are evaluated, hence the term

ROLLING 12-MONTH TOTAL RATE OF RETURN FOR THE MUTUAL FUND OVER TIME

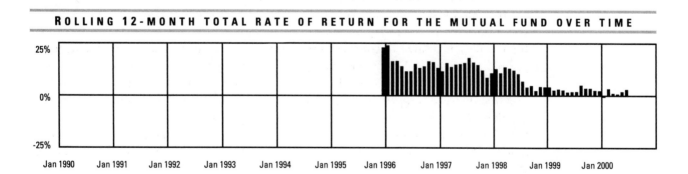

25%

0%

-25%

Jan 1990 Jan 1991 Jan 1992 Jan 1993 Jan 1994 Jan 1995 Jan 1996 Jan 1997 Jan 1998 Jan 1999 Jan 2000

rolling period returns. Moving progressively to the right, the bars illustrate the performance of the fund as it approaches the current date. The return for the Trimark Advantage Bond Fund for the one-year period ending June 30, 2000, is 2.7 per cent, and the bar at the far right illustrates this performance. Investors should note that some investments experience large swings in performance from one period to the next.

Portfolio Building

Asset allocation has been an intrinsic element in the investing process since the 1950s, when Harry Markowitz showed mathematically exactly how diversification reduced volatility without sacrificing return. Markowitz called the process of constructing a portfolio with the highest return for a given level of risk "mean variance optimization" or Modern Portfolio Theory (MPT). It has become the heart of the asset allocation process. Different combinations of assets invested in a portfolio generate different return and risk characteristics.

Investors approach asset allocation in different ways, depending on how they measure returns and risk and define different asset classes and securities. But the single most important variable in investing is choosing the right combination of assets. Research shows that variations in the weights given to different asset classes to determine how to divide the available money account for 90 per cent of the variance of investment returns. Investors will have an opportunity to build their own portfolios at the end of this chapter, using a short comprehensive questionnaire that will help you make appropriate asset-allocation decisions.

Relative Portfolio Theory introduced

Many investors optimize their portfolios by measuring the risk and reward characteristics of an investment. They measure risk using a tool called standard deviation, and measure reward using time-weighted rates of return.

Relative Portfolio Theory (RPT) takes a different approach. Its objective is to deliver consistent predictable performance after 12 months relative to other investments. It aims to add value by creating a combination of investments that outperforms the average mutual fund consistently after 12 months. Unlike Modern Portfolio Theory, RPT creates a portfolio of funds that perform individually and follow different trends and influences so that they don't rise or fall in value together. Together, they deliver optimal performance over more than one period. Conversely, MPT defines an optimal portfolio of funds by the upward and downward movements of its individual investments together over one period. Thus, RPT solves some of the deficiencies associated with the measurement of risk and reward in MPT.

Introduction to the portfolios

To build an optimized and diversified portfolio, we have focused on eight generic investment categories. To help investors build a better portfolio, we will also provide a comprehensive analysis of four portfolios based on their historical results. This method illustrates the importance of selecting an appropriate asset mix and why diversification is key to investment success.

Alternatively, investors can simply select any of the top-performing investments in this book to complement their asset mix with their own investment ideas.

The last section of this chapter introduces a questionnaire that will enable investors to determine the asset mix appropriate for their own risk and reward profile.

When investors build a portfolio they will not need to rely on a single top-performing mutual fund, which could underperform over the short term. Instead, a well diversified portfolio of mutual funds should generate above-average consistent performance.

First, an asset mix was determined for each of the four portfolios based on the questionnaire at the end of this chapter. Each portfolio in the following examples was then optimized based on the relative performance of each of the eight investment categories. (For each investment category, the average was used.) Using the averages, each portfolio was compared with Canadian balanced mutual funds over a period ranging from December 1987 to June 2000. Each portfolio's objective was to provide the highest rate of return for the given level of risk, and each portfolio aimed to achieve top-quartile performance after 12 months relative to Canadian balanced mutual funds. This isn't always possible, since the portfolio's first objective is to adhere to the investment objective, as determined by the asset mix, and the asset mix is constrained by the level of risk investors are willing to accept. In addition, the portfolios are optimized based on the average return for the investment category. These portfolios could not invest in all investment categories or take advantage of active investment management, which has added value over the long term. Nevertheless, they generated some very impressive risk and reward profiles, indicating the importance of asset allocation.

Investors could consider changing some of the underlying investment categories or altering the weights of the current investment categories (see the end of the chapter) to suit their own risk and return profiles. They should also consider any new information that is available at the time of reading.

An investment in a category or mutual fund that accounts for less than 5 per cent of your total portfolio will not have a significant impact on the overall risk and return profile of your portfolio. Also, an investor can limit his or her selection of mutual funds and still have a well-diversified portfolio. By limiting the number of funds, you can usually meet a fund's minimum investment requirement, if applicable. In addition, investors should remember that some funds are available only through a particular company. For example, if you wish to purchase a mutual fund from Investors Group, you have to contact an Investors Group representative directly.

A word of caution

An investor can construct an infinite number of portfolios depending on his or her risk and reward profile. This summary includes only four sample portfolios to illustrate the objective behind portfolio building. In all four, the investor would have enjoyed excellent returns for the given level of risk incurred. Investors have to remember that it's the asset mix that counts; fund selection is just a bonus.

The portfolios have been constructed to achieve superior performance for investors who want to achieve their investment objective with the highest level of diversification. These portfolios clearly demonstrate the benefits of diversification, which can limit risk without sacrificing reward. These portfolios are all RRSP-eligible, although investors may have to invest in RRSP-eligible foreign equity funds in certain circumstances. These portfolios would be appropriate inside or outside an RRSP, but unfortunately taxable investors will earn a lower rate of return because they have to pay tax.

To develop your own optimal portfolio, you can simply study the questionnaire at the end of this chapter and select the top-performing mutual funds in this book or supplement them with your own choices. Regardless of which option you choose, the key is the diversification achieved through asset allocation. You don't need a sophisticated computer program such as the one we used to generate these portfolios. Simply keep in mind that the objective is to invest in two (or more) mutual funds that perform very differently from each other during various time periods.

Summary of the portfolios

The following table is a short summary of the four portfolios reviewed in the following pages. First we review the asset allocation and then how each fund scored based on the Vos Value Rating (VVR) methodology. To determine the appropriate asset mix for yourself, you should see the questionnaire at the end of this chapter. (Note: The following portfolios scored 15, 20, 25, and 30 respectively on the questionnaire at the end of this chapter.)

Portfolio	Cash	Bonds	High-Yield Bonds	Balanced	Domestic Equity	Global Equity	U.S. Equity	International Equity
Conservative	40%	25%	1%	18%	4%	12%		
Moderate		35%	7%	18%	14%		11%	15%
Aggressive		25%	12%	6%	21%		16%	20%
Very Aggressive		15%	10%		27%		22%	26%

From the table above you can see that investors who can withstand risk invest a large part of their investments in equity mutual funds, and investors who dislike risk invest a large portion of their investments in cash and bonds. Make sure that you know how much risk you can comfortably incur. Investors should remember that a diversified portfolio would reduce risk and increase the probability that you'll achieve your investment objective.

The table below illustrates the performance of each portfolio based on the Vos Value Rating methodology. The most conservative portfolio scores very high based on the risk rating, but sacrifices a lot of return potential to meet its primary objective of preserving capital. The very aggressive portfolio scores much higher based on the reward rating, but scores a lot lower based on the risk rating.

VOS VALUE RATING			
Portfolio	Reward	Risk	Best balance
Conservative	★★	★★★★★	★
Moderate	★★★	★★★★★	★★★★★
Aggressive	★★★★	★★★★★	★★★★★
Very Aggressive	★★★★★	★★★	★★★★★

Conservative portfolio

This portfolio focuses heavily on Canadian investments, including bonds and money market mutual funds. The portfolio is also heavily weighted toward interest-rate-sensitive securities and income-producing stocks. Investors who wish to reduce the risk in this portfolio even further could consider investing in an international bond or money market mutual fund. This would reduce the risk of a declining Canadian dollar and achieve a higher level of income. These changes wouldn't alter the risk-and-return profile of the portfolio significantly unless there were a large divergence between the performance of Canadian and international bonds, as occurred in 1999.

Investors can choose any of the funds listed in this book or choose their own. Conservative investors who require income or who travel outside the country for long periods could consider an international bond or money market mutual fund to reduce the risk of a declining Canadian dollar—when they travel they can use these investments for their travel expenditures if the U.S. dollar is too expensive. When the Canadian dollar declines, their investments increase in value; when the Canadian currency increases, their travel costs decrease (assuming that the currency risk of the mutual fund selected isn't hedged).

Portfolio profile

The Conservative portfolio is a compilation of six investment categories from which investors can select their own investments. This portfolio has historically achieved top results and has added value consistently. Investors can add even more value themselves by investing in top-performing mutual funds featured in this book. This portfolio is less risky than the moderate and aggressive portfolios, but has still displayed upside potential in the past. The portfolio's largest three holdings include a money market, bond, and balanced mutual fund. It is highly suitable for investors who dislike risk completely and require less growth.

Portfolio performance

If this portfolio were a Canadian balanced mutual fund, it would have scored a poor Vos Value Rating for reward because of its very conservative risk profile. Most Canadian balanced funds take a lot more risk. Nevertheless, investors still enjoyed upside potential and outperformed a Guaranteed Investment Certificate (GIC). This portfolio has added value consistently. Its average 12-month rate of return was a gain of 8.5 per cent, and its best 12-month rate of return was a gain of 16.6 per cent. Over the long term it generated an average 10-year rate of return of 8.3 per cent, an excellent result considering the portfolio's low risk profile.

Portfolio risks

The worst 12-month rate of return for this portfolio was a decline of 2.4 per cent, and it posted negative rates of return after 12 months only 1 per cent of the time. During the bear market of 1994, it declined in value by 4.9 per cent, significantly less than the average Canadian balanced fund. After incurring the setback, the portfolio took nine months to recover. In short, the portfolio has done an excellent job of preserving capital. The value at risk of $1,000 after one year was $1,026, meaning that the value of an investor's portfolio was more than $1,026 after one year at least 95 per cent of the time.

Future prospects

Relative Portfolio Theory assumes that a portfolio of investment categories that has historically added value consistently will continue to outperform in the future. This portfolio has demonstrated its capability to add value in the past, adjusted for risk, and it could make an excellent investment for the future for conservative investors.

FUND DETAILS

Fund name	**Conservative Portfolio**	Fund size (in $ millions)	$209
Fund family	Weight	Percentage in foreign holdings	10.36%
Mutual fund investment category	Canadian Balanced	RRSP eligible	92%
Start date for data shown	December 1987	Sales charge	Optional
Number of funds in investment category	383	Redemption charge	Optional
Dividend frequency	Monthly	Management expense ratio	1.51%

FUND PERFORMANCE

	1 month	6 months	1 year	3 years	5 years	10 years
Returns ending June 2000	1.4%	4.4%	8.3%	6.5%	7.8%	8.3%
Best historical return	3.2%	9.9%	16.6%	12.4%	10.6%	9.2%
Average historical return	0.7%	4.2%	8.5%	8.6%	8.6%	8.5%
Worst historical return	-4.2%	-3.6%	-2.4%	5.5%	6.4%	7.9%
Value at risk of $1,000	$989	$1,001	$1,026	$1,206	$1,390	$2,144

RETURNS GREATER THAN

	1 month	6 months	1 year	3 years	5 years	10 years
10 per cent	0%	39%	35%	14%	8%	0%
Zero	74%	95%	99%	100%	100%	100%
Percentage of time fund lost $	26%	5%	1%	0%	0%	0%
Number of periods evaluated	151	146	140	116	92	32

DOWNSIDE RISK

	Worst setback since start date	In bear 1987	In bear 1990	In bear 1994	In bear 1998
Setback for mutual fund	-4.9%		-2.4%	-4.9%	-4.5%
Setback for peer group	-8.7%		-7.2%	-8.7%	-13.4%
Setback ended in	June 1994		April 1990	June 1994	Aug. 1998
Months to recover from loss	9		1	9	4

ROLLING 12-MONTH QUARTILE RANKING OF MUTUAL FUND PERFORMANCE OVER TIME

Canadian balanced

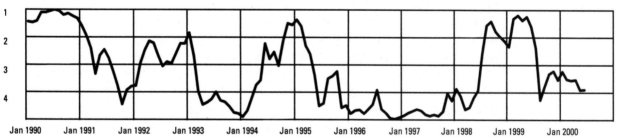

1 is first quartile; 2 is second quartile; 3 is third quartile; 4 is fourth quartile. First quartile means that the fund outperformed 75 per cent of other similar funds after 12 months.

ROLLING 12-MONTH TOTAL RATE OF RETURN FOR THE MUTUAL FUND OVER TIME

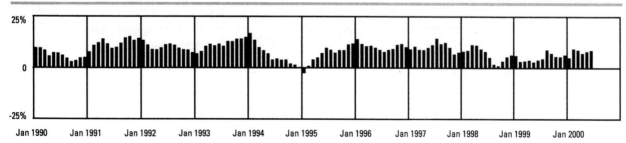

Moderate portfolio

The Moderate portfolio is a compilation of six different investment categories. It focuses largely on bonds and equities that trade in the North American stock market. Investors might consider investing in an international bond or money market fund to reduce the risk of a declining Canadian dollar and achieve a higher level of income. Investors could also invest a portion of their holdings in an Asia and Pacific Rim mutual fund as a portion of their international investments. This portfolio is suitable for investors who require both income and growth. It holds a large investment in bonds, which will provide income, and has also invested in equities, which will provide growth.

Portfolio profile

This portfolio has historically achieved top results and has added value consistently. It holds a diverse number of investments and has outperformed the average Canadian balanced fund by investing in foreign equities.

It is more risky than the Conservative portfolio but less risky than the Aggressive portfolio and has displayed an excellent risk-and-return profile in the past. The portfolio's largest three holdings include a bond, balanced fund, and international equity fund.

Portfolio performance

If this portfolio were a Canadian balanced mutual fund, it would have scored a five-star Vos Value Rating for best balance between risk and reward. This indicates that the portfolio has added value consistently. Its best 12-month rate of return was a gain of 26.3 per cent, and the average 12-month rate of return was 10.3 per cent. It posted positive rates of return after 12 months 93 per cent of the time. It would have been consistently first quartile or second quartile after 12 months. During the previous year, this portfolio would have posted a gain of 11.5 per cent.

Portfolio risks

The worst 12-month rate of return for this portfolio was a decline of 6.8 per cent, and it posted negative rates of return after 12 months 7 per cent of the time. During the bear market of 1994, it declined in value by 8.7 per cent, less than the average Canadian balanced fund. After incurring the setback, the portfolio took 11 months to recover its loss. In short, the portfolio has done an excellent job of preserving capital, outperforming during the previous three bear markets.

Future prospects

This portfolio has demonstrated its capability of outperforming in the past. It could make an excellent investment for the future if the underlying investment categories and mutual funds continue to add value. It does incur more risk than the Conservative portfolio but investors looking to achieve higher returns than a fixed-income investment can achieve that goal with this portfolio. While they will incur more risk, historically it has been nominal.

FUND DETAILS

Fund name	**Moderate Portfolio**	Fund size (in $ millions)	$154
Fund family	Investment Category Portfolio	Percentage in foreign holdings	21.74%
Mutual fund investment category	Canadian Balanced	RRSP eligible	82%
Start date for data shown	December 1987	Sales charge	Optional
Number of funds in investment category	383	Redemption charge	Optional
Dividend frequency	Monthly	Management expense ratio	1.85%

FUND PERFORMANCE

	1 month	6 months	1 year	3 years	5 years	10 years
Returns ending June 2000	2.2%	5.2%	11.5%	9.1%	11.3%	10.6%
Best historical return	5.1%	14.3%	26.3%	15.8%	12.8%	11.1%
Average historical return	0.9%	5.1%	10.3%	10.5%	10.6%	10.3%
Worst historical return	-8.0%	-6.9%	-6.8%	7.2%	8.1%	9.4%
Value at risk of $1,000	$976	$977	$991	$1,239	$1,499	$2,486

RETURNS GREATER THAN

	1 month	6 months	1 year	3 years	5 years	10 years
10 per cent	0%	55%	56%	53%	71%	69%
Zero	70%	86%	93%	100%	100%	100%
Percentage of time fund lost $	30%	14%	7%	0%	0%	0%
Number of periods evaluated	151	146	140	116	92	32

DOWNSIDE RISK

	Worst setback since start date	In bear 1987	In bear 1990	In bear 1994	In bear 1998
Setback for mutual fund	-8.7%		-6.5%	-8.7%	-8.6%
Setback for peer group	-8.7%		-7.2%	-8.7%	-13.4%
Setback ended in	June 1994		April 1990	June 1994	Aug. 1998
Months to recover from loss	11		3	11	4

ROLLING 12-MONTH QUARTILE RANKING OF MUTUAL FUND PERFORMANCE OVER TIME

Canadian balanced

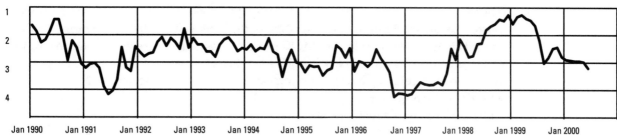

1 is first quartile; 2 is second quartile; 3 is third quartile; 4 is fourth quartile. First quartile means that the fund outperformed 75 per cent of other similar funds after 12 months.

ROLLING 12-MONTH TOTAL RATE OF RETURN FOR THE MUTUAL FUND OVER TIME

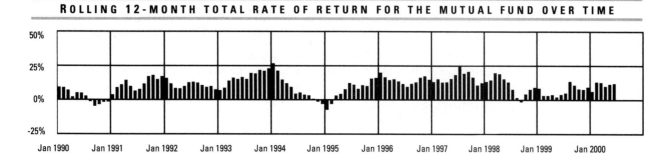

Aggressive portfolio

The Aggressive portfolio is a compilation of six different investment categories. It focuses on bonds and equities, including U.S. and international equities. Investors could consider investing in an international bond or money market mutual fund to reduce the risk of a declining Canadian dollar and achieve a higher level of income. Investors could also invest in other investment categories to reduce risk.

More aggressive investors who want to achieve higher rates of return with more risk over the long term could consider increasing their equity exposure by investing in international equity funds that are RRSP-eligible or investing in some specialty mutual funds.

Portfolio profile

This portfolio has historically achieved top results and has added value consistently for investors. It holds a diverse number of investments and has outperformed the average Canadian balanced mutual fund.

It is more risky than the Conservative and Moderate portfolios, but less risky than the Very Aggressive portfolio. It has displayed more upside potential in the past. Its largest three holdings include domestic, U.S., and international equities.

Portfolio performance

If this portfolio were a Canadian balanced mutual fund it would have scored a five-star Vos Value Rating for the best balance between risk and reward. This indicates that the portfolio has added value consistently on a risk-adjusted basis more than other Canadian balanced funds over the previous three years. Its best 12-month rate of return was a gain of 28.1 per cent, and its average 12-month rate of return was 10.8 per cent. The portfolio posted positive rates of return after 12 months 93 per cent of the time, and it would have been consistently first or second quartile after 12 months, although it did slip into fourth quartile briefly in 1991.

Portfolio risks

The worst 12-month rate of return for this portfolio was a decline of 6.9 per cent, and it posted negative rates of return after 12 months 7 per cent of the time. During the bear market of 1994, it declined in value by 8.4 per cent, less than the average Canadian balanced fund. After incurring this setback it took 11 months to recover its loss. In short, the portfolio has done an excellent job of preserving capital, but underperformed the Conservative and Moderate portfolios on occasion. In addition, investors incur a lower value at risk in the short term, implying more risk.

Future prospects

Relative Portfolio Theory assumes that a portfolio of investment categories that has historically outperformed consistently will continue to add value in the future, if the underlying portfolio's investment categories and mutual funds continue to add value. Investors with this aggressive asset mix should realize that it did not outperform consistently, but has added value over the long term. This portfolio is suitable for investors seeking the higher returns offered by equity investments without incurring an excessive amount of downside risk. Over the long term this portfolio will be very competitive with most Canadian balanced mutual funds.

FUND DETAILS

Fund name	**Aggressive Portfolio**	Fund size (in $ millions)	$152
Fund family	Investment Category Portfolio	Percentage in foreign holdings	27.71%
Mutual fund investment category	Canadian Balanced	RRSP eligible	76%
Start date for data shown	December 1987	Sales charge	Optional
Number of funds in investment category	383	Redemption charge	Optional
Dividend frequency	Monthly	Management expense ratio	1.88%

FUND PERFORMANCE

	1 month	6 months	1 year	3 years	5 years	10 years
Returns ending June 2000	2.3%	4.6%	12.8%	10.2%	12.3%	11.1%
Best historical return	5.6%	15.8%	28.1%	16.3%	13.5%	11.6%
Average historical return	0.9%	5.3%	10.8%	10.9%	11.0%	10.7%
Worst historical return	-9.2%	-7.6%	-6.9%	6.4%	8.1%	9.7%
Value at risk of $1,000	$973	$971	$981	$1,225	$1,508	$2,572

RETURNS GREATER THAN

	1 month	6 months	1 year	3 years	5 years	10 years
10 per cent	0%	58%	57%	65%	73%	88%
Zero	70%	85%	93%	100%	100%	100%
Percentage of time fund lost $	30%	15%	7%	0%	0%	0%
Number of periods evaluated	151	146	140	116	92	32

DOWNSIDE RISK

	Worst setback since start date	In bear 1987	In bear 1990	In bear 1994	In bear 1998
Setback for mutual fund	-9.6%		-7.7%	-8.4%	-9.6%
Setback for peer group	-13.4%		-7.2%	-8.7%	-13.4%
Setback ended in	Aug. 1998		Sept. 1990	June 1994	Aug. 1998
Months to recover from loss	4		5	11	4

ROLLING 12-MONTH QUARTILE RANKING OF MUTUAL FUND PERFORMANCE OVER TIME

Canadian balanced

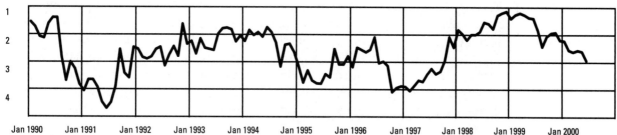

1 is first quartile; 2 is second quartile; 3 is third quartile; 4 is fourth quartile. First quartile means that the fund outperformed 75 per cent of other similar funds after 12 months.

ROLLING 12-MONTH TOTAL RATE OF RETURN FOR THE MUTUAL FUND OVER TIME

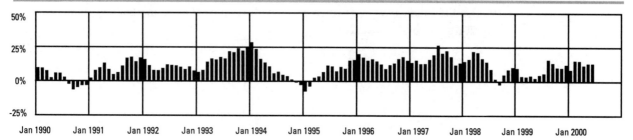

Very Aggressive portfolio

The Very Aggressive portfolio is a compilation of six different investment categories. It focuses on bonds and equities, including U.S. and international equities. Investors could consider investing in an international bond or money market mutual fund to reduce the risk of a declining Canadian dollar. In addition, investors could invest in one or more specialty, region, or country fund to reduce geographic and political risk but increase their return. Investors should not ignore the aggressive nature of this portfolio, which may not make it suitable for all investors. But individuals seeking more growth and less income will find this portfolio suitable for their needs.

Portfolio profile

This portfolio has historically achieved top results and has added value consistently for investors. It holds a diverse number of investments and has outperformed the average Canadian balanced mutual fund.

It is more risky than the Conservative, Moderate, and Aggressive portfolios, although it has also displayed more upside potential in the past. The portfolio's largest three holdings include domestic, U.S., and international equities. It has very little invested in bonds, which provide income and diversification.

Portfolio performance

If this portfolio were a Canadian balanced mutual fund, it would have scored a five-star Vos Value Rating for reward and best balance between risk and reward. This indicates that the portfolio has added value consistently on a risk-adjusted basis more than other Canadian balanced funds over the previous three years. Its best 12-month rate of return was a gain of 29.9 per cent, and its average 12-month rate of return was 11.5 per cent. The portfolio posted positive rates of return after 12 months 93 per cent of the time. It would have been consistently first or second quartile after 12 months, although it did slip into fourth quartile briefly in 1991.

Portfolio risks

The worst 12-month rate of return for this portfolio was a decline of 8.4 per cent, and it posted negative rates of return after 12 months 7 per cent of the time. During the bear market of 1994, the portfolio declined in value by 7.3 per cent, less than the average Canadian balanced fund. After incurring this setback the portfolio took 11 months to recover. In short, the portfolio has done an excellent job of preserving capital, but underperformed the Conservative and Moderate portfolios on occasion. In addition, investors incurred a lower value at risk in the short term, implying more risk.

Future prospects

Investors with this aggressive asset mix should realize that this portfolio did not outperform consistently, but has added value over the long term. This portfolio lost some of its upside potential during the previous year, because Canadian equities outperformed global equity funds. However much of the performance of the Canadian equity market can be attributed to one stock, Nortel.

FUND DETAILS

Fund name	**Very Aggressive Portfolio**	Fund size (in $ millions)	$158
Fund family	Investment Category Portfolio	Percentage in foreign holdings	34.54%
Mutual fund investment category	Canadian Balanced	RRSP eligible	69%
Start date for data shown	December 1987	Sales charge	Optional
Number of funds in investment category	383	Redemption charge	Optional
Dividend frequency	Monthly	Management expense ratio	1.91%

FUND PERFORMANCE

	1 month	6 months	1 year	3 years	5 years	10 years
Returns ending June 2000	2.4%	4.5%	15.0%	11.7%	13.7%	11.7%
Best historical return	6.3%	17.4%	29.9%	17.7%	14.7%	12.2%
Average historical return	1.0%	5.7%	11.5%	11.3%	11.5%	11.1%
Worst historical return	-10.8%	-9.6%	-8.4%	5.0%	8.0%	10.0%
Value at risk of $1,000	$971	$958	$970	$1,194	$1,503	$2,653

RETURNS GREATER THAN

	1 month	6 months	1 year	3 years	5 years	10 years
10 per cent	0%	58%	59%	66%	76%	100%
Zero	70%	85%	93%	100%	100%	100%
Percentage of time fund lost $	30%	15%	7%	0%	0%	0%
Number of periods evaluated	151	146	140	116	92	32

DOWNSIDE RISK

	Worst setback since start date	In bear 1987	In bear 1990	In bear 1994	In bear 1998
Setback for mutual fund	-11.1%	-0.3%	-9.6%	-7.3%	-11.1%
Setback for peer group	-13.4%		-7.2%	-8.7%	-13.4%
Setback ended in	Aug. 1998	Jan. 1988	Sept. 1990	June 1994	Aug. 1998
Months to recover from loss	4	1	5	11	4

ROLLING 12-MONTH QUARTILE RANKING OF MUTUAL FUND PERFORMANCE OVER TIME

Canadian balanced

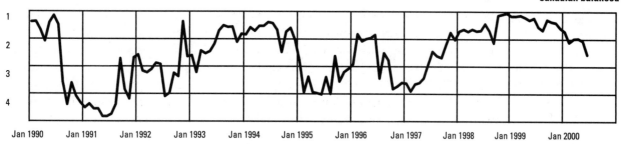

1 is first quartile; 2 is second quartile; 3 is third quartile; 4 is fourth quartile. First quartile means that the fund outperformed 75 per cent of other similar funds after 12 months.

ROLLING 12-MONTH TOTAL RATE OF RETURN FOR THE MUTUAL FUND OVER TIME

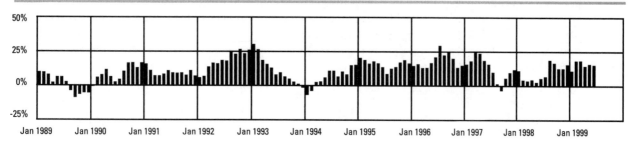

A guide to determining your asset mix

Portfolio performance depends more on the mix of investments you select than on the individual securities you hold over the long term. It's more important, for example, to invest the right amount of your portfolio in U.S. equities than to invest in the best U.S. mutual fund over the long term. Getting the right asset mix will add more value for investors than selecting the best mutual funds. In fact, when two portfolios perform differently, the difference is usually attributable to the mix of assets held in each one.

The following questionnaire will help you determine your risk and reward profile. Developed by William Droms of Georgetown University in Washington, D.C., it helps investors determine their tolerance for risk and the price they'll pay for potential gains.

Investors with a high score (above 30) are more aggressive and could tolerate a more equity-oriented investment portfolio. Investors with a low score should consider a less risky portfolio.

Once you've completed the questionnaire you can check your recommended long-term strategic asset mix in the recommended asset mix table that follows.

Investment Objective	Strongly Agree	Agree	Neutral	Disagree	Strongly Disagree
1. Earning a high long-term rate of return that will allow my investment to grow faster than inflation is a very important objective for me.	5	4	3	2	1
2. I'd like an investment that provides me with an opportunity to defer taxation of capital gains and/or interest income to future years.	5	4	3	2	1
3. I don't require a high level of current income from my investments.	5	4	3	2	1
4. My major investment goals are relatively long term.	5	4	3	2	1
5. I'm willing to tolerate sharp up and down swings in the return on my investment in order to seek a potentially higher return than would normally be expected from more stable investments.	5	4	3	2	1
6. I'm willing to risk a short-term loss in return for a potentially higher long-run rate of return.	5	4	3	2	1
7. I'm financially able to accept a low level of liquidity in my investment portfolio.	5	4	3	2	1

Total _____

Source: William G. Droms, Copyright © 1988.

Once you've completed the questionnaire simply add up your answers for questions 1 to 7. Then check your score between 7 and 35 on the corresponding table below. After you match your score with the recommended asset mix you can begin building a portfolio, or adjusting your current portfolio with investments recommended in this book or that you've selected on your own. The choices range from the very conservative to the very aggressive.

| | | | | | Asset Class | | | | |
Score	Cash	Bonds	High Yield Bonds	Balanced	Domestic Equity	Global Equity	U.S. Equity	International Equity	Historical Return
5	95%	5%							8.6%
6	90%	7%				3%			8.8%
7	85%	9%		2%		4%			9.0%
8	80%	11%		4%		5%			9.1%
9	75%	13%		6%		6%			9.3%
10	70%	15%		8%		7%			9.4%
11	65%	17%		10%		8%			9.6%
12	60%	19%		12%		9%			9.7%
13	55%	21%		14%		10%			9.9%
14	50%	23%		16%		11%			10.1%
15	40%	25%	1%	18%	4%	12%			10.4%
16	30%	27%	2%	20%	6%	15%			10.7%
17	20%	29%	3%	22%	8%	18%			11.1%
18	10%	31%	4%	23%	10%		9%	13%	11.2%
19	0%	33%	6%	25%	12%		10%	14%	11.5%
20		35%	7%	18%	14%		11%	15%	11.6%
21		33%	8%	15%	16%		12%	16%	11.7%
22		31%	9%	12%	18%		13%	17%	11.7%
23		29%	10%	10%	19%		14%	18%	11.8%
24		27%	11%	8%	20%		15%	19%	11.8%
25		25%	12%	6%	21%		16%	20%	11.9%
26		23%	13%	4%	22%		17%	21%	12.0%
27		21%	12%	4%	23%		18%	22%	12.0%
28		19%	12%		25%		20%	24%	12.1%
29		17%	11%		26%		21%	25%	12.2%
30		15%	10%		27%		22%	26%	12.3%
31		13%	9%		28%		23%	27%	12.3%
32		11%	8%		29%		24%	28%	12.4%
33		9%	7%		30%		25%	29%	12.5%
34		7%	6%		31%		26%	30%	12.5%
35		5%	5%		32%		27%	31%	12.6%

Please refer to pp. 17–24 for a complete description of each investment category.

Best of the Best Mutual Funds for Canadians

On the following pages is a comprehensive set of mutual funds selected for their excellent performance during the life of the fund. The funds were also evaluated on their management process, people, and philosophy. (With some exceptions, a fund needs a three-year track record to be eligible.) When two mutual funds exhibited similar risk and return patterns, we selected the fund that's more widely available to investors. The selection criteria include the Vos Value Rating, the All Time Periods (ATP) chart, diversifiable risk, and a qualitative assessment of the mutual fund and fund company.

These 100 funds have displayed superior performance relative to similar mutual funds. With over 3,000 mutual funds to choose from we could have included more than 100, but we had to draw the line there to keep the list manageable. With this in mind, we featured only 60 of these 100 funds in this book. If a fund is featured, it is accompanied by a page number. The funds selected are listed and described in a systematic order to allow investors to easily build a mutual fund portfolio based on the previous questionnaire.

If you want to invest in more than one mutual fund, you should review the previous sections on portfolio building. This will help you to select a combination of mutual funds to achieve a superior risk and return profile.

TOP FUNDS FOR THE NEW MILLENNIUM

Investment Category	Fund Name	RRSP Eligibility	Phone Number	Page Number
Cash				
Canadian money market	Scudder Canadian Money Mkt	Yes	888-4MAXXUM	n/a
	Trimark Interest	Yes	800-387-9845	50
Foreign money market	Guardian RSP US M-Mkt Classic	Yes	800-668-7327	n/a
	PH & N US$ Money Market	Yes	800-661-6141	52
Bonds				
Canadian short-term bond	CIBC Cdn S-T Bd Ind	Yes	800-465-3863	n/a
	Fidelity Canadian S-Term Bond	Yes	800-263-4077	54
	PH & N S-T Bond & Mortgage	Yes	800-661-6141	56
Canadian mortgage	HSBC Mortgage	Yes	800-830-8888	n/a
Canadian bond	Altamira Bond	Yes	800-263-2824	58
	C.I. Canadian Bond	Yes	800-563-5181	60
	Green Line Cdn. Bond	Yes	800-268-8166	n/a
	PH & N Bond	Yes	800-661-6141	62
Foreign bond	AGF Global Government Bond	Foreign	800-268-8583	64
	Guardian Foreign Income CI A	Yes	800-668-7327	n/a
	MD Global Bond	Foreign	800-267-4022	n/a
	Talvest Global Bond RSP	Yes	800-268-8258	n/a
High Yield Bonds				
High yield bond	Trimark Advantage Bd	Yes	800-387-9845	66
Foreign high yield bond	C.I. Global High Yield	Foreign	800-563-5181	n/a

Investment Category	Fund Name	RRSP Eligibility	Phone Number	Page Number
Balanced				
Canadian balanced	Atlas Canadian Balanced	Yes	800-463-2857	68
	Fidelity Cdn Asset Alloc	Yes	800-263-4077	70
	Royal & SunAlliance Balanced	Yes	800-263-1747	n/a
	Scotia Canadian Balanced	Yes	800-268-9269	72
	Standard Life Balanced	Yes	888-841-6633	74
	Transamerica Growsafe Cdn Bal	Yes	416-290-6221	76
Global balanced	AGF American T.A. Alloc	Foreign	800-268-8583	78
	C.I. International Balanced	Foreign	800-563-5181	80
	Fidelity Glo Asset Alloc	Foreign	800-263-4077	82
	Spectrum United Global Divr	Foreign	877-732-8786	84
Domestic Equity				
Canadian dividend income	BMO Dividend	Yes	800-665-7700	86
	HSBC Dividend Income	Yes	800-830-8888	n/a
	PH & N Dividend Income	Yes	800-661-6141	88
Canadian diversified equity	AGF Canadian Stock	Yes	800-268-8583	90
	AIM Canada Growth Class	Yes	877-468-2468	92
	AIM Canada Value Class	Yes	877-468-2468	94
	BMO Equity	Yes	800-665-7700	96
	Fidelity Disciplined Equity	Yes	800-263-4077	98
	Fidelity True North	Yes	800-263-4077	n/a
	Investors Summa	Yes	888-746-6344	100
	Spectrum United Cdn Stock	Yes	877-732-8786	n/a
	Synergy Cdn. Momentum Cl	Yes	888-664-4784	n/a
	Talvest Cdn. Equity Growth	Yes	800-268-8258	n/a
	Universal Future	Yes	800-387-0614	102
Canadian small/mid-cap equity	CIBC Cdn Small Cos	Yes	800-465-3863	104
	Cundill Cdn Security Series A	Yes	800-387-0614	n/a
	Fidelity Cdn Growth Company	Yes	800-263-4077	106
	GBC Canadian Growth	Yes	800-668-7383	n/a
	Saxon Small Cap	Yes	888-287-2966	108
	YMG Emerging Companies	Yes	888-964-3533	n/a
Global Equity				
Global equity	AGF International Value	Foreign/Yes	800-268-8583	110
	AIM Global Theme Class	Foreign	877-468-2468	n/a
	Atlas Global Value	Foreign	800-463-2857	112
	BPI Global Equity Value	Foreign/Yes	800-563-5181	114
	C.I. Global	Foreign/Yes	800-563-5181	116
	Fidelity Intl Portfolio	Foreign/Yes	800-263-4077	118
	Janus Global Equity	Foreign/Yes	888-4MAXXUM	120
	MB Global Equity	Foreign	800-267-4022	n/a
	Spectrum United Global Growth	Foreign	877-732-8786	122
	Talvest Global Small Cap	Foreign/Yes	800-268-8258	124
	Universal Select Managers	Foreign/Yes	800-387-0614	126
U.S. Equity				
U.S. diversified equity	AGF Intl - American Gth Class	Foreign/Yes	800-268-8583	n/a
	AIM American Blue Chip Growth	Foreign/Yes	877-468-2468	128
	BPI American Equity Value	Foreign/Yes	800-563-5181	n/a
	CIBC U.S. Index RRSP	Yes	800-465-3863	130
	Ethical North American Equity	Foreign/Yes	877-384-4225	132
	Janus American Equity	Foreign/Yes	888-4MAXXUM	134
	VistaFund 2 American Stock	Foreign	800-661-6464	n/a
U.S. small/mid-cap equity	AGF Aggressive Growth	Foreign	800-268-8583	136
	Clarington US Smaller Co Gth	Foreign	888-860-9888	n/a
	Elliott & Page U.S. Mid-Cap	Foreign	888-588-7999	n/a
	Franklin U.S. Small Cap Gth	Foreign	800-387-0830	n/a
International Equity				
International equity	AGF Intl - Intl Stock Class	Foreign	800-268-8583	138
	Atlas Intl Large Cap Growth	Foreign/Yes	800-463-2857	n/a
	C.I. International	Foreign/Yes	800-563-5181	n/a
	CIBC International Small Companies Fund	Foreign	800-465-3863	140
	GWL Intl Equity (P) Opt A	Foreign	204-946-1190	142

Investment Category	Fund Name	RRSP Eligibility	Phone Number	Page Number
European equity	AIM European Growth	Foreign/Yes	877-468-2468	144
	HSBC European Growth	Foreign	800-830-8888	n/a
	Universal Euro. Opportunities	Foreign/Yes	800-387-0614	146
Japanese equity	AGF Intl - Japan Class	Foreign/Yes	800-268-8583	n/a
	Altamira Japanese Opportunity	Foreign/Yes	800-263-2824	n/a
	Fidelity Japanese Growth	Foreign/Yes	800-263-4077	148
Asia ex-Japan equity	Fidelity Far East	Foreign/Yes	800-263-4077	150
	Green Line Asian Growth	Foreign	800-268-8166	n/a
Asia-Pacific Rim equity	Scudder Pacific	Foreign	888-4MAXXUM	152
Latin American equity	Atlas Latin American Value	Foreign	800-463-2857	n/a
	Green Line Latin American Gth	Foreign	800-268-8166	154
Emerging markets equity	Green Line Emerging Mkts	Foreign	800-268-8166	156
	Spectrum United Emerging Mkts	Foreign	877-732-8786	n/a
Special Equity				
Specialty - Financial	CIBC Financial Companies	Yes	800-465-3863	n/a
Specialty - Natural resources	Investors Cdn Nat Resource	Yes	888-746-6344	n/a
	Royal Energy	Yes	800-463-3863	158
Specialty - Precious metals	Green Line Precious Metals	Yes	800-268-8166	160
Specialty - Health Care	Talvest Global Health Care	Foreign/Yes	800-268-8258	162
Specialty - Science & Technology	AIM Global Technology	Foreign/Yes	877-468-2468	164
	CIBC Glo Technology	Foreign	800-465-3863	n/a
	Talvest Global Science & Tech	Foreign/Yes	800-268-8258	166
Specialty - Telecommunications	C.I. Global Telecom Sector	Foreign/Yes	800-563-5181	n/a
	Spectrum United Glo Telecom	Foreign/Yes	877-732-8786	168
Country-Specific	Talvest China Plus	Foreign/Yes	800-268-8258	n/a
Specialty and Miscellaneous	C.I. Glo Consumer Prod Sector	Foreign/Yes	800-563-5181	n/a
	Green Line Entertain. & Comm.	Foreign	800-268-8166	n/a

TRIMARK INTEREST FUND

Vos value rating		
Reward	**Risk**	**Best balance**
★★★★	★★★★★	★★★★★

Fund profile

The Trimark Interest Fund aims to achieve a high level of current income by investing in Government of Canada T-bills, banker's acceptances, and other short-term corporate obligations, including short-term discount notes issued by the Bank of Montreal and the Royal Bank of Canada, two of Canada's largest banks. It is an excellent investment for those who require a high level of interest income, have a short-term time horizon, or desire a high level of capital preservation. It is comparable to a six-month GIC. Patrick Farmer and Rex Chong manage this fund along with other fixed income funds within the AIM fund family.

Fund performance

Investors should have realistic expectations about the rates of return posted by money market funds. You should never expect 20 per cent returns in a single year, but you should never encounter a loss either. Over the long term, these funds will generate a return of 6 to 7 per cent. However, investors should remember that, after inflation and taxes, their real purchasing power will not increase significantly. This fund's best 12-month rate of return was a gain of 13 per cent, and its average rate of return after 12 months was 6.7 per cent. During the previous 10 years, this fund has appreciated in value by an average of 5.4 per cent per year. It invests in interest-bearing securities and pays a distribution each month equal to its earned income. This strategy allows the fund's net asset value (NAV) to remain fixed at $10 per unit.

Fund risks

Investors who have an aversion to losing money will appreciate the security and stability of a money market fund. Money market funds haven't declined in value, in turn this fund has appreciated in value each month during the previous 162 months. The managers have done a good job and have earned a more predictable and consistent level of income each month than comparable funds. In turn, the fund scored a five-star Vos Value Rating for risk. Its worst 12-month return was a gain of 2.6.

Fund prospects

When it comes to investing, you won't lose money with this investment. Each month investors receive income, and each month their investment grows, but at a very slow rate. Money market funds don't incur risk, and investments that don't incur risk will not generate very high rates of return, although they won't lose a lot of money either. Investors looking for income, safety, and capital preservation should consider the Trimark Interest Fund for a portion of their portfolio. It will ensure your money is there when you need it, so it's an ideal investment for conservative investors or investors saving for short-term goals.

FUND DETAILS

Fund name	**Trimark Interest**	Fund size (in $ millions)	$956
Fund family	Trimark Investment Management Inc.	Percentage in foreign holdings	0.00%
Mutual fund investment category	Canadian Money Market	RRSP eligible	100%
Start date for data shown	January 1987	Sales charge	Yes
Number of funds in investment category	172	Redemption charge	None
Dividend frequency	Monthly	Management expense ratio	0.87%

FUND PERFORMANCE

	1 month	6 months	1 year	3 years	5 years	10 years
Returns ending June 2000	0.4%	2.3%	4.4%	4.1%	4.1%	5.4%
Best historical return	1.1%	6.6%	13.0%	11.3%	10.0%	7.6%
Average historical return	0.5%	3.3%	6.7%	6.7%	6.5%	6.6%
Worst historical return	0.2%	1.2%	2.6%	3.6%	4.1%	5.4%
Value at risk of $1,000	$1,002	$1,014	$1,029	$1,113	$1,235	$1,724

RETURNS GREATER THAN

	1 month	6 months	1 year	3 years	5 years	10 years
10 per cent	0%	15%	17%	22%	3%	0%
Zero	100%	100%	100%	100%	100%	100%
Percentage of time fund lost $	0%	0%	0%	0%	0%	0%
Number of periods evaluated	162	157	151	127	103	43

DOWNSIDE RISK

	Worst setback since start date	In bear 1987	In bear 1990	In bear 1994	In bear 1998
Setback for mutual fund	n/a				
Setback for peer group	n/a				
Setback ended in	Jan. 2000				
Months to recover from loss	n/a				

ROLLING 12-MONTH QUARTILE RANKING OF MUTUAL FUND PERFORMANCE OVER TIME

Canadian money market

1 is first quartile; 2 is second quartile; 3 is third quartile; 4 is fourth quartile. First quartile means that the fund outperformed 75 per cent of other similar funds after 12 months.

ROLLING 12-MONTH TOTAL RATE OF RETURN FOR THE MUTUAL FUND OVER TIME

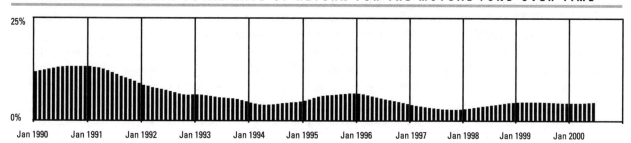

PHILLIPS, HAGER & NORTH US$ MONEY MARKET FUND

Vos value rating		
Reward	**Risk**	**Best balance**
★★★★★	★★★★★	★★★★★

Fund profile

Snowbirds or investors who expect a steep decline in the value of the Canadian dollar might consider a foreign money market fund, which reduces risk by investing outside of Canada when the currency starts to drop. This fund invests in Canadian money-market investments such as Government of Canada T-bills and corporate short-term notes denominated in U.S. dollars. This makes the fund 100-per-cent RRSP-eligible and suitable for a retirement account.

Foreign money-market funds have generated good returns in U.S. dollars, but the increase in value of the Canadian dollar in 1999 would have eroded the gains. Lynn Delahey of Phillips, Hager & North Investment Management manages this fund.

Fund performance

This fund is valued in U.S. dollars, so performance numbers don't take into account the value added or deleted by Canadian currency fluctuations. Investors in this fund have benefited from a below-average management fee and above-average investment management capability. The fund has been first quartile after 12 months frequently compared to similar funds. Its best 3-year rate of return was a gain of 5.2 per cent annualized, and its average annualized 3-year rate of return was 4.5 per cent. During the previous five years, this fund has appreciated in value by an average of 5 per cent per year. In 1998, the fund benefited from a decline in the value of the Canadian dollar, but currency appreciation hurt it in 1999.

The fund has made a 77 per cent investment in Canadian T-bills. The majority of the remaining portfolio is invested in various short-term discount notes of organizations such as Chevron, Export Development Corporation, and Westcoast Energy.

Fund risks

A money-market fund is great for people who need stability and capital preservation. Investors can feel reassured that a good money-market fund won't decline in value during the short or long term. This particular fund has posted gains after one month 100 per cent of the time (in U.S. dollars). This makes it ideal for very conservative investors, who should remember, however, that it doesn't eliminate currency risk. Its portfolio will fluctuate with the value of the Canadian dollar after considering its return. If the Canadian dollar appreciates, investors lose and vice versa.

Future prospects

Money market mutual funds are for investors whose number-one priority is the safety of their investment. This fund is unique because it doesn't eliminate the currency risk. Large differences in inflation, interest, and unemployment rates between the U.S. and Canada, along with higher commodity prices, mean that the Canadian dollar could remain volatile in the short term. Regardless of currency fluctuations, this fund should still make a good investment for conservative investors seeking income and a hedge against a declining Canadian dollar. It can come in handy if you plan a trip south of the border.

FUND DETAILS

Fund name	**PH & N US$ Money Market**	Fund size (in $ millions)	$51
Fund family	Phillips, Hager & North Ltd.	Percentage in foreign holdings	0.00%
Mutual fund investment category	Foreign Money Market	RRSP eligible	100%
Start date for data shown	December 1990	Sales charge	None
Number of funds in investment category	22	Redemption charge	None
Dividend frequency	Monthly	Management expense ratio	0.52%

FUND PERFORMANCE

	1 month	6 months	1 year	3 years	5 years	10 years
Returns ending June 2000	0.5%	2.7%	5.3%	5.0%	5.1%	
Best historical return	0.6%	3.2%	6.0%	5.2%	5.1%	
Average historical return	0.4%	2.3%	4.5%	4.5%	4.6%	
Worst historical return	0.2%	1.3%	2.6%	3.3%	4.1%	
Value at risk of $1,000	$1,002	$1,013	$1,027	$1,104	$1,222	

RETURNS GREATER THAN

	1 month	6 months	1 year	3 years	5 years	10 years
10 per cent	0%	0%	0%	0%	0%	
Zero	100%	100%	100%	100%	100%	
Percentage of time fund lost $	0%	0%	0%	0%	0%	
Number of periods evaluated	115	110	104	80	56	

DOWNSIDE RISK

	Worst setback since start date	In bear 1987	In bear 1990	In bear 1994	In bear 1998
Setback for mutual fund	n/a			n/a	n/a
Setback for peer group	n/a			n/a	n/a
Setback ended in	Jan. 2000			n/a	n/a
Months to recover from loss	n/a			n/a	n/a

ROLLING 12-MONTH QUARTILE RANKING OF MUTUAL FUND PERFORMANCE OVER TIME

Foreign money market

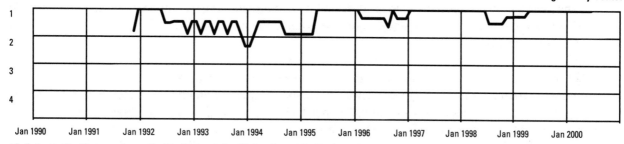

1 is first quartile; 2 is second quartile; 3 is third quartile; 4 is fourth quartile. First quartile means that the fund outperformed 75 per cent of other similar funds after 12 months.

ROLLING 12-MONTH TOTAL RATE OF RETURN FOR THE MUTUAL FUND OVER TIME

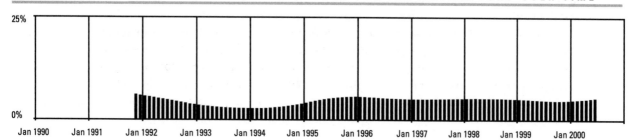

FIDELITY CANADIAN SHORT-TERM BOND FUND

Vos value rating		
Reward	**Risk**	**Best balance**
★★★★	★	★★★★

Fund profile

This fund aims to provide investors with a high level of income while protecting capital by investing in Canadian government, provincial, or corporate bonds. It invests primarily in short- and medium-term bonds, as well as various preferred, convertible, and mortgage-backed securities that will mature in less than five years. This fund is ideally suited for conservative investors who require stability and consistency in their investment portfolios. It aims to incur very little interest-rate risk by investing in bonds that have a similar maturity and duration to the index. Although the fund incurs more credit risk than other short-term Canadian bond funds, the risk is nominal. It makes an ideal addition to any conservative income-oriented portfolio. Ford O'Neal and Jeff Moore manage its portfolio.

Fund performance

The fund's recent performance has been affected by higher economic growth in North America. Higher growth leads to higher inflation and, in turn, higher short-term interest rates, which aren't good for bonds. However, the fund has delivered excellent long-term returns while reducing risk. The best 3-year rate of return for this fund was a gain of 9.6 per cent annualized, and the average annualized 3-year rate of return was 6.2 per cent. During the previous 5 years, this fund has appreciated in value by an average of 6 per cent per year. The fund scored high marks for performance, earning a four-star Vos Value Rating for reward. The managers add value by investing in higher-yielding provincial and corporate bonds when prudent. This strategy allows the fund to earn higher rates of return by capitalizing on different yield spreads. The fund has made investments in discount notes issued by companies such as Trizec Hahn, a major real estate company, and Mackenzie Financial. It will underperform longer-term bond funds when interest rates decline and outperform them when interest rates increase.

Fund risks

Since its inception the fund has maintained a very conservative risk profile relative to most mutual funds (but not to other short-term bond funds), and so has earned a poor one-star Vos Value Rating for risk. In addition, the fund declined in value by 0.7 per cent during the bear market of 1998, almost twice the decline posted by similar funds.

Future prospects

If economic growth slows in Canada, the environment for bonds will improve. With no threat of inflation, bond investors should fare well throughout the upcoming year. Unfortunately inflation reappears occasionally, which can send large shock waves through bond and stock markets. Currently, the short end of the interest rate curve is very steep compared to bonds with a longer maturity. This is an unusual situation for the bond market. Conservative investors who want to diversify their portfolio and avoid the above-average volatility associated with the stock market should consider investing a portion of it in a top-performing short-term bond fund like the Fidelity Canadian Short-Term Bond Fund.

FUND DETAILS

Fund name	**Fidelity Canadian Short-Term Bond**	Fund size (in $ millions)	$89
Fund family	Fidelity Investments Canada Limited	Percentage in foreign holdings	0.00%
Mutual fund investment category	Canadian Short-Term Bond	RRSP eligible	100%
Start date for data shown	February 1995	Sales charge	Optional
Number of funds in investment category	36	Redemption charge	Optional
Dividend frequency	Monthly	Management expense ratio	1.25%

FUND PERFORMANCE

	1 month	6 months	1 year	3 years	5 years	10 years
Returns ending June 2000	1.1%	2.9%	3.6%	4.2%	6.0%	
Best historical return	2.8%	9.3%	15.3%	9.6%	6.7%	
Average historical return	0.6%	3.1%	6.2%	6.2%	6.3%	
Worst historical return	-1.2%	-0.6%	-0.1%	3.4%	5.9%	
Value at risk of $1,000	$991	$1,002	$1,012	$1,113	$1,336	

RETURNS GREATER THAN

	1 month	6 months	1 year	3 years	5 years	10 years
10 per cent	0%	23%	15%	0%	0%	
Zero	72%	97%	98%	100%	100%	
Percentage of time fund lost $	28%	3%	2%	0%	0%	
Number of periods evaluated	65	60	54	30	6	

DOWNSIDE RISK

	Worst setback since start date	In bear 1987	In bear 1990	In bear 1994	In bear 1998
Setback for mutual fund	-1.3%				-0.7%
Setback for peer group	-0.7%				-0.4%
Setback ended in	March 1997				Dec. 1997
Months to recover from loss	2				1

ROLLING 12-MONTH QUARTILE RANKING OF MUTUAL FUND PERFORMANCE OVER TIME

Canadian short-term bond

1 is first quartile; 2 is second quartile; 3 is third quartile; 4 is fourth quartile. First quartile means that the fund outperformed 75 per cent of other similar funds after 12 months.

ROLLING 12-MONTH TOTAL RATE OF RETURN FOR THE MUTUAL FUND OVER TIME

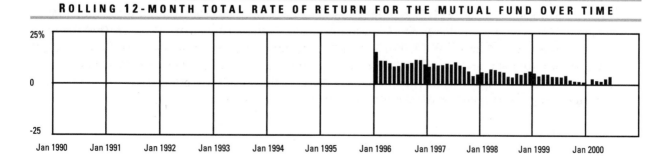

PHILLIPS, HAGER & NORTH SHORT-TERM BOND AND MORTGAGE FUND

Vos value rating		
Reward	**Risk**	**Best balance**
★★★★★	★★★	★★★★★

Fund profile

When it comes to short-term bond funds, this one is second to none, a reputation earned by delivering above-average performance and a rock-bottom management fee. Managed by Scott Lamont of Phillips, Hager & North Investment Management, the fund aims to provide income and capital preservation by investing in government and corporate bonds. It also invests in conventional first mortgages and mortgages guaranteed under the National Housing Act (NHA). To provide safety of capital the majority of the fund is invested in short-term bonds. During the previous year interest rates increased marginally, so short-term bond funds did very well in a difficult economic environment.

Fund performance

This is an excellent mutual fund that provides income while preserving the value of an investment. Therefore, it will outperform Canadian bond funds when interest rates go up and underperform them when interest rates go down. This fund has consistently posted first-quartile results when compared to similar funds after 12 months and has earned a five-star Vos Value Rating for reward and the best balance between risk and reward. Its best 3-year rate of return was a gain of 10.5 per cent annualized, and its average annualized 3-year rate of return was 7.4 per cent. During the last five years, the fund has appreciated in value by an average of 6.7 per cent per year.

It has invested 58 per cent of its portfolio in Government of Canada bonds and has also invested in discount notes issued by the Bank of Montreal and the Toronto Dominion Bank, among other issuers.

Fund risk

This fund aims to preserve capital while providing income regardless of current economic conditions. It has done a good job of preserving capital by rarely posting losses. Its worst 12-month rate of return was a loss of 2 per cent. Inherently, the fund is not very risky because its manager maintains a portfolio of investments with an average term to maturity of approximately three years. This means that the fund doesn't incur a significant amount of interest-rate risk, because its portfolio isn't as interest-rate sensitive as other bond funds.

Future prospects

There is currently a lot of upward pressure on interest rates in the United States, but the worst is likely over. The U.S. economy is growing at a very high pace, unemployment is low, and inflation could be re-emerging, but the Federal Reserve Board has done a good job of slowing the economy without stalling it. Higher interest rates are bad for bond investments, but investors in this fund have a lot more downside protection than they'd receive from a traditional bond fund. Since this fund is less sensitive to changes in interest rates, it is very suitable for investors who require income and safety of capital.

FUND DETAILS

Fund name	**PH & N S-T Bond & Mortgage**	Fund size (in $ millions)	$278
Fund family	Phillips, Hager & North Ltd.	Percentage in foreign holdings	0.00%
Mutual fund investment category	Canadian Short-Term Bond	RRSP eligible	100%
Start date for data shown	January 1994	Sales charge	None
Number of funds in investment category	36	Redemption charge	None
Dividend frequency	Quarterly	Management expense ratio	0.64%

FUND PERFORMANCE

	1 month	6 months	1 year	3 years	5 years	10 years
Returns ending June 2000	1.0%	3.6%	4.4%	4.9%	6.7%	
Best historical return	3.4%	9.1%	16.3%	10.5%	8.3%	
Average historical return	0.5%	3.3%	7.2%	7.4%	7.4%	
Worst historical return	-3.2%	-5.3%	-2.0%	3.9%	6.6%	
Value at risk of $1,000	$990	$1,002	$1.021	$1,135	$1,383	

RETURNS GREATER THAN

	1 month	6 months	1 year	3 years	5 years	10 years
10 per cent	0%	23%	28%	12%	0%	
Zero	77%	95%	97%	100%	100%	
Percentage of time fund lost $	23%	5%	3%	0%	0%	
Number of periods evaluated	78	73	67	43	19	

DOWNSIDE RISK

	Worst setback since start date	In bear 1987	In bear 1990	In bear 1994	In bear 1998
Setback for mutual fund	-6.4%			-6.4%	-0.4%
Setback for peer group	-6.0%			-6.0%	-0.4%
Setback ended in	June 1994			June 1994	Aug. 1998
Months to recover from loss	8			8	1

ROLLING 12-MONTH QUARTILE RANKING OF MUTUAL FUND PERFORMANCE OVER TIME

Canadian short-term bond

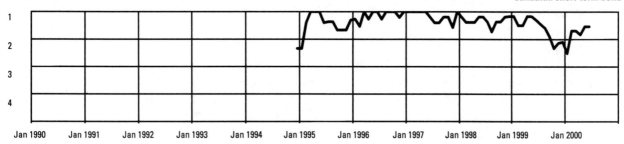

1 is first quartile; 2 is second quartile; 3 is third quartile; 4 is fourth quartile. First quartile means that the fund outperformed 75 per cent of other similar funds after 12 months.

ROLLING 12-MONTH TOTAL RATE OF RETURN FOR THE MUTUAL FUND OVER TIME

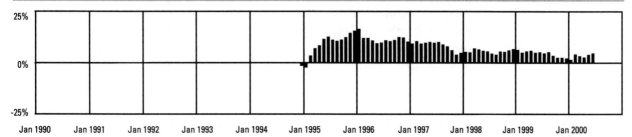

ALTAMIRA BOND FUND

Vos value rating		
Reward	**Risk**	**Best balance**
★★★★★	★	★★★★

Fund profile

Over the long term the more risk that you incur the higher the return you should receive. This is the basic principal of Finance 101. This fund has incurred more risk than many Canadian bond funds, but it has also posted the best 10-year rate of return. Managed by Robert Marcus of Altamira Management Ltd., the fund aims to provide investors with superior returns over the long term, and it has achieved this objective. The fund also aims to reduce risk by investing in Canadian government and provincial bonds, but it maintains a bias toward long-term bonds, which did not fare well in 1999 because of an increase in interest rates.

Fund performance

The fund holds long-term bonds, so when interest rates go down this fund goes up in value and vice versa. During the previous year interest rates went up, and long-term bonds underperformed their short-term counterparts. In fact, the fund was lucky to post a positive rate of return. The fund has been first and fourth quartile after 12 months frequently, depending on the direction of interest rates. The fund's best 12-month rate of return has been a gain of 28.5 per cent during 1995. Over the past year, the fund earned a return of 2.3 per cent, less than the average bond fund. But it has earned an annualized return of 11.5 per cent over the past 10 years. With such sensational performance, the fund has earned a five-star Vos Value Rating for reward.

The fund has made four significant investments. It invested 26.7 per cent of its assets in Government of Canada December 1, 2015 strip bonds, 19.4 per cent in Canada Treasury Bills, 13.4 per cent in Province of Ontario 6.2 June 2, 2031 bonds, and Government of Canada 5.5 June 1, 2009 bonds.

Fund risks

The fund will benefit from the higher yield to maturity earned from investing in longer-term bonds, but it is more sensitive to changes in interest rates than the average bond fund. Thus it earns only a one-star Vos Value Rating for risk. The fund declines more than the average bond fund in difficult economic environments. During the bear market of 1994 it declined in value by 17.3 per cent, 60 per cent more than the average bond fund, but it took only 11 months to recover the loss.

Fund prospects

Currently, there is a lot of upward pressure on interest rates in the United States, which could have negative implications on interest rates in Canada. In the U.S. the economy is growing at a very fast pace, unemployment is low, and inflation could be re-emerging. Higher interest rates are bad for bond investments, and investors should diversify their portfolio. Aggressive investors who are looking for a good long-term bond fund should consider the Altamira Bond Fund for their mutual fund portfolio.

FUND DETAILS

Fund name	**Altamira Bond**	Fund size (in $ millions)	$419
Fund family	Altamira Investment Services Inc.	Percentage in foreign holdings	20.00%
Mutual fund investment category	Canadian Bond	RRSP eligible	100%
Start date for data shown	December 1987	Sales charge	None
Number of funds in investment category	234	Redemption charge	None
Dividend frequency	Quarterly	Management expense ratio	1.37%

FUND PERFORMANCE

	1 month	6 months	1 year	3 years	5 years	10 years
Returns ending June 2000	1.7%	7.8%	2.3%	8.5%	9.8%	11.5%
Best historical return	7.5%	18.4%	28.5%	19.4%	14.4%	12.9%
Average historical return	0.9%	5.4%	11.2%	12.2%	12.1%	12.0%
Worst historical return	-6.0%	-15.6%	-10.3%	6.8%	9.0%	10.7%
Value at risk of $1,000	$975	$949	$933	$1,244	$1,592	$2,785

RETURNS GREATER THAN

	1 month	6 months	1 year	3 years	5 years	10 years
10 per cent	0%	55%	59%	71%	89%	100%
Zero	66%	84%	88%	100%	100%	100%
Percentage of time fund lost $	34%	16%	12%	0%	0%	0%
Number of periods evaluated	151	146	140	116	92	32

DOWNSIDE RISK

	Worst setback since start date	In bear 1987	In bear 1990	In bear 1994	In bear 1998
Setback for mutual fund	-17.3%		-4.2%	-17.3%	-1.2%
Setback for peer group	-11.4%		-5.0%	-11.4%	-1.8%
Setback ended in	June 1994		April 1990	June 1994	Oct. 1998
Months to recover from loss	11		2	11	1

ROLLING 12-MONTH QUARTILE RANKING OF MUTUAL FUND PERFORMANCE OVER TIME

Canadian bond

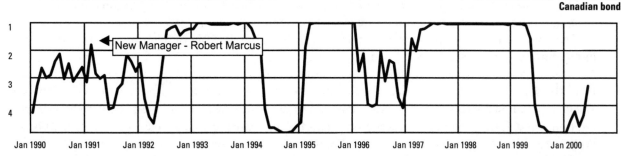

1 is first quartile; 2 is second quartile; 3 is third quartile; 4 is fourth quartile. First quartile means that the fund outperformed 75 per cent of other similar funds after 12 months.

ROLLING 12-MONTH TOTAL RATE OF RETURN FOR THE MUTUAL FUND OVER TIME

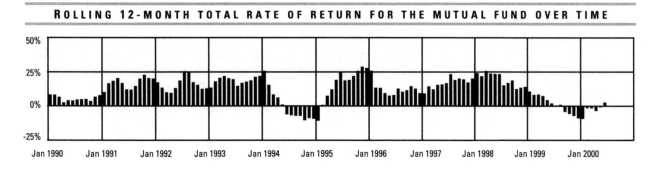

C.I. CANADIAN BOND FUND

Vos value rating		
Reward	**Risk**	**Best balance**
★★★★	★★★★	★★★★★

Fund profile

Jeffery Herold of J. Zechner & Associates manages the C.I. Canadian Bond Fund. He invests in high-quality fixed-income securities of Canadian issuers, including federal, provincial, and corporate bonds, that provide an attractive yield and offer capital appreciation.

Since bond yields are at historic lows, it's difficult to earn rates of return of more than 10 per cent. Bonds still make a very attractive investment in a diversified portfolio, but investors should remember that an increase in interest rates could generate capital losses for bond fund investors. This occurred recently when the U.S. Federal Reserve Board and the Bank of Canada raised short-term interest rates to combat fears of inflation. Through interest-rate anticipation and extensive monitoring of market conditions the manager adds value by capitalizing on various investment opportunities when they become available.

Fund performance

This fund outperformed similar funds frequently over 12-month periods, but during the previous year it managed a gain of only 2.4 per cent and thus underperformed the majority of similar investments during this time frame. Investors have been rewarded for holding bonds over the last three years as interest rates declined. They have also benefited from a narrowing of the spread between government and corporate bonds. This fund has outperformed other bond funds over the longer term by strategically investing in some corporate bonds. This was a prudent strategy in the past and, if credit spreads remain stable, investors will be rewarded again in the future. This fund's best 3-year rate of return was a gain of 14.5 per cent annualized, and the average annualized 3-year rate of return was 9.8 per cent. During the previous five years, this fund has appreciated in value by an average of 8.3 per cent per year.

The fund has made a 21 per cent investment in corporate bonds, 7 per cent in provincial bonds, and 70 per cent in Government of Canada bonds.

Fund risks

The C.I. Canadian Bond Fund emphasizes safety of investment. Therefore it invests only in the very best Government of Canada and corporate bonds such as 407 International bonds, Investors Group, and Oxford Properties. The fund's worst 12-month rate of return was a loss of 4.9 per cent. Its 12-month value at risk per $1,000 was $965, indicating that the value of a $1,000 investment in the fund after 12 months was greater than $965 at least 95 per cent of the time.

Future prospects

Since interest rates aren't likely to decline significantly, the likelihood of capital gains is minimal. Investors can benefit from the corporate bond exposure if credit spreads remain stable. While investors should expect to receive a lower rate of return going forward than in the past, they should still earn adequate rates of return for the given level of risk within this fund. Those looking for a value-added Canadian bond fund should consider the C.I. Canadian Bond Fund for a portion of their portfolios.

FUND DETAILS

Fund name	**C.I. Canadian Bond**	Fund size (in $ millions)	$324
Fund family	C.I. Mutual Funds Inc.	Percentage in foreign holdings	0.00%
Mutual fund investment category	Canadian Bond	RRSP eligible	100%
Start date for data shown	February 1993	Sales charge	Optional
Number of funds in investment category	234	Redemption charge	Optional
Dividend frequency	Monthly	Management expense ratio	1.60%

FUND PERFORMANCE

	1 month	6 months	1 year	3 years	5 years	10 years
Returns ending June 2000	1.4%	3.7%	2.4%	5.1%	8.3%	
Best historical return	4.2%	14.6%	20.2%	14.5%	10.7%	
Average historical return	0.6%	3.9%	7.9%	9.8%	9.4%	
Worst historical return	-3.4%	-8.2%	-4.9%	4.6%	8.1%	
Value at risk of $1,000	$983	$971	$965	$1,160	$1,496	

RETURNS GREATER THAN

	1 month	6 months	1 year	3 years	5 years	10 years
10 per cent	0%	40%	47%	48%	17%	
Zero	71%	81%	82%	100%	100%	
Percentage of time fund lost $	29%	19%	18%	0%	0%	
Number of periods evaluated	89	84	78	54	30	

DOWNSIDE RISK

	Worst setback since start date	In bear 1987	In bear 1990	In bear 1994	In bear 1998
Setback for mutual fund	-9.2%			-9.2%	-1.8%
Setback for peer group	-11.4%			-11.4%	-1.8%
Setback ended in	June 1994			June 1994	Aug. 1998
Months to recover from loss	10			10	1

ROLLING 12-MONTH QUARTILE RANKING OF MUTUAL FUND PERFORMANCE OVER TIME

Canadian bond

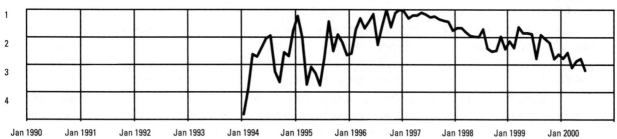

1 is first quartile; 2 is second quartile; 3 is third quartile; 4 is fourth quartile. First quartile means that the fund outperformed 75 per cent of other similar funds after 12 months.

ROLLING 12-MONTH TOTAL RATE OF RETURN FOR THE MUTUAL FUND OVER TIME

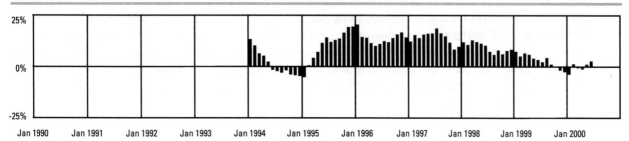

PHILLIPS, HAGER & NORTH BOND FUND

Vos value rating		
Reward	**Risk**	**Best balance**
★★★★★	★★★★★	★★★★★

Fund profile

There is only one word to describe this fund—sensational. Its historical track record is second to none, with consistent value-added performance year in and year out. Investors looking for a good bond fund should stop here and look no further. Managed by Scott Lamont of Phillips, Hager & North Investment Management, the fund pursues high returns through a combination of interest income and capital growth, investing in high-quality, fixed-income government and corporate bonds.

Investors in the Phillips Hager & North Bond Fund have enjoyed exceptional returns during the life of the fund and can expect similar results in the future. In addition, the fund has an advantage over other bond funds with its rock-bottom management fee. Investors seeking income with some conservative growth won't be disappointed with this fund over the longer term.

Fund performance

The fund has earned a five-star Vos Value Rating for reward, risk, and the best balance between risk and reward. During the previous year the fund posted a 4.6 per cent rate of return. Investors should expect a little more in this low-interest-rate environment. The best 12-month rate of return for this fund was a gain of 45.3 per cent, and the average rate of return after 12 months was 11.8 per cent.

This fund has invested 52 per cent of its portfolio in government bonds, with an additional 29 per cent in corporate bonds. It has invested 22 per cent in mid-term bonds, 25 per cent in short-term, and 51 per cent in long-term bonds respectively.

Fund risks

The fund has displayed very little downside risk and has performed in line with expectations during each of the last four bear markets. The fund's worst 12-month rate of return was a loss of 6.1 per cent, and it posted positive rates of return after 12 months 94 per cent of the time. Investing in Canadian bonds isn't a risk-free venture, but within a well-diversified portfolio of mutual funds the risk can be manageable. The worst setback that this fund has ever incurred was a loss of 11.2 per cent. During the same period the average Canadian bond fund declined in value by 11.4 per cent. The fund took 10 months to recover from its loss.

Future prospects

Fixed-income markets have endured some pressure because of a poor interest-rate outlook in the United States, which could have negative implications for interest rates in Canada. The U.S. economy is experiencing a very high rate of economic growth, low unemployment, and higher inflation, but the Federal Reserve Board has managed to slow the economy without stalling growth.

The PH & N Bond Fund should continue to generate above-average results. Investors looking for a good Canadian bond fund with an excellent reputation and long-term track record should consider it.

FUND DETAILS

Fund name	**PH & N Bond**	Fund size (in $ millions)	$2,581
Fund family	Phillips, Hager & North Ltd.	Percentage in foreign holdings	0.00%
Mutual fund investment category	Canadian Bond	RRSP eligible	100%
Start date for data shown	July 1982	Sales charge	None
Number of funds in investment category	234	Redemption charge	None
Dividend frequency	Quarterly	Management expense ratio	0.57%

FUND PERFORMANCE

	1 month	6 months	1 year	3 years	5 years	10 years
Returns ending June 2000	1.6%	5.4%	4.6%	6.2%	8.3%	10.4%
Best historical return	8.0%	37.2%	45.3%	23.6%	19.7%	15.9%
Average historical return	1.0%	5.9%	11.8%	12.0%	11.7%	11.9%
Worst historical return	-4.7%	-9.9%	-6.1%	4.9%	8.1%	9.9%
Value at risk of $1,000	$980	$975	$994	$1,215	$1,524	$2,627

RETURNS GREATER THAN

	1 month	6 months	1 year	3 years	5 years	10 years
10 per cent	0%	53%	59%	67%	84%	97%
Zero	69%	88%	94%	100%	100%	100%
Percentage of time fund lost $	31%	12%	6%	0%	0%	0%
Number of periods evaluated	216	211	205	181	157	97

DOWNSIDE RISK

	Worst setback since start date	In bear 1987	In bear 1990	In bear 1994	In bear 1998
Setback for mutual fund	-11.2%	-4.1%	-5.4%	-11.2%	-1.5%
Setback for peer group	-11.4%	-5.3%	-5.0%	-11.4%	-1.8%
Setback ended in	June 1994	Sept. 1987	April 1990	June 1994	Aug. 1998
Months to recover from loss	10	3	3	10	1

ROLLING 12-MONTH QUARTILE RANKING OF MUTUAL FUND PERFORMANCE OVER TIME

Canadian bond

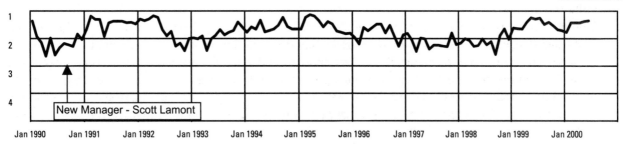

1 is first quartile; 2 is second quartile; 3 is third quartile; 4 is fourth quartile. First quartile means that the fund outperformed 75 per cent of other similar funds after 12 months.

ROLLING 12-MONTH TOTAL RATE OF RETURN FOR THE MUTUAL FUND OVER TIME

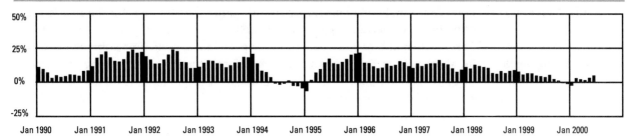

AGF GLOBAL GOVERNMENT BOND FUND

Vos value rating		
Reward	**Risk**	**Best balance**
★★★★	★★★★★	★★★★★

Fund profile

This fund aims to provide investors with a high level of monthly income and the potential for capital appreciation by investing in a diversified portfolio of government bonds from developed nations. Foreign bond funds invest in bonds that pay their interest payments in a currency other than the Canadian dollar. In this way they provide currency diversification and the potential for higher returns than Canadian bonds. They also make an excellent contribution to a well-diversified portfolio for income-oriented investors, since they tend to go up when everything else is going down and vice versa. In 1999 and 2000 the value of the Canadian dollar appreciated, and foreign bond funds have depreciated as a result. Nevertheless, foreign bonds can be a very profitable component over the long term. In 1998, for example, this was one of the best-performing investment categories.

Warren Goldring and Clive Coombs of AGF Funds manage the AGF Global Government Bond Fund. AGF has also introduced the AGF RSP Global Government Bond Fund, which is RRSP-eligible and is not considered to be foreign content within an RRSP.

Fund performance

Like most top-performing bond funds, this one had a dismal year, underperforming similar funds and posting a loss of 4.9 per cent. As a result, it earned a four-star Vos Value Rating for reward. During favourable economic conditions the fund has posted gains in excess of 20 per cent, although the average 12-month rate of return is only 7.6 per cent. The fund maintains an active currency exposure, so a depreciating Canadian dollar will help this fund's performance.

Fund risks

The volatility associated with investing in foreign bonds is highly correlated with fluctuations in foreign currencies and the Canadian dollar. When the Canadian dollar appreciates, these funds tend to decline in value. This fund's worst 12-month rate of return was a loss of 13.4 per cent, and the fund has posted losses after 12 months 85 per cent of the time. The worst setback that this fund has ever incurred was a loss of 14.7 per cent. During the same period the average foreign bond fund declined in value by 12.8 per cent. Unfortunately, the fund hasn't recovered the loss yet.

Future prospects

Fixed-income markets have endured some pressure because of a poor interest-rate outlook in the United States and an appreciating Canadian dollar. This has had a very negative impact on the performance of these funds. However, investors should remember that it's only the future that counts, and the future looks brighter than the past. With the U.S. economy slowing down and unemployment stabilizing, interest rates should stabilize as well, and these bonds should regain their appeal. It is uncertain how these factors will affect foreign bonds in the short term, but investors should never forget foreign bonds' strongest attribute: diversification. When the going gets tough, foreign bonds get going. If you're looking for a tough foreign bond fund consider the AGF Global Government Bond Fund.

FUND DETAILS

Fund name	**AGF Global Government Bond**	Fund size (in $ millions)	$179
Fund family	AGF Funds Inc.	Percentage in foreign holdings	31.34%
Mutual fund investment category	Foreign Bond	RRSP eligible	20%
Start date for data shown	November 1986	Sales charge	Optional
Number of funds in investment category	82	Redemption charge	Optional
Dividend frequency	Monthly	Management expense ratio	1.86%

FUND PERFORMANCE

	1 month	6 months	1 year	3 years	5 years	10 years
Returns ending June 2000	1.2%	0.7%	-4.9%	3.2%	4.3%	7.5%
Best historical return	10.2%	21.7%	28.7%	16.1%	11.9%	10.1%
Average historical return	0.6%	3.6%	7.6%	8.4%	8.7%	8.6%
Worst historical return	-6.4%	-11.1%	-13.4%	0.6%	4.2%	7.3%
Value at risk of $1,000	$971	$931	$928	$1,099	$1,276	$2,064

RETURNS GREATER THAN

	1 month	6 months	1 year	3 years	5 years	10 years
10 per cent	1%	43%	35%	29%	31%	4%
Zero	61%	72%	85%	100%	100%	100%
Percentage of time fund lost $	39%	28%	15%	0%	0%	0%
Number of periods evaluated	164	159	153	129	105	45

DOWNSIDE RISK

	Worst setback since start date	In bear 1987	In bear 1990	In bear 1994	In bear 1998
Setback for mutual fund	-14.7%	-9.6%	-4.1%	-3.6%	-1.3%
Setback for peer group	-12.8%	-7.5%	-5.1%	-5.1%	-1.9%
Setback ended in	Jan. 2000	Sept. 1987	April 1990	Sept. 1994	Feb. 1998
Months to recover from loss	?	3	2	4	2

ROLLING 12-MONTH QUARTILE RANKING OF MUTUAL FUND PERFORMANCE OVER TIME

Foreign bond

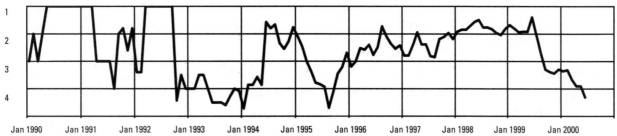

1 is first quartile; 2 is second quartile; 3 is third quartile; 4 is fourth quartile. First quartile means that the fund outperformed 75 per cent of other similar funds after 12 months.

ROLLING 12-MONTH TOTAL RATE OF RETURN FOR THE MUTUAL FUND OVER TIME

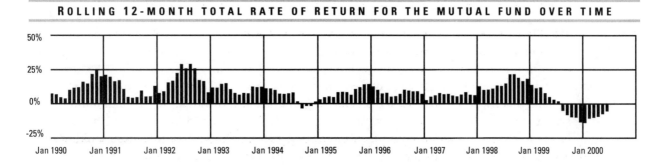

TRIMARK ADVANTAGE BOND

Vos value rating		
Reward	**Risk**	**Best balance**
★★★★★	★★★★★	★★★★★

Fund profile

This fund invests in a combination of high-yield and government bonds. High-yield bonds carry a Standard & Poor's credit rating below BBB and are issued to raise capital by companies with less financial strength and more business risk than their larger competitors. Fund managers Patrick Farmer and Rex Chong use fundamental value analysis to uncover above-average investment opportunities and reduce risk.

High-yielding bonds have generated some very impressive rates of return, although recently the Canadian market has experienced some short-term volatility. Investors should remember that over the longer term corporate bonds should continue to generate reasonable rates of return. The Trimark Advantage Bond Fund should be considered by most investors and by all bond investors to improve their returns and reduce their risk.

Fund performance

Historically this fund has added value for investors by improving returns while significantly reducing risk, and it has earned a triple five-star Vos Value Rating for reward, risk, and the best balance between risk and reward. The fund has been in the first quartile frequently when compared to similar funds after 12 months. Its best 12-month rate of return was a gain of 23.6 per cent, earned by investing in the corporate bonds of companies such as Rogers Cable Systems, Air Canada, and Silicon Graphics.

The fund has invested 20 per cent of its holdings in foreign bonds to take advantage of international opportunities, but this could also increase the risk. It has also invested in government and corporate bonds. This three-pronged strategy creates a powerful combination for conservative investors. During volatile markets, this fund should outperform; during favourable markets, it will underperform, but over the long term it should consistently deliver above-average risk-adjusted performance and outperform the competition.

Fund risks

Investing in various categories is an excellent strategy to reduce risk, and high-yield bonds are an excellent way to diversify your fixed income and equity investments. The worst 12-month return posted by this fund was a decline of 0.5 per cent, and it declined in value after 12 months only 2 per cent of the time. During the bear market of 1998, it declined in value by 3.1 per cent. During the same period, the average high-yield bond fund declined in value by 4.2 per cent, but this fund took only five months to recover its loss.

Fund prospects

High-yield bonds respond to company-specific results and changes in interest rates. If a company's fundamentals improve, it will receive a higher credit rating and, with an improved rating, the bond will increase in value. This makes high-yield bonds unique compared to high-grade or government bonds and offers investors the opportunity for higher absolute rates of return than traditional bond funds. Investors should not restrict their investments to just this fund but should invest in a combination of mutual funds to reduce their risk without sacrificing their return potential. Investors looking for a conservative high-yield bond fund should consider the Trimark Advantage Bond Fund.

FUND DETAILS

Fund name	**Trimark Advantage Bond**	Fund size (in $ millions)	$618
Fund family	Trimark Investment Management Inc.	Percentage in foreign holdings	20.00%
Mutual fund investment category	High Yield Bond	RRSP eligible	100%
Start date for data shown	January 1995	Sales charge	Optional
Number of funds in investment category	18	Redemption charge	Optional
Dividend frequency	Monthly	Management expense ratio	1.30%

FUND PERFORMANCE

	1 month	6 months	1 year	3 years	5 years	10 years
Returns ending June 2000	1.3%	2.2%	2.7%	4.8%	8.1%	
Best historical return	4.3%	13.2%	23.6%	15.7%	10.2%	
Average historical return	0.8%	4.5%	9.1%	9.3%	9.0%	
Worst historical return	-3.1%	-1.4%	-0.5%	4.8%	8.0%	
Value at risk of $1,000	$984	$994	$1,012	$1,152	$1,474	

RETURNS GREATER THAN

	1 month	6 months	1 year	3 years	5 years	10 years
10 per cent	0%	39%	55%	32%	14%	
Zero	73%	90%	98%	100%	100%	
Percentage of time fund lost $	27%	10%	2%	0%	0%	
Number of periods evaluated	66	61	55	31	7	

DOWNSIDE RISK

	Worst setback since start date	In bear 1987	In bear 1990	In bear 1994	In bear 1998
Setback for mutual fund	-3.1%				-3.1%
Setback for peer group	-3.5%				-4.2%
Setback ended in	Aug. 1998				Aug. 1998
Months to recover from loss	5				5

ROLLING 12-MONTH QUARTILE RANKING OF MUTUAL FUND PERFORMANCE OVER TIME

High yield bond

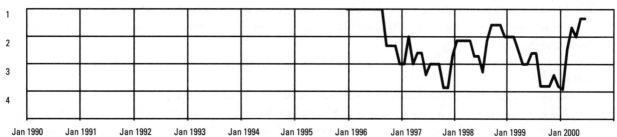

1 is first quartile; 2 is second quartile; 3 is third quartile; 4 is fourth quartile. First quartile means that the fund outperformed 75 per cent of other similar funds after 12 months.

ROLLING 12-MONTH TOTAL RATE OF RETURN FOR THE MUTUAL FUND OVER TIME

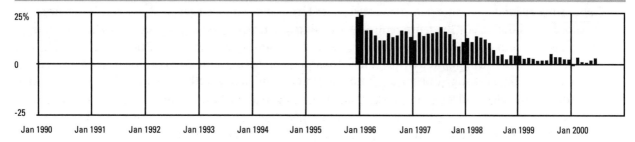

ATLAS CANADIAN BALANCED FUND

Vos value rating		
Reward	**Risk**	**Best balance**
★★★	★★★★	★★★★

Fund profile

All great funds stumble from time to time, and this fund has been no exception. Still, its long-term fundamentals remain intact. The Atlas Canadian Balanced Fund aims to provide investors with a high level of return by investing in both fixed-income and equity investments. This provides investors with a nominal level of income while they participate in the long-term growth of equity markets. The fund invests primarily in high-quality government and corporate bonds and common stock of Canadian blue-chip companies. The fund is managed Len Racioppo of Jarislowsky Fraser Ltd, the fund's sub-advisor, who relies on fundamental analysis to buy investments at reasonable prices and ensure success over the long term, a strategy that paid a handsome dividend over the long term but not during the previous year, when growth stocks led the charge.

Balanced funds are a popular investment for mutual fund investors, because they offer a high degree of diversification and growth potential. These attributes ensure that investors don't incur an excessive amount of volatility.

Fund performance

During the previous year the fund posted a dismal rate of return compared to similar funds. It was third quartile, under-performing more than 50 per cent of similar funds. Its only saving grace was generating a return of 8.3 per cent, and the fund lost its five-star Vos Value Rating for reward. Investors should remember, however, that the fund has frequently been in the first quartile after 12 months, although it has had difficulties from time to time. Its best 12-month rate of return was a gain of 29.3 per cent.

The fund has invested almost 19.99 per cent of its assets outside of Canada, but also holds Canadian companies like Loblaw, a major food retailer, and Toronto-Dominion Bank, one of Canada's largest chartered banks.

Fund risks

Jarislowsky Fraser Ltd., the sub-advisor to the fund, emphasizes risk control in its investments. These efforts have added value for investors, as the fund has displayed less downside risk than the average Canadian balanced fund. The fund declined in value by 8.3 per cent during the bear of 1998, for example, while the average Canadian balanced fund declined by 13.4 per cent. However, this strategy will also cause the fund to underperform occasionally—usually when growth stocks perform well.

Fund prospects

Good mutual funds like this one encounter short-term performance issues. However, it has done an excellent job of addressing them prudently by adopting and retaining an appropriate investment strategy. In turn, this fund has generated excellent results for investors. Patient investors who invest in a balanced fund should not be disappointed by the Atlas Canadian Balanced Fund. With value-added management and better capital market prospects, the fund should continue to do well in the future. More aggressive investors should also consider a more aggressive fund to complement this one.

FUND DETAILS

Fund name	**Atlas Canadian Balanced**	Fund size (in $ millions)	$496
Fund family	Atlas Asset Management Inc.	Percentage in foreign holdings	19.99%
Mutual fund investment category	Canadian Balanced	RRSP eligible	100%
Start date for data shown	September 1989	Sales charge	Optional
Number of funds in investment category	383	Redemption charge	Optional
Dividend frequency	Quarterly	Management expense ratio	2.32%

FUND PERFORMANCE

	1 month	6 months	1 year	3 years	5 years	10 years
Returns ending June 2000	0.7%	7.3%	8.3%	9.1%	12.3%	10.2%
Best historical return	5.0%	15.2%	29.3%	18.2%	13.8%	10.4%
Average historical return	0.8%	4.6%	9.8%	10.7%	10.7%	9.5%
Worst historical return	-7.2%	-6.5%	-6.5%	4.9%	5.4%	8.9%
Value at risk of $1,000	$974	$971	$989	$1,169	$1,325	$2,351

RETURNS GREATER THAN

	1 month	6 months	1 year	3 years	5 years	10 years
10 per cent	0%	51%	45%	51%	62%	27%
Zero	68%	81%	93%	100%	100%	100%
Percentage of time fund lost $	32%	19%	7%	0%	0%	0%
Number of periods evaluated	130	125	119	95	71	11

DOWNSIDE RISK

	Worst setback since start date	In bear 1987	In bear 1990	In bear 1994	In bear 1998
Setback for mutual fund	-8.5%		-6.9%	-8.5%	-8.3%
Setback for peer group	-8.7%		-7.2%	-8.7%	-13.4%
Setback ended in	June 1994		Sept. 1990	June 1994	Aug. 1998
Months to recover from loss	9		5	9	4

ROLLING 12-MONTH QUARTILE RANKING OF MUTUAL FUND PERFORMANCE OVER TIME

Canadian balanced

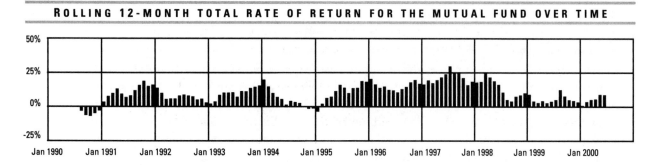

1 is first quartile; 2 is second quartile; 3 is third quartile; 4 is fourth quartile. First quartile means that the fund outperformed 75 per cent of other similar funds after 12 months.

ROLLING 12-MONTH TOTAL RATE OF RETURN FOR THE MUTUAL FUND OVER TIME

FIDELITY CANADIAN ASSET ALLOCATION FUND

Vos value rating		
Reward	**Risk**	**Best balance**
★★★★★	★★	★★★★

Fund profile

It was a good year for Canadian balanced funds, and this one participated in the gains. It aims to provide high returns by investing in a combination of Canadian stocks, bonds, and money-market instruments. This strategy allows investors to earn a higher rate of return without incurring excessive risk. It's more aggressive than a traditional balanced fund and considers a 65-per-cent weight in equities neutral, compared to a 50-per-cent weight for the average Canadian balanced fund. So it can add value by aggressively changing the mix between equities and bonds. Investors who require income and capital preservation with upside potential have been quite pleased with this fund over the longer term. It's managed by the investment team of Richard Habermann, Alan Radlo, and Ford O'Neil, who have done an excellent job of adding value through difficult capital markets.

Fund performance

The managers generate above-average performance by evaluating a broad range of economic and market factors to determine the preferred asset mix between equities and bonds. They select individual securities using a bottom-up approach, which entails finding good companies at reasonable prices. The fund has earned a five-star Vos Value Rating for reward by generating an above-average rate of return during the previous three years and has consistently been first quartile after 12 months compared to similar funds. Its best 12-month rate of return was a gain of 41.6 per cent, and the fund's average 12-month rate of return was 17.2 per cent.

The fund maintains an aggressive equity bias: 50 per cent is currently invested in such Canadian equities as BCE, Canada's largest telecommunications company, and Onex Corporation, a large holding company.

Fund risks

The fund is more risky than the average Canadian balanced fund and has earned a two-star Vos Value Rating for risk, which indicates that, in the short term, it has displayed more risk than similar funds. Over the medium term, however, the fund managers have done an excellent job of managing the risk associated with investing in Canadian capital markets.

Investors should realize that they'll inevitably encounter above-average risk with a balanced fund that can aggressively change its asset mix. Investors benefit if the managers make the correct decision; if they make the wrong decision, investors could experience new levels of downside risk. The fund has earned money frequently and still exhibits significantly less risk than a traditional equity fund.

Fund prospects

Economic growth in North America is strong, and this could stimulate further volatility in capital markets. Higher economic growth could continue to generate havoc in the bond markets, and stock markets are establishing new highs on a daily basis, which could be a prelude to a market correction. However, investors who patiently invest in a balanced fund should not be disappointed over the long term. Investors looking for a more aggressive Canadian balanced fund with value-added management should consider the Fidelity Canadian Tactical Asset Allocation Fund.

FUND DETAILS

Fund name	**Fidelity Canadian Asset Allocation**	Fund size (in $ millions)	$6,650
Fund family	Fidelity Investments Canada Limited	Percentage in foreign holdings	15.17%
Mutual fund investment category	Canadian Balanced	RRSP eligible	100%
Start date for data shown	January 1995	Sales charge	Optional
Number of funds in investment category	383	Redemption charge	Optional
Dividend frequency	Quarterly	Management expense ratio	2.41%

FUND PERFORMANCE

	1 month	6 months	1 year	3 years	5 years	10 years
Returns ending June 2000	5.5%	6.0%	18.6%	13.2%	16.7%	
Best historical return	9.3%	22.3%	41.6%	23.9%	18.9%	
Average historical return	1.4%	8.7%	17.2%	17.6%	17.6%	
Worst historical return	-9.8%	-8.9%	-1.5%	12.2%	16.1%	
Value at risk of $1,000	$969	$951	$1,022	$1,438	$2,124	

RETURNS GREATER THAN

	1 month	6 months	1 year	3 years	5 years	10 years
10 per cent	0%	77%	75%	100%	100%	
Zero	67%	89%	98%	100%	100%	
Percentage of time fund lost $	33%	11%	2%	0%	0%	
Number of periods evaluated	66	61	55	31	7	

DOWNSIDE RISK

	Worst setback since start date	In bear 1987	In bear 1990	In bear 1994	In bear 1998
Setback for mutual fund	-11.8%			-1.1%	-11.8%
Setback for peer group	-13.4%			-1.5%	-13.4%
Setback ended in	Aug. 1998			Jan. 1995	Aug. 1998
Months to recover from loss	5			1	5

ROLLING 12-MONTH QUARTILE RANKING OF MUTUAL FUND PERFORMANCE OVER TIME

Canadian balanced

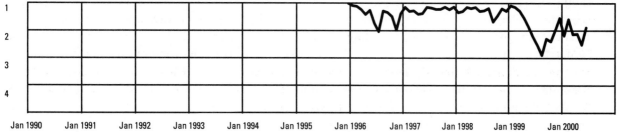

1 is first quartile; 2 is second quartile; 3 is third quartile; 4 is fourth quartile. First quartile means that the fund outperformed 75 per cent of other similar funds after 12 months.

ROLLING 12-MONTH TOTAL RATE OF RETURN FOR THE MUTUAL FUND OVER TIME

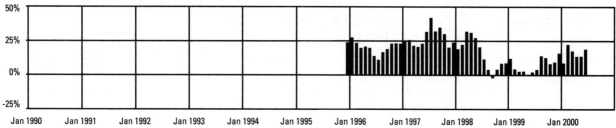

SCOTIA CANADIAN BALANCED FUND

Vos value rating		
Reward	**Risk**	**Best balance**
★★★★★	★★★★★	★★★★★

Fund profile

The Scotia Canadian Balanced Fund, formerly known as the National Trust Balanced Fund, invests in a diversified portfolio of investments to achieve a consistent rate of return and is ideal for conservative investors looking for a core investment in their mutual fund portfolio. It invests in international and domestic equities, domestic bonds, and cash to diversify the portfolio while achieving consistent rates of return. Managed by Scotia Cassels Investment Counsel Ltd., it maintains a low management fee and avoids large risks.

During the previous year Canadian balanced funds have had a good year. Many have appreciated in value by more than 15 per cent, a very impressive return compared to 1998.

Fund performance

This fund won't deliver any surprises. It maintains a consistent asset mix and invests in large blue-chip and international companies. It has generated above-average performance during the previous three years and has earned a triple five-star Vos Value Rating for reward, risk, and the best balance between risk and reward. During the past year, it earned a return of 15 per cent. Its best 12-month rate of return was a gain of 32.8 per cent, and the its average 12-month rate of return was a gain of 11.7 per cent.

The fund holds 18.57 per cent of its assets in foreign investments, 40 per cent in Canadian bonds, and 30-plus per cent in Canadian equities. It has invested in two of Canada's largest chartered banks, Royal Bank and TD, and in Bombardier, one of Canada's most dynamic companies.

Fund risks

The fund will incur very little company-specific risk. It avoids making aggressive investments, so investors incur only the risk associated with investing in capital markets. During the bear market of 1998, the fund declined by 11 per cent, while the average Canadian balanced fund declined by 13.4 per cent. But this fund took only five months to recover. Thus, the fund has delivered average performance during periods of capital-market volatility and downside risk. Conservative investors will appreciate the fund's emphasis on risk control.

Future prospects

Investing in Canadian balanced funds doesn't work each year, but over time they'll add value for conservative investors. Balanced-fund investors participate in the growth potential of the stock market while preserving their capital by investing in bonds and other fixed-income investments. Canadian capital markets will continue to be volatile—more so than ever before. However, with good economic growth, a stronger dollar, and low interest rates, capital markets should appreciate over the long term. Investors who use a balanced approach should not be disappointed with their results. Investors looking for a fund that has a high probability of achieving good results should consider the Scotia Canadian Balanced Fund.

FUND DETAILS

Fund name	**Scotia Canadian Balanced**	Fund size (in $ millions)	$1,198
Fund family	The Bank of Nova Scotia	Percentage in foreign holdings	18.57%
Mutual fund investment category	Canadian Balanced	RRSP eligible	100%
Start date for data shown	July 1990	Sales charge	None
Number of funds in investment category	383	Redemption charge	None
Dividend frequency	Quarterly	Management expense ratio	1.64%

FUND PERFORMANCE

	1 month	6 months	1 year	3 years	5 years	10 years
Returns ending June 2000	3.6%	7.7%	15.0%	10.9%	13.3%	11.5%
Best historical return	5.6%	17.2%	32.8%	18.2%	13.9%	11.5%
Average historical return	0.9%	5.8%	11.7%	11.6%	11.5%	11.5%
Worst historical return	-9.4%	-8.9%	-9.3%	4.7%	8.8%	11.5%
Value at risk of $1,000	$972	$967	$984	$1,210	$1,578	$2,967

RETURNS GREATER THAN

	1 month	6 months	1 year	3 years	5 years	10 years
10 per cent	0%	60%	63%	64%	80%	100%
Zero	68%	87%	93%	100%	100%	100%
Percentage of time fund lost $	33%	13%	7%	0%	0%	0%
Number of periods evaluated	120	115	109	85	61	1

DOWNSIDE RISK

	Worst setback since start date	In bear 1987	In bear 1990	In bear 1994	In bear 1998
Setback for mutual fund	-11.4%		-5.7%	-11.4%	-11.0%
Setback for peer group	-8.7%		-4.3%	-8.7%	-13.4%
Setback ended in	June 1994		Oct. 1990	June 1994	Aug. 1998
Months to recover from loss	11		2	11	5

ROLLING 12-MONTH QUARTILE RANKING OF MUTUAL FUND PERFORMANCE OVER TIME

Canadian balanced

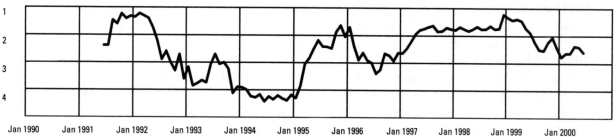

1 is first quartile; 2 is second quartile; 3 is third quartile; 4 is fourth quartile. First quartile means that the fund outperformed 75 per cent of other similar funds after 12 months.

ROLLING 12-MONTH TOTAL RATE OF RETURN FOR THE MUTUAL FUND OVER TIME

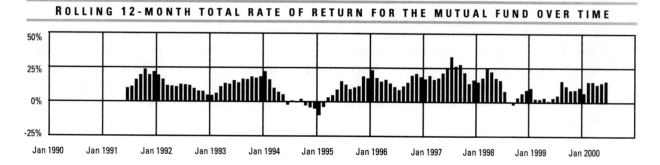

STANDARD LIFE BALANCED FUND

Vos value rating		
Reward	**Risk**	**Best balance**
★★★★★	★★★★★	★★★★★

Fund profile

The Standard Life Balanced Fund, managed by Peter Hill, Norman Raschkowan, and William MacDonald of Standard Life Portfolio Management Limited, aims to provide investors with steady income and the potential for long-term capital gains while minimizing short-term risk. Canadian balanced funds were very kind to investors during the previous year. Many of them appreciated in value by more than 15 per cent.

This fund has invested in large blue-chip Canadian companies and Canadian government bonds. It has also invested 15.43 per cent of its assets in foreign investments to reduce risk through diversification. These characteristics make this fund ideal for conservative investors looking for a core investment in their portfolio.

Fund performance

This fund has delivered consistent results and has earned a triple five-star rating for reward, risk, and the best balance between risk and reward. The fund has been first quartile after 12 months frequently when compared to similar funds, although it was fourth quartile during 1994. The fund's best 12-month rate of return was a gain of 29.7 per cent, and its average rate of return was a gain of 11.2 per cent. During the previous year the fund generated a return of 20.1 per cent—a very impressive return.

The fund has invested 41 per cent of its assets in Canadian equities and 37 per cent in Canadian bonds. The remainder is invested in cash and foreign equities. In Canadian equities, the fund has invested 16 per cent of its assets in the industrial-products sector and an additional 4 per cent in financial services. The fund has invested in companies like Nortel Networks, Royal Bank of Canada, BCE, and Toronto Dominion Bank.

Fund risks

The fund has done a good job managing the risk associated with Canadian balanced funds. It declined in value less than the average fund during the bear market of 1998, and its worst 12-month rate of return was a loss of 7.2 per cent. The fund's one-year value at risk was $981, indicating that after one year an investor's initial $1,000 investment would have been worth more than $981 at least 95 per cent of the time.

Fund prospects

The managers of this balanced fund have done a good job of balancing risk and growth. But investors should remember that capital markets in general and this fund in particular could exhibit more downside risk. With inflation inching upward and economic growth still robust, they should be realistic about future returns. Higher inflation may force interest rates up in the short term, which would cause stock markets to go down in value. The fund makes a good core fund or a nice complement to a well-diversified portfolio. In the short term, capital markets will be volatile, but short-term problems will be resolved over the longer term, and capital markets will appreciate. Investors looking for a value-added balanced fund should consider the Standard Life Balanced Fund.

FUND DETAILS

Fund name	**Standard Life Balanced**	Fund size (in $ millions)	$34
Fund family	The Standard Life Assurance Company	Percentage in foreign holdings	15.43%
Mutual fund investment category	Canadian Balanced	RRSP eligible	100%
Start date for data shown	November 1992	Sales charge	None
Number of funds in investment category	383	Redemption charge	Deferred
Dividend frequency	Quarterly	Management expense ratio	2.00%

FUND PERFORMANCE

	1 month	6 months	1 year	3 years	5 years	10 years
Returns ending June 2000	4.5%	11.8%	20.1%	11.4%	13.7%	
Best historical return	5.8%	16.1%	29.7%	18.2%	13.9%	
Average historical return	1.0%	5.7%	11.2%	12.3%	12.0%	
Worst historical return	-9.7%	-8.8%	-7.2%	7.8%	8.9%	
Value at risk of $1,000	$973	$945	$981	$1,259	$1,588	

RETURNS GREATER THAN

	1 month	6 months	1 year	3 years	5 years	10 years
10 per cent	0%	64%	59%	72%	85%	
Zero	67%	85%	85%	100%	100%	
Percentage of time fund lost $	33%	15%	15%	0%	0%	
Number of periods evaluated	92	87	81	57	33	

DOWNSIDE RISK

	Worst setback since start date	In bear 1987	In bear 1990	In bear 1994	In bear 1998
Setback for mutual fund	-11.9%			-10.1%	-11.9%
Setback for peer group	-13.4%			-8.7%	-13.4%
Setback ended in	Aug. 1998			June 1994	Aug. 1998
Months to recover from loss	10			11	10

ROLLING 12-MONTH QUARTILE RANKING OF MUTUAL FUND PERFORMANCE OVER TIME

Canadian balanced

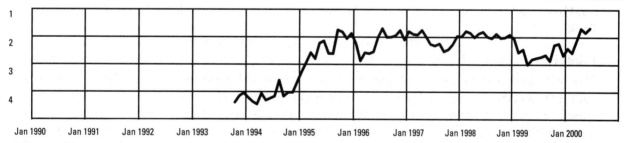

1 is first quartile; 2 is second quartile; 3 is third quartile; 4 is fourth quartile. First quartile means that the fund outperformed 75 per cent of other similar funds after 12 months.

ROLLING 12-MONTH TOTAL RATE OF RETURN FOR THE MUTUAL FUND OVER TIME

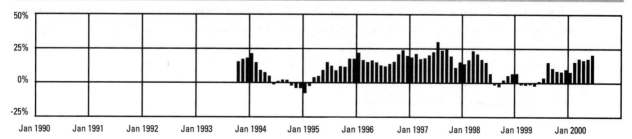

TRANSAMERICA GROWSAFE CANADIAN BALANCED FUND

Vos value rating		
Reward	**Risk**	**Best balance**
★★★★★	★	★★★★

Fund profile

Stop—look twice before you consider investing in this fund. This fund was one of the best-performing Canadian balanced funds during the previous year and generated higher returns than some Canadian equity funds. It aims to provide a long-term stable rate of return while maintaining a reasonable degree of diversification, investing prudently in an array of Canadian and foreign securities.

This fund consistently underperformed similar funds until Mark Jackson took over the day-to-day activities in October 1998. Since then, the fund has completed a transformation and is now posting first quartile performance. Investors should realize that the fund manager didn't generate such sensational rates of return without incurring more risk than similar funds. But if they're willing to endure this higher level of risk, they should consider the merits of this fund.

Fund performance

With some prudent stock selection like JDS Uniphase, Certicom, Celestica, and PMC-Sierra, this fund generated a return of 63.5 per cent during the previous year and earned a five-star Vos Value Rating for reward. Since Mark Jackson started managing the fund, it has generated first-quartile performance after 12 months relative to similar funds. Its best 12-month rate of return was a gain of 106.7 per cent, and its average rate of return after 12 months was 17.7 per cent. The fund continues to invest aggressively in high-technology companies but has also invested in several blue-chip Canadian companies.

Fund risks

The fund's worst setback ever was a loss of 17.2 per cent. During the same period the average Canadian balanced fund did not decline in value. The fund still hasn't recovered. It has earned a one-star Vos Value Rating for risk, because it incurs an excessive amount of short-term risk, of which investors should be aware.

Fund prospects

In future, the fund isn't likely to post another gain of 63 per cent, but the manager has displayed some talent for selecting stocks in the short term. However, this short-term trend may not translate into a long-term consistent track record. A fund that can outperform by such large margins can also underperform by similar margins. For investors who can withstand some short-term risk, this fund has upside potential. After all, a $1,000 investment that appreciates by 63 per cent is worth $1,630—not bad. Investors looking for a little spice could consider the Transamerica Growsafe Canadian Balanced Fund for a portion of their portfolio, which could make a big difference to their overall gains.

FUND DETAILS

Fund name	Transamerica Growsafe Canadian Balanced	Fund size (in $ millions)	$477
Fund family	Transamerica Life Insurance Co. of Canada	Percentage in foreign holdings	12.08%
Mutual fund investment category	Canadian Balanced	RRSP eligible	100%
Start date for data shown	April 1994	Sales charge	None
Number of funds in investment category	383	Redemption charge	Deferred
Dividend frequency	N	Management expense ratio	2.46%

FUND PERFORMANCE

	1 month	6 months	1 year	3 years	5 years	10 years
Returns ending June 2000	8.1%	16.5%	63.6%	26.6%	20.5%	
Best historical return	21.2%	80.3%	106.7%	32.6%	24.3%	
Average historical return	1.4%	9.9%	17.7%	13.4%	15.3%	
Worst historical return	-10.0%	-10.2%	-7.4%	5.3%	9.3%	
Value at risk of $1,000	$952	$963	$1,003	$1,223	$1,602	

RETURNS GREATER THAN

	1 month	6 months	1 year	3 years	5 years	10 years
10 per cent	4%	54%	63%	75%	94%	
Zero	65%	89%	95%	100%	100%	
Percentage of time fund lost $	35%	11%	5%	0%	0%	
Number of periods evaluated	75	70	64	40	16	

DOWNSIDE RISK

	Worst setback since start date	In bear 1987	In bear 1990	In bear 1994	In bear 1998
Setback for mutual fund	-17.2%			-4.4%	-13.0%
Setback for peer group	0.0%			-4.7%	-13.4%
Setback ended in	May 2000			June 1994	Aug. 1998
Months to recover from loss	?			8	5

ROLLING 12-MONTH QUARTILE RANKING OF MUTUAL FUND PERFORMANCE OVER TIME

Canadian balanced

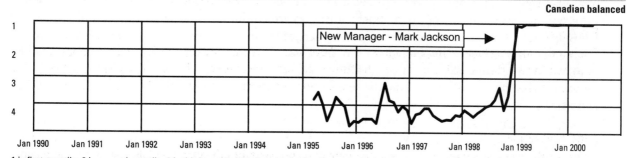

1 is first quartile; 2 is second quartile; 3 is third quartile; 4 is fourth quartile. First quartile means that the fund outperformed 75 per cent of other similar funds after 12 months.

ROLLING 12-MONTH TOTAL RATE OF RETURN FOR THE MUTUAL FUND OVER TIME

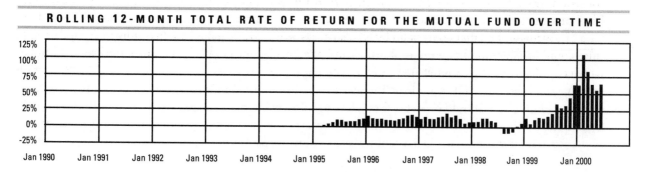

AGF AMERICAN TACTICAL ASSET ALLOCATION FUND

Vos value rating		
Reward	**Risk**	**Best balance**
★★★★★	★★★★	★★★★★

Fund profile

The AGF American Tactical Allocation Fund has been managed by Barclays Global Investors since June 1996. It invests in a combination of shares from the Standard and Poor's 500 index, using a qualitative model to move from equity to bond investments when economic conditions change. The bond portion of the fund is invested in long-term and U.S. Treasury bonds.

Investors who want to participate in the growth of the U.S. stock market with less risk will find this fund suitable. However, unlike other foreign balanced funds, this fund focuses only on U.S. stocks and so does not have the same degree of geographic diversification. U.S. stocks currently trade at a high premium and, with inflation rates inching upwards, the U.S. stock market could become riskier. However, if the manager continues to make prudent asset-class decisions, investors should not experience any adverse downside risk.

Fund performance

This fund has participated in the growth of the U.S. stock market and has earned a five-star Vos Value Rating for reward and the best balance between risk and reward. It has frequently been first quartile after 12 months, but not during the previous year. The fund also encountered some performance issues during 1994, a period of rising interest rates and lower equity returns. The fund's best 12-month rate of return was a gain of 36.6 per cent. During the last year, it posted a gain of 6 per cent, respectable but not very good considering the economic environment for international stocks, in which this fund doesn't invest. Similar funds do invest in international stocks and were able to outperform in the short term because of these investments.

The fund has currently invested 60 per cent of its assets in equities such as Microsoft, General Electric, Intel, Wal-Mart, Exxon, Merck & Co, IBM, Coca-Cola, and Pfizer, with the remainder in bonds.

Fund risks

During the bear market of 1998 the fund declined by 6.2 per cent, less than the average foreign balanced fund, which declined in value by 7.6 per cent. The fund took only two months to recover. The worst 12-month return posted by this fund was a decline of 5.1 per cent, and it declined in value after 12 months only 3 per cent of the time.

Fund prospects

This fund is ideal for conservative investors. The fund's ability to switch back and forth from bonds to equities should generate less volatility than a pure U.S. equity fund, but it could also generate lower returns. This ability to switch is an attractive feature, considering the current volatility associated with the stock market. The AGF American Tactical Allocation Fund should continue to generate acceptable returns, but investors should expect some short-term downside risk. The risk associated with investing in U.S. equities is increasing, because short-term interest rates are rising as the economy rages ahead. To avoid a market correction, the U.S. economy has to slow down without stagnating.

FUND DETAILS

Fund name	**AGF American T.A. Allocation**	Fund size (in $ millions)	$694
Fund family	AGF Funds Inc.	Percentage in foreign holdings	100.00%
Mutual fund investment category	Global Balanced	RRSP eligible	20%
Start date for data shown	November 1988	Sales charge	Optional
Number of funds in investment category	81	Redemption charge	Optional
Dividend frequency	Annual	Management expense ratio	2.85%

FUND PERFORMANCE

	1 month	6 months	1 year	3 years	5 years	10 years
Returns ending June 2000	0.9%	5.8%	6.0%	17.4%	16.0%	14.7%
Best historical return	9.4%	18.0%	36.6%	22.1%	18.5%	15.0%
Average historical return	1.1%	6.7%	14.1%	14.9%	14.4%	14.4%
Worst historical return	-6.2%	-4.2%	-5.1%	5.7%	9.9%	13.7%
Value at risk of $1,000	$977	$984	$1,006	$1,282	$1,685	$3,630

RETURNS GREATER THAN

	1 month	6 months	1 year	3 years	5 years	10 years
10 per cent	0%	59%	64%	85%	99%	100%
Zero	69%	88%	97%	100%	100%	100%
Percentage of time fund lost $	31%	12%	3%	0%	0%	0%
Number of periods evaluated	140	135	129	105	81	21

DOWNSIDE RISK

	Worst setback since start date	In bear 1987	In bear 1990	In bear 1994	In bear 1998
Setback for mutual fund	-7.3%		-2.9%	-7.3%	-6.2%
Setback for peer group	-3.4%		-7.6%	-4.1%	-7.6%
Setback ended in	Sept. 1994		Sept. 1990	Sept. 1994	Aug. 1998
Months to recover from loss	4		2	4	2

ROLLING 12-MONTH QUARTILE RANKING OF MUTUAL FUND PERFORMANCE OVER TIME

Global balanced

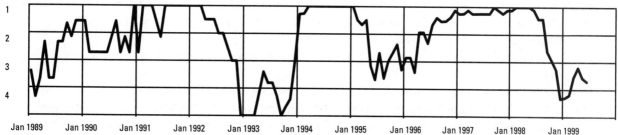

1 is first quartile; 2 is second quartile; 3 is third quartile; 4 is fourth quartile. First quartile means that the fund outperformed 75 per cent of other similar funds after 12 months.

ROLLING 12-MONTH TOTAL RATE OF RETURN FOR THE MUTUAL FUND OVER TIME

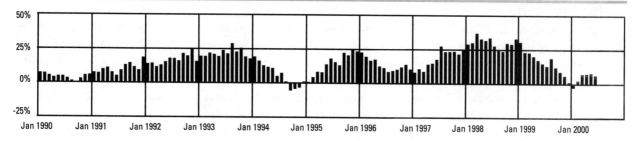

C.I. INTERNATIONAL BALANCED

Vos value rating		
Reward	**Risk**	**Best balance**
★★★★★	★★★★★	★★★★★

Fund profile

This fund is ideally suited for conservative investors who want to participate in both fixed-income and equity markets around the world. It invests internationally to increase investment opportunities and upside potential while reducing risk. In general, global balanced funds can deliver higher and more consistent returns than their domestic counterparts, because global capital markets go up and down according to different influences and at different times. Canadian balanced funds must invest a large portion of their investments in Canada, and Canadian capital markets don't always appreciate at the same rate as global markets or in the same manner.

Managed by Bill Sterling of C.I. Global Advisors, this fund invests worldwide, in both developed and emerging markets, and holds a diversified mix of stocks and bonds. The manager employs a top-down analysis of global macro-economic and market trends to determine the asset mix. In turn, he uses bottom-up fundamental research to select individual securities.

Fund performance

The fund continues to invest heavily in bonds and equities of companies that operate in the technology or telecommunications industries. In turn, the fund's performance has been sensational. It received a triple five-star Vos Value Rating for reward, risk, and the best balance between risk and reward. The fund has been consistent and has avoided surprises. During the previous year, it gained in value by 23.4 per cent, an excellent return for a balanced fund. Its best 12-month rate of return was a gain of 29.8 per cent, while the average 12-month rate of return has been 16 per cent.

With a 47 per cent investment in foreign equities, the fund has participated in the success of companies like Nokia, PMC-Sierra, and Corning, which have all generated some very impressive results for shareholders during the recent year.

Fund risks

Relative to similar mutual funds, this one has not displayed any above-average short-term risk. The manager has done an excellent job of preserving capital, and the fund has shown below-average downside risk. It hasn't lost money over any 6-month period, an excellent result considering that it has posted 63 rolling 6-month periods. In addition, the fund's worst setback was a loss of 5.4 per cent. During the same period the average global balanced fund declined in value by 6.2 per cent, but this fund took only three months to recover its loss.

Fund prospects

Global investing is an excellent way for Canadian investors to increase returns and reduce risk. During the previous year economic conditions were very robust, and investors participated by earning good returns. However, with a robust economy comes pressure. A high-growth economy can lead to higher inflation, which could lead to higher interest rates and additional volatility in capital markets. However, prudent investors with a long-term horizon should not be discouraged by a short-term event. Over the long-term, these events will work themselves out and generate higher returns. Conservative investors should invest in a foreign balanced fund to reduce the risk of their portfolios, and the C.I. International Balanced Fund is an excellent choice.

FUND DETAILS

Fund name	C.I. International Balanced	Fund size (in $ millions)	$1,603
Fund family	C.I. Mutual Funds Inc.	Percentage in foreign holdings	47.00%
Mutual fund investment category	Global Balanced	RRSP eligible	20%
Start date for data shown	November 1994	Sales charge	Optional
Number of funds in investment category	81	Redemption charge	Optional
Dividend frequency	Annual	Management expense ratio	2.35%

FUND PERFORMANCE

	1 month	6 months	1 year	3 years	5 years	10 years
Returns ending June 2000	2.3%	3.8%	23.4%	16.0%	16.1%	
Best historical return	8.6%	25.5%	29.8%	20.1%	18.0%	
Average historical return	1.3%	8.2%	16.0%	16.1%	16.4%	
Worst historical return	-5.4%	0.0%	5.2%	13.3%	13.9%	
Value at risk of $1,000	$972	$1,013	$1,075	$1,472	$1,969	

RETURNS GREATER THAN

	1 month	6 months	1 year	3 years	5 years	10 years
10 per cent	0%	75%	84%	100%	100%	
Zero	76%	100%	100%	100%	100%	
Percentage of time fund lost $	24%	0%	0%	0%	0%	
Number of periods evaluated	68	63	57	33	9	

DOWNSIDE RISK

	Worst setback since start date	In bear 1987	In bear 1990	In bear 1994	In bear 1998
Setback for mutual fund	-5.4%				-5.4%
Setback for peer group	-6.2%				-7.6%
Setback ended in	Aug. 1998				Aug. 1998
Months to recover from loss	3				3

ROLLING 12-MONTH QUARTILE RANKING OF MUTUAL FUND PERFORMANCE OVER TIME

Global balanced

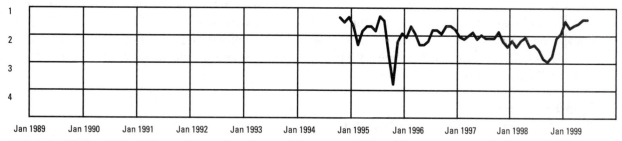

1 is first quartile; 2 is second quartile; 3 is third quartile; 4 is fourth quartile. First quartile means that the fund outperformed 75 per cent of other similar funds after 12 months.

ROLLING 12-MONTH TOTAL RATE OF RETURN FOR THE MUTUAL FUND OVER TIME

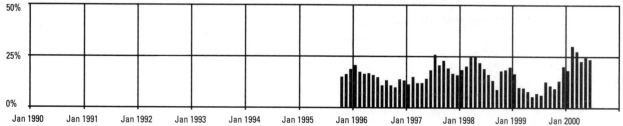

FIDELITY GLOBAL ASSET ALLOCATION FUND

Vos value rating		
Reward	**Risk**	**Best balance**
★★★★★	★★★★	★★★★★

Fund profile

Foreign bond funds had a great run during the previous year as equity markets rallied. This fund invests in a variety of equities and bonds issued by various companies and governments around the world. This ensures that the fund generates good rates of return without incurring an excessive amount of volatility. Therefore, this fund is ideally suited for investors looking for consistent growth and income. Managers Dick Habermann, Charles Morrisson, and Robert Kuo of Fidelity Management and Research utilize Fidelity's traditional bottom-up approach to stock and bond selection while relying on Fidelity's vast global resources.

Fund performance

During the previous year the fund earned a return of 16.7 per cent. Its best three-year rate of return was a gain of 20 per cent annualized, and its average annualized three-year rate of return is 14.5 per cent. During the previous five years, this fund has appreciated in value by an average of 16.6 per cent per year, an excellent result for a balanced fund. With value-added performance the fund has earned a five-star Vos Value Rating for reward and the best balance between reward and risk.

The fund continues to have a bias towards equities, which currently account for more than 70 per cent of its assets, but it also invests an above-average amount in corporate bonds. The fund has invested in companies like Nokia, Wal-Mart, Microsoft, and General Electric; the fund has invested heavily in technology and telecommunications, two of the hottest investment sectors during the previous year.

Fund risks

Balanced funds usually incur only minimal absolute losses, which makes them ideal for more conservative investors or investors looking for a core fund in their portfolio. The worst 12-month return posted by this fund was a decline of 7.3 per cent. It declined in value after 12 months 9 per cent of the time. During the bear market of 1998, it declined in value by 9 per cent, while the average global balanced fund declined in value by 7.6 per cent. But the fund took only two months to recover its loss.

Fund prospects

The outlook for this fund remains robust. With a large investment in technology and telecommunications, the fund can continue to generate above-average rates of return but with more short-term risk. The expertise and resources of the world's largest mutual fund company have allowed the fund managers to generate exceptional results for a foreign balanced fund. In the future capital markets will become more volatile, but this diversified fund should manage the volatility while participating in the gains. Investors looking for a good foreign balanced fund should consider the Fidelity Global Asset Allocation Fund for a portion of their investment portfolio.

FUND DETAILS

Fund name	**Fidelity Global Asset Allocation**	Fund size (in $ millions)	$1,118
Fund family	Fidelity Investments Canada Limited	Percentage in foreign holdings	88.98%
Mutual fund investment category	Global Balanced	RRSP eligible	20%
Start date for data shown	February 1993	Sales charge	Optional
Number of funds in investment category	81	Redemption charge	Optional
Dividend frequency	Annual	Management expense ratio	2.59%

FUND PERFORMANCE

	1 month	6 months	1 year	3 years	5 years	10 years
Returns ending June 2000	3.0%	0.4%	16.7%	14.7%	16.6%	
Best historical return	6.7%	18.1%	33.5%	20.0%	17.3%	
Average historical return	1.1%	6.9%	13.6%	14.5%	14.0%	
Worst historical return	-8.0%	-5.5%	-7.3%	5.4%	10.7%	
Value at risk of $1,000	$968	$978	$991	$1,213	$1,709	

RETURNS GREATER THAN

	1 month	6 months	1 year	3 years	5 years	10 years
10 per cent	0%	60%	69%	74%	100%	
Zero	66%	88%	91%	100%	100%	
Percentage of time fund lost $	34%	12%	9%	0%	0%	
Number of periods evaluated	89	84	78	54	30	

DOWNSIDE RISK

	Worst setback since start date	In bear 1987	In bear 1990	In bear 1994	In bear 1998
Setback for mutual fund	-9.0%			-7.3%	-9.0%
Setback for peer group	-7.6%			-4.1%	-7.6%
Setback ended in	Sept. 1998			Jan. 1995	Sept. 1998
Months to recover from loss	2			11	2

ROLLING 12-MONTH QUARTILE RANKING OF MUTUAL FUND PERFORMANCE OVER TIME

Global balanced

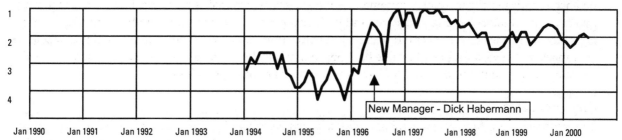

1 is first quartile; 2 is second quartile; 3 is third quartile; 4 is fourth quartile. First quartile means that the fund outperformed 75 per cent of other similar funds after 12 months.

ROLLING 12-MONTH TOTAL RATE OF RETURN FOR THE MUTUAL FUND OVER TIME

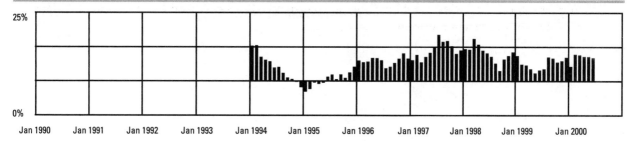

SPECTRUM UNITED GLOBAL DIVERSIFIED FUND

Vos value rating		
Reward	**Risk**	**Best balance**
★★★★	★★★★★	★★★★★

Fund profile

This foreign balanced fund offers investors the opportunity for growth potential and income while retaining a prudent level of diversification. It invests in a variety of stocks and bonds issued by various companies and governments throughout the world. During the previous year, capital markets have been favourable, and this fund participated in the gains. Managed by Ken Yoshida and Charles Prideaux of Mercury Asset Management in London, England, sub-advisor to the fund, it is ideally suited for more conservative investors looking for a good core fund for a diversified mutual fund portfolio.

Fund performance

This fund has generated excellent results during the last three years and earned a five-star Vos Value Rating for best balance between risk and reward. Its best 12-month rate of return was a gain of 23.7 per cent, and the average rate of return after 12 months was 10.4 per cent. During the previous 10 years, this fund has appreciated in value by an average of 10.7 per cent a year. It has been first quartile after 12 months frequently when compared to similar funds, but has been fourth quartile on occasion as well.

The fund has invested 59 per cent of its holdings in equities, and 29 per cent is invested in the United States alone. The fund has also invested 30 per cent of its holdings in fixed-income products, the majority also in the United States. The fund has invested in companies like General Electric and Cisco Systems.

Fund risks

This fund scores high marks for managing short-term risk and earned a five-star Vos Value Rating for risk. Its worst 12-month return was a decline of 8.6 per cent, and it declined in value after 12 months 8 per cent of the time. During the bear market of 1998, it declined in value by 5.3 per cent, while the average global balanced fund declined in value by 7.6 per cent. But it took only two months to recover. In short, the absolute risk associated with this fund is not excessive.

Fund prospects

Recently, capital markets have been very favourable and investors participated in some very impressive gains. This fund has encountered some short-term performance issues, but they should not translate into long-term concerns. Among this fund's combination of investments some will appreciate in value, offsetting the losses incurred by other investments. Conservative investors looking for a value-added fund that displays its own unique risk-and-return characteristics should consider Spectrum United Global Diversified for a portion of their mutual fund portfolio. It won't deliver triple-digit returns, but it will provide consistent growth and income—two essential factors to investment success.

FUND DETAILS

Fund name	**Spectrum United Global Diversified**	Fund size (in $ millions)	$57
Fund family	Spectrum Investment Management Limited	Percentage in foreign holdings	90.70%
Mutual fund investment category	Global Balanced	RRSP eligible	20%
Start date for data shown	January 1989	Sales charge	Optional
Number of funds in investment category	81	Redemption charge	Optional
Dividend frequency	Semi-Annually	Management expense ratio	2.41%

FUND PERFORMANCE

	1 month	6 months	1 year	3 years	5 years	10 years
Returns ending June 2000	1.0%	-2.8%	9.3%	10.7%	11.3%	10.7%
Best historical return	5.0%	15.4%	23.7%	17.5%	13.7%	11.3%
Average historical return	0.8%	5.2%	10.4%	10.8%	10.5%	10.5%
Worst historical return	-5.0%	-8.4%	-8.6%	5.0%	7.7%	9.5%
Value at risk of $1,000	$972	$967	$977	$1,231	$1,479	$2,511

RETURNS GREATER THAN

	1 month	6 months	1 year	3 years	5 years	10 years
10 per cent	0%	50%	59%	61%	65%	74%
Zero	68%	83%	92%	100%	100%	100%
Percentage of time fund lost $	32%	17%	8%	0%	0%	0%
Number of periods evaluated	138	133	127	103	79	19

DOWNSIDE RISK

	Worst setback since start date	In bear 1987	In bear 1990	In bear 1994	In bear 1998
Setback for mutual fund	-10.1		-8.6%	-10.1%	-5.3%
Setback for peer group	-3.9%		-7.6%	-4.1%	-7.6%
Setback ended in	June 1994		Sept. 1990	June 1994	Sept. 1998
Months to recover from loss	12		4	12	2

ROLLING 12-MONTH QUARTILE RANKING OF MUTUAL FUND PERFORMANCE OVER TIME

Global balanced

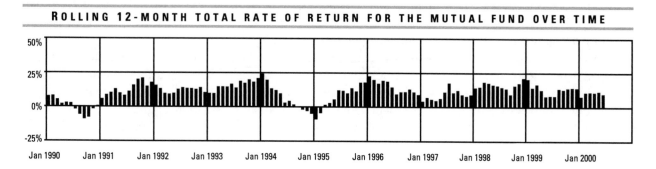

1 is first quartile; 2 is second quartile; 3 is third quartile; 4 is fourth quartile. First quartile means that the fund outperformed 75 per cent of other similar funds after 12 months.

ROLLING 12-MONTH TOTAL RATE OF RETURN FOR THE MUTUAL FUND OVER TIME

BMO DIVIDEND FUND

Vos value rating		
Reward	**Risk**	**Best balance**
★★★★★	★★★	★★★★★

Fund profile

This fund invests in common stocks and preferred shares of Canadian companies in order to provide investors with a superior after-tax rate of return. Manager Michael Stanley of Jones Heward Investment Counsel, a subsidiary of the Bank of Montreal, prefers companies with an established dividend payment record and tends to favour the financial service and utility industries, where big blue-chip, high-yielding companies provide investors with tax-advantageous income.

With a decline in value of many bank stocks caused by higher interest rates and the federal government's disallowance of bank mergers, dividend funds have had a difficult year relative to some growth funds. But many still delivered double-digit returns. Investors should experience even better results than they did in the recent past and shouldn't get discouraged with their conservative Canadian investments. Dividend funds can play an important role in a well-diversified portfolio. Investors can also benefit from favourable tax treatment through Canadian dividend funds, although they should hold their investment outside their RRSP (if possible) to take full advantage of the preferential tax rate on dividends of Canadian companies.

Fund performance

This fund has generated an above-average rate of return and an above-average amount of risk. It has frequently been first quartile, especially during bull markets, when it does particularly well. The fund has earned a five-star Vos Value Rating for reward and best balance between risk and reward. Its best 12-month rate of return was a gain of 47.9 per cent, while the average 12-month rate of return was a gain of 18.3 per cent. During the previous year the fund posted a gain of 13.8 per cent.

This fund has invested 29 per cent of its assets in the financial services sector, which boosted its absolute performance during the previous year. It has invested another 25 per cent in utilities, and only 7 per cent in pipelines. The fund has invested in companies like TD Bank, BCE, Royal Bank, Torstar (parent of the *Toronto Star*), and Enbridge.

Fund risks

This fund is riskier than the average dividend fund. During the bear market of 1998, it declined in value by 22.1 per cent, while the average dividend fund posted a loss of 17.7 per cent. The fund has underperformed during the previous two bear markets and has earned only a three-star Vos Value Rating for risk. Its worst 12-month rate of return was a loss of 8.4 per cent, and it posted a loss after 12 months 9 per cent of the time.

Fund prospects

Canadian companies have become more competitive during the previous year. Corporate profits are good, commodity prices have substantially improved, inflation is in check, and the Canadian dollar is favourable. All these factors should improve economic conditions. Investors should not lose faith in their dividend fund. Such a fund offers excellent value. Investors looking for a more aggressive dividend fund should consider the BMO Dividend Fund, which has delivered superior results consistently.

FUND DETAILS

Fund name	**BMO Dividend**	Fund size (in $ millions)	$923
Fund family	BMO Investments Inc.	Percentage in foreign holdings	0.00%
Mutual fund investment category	Canadian Dividend Income	RRSP eligible	100%
Start date for data shown	November 1994	Sales charge	None
Number of funds in investment category	75	Redemption charge	None
Dividend frequency	Quarterly	Management expense ratio	1.80%

FUND PERFORMANCE

	1 month	6 months	1 year	3 years	5 years	10 years
Returns ending June 2000	0.2%	11.5%	13.8%	13.0%	18.1%	
Best historical return	9.0%	24.4%	47.9%	30.3%	18.4%	
Average historical return	1.4%	8.6%	18.3%	20.5%	17.1%	
Worst historical return	-16.3%	-18.8%	-8.4%	11.0%	15.4%	
Value at risk of $1,000	$963	$891	$954	$1,408	$2,082	

RETURNS GREATER THAN

	1 month	6 months	1 year	3 years	5 years	10 years
10 per cent	0%	68%	65%	100%	100%	
Zero	72%	86%	91%	100%	100%	
Percentage of time fund lost $	28%	14%	9%	0%	0%	
Number of periods evaluated	68	63	57	33	9	

DOWNSIDE RISK

	Worst setback since start date	In bear 1987	In bear 1990	In bear 1994	In bear 1998
Setback for mutual fund	-22.1%			-9.0%	-22.1%
Setback for peer group	-17.7%			-2.2%	-17.7%
Setback ended in	Aug. 1998			Jan. 1995	Aug. 1998
Months to recover from loss	19			8	19

ROLLING 12-MONTH QUARTILE RANKING OF MUTUAL FUND PERFORMANCE OVER TIME

Canadian dividend income

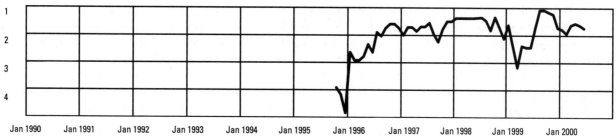

1 is first quartile; 2 is second quartile; 3 is third quartile; 4 is fourth quartile. First quartile means that the fund outperformed 75 per cent of other similar funds after 12 months.

ROLLING 12-MONTH TOTAL RATE OF RETURN FOR THE MUTUAL FUND OVER TIME

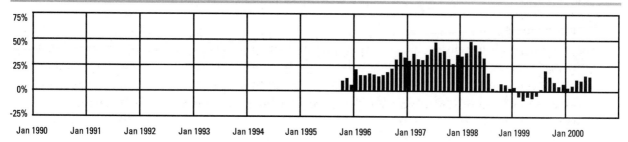

PHILLIPS, HAGER & NORTH DIVIDEND INCOME FUND

Vos value rating		
Reward	**Risk**	**Best balance**
★★★★★	★★★	★★★★★

Fund profile

The Phillips, Hager & North Dividend Income Fund is managed by Bill Slatter of Phillips, Hager & North Investment Management. The fund aims to provide long-term capital growth and income by investing primarily in relatively high-income-producing Canadian corporations.

Dividend funds have had a good year of returns, but many underperformed the general market because they don't own Nortel Networks, currently the stock-market darling. Nortel Networks has single-handedly propelled the Canadian equity market forward, but doesn't pay a very material dividend, so many dividend funds avoid the stock. Nevertheless, investors in Canadian dividend funds can benefit from the favourable tax treatment. Tax laws allow investors to pay less tax on a dollar of dividend income than on a dollar of interest income, although the investment has to be held outside of an RRSP to qualify for the beneficial tax treatment. These funds are a very good investment for investors who need regular income outside of their RRSP. They also tend to favour stable companies that trade at very reasonable valuations. This ensures a lower level of risk within the fund.

Fund performance

This fund is a little more aggressive than the average dividend fund, and its performance tends to fluctuate more, as well. It has been first quartile frequently, but will occasionally underperform similar funds. The fund has earned a five-star Vos Value Rating for reward and the best balance between risk and reward, indicating an above-average rate of return during the previous three years. Its average 12-month rate of return was a gain of 14.1 per cent, but it posted a gain of 25.7 per cent during the previous year.

The fund holds 47 per cent of its assets in the financial services sector, 8.4 per cent in the pipelines sector, and 8.6 per cent in the utility sector. It has invested in such blue-chip companies as Enbridge, Suncor Energy, CIBC, Bank of Montreal, Thomson, and Power Corporation. The fund has also made a small investment in Nortel Networks, unusual for a dividend fund but very advantageous for investors during the last year.

Fund risks

This fund has displayed more risk than the average dividend fund. During the bear market of 1998, it declined in value by 21.6 per cent. The average fund declined by 17.7 per cent. The fund has also declined in value more than the average fund during each of the last four bear markets.

Fund prospects

This fund depends heavily on the performance of the financial services sector, which should generate better performance over the next year than during the previous two years. However, investors shouldn't expect the phenomenal returns of 1996 and 1997 consistently. Dividend funds should provide a return higher than a good balanced fund but lower than a Canadian equity fund. Investors looking for an aggressive dividend fund that pays dividends regularly and has an excellent long-term track record should consider the Phillips, Hager & North Dividend Income Fund.

FUND DETAILS

Fund name	PH & N Dividend Income	Fund size (in $ millions)	$746
Fund family	Phillips, Hager & North Ltd.	Percentage in foreign holdings	0.00%
Mutual fund investment category	Canadian Dividend Income	RRSP eligible	100%
Start date for data shown	July 1982	Sales charge	None
Number of funds in investment category	75	Redemption charge	None
Dividend frequency	Quarterly	Management expense ratio	1.21%

FUND PERFORMANCE

	1 month	6 months	1 year	3 years	5 years	10 years
Returns ending June 2000	2.3%	24.4%	25.7%	17.5%	22.1%	15.6%
Best historical return	10.2%	31.1%	57.9%	33.0%	24.5%	16.5%
Average historical return	1.2%	7.2%	14.1%	13.6%	12.6%	11.7%
Worst historical return	-16.1%	-16.2%	-10.1%	2.3%	5.7%	9.1%
Value at risk of $1,000	$967	$931	$969	$1,140	$1,374	$2,438

RETURNS GREATER THAN

	1 month	6 months	1 year	3 years	5 years	10 years
10 per cent	0%	58%	57%	66%	59%	67%
Zero	70%	80%	90%	100%	100%	100%
Percentage of time fund lost $	40%	20%	10%	0%	0%	0%
Number of periods evaluated	216	211	205	181	157	97

DOWNSIDE RISK

	Worst setback since start date	In bear 1987	In bear 1990	In bear 1994	In bear 1998
Setback for mutual fund	-21.6%	-15.9%	-12.1%	-10.6%	-21.6%
Setback for peer group	-17.7%	-9.0%	-.9.2%	-8.8%	-17.7%
Setback ended in	Aug. 1998	Oct. 1987	Sept. 1990	June 1994	Aug. 1998
Months to recover from loss	19	12	6	10	19

ROLLING 12-MONTH QUARTILE RANKING OF MUTUAL FUND PERFORMANCE OVER TIME

Canadian dividend income

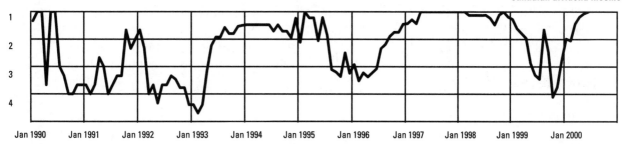

1 is first quartile; 2 is second quartile; 3 is third quartile; 4 is fourth quartile. First quartile means that the fund outperformed 75 per cent of other similar funds after 12 months.

ROLLING 12-MONTH TOTAL RATE OF RETURN FOR THE MUTUAL FUND OVER TIME

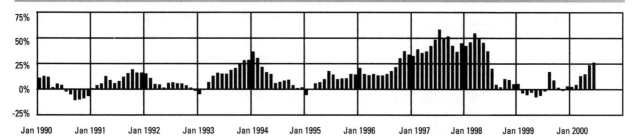

AGF CANADIAN STOCK FUND

Vos value rating		
Reward	**Risk**	**Best balance**
★★★★★	★★	★★★★

Fund profile

Canadian equities have had a great year, and this fund was among the leaders of the pack. It aims to provide investors with superior and consistent risk-adjusted returns by investing in shares of Canadian companies that exhibit excellent potential. Manager Martin Hubbes has been with AGF since 1992, and he has built a reputation as an excellent bottom-up stock picker. His philosophy paid a big dividend for investors last year, which was a great year for Canadian equities. Investors can remain optimistic about the Canadian economy's future prospects, as well, which should have a favourable impact on the Canadian stock market. In the short term, though, investors should be cautious about the volatility that could result if interest rates continue to appreciate.

Fund performance

This Canadian equity fund is currently white hot, generating top-quartile performance for investors and appreciating in value last year by 52 per cent. In turn, the fund earned a five-star Vos Value Rating for reward and the best balance between risk and reward. However, the fund has not always been first quartile. During 1996 and 1998, for example, it endured some difficult times. Its best 12-month rate of return was a gain of 57.6 per cent, and its average rate of return after 12 months was 10.9 per cent. During the previous 10 years this fund has appreciated in value by an average of 12.6 per cent per year. It has invested in companies like Nortel Networks, a fiber-optics player, and Bioval, a pharmaceutical company.

Fund risks

This fund has not always led the pack. From time to time it has underperformed similar funds and lost money. Its worst 12-month return was a decline of 21.3 per cent, and it declined in value after 12 months 22 per cent of the time. During the bear market of 1998, it declined in value by 27.5 per cent, while the average Canadian diversified equity fund declined in value by 24.6 per cent. But it took only 15 months to recover its loss.

Fund prospects

This fund has made a large investment in growth stocks, with 39 per cent of its assets invested in the industrial products sector, a sector that includes companies like Nortel Networks, JDS Uniphase, and Descartes Systems. All of these stocks have been market darlings but they are now trading at nosebleed valuations and will have to grow into their valuations very quickly. This is very possible, though, because they all lead their high-growth industries. If they can continue growing at this pace, investors will continue to participate in above-average returns. If they can't sustain this level of growth, expect a lot more volatility. Investors looking for a great Canadian Equity Fund should consider the AGF Canadian Stock Fund.

FUND DETAILS

Fund name	**AGF Canadian Stock**	Fund size (in $ millions)	$1,397
Fund family	AGF Funds Inc.	Percentage in foreign holdings	0.00%
Mutual fund investment category	Canadian Diversified Equity	RRSP eligible	100%
Start date for data shown	July 1989	Sales charge	Optional
Number of funds in investment category	446	Redemption charge	Optional
Dividend frequency	Annual	Management expense ratio	2.46%

FUND PERFORMANCE

	1 month	6 months	1 year	3 years	5 years	10 years
Returns ending June 2000	6.4%	22.7%	52.0%	19.1%	17.1%	12.6%
Best historical return	14.8%	44.8%	57.6%	21.3%	17.8%	12.6%
Average historical return	1.0%	5.8%	10.9%	10.0%	10.0%	9.9%
Worst historical return	-18.9%	-22.8%	-21.3%	0.5%	5.3%	7.6%
Value at risk of $1,000	$949	$939	$911	$1,066	$1,323	$2,078

RETURNS GREATER THAN

	1 month	6 months	1 year	3 years	5 years	10 years
10 per cent	2%	50%	48%	45%	37%	46%
Zero	60%	72%	78%	100%	100%	100%
Percentage of time fund lost $	40%	28%	22%	0%	0%	0%
Number of periods evaluated	132	127	121	97	73	13

DOWNSIDE RISK

	Worst setback since start date	In bear 1987	In bear 1990	In bear 1994	In bear 1998
Setback for mutual fund	-27.5%		-11.4%	-10.0%	-27.5%
Setback for peer group	-24.6%		-16.3%	-9.7%	-24.6%
Setback ended in	Aug. 1998		Oct. 1990	June 1994	Aug.1998
Months to recover from loss	15		5	11	15

ROLLING 12-MONTH QUARTILE RANKING OF MUTUAL FUND PERFORMANCE OVER TIME

Canadian diversified equity

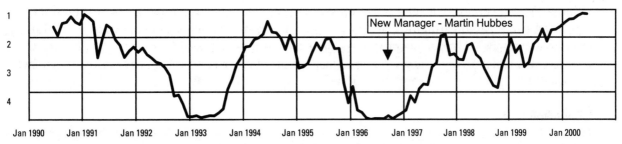

1 is first quartile; 2 is second quartile; 3 is third quartile; 4 is fourth quartile. First quartile means that the fund outperformed 75 per cent of other similar funds after 12 months.

ROLLING 12-MONTH TOTAL RATE OF RETURN FOR THE MUTUAL FUND OVER TIME

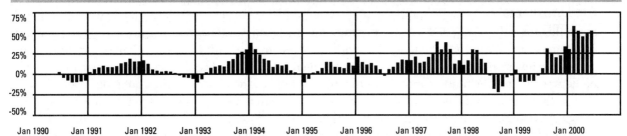

AIM CANADA GROWTH

Vos value rating		
Reward	**Risk**	**Best balance**
★★★★★	★	★★★★

Fund profile

This fund's investment objective is to provide long-term growth by investing in small, medium, and large Canadian companies with above-average growth potential. Unlike many similar Canadian equity mutual funds, the AIM Canada Growth fund aims to invest a minimum of 15 per cent in foreign equities to increase return and reduce risk.

The previous manager, Derek Webb, recently left the company. The fund is now managed by Class Olsson, who also manages the AIM Canadian Premier Fund, which has generated better performance than this one. Olsson uses a disciplined earnings-momentum investment style to add value for investors. He focuses on companies whose earnings are growing faster than similar companies. This means that he'll concentrate on companies whose stock price is likely going to appreciate more rapidly than the general stock market because of changes in the company's earnings potential. Olsson conducts a comprehensive fundamental review of a company before investing. During the previous year, Canadian equity markets have generated sensational returns. But investors should remember that it is unlikely that every year will be so prosperous. Still, over the long term the Canadian stock market should reward investors handsomely. They should nevertheless diversify outside of Canada while taking advantage of opportunities within the country.

Fund performance

This is a very aggressive growth fund, and growth funds led the pack during the previous year. During bull markets, growth funds tend to exhibit more upside potential, and this one has earned a five-star Vos Value Rating for reward. The fund is either first or fourth quartile after 12 months, a direct result of the fund's aggressive investment objective. The fund has made large investments in technology, telecommunications, and consumer products sectors, in companies such as JDS Uniphase, Bombardier, Onex, C-Mac, Clarica Life Insurance, and C.I. Fund Management. It maintains a below-average investment in the financial services industry. In short, this fund is very different from the average Canadian equity fund.

Fund risks

The fund currently scores a very low Vos Value Rating for risk, an indication of its above-average risk for above-average returns. It has the potential to either significantly outperform or significantly underperform the market. During the bear market of 1998, the fund declined in value by 24.2 per cent but recovered its loss within 10 months.

Fund prospects

Since this fund displays good discipline coupled with strong fundamental research, it should generate above-average returns over the long term with more risk than a traditional Canadian equity fund. More aggressive investors looking for a very different Canadian equity fund could consider this one for a portion of their portfolios. The fund's earnings-momentum style can add value over time, but it does not eliminate risk, as the manager may not be able to react swiftly enough with large amounts of money during times of rapid economic change. Growth investments have had a good year, but that may not occur every year. Investors looking for a great growth investment should consider the AIM Canada Growth Fund.

FUND DETAILS

Fund name	**AIM Canada Growth Class**	Fund size (in $ millions)	$1,525
Fund family	AIM Funds Management Inc.	Percentage in foreign holdings	11.96%
Mutual fund investment category	Canadian Diversified Equity	RRSP eligible	100%
Start date for data shown	February 1995	Sales charge	Optional
Number of funds in investment category	446	Redemption charge	Optional
Dividend frequency	Annual	Management expense ratio	2.38%

FUND PERFORMANCE

	1 month	6 months	1 year	3 years	5 years	10 years
Returns ending June 2000	2.4%	4.6%	44.3%	21.9%	22.5%	
Best historical return	23.5%	73.6%	85.6%	29.6%	28.1%	
Average historical return	1.9%	12.8%	23.4%	18.1%	24.5%	
Worst historical return	-17.3%	-21.9%	-21.0%	6.7%	22.5%	
Value at risk of $1,000	$935	$876	$957	$1,325	$2,757	

RETURNS GREATER THAN

	1 month	6 months	1 year	3 years	5 years	10 years
10 per cent	6%	75%	72%	93%	100%	
Zero	63%	83%	85%	100%	100%	
Percentage of time fund lost $	37%	17%	15%	0%	0%	
Number of periods evaluated	65	60	54	30	6	

DOWNSIDE RISK

	Worst setback since start date	In bear 1987	In bear 1990	In bear 1994	In bear 1998
Setback for mutual fund	-24.2%				-24.2%
Setback for peer group	-23.0%				-24.6%
Setback ended in	Sept. 1998				Sept. 1998
Months to recover from loss	10				10

ROLLING 12-MONTH QUARTILE RANKING OF MUTUAL FUND PERFORMANCE OVER TIME

Canadian diversified equity

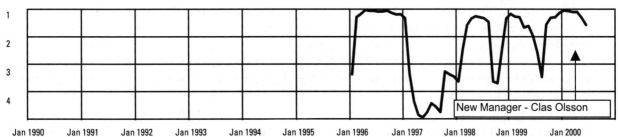

1 is first quartile; 2 is second quartile; 3 is third quartile; 4 is fourth quartile. First quartile means that the fund outperformed 75 per cent of other similar funds after 12 months.

ROLLING 12-MONTH TOTAL RATE OF RETURN FOR THE MUTUAL FUND OVER TIME

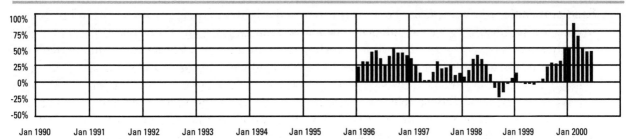

AIM CANADA VALUE CLASS FUND

Vos value rating		
Reward	**Risk**	**Best balance**

Fund profile

Canadian value companies have outperformed Canadian growth companies during the previous 10 years, but during the last year, growth outperformed value by over 60 per cent. Such a large variance in performance hasn't been seen in the Canadian marketplace since the Second World War. In turn, many investors bailed out of their value investments to chase after hot growth investments like telecommunications, media, and technology (TMT). However, investors should not ignore value investments, which have traditionally generated above-average rates of return for investors. The AIM Canada Value Class Fund aims to invest in companies that, in the opinion of the manager, Roger Mortimer of AIM Capital Management, trade below their fair market value. Like its sister fund, the AIM Canada Growth Fund, this fund also aims to invest at least 15 per cent of its portfolio outside of Canada.

Fund performance

This fund hasn't yet earned a Vos Value Rating, because it doesn't have a three-year track record. However, the fund's initial debut has been very impressive for a value fund, outperforming some growth funds as well as the stock market and almost all value funds. It has generated such an impressive rate of return through prudent stock selection and by investing in a select number of growth stocks that, in the opinion of the manager, are trading at less than their fair market value. The fund has invested in companies like Kansas City Southern, a U.S. railroad company that has an 80-per-cent interest in Janus Mutual Funds, a no-load mutual fund company that has been growing in the U.S. at a sensational pace. During the previous year, the fund posted a gain of 39.9 per cent. Its best 12-month rate of return was a gain of 51.8 per cent, and the average rate of return after 12 months was a gain of 18.2 per cent.

Fund risks

This is an aggressive value fund, and it incurs a lot of company-specific risk. Over 50 per cent of the fund is invested in only 15 companies, many of which trade at very reasonable valuations. These types of companies tend to exhibit less downside risk during difficult market environments. The fund's worst 12-month return was a decline of 13.1 per cent. During the bear market of 1998, it declined in value by 24.5 per cent. During the same period, the average Canadian diversified equity fund declined in value by 24.6 per cent.

Fund prospects

Investors who want a value-added Canadian equity fund with a different approach need look no further than the AIM Canada Value Class Fund. It is run by a disciplined manager with a proven investment process and philosophy, which should generate above-average performance over the long term, while providing diversification potential within a portfolio of mutual funds. Canadian capital markets will display more risk in future, but this fund is well positioned to manage any volatility.

FUND DETAILS

Fund name	**AIM Canada Value Class**	Fund size (in $ millions)	$181
Fund family	AIM Funds Management Inc.	Percentage in foreign holdings	19.49%
Mutual fund investment category	Canadian Diversified Equity	RRSP eligible	100%
Start date for data shown	October 1997	Sales charge	Optional
Number of funds in investment category	446	Redemption charge	Optional
Dividend frequency	Annual	Management expense ratio	2.82%

FUND PERFORMANCE

	1 month	6 months	1 year	3 years	5 years	10 years
Returns ending June 2000	1.4%	18.8%	39.9%			
Best historical return	13.5%	33.0%	51.8%			
Average historical return	1.6%	10.3%	18.2%			
Worst historical return	-17.0%	-22.0%	-13.1%			
Value at risk of $1,000	$959	$809	$894			

RETURNS GREATER THAN

	1 month	6 months	1 year	3 years	5 years	10 years
10 per cent	9%	75%	55%			
Zero	70%	79%	68%			
Percentage of time fund lost $	30%	21%	32%			
Number of periods evaluated	33	28	22			

DOWNSIDE RISK

	Worst setback since start date	In bear 1987	In bear 1990	In bear 1994	In bear 1998
Setback for mutual fund	-24.5%				-24.5%
Setback for peer group	-24.6%				-24.6%
Setback ended in	Aug. 1998				Aug. 1998
Months to recover from loss	10				10

ROLLING 12-MONTH QUARTILE RANKING OF MUTUAL FUND PERFORMANCE OVER TIME

Canadian diversified equity

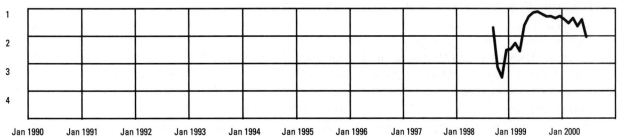

1 is first quartile; 2 is second quartile; 3 is third quartile; 4 is fourth quartile. First quartile means that the fund outperformed 75 per cent of other similar funds after 12 months.

ROLLING 12-MONTH TOTAL RATE OF RETURN FOR THE MUTUAL FUND OVER TIME

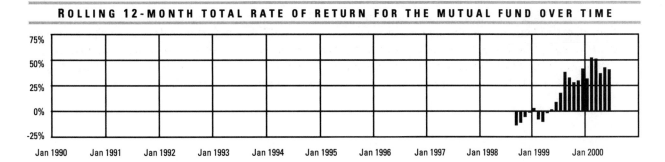

BMO EQUITY FUND

Vos value rating		
Reward	**Risk**	**Best balance**
★★★★	★★★★★	★★★★★

Fund profile

During the previous year Canadian equities were hot, and this fund was no exception. Investors in BMO mutual funds should seriously consider this fund for a portion of their portfolio. The fund invests in high-quality companies that exhibit great investment potential. Manager Michael Stanley of Jones Heward Investment Counsel relies on several strategies to identify superior investments. He examines a company's balance sheet and income statement, determines the company's growth potential, and assesses management's competence. Investors looking for a core Canadian equity fund should consider this one.

Fund performance

Through prudent stock selection and excellent management, the fund has generated good absolute and relative returns. It is frequently first or second quartile after 12 months, but never at the top or the bottom of the charts in the short term. It has earned a four-star Vos Value Rating for Reward—based on a three-year assessment of performance, not five or ten years. Its best three-year rate of return was a gain of 23.6 per cent annualized, and the average annualized three-year rate of return was 15.8 per cent. During the previous five years this fund has appreciated in value by an average of 18.1 per cent a year.

The fund has made large investments in the biggest Canadian companies like Nortel Networks, BCE, Royal Bank, Toronto Dominion Bank, CIBC, Suncor Energy, and Seagram. The fund has invested 32 per cent of its assets in the industrial sector and 15 per cent in financial services.

Fund risks

This fund does a great job of managing risk and has earned a five-star Vos Value Rating for risk and the best balance between risk and return. Its worst 12-month return was a decline of 14.5 per cent, and it declined in value after 12 months 23 per cent of the time. During the bear market of 1998, this fund declined in value by 23.8 per cent, while the average Canadian diversified equity fund declined in value by 24.6 per cent. The fund took only 14 months to recover.

Fund prospects

The outlook for Canadian equities remains robust, but investors should be prepared for some additional volatility in the short term. Companies are reporting good earnings growth, interest rates should remain stable, and economic conditions should remain favourable. All these conditions favour Canadian stock markets. Investors with a time horizon greater than five years should seriously consider investing a portion of their portfolio in the BMO Equity Fund. It will provide stability and consistency within a diversified portfolio and will also generate a higher rate of return than more conservative funds without incurring an excessive amount of risk.

FUND DETAILS

Fund name	**BMO Equity**	Fund size (in $ millions)	$1,504
Fund family	BMO Investments Inc.	Percentage in foreign holdings	6.48%
Mutual fund investment category	Canadian Diversified Equity	RRSP eligible	100%
Start date for data shown	September 1993	Sales charge	None
Number of funds in investment category	446	Redemption charge	None
Dividend frequency	Quarterly	Management expense ratio	2.35%

FUND PERFORMANCE

	1 month	6 months	1 year	3 years	5 years	10 years
Returns ending June 2000	4.9%	11.5%	30.8%	15.2%	18.1%	
Best historical return	11.8%	28.3%	46.5%	23.6%	18.8%	
Average historical return	1.2%	7.0%	14.3%	15.8%	13.8%	
Worst historical return	-18.1%	-20.0%	-14.5%	7.2%	7.6%	
Value at risk of $1,000	$952	$886	$930	$1,301	$1,514	

RETURNS GREATER THAN

	1 month	6 months	1 year	3 years	5 years	10 years
10 per cent	1%	65%	62%	94%	87%	
Zero	62%	78%	77%	100%	100%	
Percentage of time fund lost $	38%	22%	23%	0%	0%	
Number of periods evaluated	82	77	71	47	23	

DOWNSIDE RISK

	Worst setback since start date	In bear 1987	In bear 1990	In bear 1994	In bear 1998
Setback for mutual fund	-23.8%			-13.1%	-23.8%
Setback for peer group	-24.6%			-9.7%	-24.6%
Setback ended in	Aug. 1998			June 1994	Aug. 1998
Months to recover from loss	14			13	14

ROLLING 12-MONTH QUARTILE RANKING OF MUTUAL FUND PERFORMANCE OVER TIME

Canadian diversified equity

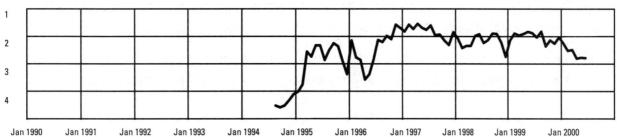

1 is first quartile; 2 is second quartile; 3 is third quartile; 4 is fourth quartile. First quartile means that the fund outperformed 75 per cent of other similar funds after 12 months.

ROLLING 12-MONTH TOTAL RATE OF RETURN FOR THE MUTUAL FUND OVER TIME

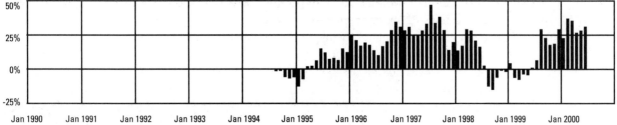

FIDELITY DISCIPLINED EQUITY FUND

Vos value rating		
Reward	**Risk**	**Best balance**

Fund profile

Over the previous year Canadian equity funds have been hot, and this fund in particular has generated some very impressive results. What makes them even more impressive is the fund's disciplined investment approach. To reduce the risk associated with investing in Canadian equities, manager Robert Haber always maintains the same sector weights as the TSE 300, thereby eliminating any sector risk. Being overweight in a sector that performs poorly can cause havoc with a fund's performance, but investors in the Fidelity Disciplined Equity Fund don't have to worry about this problem. Haber relies on the strength of the world's largest mutual fund company to identify superior investment opportunities. He uses a bottom-up stock-selection approach to identify companies that are attractively priced given their fundamentals. Considering the fund's returns, the strategy works.

Fund performance

Canadian equity funds have been hot, and, during the previous year, this particular fund gained in value by 49.3 per cent. In existence for a mere two years, it has almost doubled in value in that period. In addition, the fund has consistently been deep first quartile relative to other funds after 12 months. The best 12-month rate of return for this fund was a gain of 65.3 per cent, and the average rate of return after 12 months was 46 per cent.

The fund has made large investments in industrial products, utilities, and financial services sectors by investing in companies like Nortel Networks, Bell Canada, JDS Uniphase, and Bombardier. The top 10 holdings in the fund represent 40 per cent of the portfolio, and the fund has made 180 different investments. This feature allows the manager to diversify the portfolio but still add value by concentrating the fund's investments and participating in the success of smaller companies.

Fund risks

Inherently, this fund is less risky than similar funds, and in fact the fund currently has not displayed any real risk. Its worst 12-month rate of return is actually a gain of 31.5 per cent. In the short term, the fund's worst 1-month decline in value was a setback of 4.7 per cent.

Fund prospects

The economic outlook for Canadian equities remains robust, and this should affect Canadian capital markets favourably. Conservative investors who want to participate in the success of Canadian companies should consider the Fidelity Disciplined Equity Fund for their mutual fund portfolio. A value-added investment like this fund could do wonders for your portfolio. Investors should be aware that the fund will not likely continue delivering such exceptional performance. However, over the long term, it should make a meaningful impact on your investment returns.

FUND DETAILS

Fund name	**Fidelity Disciplined Equity**	Fund size (in $ millions)	$993
Fund family	Fidelity Investments Canada Limited	Percentage in foreign holdings	5.83%
Mutual fund investment category	Canadian Diversified Equity	RRSP eligible	100%
Start date for data shown	October 1998	Sales charge	Optional
Number of funds in investment category	446	Redemption charge	Optional
Dividend frequency	Annual	Management expense ratio	2.40%

FUND PERFORMANCE

	1 month	6 months	1 year	3 years	5 years	10 years
Returns ending June 2000	6.6%	15.0%	49.3%			
Best historical return	15.9%	44.9%	65.3%			
Average historical return	3.5%	22.3%	46.0%			
Worst historical return	-4.7%	9.4%	31.5%			
Value at risk of $1,000	$970	$1,106	$1,327			

RETURNS GREATER THAN

	1 month	6 months	1 year	3 years	5 years	10 years
10 per cent	10%	100%	100%			
Zero	71%	100%	100%			
Percentage of time fund lost $	29%	0%	0%			
Number of periods evaluated	21	16	10			

DOWNSIDE RISK

	Worst setback since start date	In bear 1987	In bear 1990	In bear 1994	In bear 1998
Setback for mutual fund	-4.8%				
Setback for peer group	0.0%				
Setback ended in	May 2000				
Months to recover from loss	1				

ROLLING 12-MONTH QUARTILE RANKING OF MUTUAL FUND PERFORMANCE OVER TIME

Canadian diversified equity

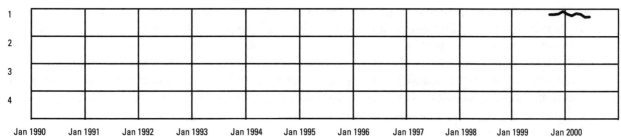

1 is first quartile; 2 is second quartile; 3 is third quartile; 4 is fourth quartile. First quartile means that the fund outperformed 75 per cent of other similar funds after 12 months.

ROLLING 12-MONTH TOTAL RATE OF RETURN FOR THE MUTUAL FUND OVER TIME

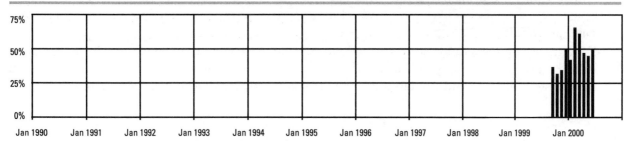

INVESTORS SUMMA FUND

Vos value rating		
Reward	**Risk**	**Best balance**
★★★★★	★★★★	★★★★★

Fund profile

There is only one word for this fund—exceptional. Allan Brown of Investors Group Inc. has managed the Investors Summa Fund since January 1997. In that period, its performance has significantly improved. Its objective is to provide capital appreciation with income generation. The fund invests in common shares of socially responsible corporations that have adopted progressive standards reflecting an awareness of economic, social, and environmental issues.

If you're an Investors Group client, and if you own a Canadian equity fund, you have to own this fund. It has a really cool investment objective in conjunction with excellent relative performance for a Canadian equity fund. What more could an investor want? The fund isn't immune to fluctuations in the Canadian economy, and investors must be aware of the underlying risks involved when investing in equity securities. But Canadian equity funds fared well during the past year, primarily through investments in technology and telecommunications, after a not-so-great 1999.

Fund performance

This fund has posted above-average performance and earned a five-star Vos Value Rating for reward and the best balance between risk and reward. The fund has been first quartile after 12 months for the last four years. During the past year it posted a gain of 43.4 per cent, a very good result, a result that allowed the fund to outperform similar funds by more than 15 per cent. The best three-year rate of return for this fund was a gain of 27.5 per cent annualized, and the average annualized three-year rate of return was 11.1 per cent. During the previous five years this fund has appreciated in value by an average of 23.5 per cent per year.

The fund has made a 30 per cent investment in financial services, 16 per cent in communications, and 10 per cent in utilities, by investing in such Canadian blue-chip companies as TD Bank, BCE, Royal Bank, Suncor Energy, and a vast array of emerging Canadian and U.S. companies. To tap these emerging U.S. companies, the fund has invested 24.83 per cent of its assets outside of Canada, a prudent diversification strategy that has added value. However, investors should consider this in their asset mix.

Fund risks

The worst 12-month rate of return for the fund was a loss of 23.5 per cent, but it has posted losses after 12 months only 23 per cent of the time. During the bear market of 1998, the fund declined in value by 24.1 per cent, less than the average Canadian equity fund, and it has done a good job of managing the risk associated with investing in Canadian equity funds.

Fund prospects

Performance for these funds has been good, and the outlook continues to be favourable, but investors should expect more volatility. Still, investors looking for a superior Canadian equity fund should consider the Investors Summa Fund, a value-added fund that is quickly building a superior track record.

FUND DETAILS

Fund name	**Investors Summa**	Fund size (in $ millions)	$2,840
Fund family	Investors Group Financial Services	Percentage in foreign holdings	24.83%
Mutual fund investment category	Canadian Diversified Equity	RRSP eligible	100%
Start date for data shown	February 1987	Sales charge	Yes
Number of funds in investment category	446	Redemption charge	Deferred
Dividend frequency	Annual	Management expense ratio	2.50%

FUND PERFORMANCE

	1 month	6 months	1 year	3 years	5 years	10 years
Returns ending June 2000	8.0%	17.7%	43.4%	23.0%	23.5%	15.0%
Best historical return	11.3%	44.9%	58.9%	27.5%	24.8%	15.3%
Average historical return	1.0%	6.2%	12.1%	11.1%	10.9%	10.9%
Worst historical return	-17.8%	-19.2%	-23.5%	-4.1%	2.4%	7.6%
Value at risk of $1,000	$959	$862	$908	$1,016	$1,150	$2,172

RETURNS GREATER THAN

	1 month	6 months	1 year	3 years	5 years	10 years
10 per cent	1%	60%	55%	48%	52%	69%
Zero	65%	77%	77%	97%	100%	100%
Percentage of time fund lost $	35%	23%	23%	3%	0%	0%
Number of periods evaluated	161	156	150	126	102	42

DOWNSIDE RISK

	Worst setback since start date	In bear 1987	In bear 1990	In bear 1994	In bear 1998
Setback for mutual fund	-24.1%	-19.7%	-23.7%	-11.4%	-24.1%
Setback for peer group	-24.6%	-23.2%	-16.3%	-9.7%	-24.6%
Setback ended in	Aug. 1998	Nov. 1987	Oct. 1990	June 1994	Aug. 1998
Months to recover from loss	10	17	14	15	10

ROLLING 12-MONTH QUARTILE RANKING OF MUTUAL FUND PERFORMANCE OVER TIME

Canadian diversified equity

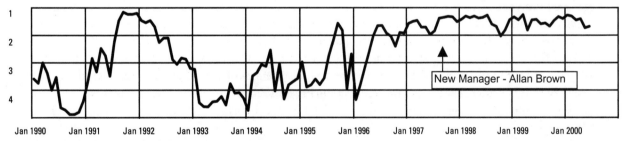

1 is first quartile; 2 is second quartile; 3 is third quartile; 4 is fourth quartile. First quartile means that the fund outperformed 75 per cent of other similar funds after 12 months.

ROLLING 12-MONTH TOTAL RATE OF RETURN FOR THE MUTUAL FUND OVER TIME

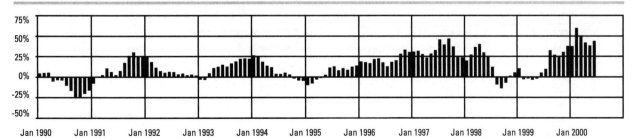

UNIVERSAL FUTURE FUND

Vos value rating		
Reward	**Risk**	**Best balance**
★★★★★	★★★★	★★★★★

Fund profile

Market conditions couldn't have been better for the Universal Future Fund than they were during the previous year, when it appreciated in value by 54.8 per cent. The fund aims to invest in companies with above-average growth potential, that lead their industries, and that export their products and services around the world. It typically places 50 per cent of its holdings in technology companies and the remaining portion in companies that exhibit excellent growth potential and financial stability. Managed by John Rohr of Mackenzie Financial Corporation, this fund is ideally suited for investors who want to invest in growth companies in Canada and in technology companies outside of Canada. This fund is more aggressive than similar funds and has displayed more risk, but investors who are bullish on technology can invest in a Canadian equity fund with a bias in that particular sector.

Fund performance

This fund is either first quartile or fourth quartile—either outperforming or underperforming similar funds by large margins. In the previous year, this fund outperformed, but investors should not expect such exceptional performance every year. Over the long term, the fund will generate above-average returns with more risk. The best 12-month rate of return for this fund was a gain of 80.3 per cent, and the average rate of return after 12 months was 14 per cent. During the previous 10 years, this fund has appreciated in value by an average of 15.6 per cent per year.

The fund continues to avoid concept stocks like e-retailers and some business-to-business companies. Instead, the fund manager invests in companies that provide the infrastructure to telecommunications companies and semi-conductor manufacturers such as ATS Automation and Tooling, Texas Instruments, and Celestica.

Fund risks

The worst 12-month return posted by this fund was a decline of 18.4 per cent, and it declined in value after 12 months 23 per cent of the time. During the bear market of 1998, this fund declined in value by 23.8 per cent, while the average Canadian diversified equity fund declined in value by 24.6 per cent. The fund took only eight months to recover its loss.

Fund prospects

This fund has outperformed similar funds in 6 out of the pervious 10 years. But it also underperformed similar funds in 4 out the previous 10 years. Nevertheless, investors can use this fund to gain access to the investment potential of high-growth technology companies on the leading edge of their respective industries. If they continue to change and grow at their current rates, investors could make a lot of money with the Universal Future Fund, but there are no guarantees.

FUND DETAILS

Fund name	**Universal Future**	Fund size (in $ millions)	$2,003
Fund family	Mackenzie Financial Corporation	Percentage in foreign holdings	19.99%
Mutual fund investment category	Canadian Diversified Equity	RRSP eligible	100%
Start date for data shown	January 1988	Sales charge	Optional
Number of funds in investment category	446	Redemption charge	Optional
Dividend frequency	Annual	Management expense ratio	2.30%

FUND PERFORMANCE

	1 month	6 months	1 year	3 years	5 years	10 years
Returns ending June 2000	6.6%	19.6%	54.8%	25.4%	21.2%	15.6%
Best historical return	12.5%	47.2%	80.3%	28.6%	23.6%	16.1%
Average historical return	1.2%	7.2%	14.0%	11.7%	12.5%	11.1%
Worst historical return	-16.6%	-20.1%	-18.4%	-6.3%	1.2%	8.1%
Value at risk of $1,000	$952	$913	$899	$901	$1,296	$2,274

RETURNS GREATER THAN

	1 month	6 months	1 year	3 years	5 years	10 years
10 per cent	2%	52%	55%	70%	65%	65%
Zero	63%	73%	77%	89%	100%	100%
Percentage of time fund lost $	37%	27%	23%	11%	0%	0%
Number of periods evaluated	150	145	139	115	91	31

DOWNSIDE RISK

	Worst setback since start date	In bear 1987	In bear 1990	In bear 1994	In bear 1998
Setback for mutual fund	-23.8%		-20.0%	-6.0%	-23.8%
Setback for peer group	-24.6%	-1.8%	-16.3%	-9.7%	-24.6%
Setback ended in	Aug. 1998		Oct. 1990	June 1994	Aug. 1998
Months to recover from loss	8		29	3	8

ROLLING 12-MONTH QUARTILE RANKING OF MUTUAL FUND PERFORMANCE OVER TIME

Canadian diversified equity

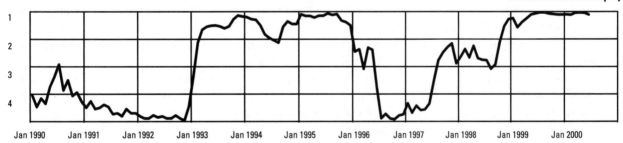

1 is first quartile; 2 is second quartile; 3 is third quartile; 4 is fourth quartile. First quartile means that the fund outperformed 75 per cent of other similar funds after 12 months.

ROLLING 12-MONTH TOTAL RATE OF RETURN FOR THE MUTUAL FUND OVER TIME

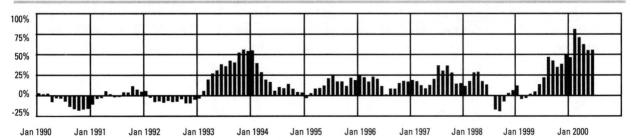

CIBC CANADIAN SMALL COMPANIES FUND

Vos value rating		
Reward	Risk	Best balance

Fund profile

When it comes to investing in Canadian small companies with excellent growth potential, you want one person in your corner: the manager of the CIBC Canadian Small Companies Fund, Virginia Wai-Ping. Hard-working, resourceful, and, most important, smart and knowledgeable about her investments, Virginia can make money and generate exceptional rates of return for unit holders. During the previous year, Canadian small-cap growth stocks were the place to be. After a couple of less-than-exceptional years, this segment of the market regained its momentum and earned big returns for investors. The aim of this fund is to invest in small or medium-sized companies that exhibit excellent growth opportunities. The fund is ideal for investors who want long-term growth and can withstand some short-term risk.

Fund performance

The fund isn't even two years old, and it has already doubled in value. During the previous year, it appreciated in value by 70.3 per cent. Its best 12-month rate of return was a gain of 100.6 per cent, and the average rate of return after 12 months was 32.6 per cent. The fund continues to emphasize companies in the technology, software, and hardware industries as well as some companies in the biotechnology and pharmaceutical industries, investing in companies like Intrawest, the owner of the Whistler ski resort; Mosaid Technologies; and GSI Lumonics.

Fund risks

Small-cap stocks are riskier than their large-cap counterparts, and investors should be aware of the potential for disappointment. This fund's worst 12-month return was a decline of 16.8 per cent, and it declined in value after 12 months 13 per cent of the time. During the bear market of 1998 it declined in value by 25.8 per cent. During the same period, the average Canadian small- to mid-cap equity fund declined in value by 28.3 per cent. The fund took only eight months to recover its loss.

Fund prospects

Investors who have a long-term view of their investments should seriously consider the benefits of a value-added and well-managed Canadian small-cap mutual fund like the CIBC Canadian Small Companies Fund. The outlook for Canadian small companies should remain robust. With a vibrant venture capital market, many of these companies are establishing the strategic partnerships they need to allow their companies to grow quickly and prudently. In turn, their stock prices are appreciating in value. There will be volatility, but by investing systematically and diversifying your portfolio, you can ensure the risk is never detrimental while participating in the success of this fund. In addition, this is a no-load mutual fund offered by a bank that charges investors a below-average management fee. The fund is also widely available from an array of financial planners and brokers.

FUND DETAILS

Fund name	**CIBC Canadian Small Companies**	Fund size (in $ millions)	$140
Fund family	CIBC Securities Inc.	Percentage in foreign holdings	14.99%
Mutual fund investment category	Canadian Small/Mid-Cap Equity	RRSP eligible	100%
Start date for data shown	September 1997	Sales charge	None
Number of funds in investment category	125	Redemption charge	None
Dividend frequency	Annual	Management expense ratio	2.40%

FUND PERFORMANCE

	1 month	6 months	1 year	3 years	5 years	10 years
Returns ending June 2000	8.6%	31.9%	70.3%			
Best historical return	23.5%	58.1%	100.6%			
Average historical return	2.6%	18.3%	32.6%			
Worst historical return	-20.8%	-22.0%	-16.8%			
Value at risk of $1,000	$935	$809	$870			

RETURNS GREATER THAN

	1 month	6 months	1 year	3 years	5 years	10 years
10 per cent	9%	79%	65%			
Zero	65%	83%	87%			
Percentage of time fund lost $	35%	17%	13%			
Number of periods evaluated	34	29	23			

DOWNSIDE RISK

	Worst setback since start date	In bear 1987	In bear 1990	In bear 1994	In bear 1998
Setback for mutual fund	-25.8%				-25.8%
Setback for peer group	-28.3%				-28.3%
Setback ended in	Aug. 1998				Aug. 1998
Months to recover from loss	8				8

ROLLING 12-MONTH QUARTILE RANKING OF MUTUAL FUND PERFORMANCE OVER TIME

Canadian small/mid-cap equity

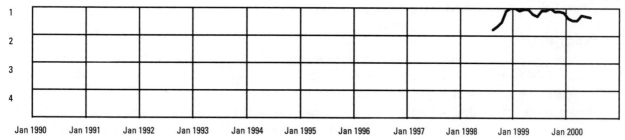

1 is first quartile; 2 is second quartile; 3 is third quartile; 4 is fourth quartile. First quartile means that the fund outperformed 75 per cent of other similar funds after 12 months.

ROLLING 12-MONTH TOTAL RATE OF RETURN FOR THE MUTUAL FUND OVER TIME

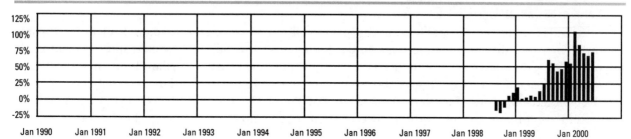

FIDELITY CANADIAN GROWTH COMPANY FUND

Vos value rating		
Reward	**Risk**	**Best balance**
★★★★★	★★★★★	★★★★★

Fund profile

This fund aims to provide above-average long-term growth primarily by investing in companies that are smaller or lesser known and that are well positioned for growth during the market cycle. It will also invest in larger companies when prudent, a feature that makes this mid-cap mutual fund unique from other mid-cap mutual funds. Manager Alan Radlo selects investments using Fidelity's bottom-up investment approach, which involves selecting companies with great fundamental value. The manager tends to invest in companies that provide innovative products or services. Each company should also exhibit superior growth potential over the long term and have a competitive and comparative advantage within their marketplace. This strategy will allow the fund to minimize the risk associated with investing in small companies in Canada, a segment of the market that generated some exceptional returns during the previous year.

Fund performance

This fund's unique investment objective has allowed it to earn a triple five-star Vos Value Rating for reward, risk, and the best balance between risk and return. The fund has frequently posted first-quartile performance after 12 months, although it tends to underperform during small-cap rallies. The fund has posted a gain of 29.1 per cent during the previous year.

This fund continues to hold large investments in industrial products, communications, and media companies, including Onex, Celestica, CGI Group, Westjet Airlines, and Biovail. You won't see these companies in other small-cap funds. The fund has made investments in 141 different companies, but the 10 top holdings of the fund represent 23 per cent of the assets.

Fund risks

Small-cap investors will have to continue to endure the volatility associated with investing in this high-growth and high-risk sector. But unlike many other small-cap funds, the Fidelity Canadian Growth Company Fund has done a good job of managing risk by investing in larger companies prudently. The fund still incurs downside risk, but it's less severe compared to similar funds. During the bear of 1998 the fund declined in value by 20.9 per cent, while the average Canadian small- to mid-cap equity funds declined by 28.3 per cent. The fund has generated positive rates of return after 12 months 88 per cent of the time. It has a value at risk of $1,000 dollars of $970 after 12 months. This means that, 95 per cent of the time, an investor's initial $1,000 investment would be worth more than $970 after one year.

Fund prospects

This fund is a good complement to other Canadian small- to mid-cap mutual funds, as it tends to go up and down in a very different pattern than similar funds. Over the long term small-cap funds will likely outperform their large-cap counterparts. However, investors must be prepared for some short-term underperformance. This fund rewards investors by investing in a mix of large and small companies. Experienced and novice small-cap investors will find that the Fidelity Canadian Growth Company Fund a useful contribution to their portfolios because of its unique investment strategy and flexibility.

FUND DETAILS

Fund name	**Fidelity Canadian Growth Company**	Fund size (in $ millions)	$2,433
Fund family	Fidelity Investments Canada Limited	Percentage in foreign holdings	8.62%
Mutual fund investment category	Canadian Small/Mid-Cap Equity	RRSP eligible	100%
Start date for data shown	August 1994	Sales charge	Optional
Number of funds in investment category	125	Redemption charge	Optional
Dividend frequency	Annual	Management expense ratio	2.45%

FUND PERFORMANCE

	1 month	6 months	1 year	3 years	5 years	10 years
Returns ending June 2000	4.2%	10.8%	29.1%	17.5%	20.1%	
Best historical return	15.1%	31.0%	42.4%	28.4%	23.7%	
Average historical return	1.7%	10.4%	20.7%	20.4%	20.0%	
Worst historical return	-15.1%	-17.6%	-12.1%	13.8%	17.3%	
Value at risk of $1,000	$956	$901	$970	$1,497	$2,256	

RETURNS GREATER THAN

	1 month	6 months	1 year	3 years	5 years	10 years
10 per cent	3%	82%	80%	100%	100%	
Zero	72%	91%	88%	100%	100%	
Percentage of time fund lost $	28%	9%	12%	0%	0%	
Number of periods evaluated	71	66	60	36	12	

DOWNSIDE RISK

	Worst setback since start date	In bear 1987	In bear 1990	In bear 1994	In bear 1998
Setback for mutual fund	-20.9%			-3.0%	-20.9%
Setback for peer group	-28.3%			-6.9%	-28.3%
Setback ended in	Aug. 1998			Nov. 1994	Aug. 1998
Months to recover from loss	11			1	11

ROLLING 12-MONTH QUARTILE RANKING OF MUTUAL FUND PERFORMANCE OVER TIME

Canadian small/mid-cap equity

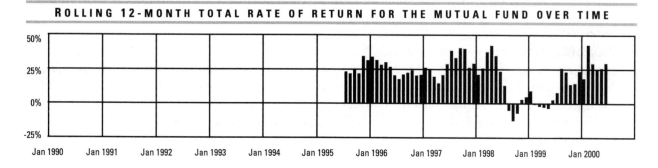

1 is first quartile; 2 is second quartile; 3 is third quartile; 4 is fourth quartile. First quartile means that the fund outperformed 75 per cent of other similar funds after 12 months.

ROLLING 12-MONTH TOTAL RATE OF RETURN FOR THE MUTUAL FUND OVER TIME

SAXON SMALL CAP FUND

Vos value rating		
Reward	**Risk**	**Best balance**
★★★★	★★★★★	★★★★★

Fund profile

Finally—an excellent year for small-cap companies. Unfortunately, small-cap value companies didn't participate in the success to the same extent as small-cap growth stocks. Nevertheless, it's the future that counts, and the future for small-cap value stocks looks good. Corporate activity is up, and companies are merging with and acquiring other companies while buying back their own shares. This fund aims for long-term growth by investing in Canadian companies with limited market capitalization. The fund is unique in that it invests only in companies with market capitalization below $150 million, often called micro-cap stocks. These stocks exhibit higher return and loss potential, and many remain small because they fail to generate any shareholder value. But some of them have growth potential, add shareholder value, and can sustain abnormal rates of growth until they become household names.

Within a micro-cap environment, prudent stock picking is key. Manager Robert Tattersall has generated an excellent reputation for identifying investment opportunities before they're fulfilled. He researches each company using a traditional bottom-up investment strategy and places heavy emphasis on statistical analysis, fundamental valuations, and manager interviews.

Fund performance

During the previous three years, this fund has been on fire and has earned a four-star Vos Value Rating for reward and a five-star Vos Value Rating for the best balance between risk and reward. During this period it consistently outperformed similar funds in first-quartile results until it lost some of its momentum and growth-oriented funds surged ahead. During the previous year the fund earned a rate of return of 13.5 per cent. It is highly diversified, investing in more than 50 companies. A majority of the fund is currently invested in industrial products and oil and gas. It tends to avoid speculative investments, choosing companies such as Canadian Western Bank, Magin Energy, Brampton Brick, and Jetform.

Fund risks

Investors should realize that some companies are small for one of two reasons: either they're poorly run and deserve to remain small or they've exhausted their growth possibilities. To achieve investment success it is essential to distinguish these companies from ones with potential for success. Robert Tattersall has a proven ability to distinguish the goose that will lay the golden egg from the ugly duckling. However, investors should be aware that the goose may not lay an egg each day, so they should expect some volatility. This point is clearly illustrated by the fund's performance in the early 1990s, when it did not generate first-quartile performance.

Fund prospects

Small-cap investing will likely be more fruitful than it is currently, and aggressive investors should allocate a portion of their investment portfolio to the Saxon Small Cap Fund to benefit from the value-added management and the unique growth potential of this market segment.

FUND DETAILS

Fund name	Saxon Small Cap	Fund size (in $ millions)	$38
Fund family	Howson Tattersall Investment Counsel Ltd.	Percentage in foreign holdings	0.00%
Mutual fund investment category	Canadian Small/Mid-Cap Equity	RRSP eligible	100%
Start date for data shown	January 1986	Sales charge	None
Number of funds in investment category	125	Redemption charge	None
Dividend frequency	Annual	Management expense ratio	1.75%

FUND PERFORMANCE

	1 month	6 months	1 year	3 years	5 years	10 years
Returns ending June 2000	2.2%	11.5%	13.5%	12.2%	17.3%	13.3%
Best historical return	11.9%	32.4%	57.2%	27.5%	22.4%	13.3%
Average historical return	0.8%	5.2%	10.5%	9.8%	9.5%	9.2%
Worst historical return	-19.6%	-20.6%	-25.9%	-8.9%	-2.6%	5.7%
Value at risk of $1,000	$962	$847	$858	$880	$931	$1,785

RETURNS GREATER THAN

	1 month	6 months	1 year	3 years	5 years	10 years
10 per cent	1%	57%	52%	55%	51%	44%
Zero	60%	73%	73%	76%	83%	100%
Percentage of time fund lost $	40%	27%	27%	24%	17%	0%
Number of periods evaluated	174	169	163	139	115	55

DOWNSIDE RISK

	Worst setback since start date	In bear 1987	In bear 1990	In bear 1994	In bear 1998
Setback for mutual fund	-27.9%	-21.4%	-27.9	-15.3%	-22.0%
Setback for peer group	-13.8%	-23.0%	-14.7%	-14.4%	-28.3%
Setback ended in	Nov. 1990	Nov. 1987	Nov. 1990	Feb. 1995	Aug. 1998
Months to recover from loss	28	64	28	12	11

ROLLING 12-MONTH QUARTILE RANKING OF MUTUAL FUND PERFORMANCE OVER TIME

Canadian small/mid-cap equity

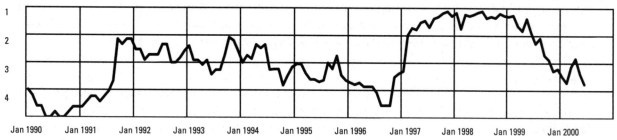

1 is first quartile; 2 is second quartile; 3 is third quartile; 4 is fourth quartile. First quartile means that the fund outperformed 75 per cent of other similar funds after 12 months.

ROLLING 12-MONTH TOTAL RATE OF RETURN FOR THE MUTUAL FUND OVER TIME

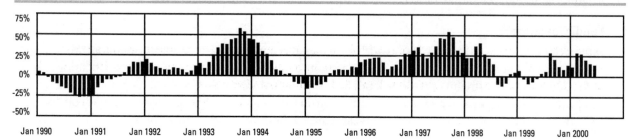

AGF INTERNATIONAL VALUE FUND

Vos value rating		
Reward	**Risk**	**Best balance**
★★★	★	★★★

Fund profile

This fund aims to provide investors with a superior rate of return, while controlling risk and preserving capital. It invests in companies from various industries and countries that exhibit above-average growth potential. Charles Brandes and Jeff Busby of Brandes Investment Partners have managed the fund since November 1994. The money mangers use a bottom-up, value-investing strategy to identify companies that are trading below their true intrinsic value. This investment philosophy usually identifies a lot of value companies that are trading at very reasonable valuations and over the long-term this strategy has provided investors with very attractive rates of return.

In the global economy you frequently hear terms like integration, trade regulation, currency devaluation, deregulation, inflation, and debt crisis. All these terms refer to situations that adversely affect stock-price valuations. But they also refer to short-term problems that don't affect the average investor. Ten years from now few people will remember what was moving capital markets today. Let's use AGF International Value Fund to illustrate the point: during the previous 10 years this fund generated an average annual return of 14.8 per cent. A $1,000 investment would have grown to $3,975 over that period. In short, you shouldn't worry about timing the market, but about how long you'll be invested in it. Don't miss out on long-term gains by concerning yourself over short-term problems. These problems will resolve themselves.

Fund performance

The managers have made investments throughout the world, including Mexico, Italy, Germany, France, and the United States, and have made larger investments than comparable funds in the U.K. and the States. It has also avoided the technology sector, which has affected its short-term performance. Instead the managers prefer to invest in companies at reasonable prices. This strategy has added value for investors over the long term and has allowed the fund to generate above-average performance over this time period. The fund has invested in companies like Boeing, Philip Morris, and Metlife, which haven't allowed the fund to generate top-quartile performance in the short term but have generated excellent results over the long term.

Fund risks

The fund has displayed above-average risk, but it's very nominal. The fund has posted gains after 12 months 94 per cent of the time, and the worst 12-month loss was 5.1 per cent. Investing in companies at reasonable prices reduces the risk associated with equities. The fund's investment objective of investing around the world has allowed for additional diversification and reduced risk.

Fund prospects

International diversification and value-added management make this fund ideal for almost any mutual-fund investor. Global investing allows the manager to fully utilize the benefit of diversification. Those with a long-term investment horizon will not be disappointed with the benefits of global investing, which can lead to higher returns while reducing risk. Conservative global equity investors should consider the AGF International Value Fund as a core investment for their mutual fund portfolios.

FUND DETAILS

Fund name	**AGF International Value**	Fund size (in $ millions)	$4,125
Fund family	AGF Funds Inc.	Percentage in foreign holdings	0.00%
Mutual fund investment category	Global Equity	RRSP eligible	20%
Start date for data shown	July 1989	Sales charge	Optional
Number of funds in investment category	281	Redemption charge	Optional
Dividend frequency	Annual	Management expense ratio	2.77%

FUND PERFORMANCE

	1 month	6 months	1 year	3 years	5 years	10 years
Returns ending June 2000	-0.1%	4.0%	4.4%	15.3%	18.0%	14.8%
Best historical return	14.6%	24.0%	39.4%	25.7%	19.5%	15.4%
Average historical return	1.2%	7.1%	14.9%	15.6%	15.0%	14.6%
Worst historical return	-14.3%	-12.1%	-5.1%	6.9%	10.7%	13.6%
Value at risk of $1,000	$956	$940	$992	$1,318	$1,704	$3,680

RETURNS GREATER THAN

	1 month	6 months	1 year	3 years	5 years	10 years
10 per cent	1%	60%	69%	90%	100%	100%
Zero	61%	83%	94%	100%	100%	100%
Percentage of time fund lost $	39%	17%	6%	0%	0%	0%
Number of periods evaluated	132	127	121	97	73	13

DOWNSIDE RISK

	Worst setback since start date	In bear 1987	In bear 1990	In bear 1994	In bear 1998
Setback for mutual fund	-14.3%		-11.0%	-8.7%	-14.3%
Setback for peer group	-11.4%		-14.6%	-5.9%	-13.6%
Setback ended in	Aug. 1998		Oct. 1990	June 1994	Aug. 1998
Months to recover from loss	3		4	2	3

ROLLING 12-MONTH QUARTILE RANKING OF MUTUAL FUND PERFORMANCE OVER TIME

Global equity

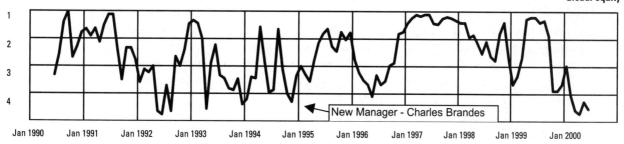

1 is first quartile; 2 is second quartile; 3 is third quartile; 4 is fourth quartile. First quartile means that the fund outperformed 75 per cent of other similar funds after 12 months.

ROLLING 12-MONTH TOTAL RATE OF RETURN FOR THE MUTUAL FUND OVER TIME

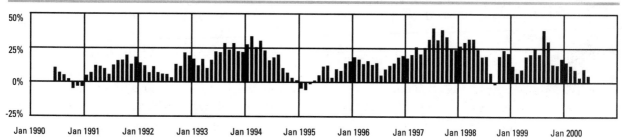

ATLAS GLOBAL VALUE FUND

Vos value rating		
Reward	**Risk**	**Best balance**
★★★★★	★★★	★★★★★

Fund profile

It was a good year for global equity funds. Okay, most Canadian equity funds performed better, but that was because of the exceptional performance of one stock, Nortel. If you want to invest in one stock and receive the risk and rewards associated with one stock, then you may invest in one stock. If you want the proven expertise of a global portfolio manager with a proven track record, then you should consider the Atlas Global Value Fund. Anthony Rawlinson is the managing director of the Global Value Investment Portfolio Management Pte. Ltd. in Singapore. As manager of the Atlas Global Value Fund, he has built an international reputation for his strict adherence to his firm's investment process, a disciplined bottom-up approach to selecting companies. This fund is ideal for investors who want to reduce the volatility associated with capital markets. Investors who invest in a great global equity fund with a value bias can diversify their investment portfolio while retaining their ability to earn higher rates of return.

Fund performance

During the previous year the fund posted a great gain of 44 per cent. Its best 12-month rate of return was a gain of 72.1 per cent, and the average rate of return after 12 months was 16 per cent. During the previous 10 years, this fund has appreciated in value by an average of 14.9 per cent per year. With such great results the fund earned a five-star Vos Value Rating for reward.

The fund has made large investments in Canada, the Pacific Rim, the United Kingdom, and the United States, in companies like Oxford Health, Avis Rent-A-Car, and Flextronics International.

Fund risks

This fund has had a period of prolonged underperformance, and that could occur again, so investors should monitor their investments carefully. Its worst 12-month return was a decline of 7.3 per cent, and it declined in value after 12 months 9 per cent of the time. During the bear market of 1998, the fund declined in value by 12.8 per cent, while the average global equity fund declined in value by 13.6 per cent. But the fund took only three months to recover its loss.

Fund prospects

The outlook for global equity funds is always favourable, because the manager has the whole world at his disposal. Capital markets have appreciated in value recently, although they will eventually incur a setback. Short-term problems will be resolved, however, and over the long term your investments will grow at a faster rate. The Atlas Global Value Fund provides unique risk-and-reward characteristics that will increase the level of diversification and return potential in a mutual fund portfolio.

FUND DETAILS

Fund name	**Atlas Global Value**	Fund size (in $ millions)	$122
Fund family	Atlas Asset Management Inc.	Percentage in foreign holdings	79.30%
Mutual fund investment category	Global Equity	RRSP eligible	20%
Start date for data shown	April 1990	Sales charge	Optional
Number of funds in investment category	281	Redemption charge	Optional
Dividend frequency	Annual	Management expense ratio	2.68%

FUND PERFORMANCE

	1 month	6 months	1 year	3 years	5 years	10 years
Returns ending June 2000	6.7%	-2.5%	44.0%	25.0%	20.5%	14.9%
Best historical return	25.5%	59.8%	72.1%	33.3%	23.3%	16.5%
Average historical return	1.3%	8.1%	16.2%	14.1%	13.0%	15.2%
Worst historical return	-11.5%	-10.2%	-7.3%	5.8%	7.9%	14.1%
Value at risk of $1,000	$950	$935	$980	$1,212	$1,577	$3,791

RETURNS GREATER THAN

	1 month	6 months	1 year	3 years	5 years	10 years
10 per cent	3%	58%	60%	75%	86%	100%
Zero	59%	74%	91%	100%	100%	100%
Percentage of time fund lost $	41%	26%	9%	0%	0%	0%
Number of periods evaluated	123	118	112	88	64	4

DOWNSIDE RISK

	Worst setback since start date	In bear 1987	In bear 1990	In bear 1994	In bear 1998
Setback for mutual fund	-14.6%		-12.2%	-7.6%	-12.8%
Setback for peer group	-5.1%		-14.6%	-5.9%	-13.6%
Setback ended in	May 2000		Sept. 1990	Jan. 1995	Sept. 1998
Months to recover from loss	?		15	6	3

ROLLING 12-MONTH QUARTILE RANKING OF MUTUAL FUND PERFORMANCE OVER TIME

Global equity

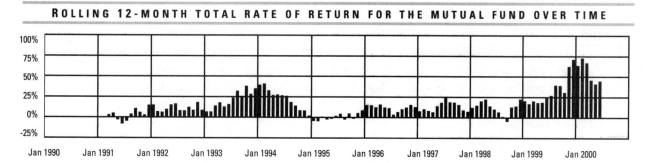

Jan 1990 Jan 1991 Jan 1992 Jan 1993 Jan 1994 Jan 1995 Jan 1996 Jan 1997 Jan 1998 Jan 1999 Jan 2000

1 is first quartile; 2 is second quartile; 3 is third quartile; 4 is fourth quartile. First quartile means that the fund outperformed 75 per cent of other similar funds after 12 months.

ROLLING 12-MONTH TOTAL RATE OF RETURN FOR THE MUTUAL FUND OVER TIME

Jan 1990 Jan 1991 Jan 1992 Jan 1993 Jan 1994 Jan 1995 Jan 1996 Jan 1997 Jan 1998 Jan 1999 Jan 2000

BPI GLOBAL EQUITY FUND

Vos value rating		
Reward	Risk	Best balance
★★★★★	★★	★★★★★

Fund profile

When the entire world is your playground, you should be able to uncover some gems, and the BPI Global Equity Fund has earned an excellent reputation by investing in leading international and North American companies. The new portfolio managers, Daniel Jaworski, Paul Holland, and John Hudson, have found some of those gems and revised the portfolio's holdings, thereby creating significant value for investors.

Global investing has been profitable for Canadian investors as major global equity markets have appreciated in value in a robust economic environment. With its value-added management and global investment focus, this fund has increased returns and reduced risk for investors. It is ideal for investors looking for a good core global equity fund that is a little more aggressive than the norm. It identifies companies with strong fundamentals, good financial statements, and sustainable competitive and comparative advantages and focuses on the world's largest companies—household names with solid financial results.

Fund performance

With superior performance over the previous three years, this fund has earned a five-star Vos Value Rating for reward. It has frequently been in the first 12-month quartile. Mutual funds that have the ability and flexibility to invest in any company in the world can add value for investors, by earning higher returns and reducing risk through diversification. During the previous year this fund posted a gain of 32.8 per cent. Its best 12-month rate of return was a gain of 55.8 per cent, and the average rate of return after 12 months was 16.8 per cent. During the previous 10 years it has appreciated in value by an average of 15.8 per cent per year.

The fund has made large investments in the U.S. and Europe while favouring companies that provide technology or consumer products, such as Cisco Systems, Philips Electronics, and Nokia. All of these companies have exhibited strong business fundamentals and excellent price appreciation.

Fund risks

The fund hasn't added value by reducing risk, and so earned only a two-star Vos Value Rating for risk, although the risk was nominal. The fund's worst 12-month rate of return was a loss of 3.4 per cent, and it posted a gain after 12 months 95 per cent of the time. Its global investing strategy provides investors with excellent diversification, and it has experienced very few setbacks. Conservative equity investors will not be disappointed with this fund's risk profile.

Fund prospects

Investors should be prepared for some additional volatility but should also remember that absolute losses generated by this fund in the past have been very realistic. The risk associated with this fund is an excellent example of how diversification works—higher returns with less risk through global investing. Investors looking for a good global equity fund should consider the BPI Global Equity Value Fund for a portion of their portfolio.

FUND DETAILS

Fund name	**BPI Global Equity Value**	Fund size (in $ millions)	$2,062
Fund family	C.I. Mutual Funds Inc.	Percentage in foreign holdings	95.40%
Mutual fund investment category	Global Equity	RRSP eligible	20%
Start date for data shown	July 1988	Sales charge	Optional
Number of funds in investment category	281	Redemption charge	Optional
Dividend frequency	Annual	Management expense ratio	2.48%

FUND PERFORMANCE

	1 month	6 months	1 year	3 years	5 years	10 years
Returns ending June 2000	3.1%	-1.9%	32.8%	24.7%	22.6%	15.8%
Best historical return	14.2%	44.7%	55.8%	33.9%	26.5%	17.5%
Average historical return	1.3%	8.3%	16.8%	14.9%	14.4%	14.9%
Worst historical return	-11.9%	-8.3%	-3.4%	4.9%	8.6%	12.7%
Value at risk of $1,000	$950	$968	$1,004	$1,175	$1,559	$3,488

RETURNS GREATER THAN

	1 month	6 months	1 year	3 years	5 years	10 years
10 per cent	2%	62%	65%	81%	87%	100%
Zero	65%	81%	95%	100%	100%	100%
Percentage of time fund lost $	35%	19%	5%	0%	0%	0%
Number of periods evaluated	144	139	133	109	85	25

DOWNSIDE RISK

	Worst setback since start date	In bear 1987	In bear 1990	In bear 1994	In bear 1998
Setback for mutual fund	-14.3%		-7.1%	-8.6%	-14.3%
Setback for peer group	-13.6%		-14.6%	-5.9%	-13.6%
Setback ended in	Sept. 1998		Sept. 1990	Jan. 1995	Sept. 1998
Months to recover from loss	3		5	6	3

ROLLING 12-MONTH QUARTILE RANKING OF MUTUAL FUND PERFORMANCE OVER TIME

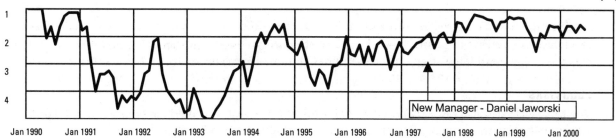

1 is first quartile; 2 is second quartile; 3 is third quartile; 4 is fourth quartile. First quartile means that the fund outperformed 75 per cent of other similar funds after 12 months.

ROLLING 12-MONTH TOTAL RATE OF RETURN FOR THE MUTUAL FUND OVER TIME

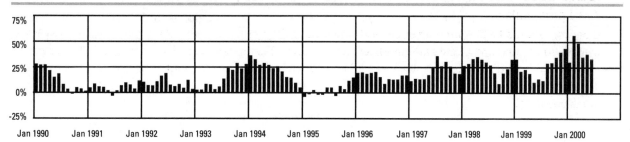

C.I. GLOBAL FUND

Vos value rating		
Reward	**Risk**	**Best balance**
★★★★★	★★★★	★★★★★

Fund profile

Bill Sterling, lead investment manager for the C.I. Global Fund, has earned an excellent reputation for being an authority on global investing. This fund aims to invest in high-quality companies to generate long-term capital growth while providing a minimum level of diversification. The fund is ideally suited for conservative investors who want equity exposure in global markets, or for more aggressive investors who want to diversify the risk associated with a more aggressive fund or their domestic investments. In any case, a global fund should be included in any portfolio. Canadian markets exhibit their own unique risk and reward characteristics. When rewards occur, diversification may seem less prudent. But when the risk comes to fruition, as it always does, you'll be glad you diversified. Plan ahead and you will get ahead with your investment.

Fund performance

During the previous year this fund generated some very impressive results, appreciating in value by 36.3 per cent. The best 12-month rate of return for this fund was a gain of 55.7 per cent, and the average rate of return after 12 months was 13 per cent. During the previous 10 years, this fund has appreciated in value by an average of 16 per cent per year. With such exceptional performance, the fund has earned a five-star Vos Value Rating for reward and best balance between risk and reward.

The fund has made a 60 per cent investment in the United States, with an additional 21 per cent in Europe and 12 per cent in Japan. It has invested in companies like Corning, PMC Sierra, Vodafone, Nokia, and Royal Dutch Petroleum.

Fund risks

The fund has incurred some short-term setbacks, but they have been manageable, and the fund earned a four-star Vos Value Rating for risk. Its worst 12-month return was a decline of 18.7 per cent, and it declined in value after 12 months 18 per cent of the time. During the bear market of 1998, this fund declined in value by 12 per cent. During the same period, the average global equity fund declined in value by 13.6 per cent, and this fund took only three months to recover its loss. Investors should remember that risk associated with a well-diversified global equity fund is very nominal.

Fund prospects

The outlook for global equities continues to be favourable, but investors should expect more volatility in the future. Over the long term, 15 per cent is realistic but 30 per cent per year is not. Investors looking to build a diversified portfolio of mutual funds should start with a good global equity fund and build from there, and this fund is an excellent choice. A capable management team and a proven track record will provide some reassurance when you make your investment.

FUND DETAILS

Fund name	**C.I. Global**	Fund size (in $ millions)	$2,996
Fund family	C.I. Mutual Funds Inc.	Percentage in foreign holdings	90.30%
Mutual fund investment category	Global Equity	RRSP eligible	20%
Start date for data shown	July 1986	Sales charge	Optional
Number of funds in investment category	281	Redemption charge	Optional
Dividend frequency	Annual	Management expense ratio	2.40%

FUND PERFORMANCE

	1 month	6 months	1 year	3 years	5 years	10 years
Returns ending June 2000	3.8%	1.8%	36.3%	22.8%	20.4%	16.0%
Best historical return	14.1%	44.9%	55.7%	29.8%	23.6%	17.3%
Average historical return	1.1%	6.8%	13.0%	12.2%	12.1%	11.9%
Worst historical return	-20.7%	-17.6%	-18.7%	-5.9%	2.9%	8.4%
Value at risk of $1,000	$949	$905	$9901	$1,030	$1,267	$2,278

RETURNS GREATER THAN

	1 month	6 months	1 year	3 years	5 years	10 years
10 per cent	2%	55%	59%	56%	79%	67%
Zero	63%	78%	82%	97%	100%	100%
Percentage of time fund lost $	37%	22%	18%	3%	0%	0%
Number of periods evaluated	168	163	157	133	109	49

DOWNSIDE RISK

	Worst setback since start date	In bear 1987	In bear 1990	In bear 1994	In bear 1998
Setback for mutual fund	-22.8%	-22.8%	-14.6%	-12.7%	-12.0%
Setback for peer group	-24.2%	-24.2%	-14.6%	-5.9%	-13.6%
Setback ended in	Nov. 1987	Nov. 1987	Sept. 1990	Feb. 1995	Sept. 1998
Months to recover from loss	42	42	8	11	3

ROLLING 12-MONTH QUARTILE RANKING OF MUTUAL FUND PERFORMANCE OVER TIME

Global equity

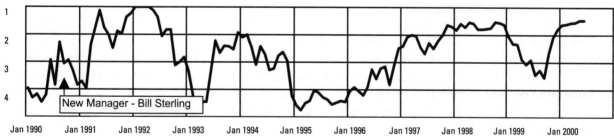

1 is first quartile; 2 is second quartile; 3 is third quartile; 4 is fourth quartile. First quartile means that the fund outperformed 75 per cent of other similar funds after 12 months.

ROLLING 12-MONTH TOTAL RATE OF RETURN FOR THE MUTUAL FUND OVER TIME

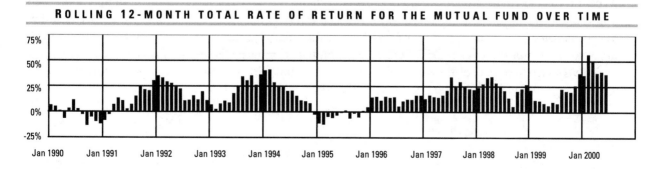

FIDELITY INTERNATIONAL PORTFOLIO FUND

Vos value rating		
Reward	**Risk**	**Best balance**
★★★★	★★★★★	★★★★★

Fund profile

This fund aims to achieve long-term growth by investing in leading global companies from different industries and countries while maintaining a prudent level of diversification. Manager Richard Habermann capitalizes on Fidelity's strong research capabilities to employ a bottom-up approach, investing in companies that can generate above-average earnings momentum and capital appreciation.

Global equity markets are an excellent place to invest, since an investment somewhere in the world is usually going up. A higher level of diversification allows investors to earn comparable rates of return with less risk. Thus, this fund is ideally suited for investors seeking a good core global equity fund to better diversify their mutual fund portfolios.

Fund performance

During the previous three years the fund has earned an above-average rate of return. The best three-year rate of return for this fund was a gain of 23.6 per cent annualized, and the average annualized three-year rate of return was 14.3 per cent. During the previous five years, this fund has appreciated in value by an average of 18.5 per cent per year, and the fund has been consistently first quartile after 12 months compared to similar funds.

The fund has invested 43 per cent of its assets in the U.S. stock market, 15 per cent in Japan, and 9 per cent in the United Kingdom, in companies like Microsoft, General Electric, Intel, Exxon Mobil, and Cisco. Altogether, the fund has invested in 597 different companies. With such a large number of holdings, it won't be number one consistently in the short term, but it has generated above-average returns over the long term.

Fund risks

This fund displays average downside risk. During the bear market of 1998 it declined by 13 per cent, the same amount as the average global equity fund. Its worst 12-month decline in value was a loss of 14.2 per cent. With 597 holdings the fund maintains a high level of diversification, and worldwide economic conditions would have to be very unfavourable before it experienced a significant setback. Such a scenario isn't likely in the short term.

Fund prospects

With strong growth in the North American economy, investors will be monitoring inflation and interest rates closely. Many investors are cautiously optimistic about capital market conditions in the near term. The performance of the U.S. stock market relative to other major stock markets will be key to this fund's relative performance. Those seeking long-term growth in a stable global equity fund should consider the Fidelity International Portfolio Fund. With this fund, you could invest your money and forget about it for 10 years, knowing it's in good hands with the world's largest mutual fund company.

FUND DETAILS

Fund name	**Fidelity International Portfolio**	Fund size (in $ millions)	$7,601
Fund family	Fidelity Investments Canada Limited	Percentage in foreign holdings	93.05%
Mutual fund investment category	Global Equity	RRSP eligible	20%
Start date for data shown	December 1987	Sales charge	Optional
Number of funds in investment category	281	Redemption charge	Optional
Dividend frequency	Annual	Management expense ratio	2.58%

FUND PERFORMANCE

	1 month	6 months	1 year	3 years	5 years	10 years
Returns ending June 2000	2.9%	-1.0%	16.8%	16.5%	18.5%	14.0%
Best historical return	10.1%	27.3%	41.3%	23.6%	20.9%	15.3%
Average historical return	1.1%	7.0%	14.8%	14.3%	14.5%	14.1%
Worst historical return	-12.3%	-13.2%	-14.2%	2.5%	6.6%	12.3%
Value at risk of $1,000	$950	$946	$958	$1,134	$1,517	$3,359

RETURNS GREATER THAN

	1 month	6 months	1 year	3 years	5 years	10 years
10 per cent	1%	62%	64%	74%	87%	100%
Zero	66%	82%	90%	100%	100%	100%
Percentage of time fund lost $	34%	18%	10%	0%	0%	0%
Number of periods evaluated	151	146	140	116	92	32

DOWNSIDE RISK

	Worst setback since start date	In bear 1987	In bear 1990	In bear 1994	In bear 1998
Setback for mutual fund	-19.5%	-5.0%	-19.5%	-9.7%	-13.0%
Setback for peer group	-14.6%	-0.2%	-14.6%	-5.9%	-13.6%
Setback ended in	Sept. 1990	Dec. 1987	Sept. 1990	Feb. 1995	Sept. 1998
Months to recover from loss	15	13	15	5	3

ROLLING 12-MONTH QUARTILE RANKING OF MUTUAL FUND PERFORMANCE OVER TIME

Global equity

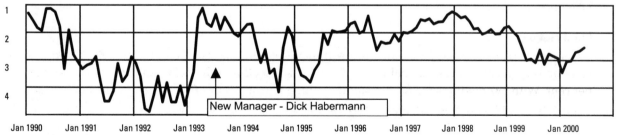

1 is first quartile; 2 is second quartile; 3 is third quartile; 4 is fourth quartile. First quartile means that the fund outperformed 75 per cent of other similar funds after 12 months.

ROLLING 12-MONTH TOTAL RATE OF RETURN FOR THE MUTUAL FUND OVER TIME

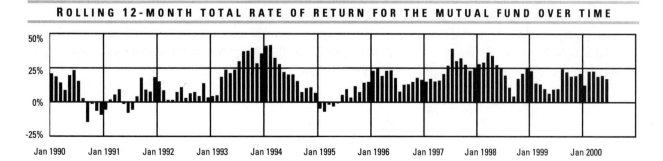

JANUS GLOBAL EQUITY FUND

Vos value rating		
Reward	Risk	Best balance
★★★★★	★★	★★★★★

Fund profile

If you're looking for an aggressive global equity fund with value-added performance and a capable management team, look no further than the Janus Global Equity Fund. It's managed by Helen Young Hayes of Janus Capital of Denver. Janus Capital has been managing money since 1970 and currently manages more than $450 billion, which exceeds the value of the entire Canadian mutual fund industry. Janus invests exclusively in equities and corporate bonds; they specialize in investing in companies that exhibit excellent growth potential to obtain above-average rates of return. This fund is suitable for more aggressive investors who can withstand higher volatility. In return for accepting a higher level of risk, investors have been rewarded. In fact, since the new manager took over day-to-day operations in 1997, the fund has done nothing but head north.

Fund performance

Wow! This fund appreciated in value during the previous year by 42.8 per cent, earning a five-star Vos Value Rating for reward, and it has frequently been first quartile relative to other funds after 12 months. Its best three-year rate of return was a gain of 36.4 per cent annualized, and the average annualized three-year rate of return was 21.6 per cent. During the previous five years this fund has appreciated in value by an average of 21.6 per cent per year.

The fund has invested 23 per cent of its assets in the United States, 21 per cent in Europe, and 10 per cent in Japan. The manager has invested 30 per cent of the fund in the telecommunications industry through cellular equipment and service companies such as China Telecommunications, Vodafone, NTT Docomo, Telefonos De Mexico, and Nokia.

Fund risks

The fund has displayed more downside risk than similar funds, but most investors wouldn't complain. Its worst 12-month return was a gain of 0.6 per cent. During the bear market of 1998, this fund declined in value by 16 per cent. During the same period, the average global equity fund declined in value by 13.6 per cent but this fund took only three months to recover the loss.

Fund prospects

This fund's performance will depend on the performance of telecommunications and technology stocks. These investments have allowed the fund to appreciate in value significantly and will allow it to continue to appreciate if these companies continue to grow at a fast pace. In the short term, there will be some pressure on interest rates but, over the long term, these issues will work themselves out and capital markets will appreciate in value. Investors looking for a superior global equity fund with very capable managers should consider the Janus Global Equity Fund.

FUND DETAILS

Fund name	Janus Global Equity	Fund size (in $ millions)	$231
Fund family	Scudder Maxxum Co.	Percentage in foreign holdings	75.28%
Mutual fund investment category	Global Equity	RRSP eligible	20%
Start date for data shown	February 1995	Sales charge	Optional
Number of funds in investment category	281	Redemption charge	Optional
Dividend frequency	Annual	Management expense ratio	2.90%

FUND PERFORMANCE

	1 month	6 months	1 year	3 years	5 years	10 years
Returns ending June 2000	3.6%	2.7%	42.8%	27.2%	21.6%	
Best historical return	14.3%	55.2%	66.2%	36.4%	28.8%	
Average historical return	2.0%	12.6%	23.2%	21.6%	25.3%	
Worst historical return	-11.1%	-5.6%	0.6%	11.4%	21.6%	
Value at risk of $1,000	$946	$991	$1,051	$1,486	$2,686	

RETURNS GREATER THAN

	1 month	6 months	1 year	3 years	5 years	10 years
10 per cent	5%	67%	80%	100%	100%	
Zero	69%	92%	100%	100%	100%	
Percentage of time fund lost $	31%	8%	0%	0%	0%	
Number of periods evaluated	65	60	54	30	6	

DOWNSIDE RISK

	Worst setback since start date	In bear 1987	In bear 1990	In bear 1994	In bear 1998
Setback for mutual fund	-16.0%				-16.0%
Setback for peer group	-13.6%				-13.6%
Setback ended in	Sept. 1998				Sept. 1998
Months to recover from loss	3				3

ROLLING 12-MONTH QUARTILE RANKING OF MUTUAL FUND PERFORMANCE OVER TIME

Global equity

New Manager - Helen Young Hayes

Jan 1990   Jan 1991   Jan 1992   Jan 1993   Jan 1994   Jan 1995   Jan 1996   Jan 1997   Jan 1998   Jan 1999   Jan 2000

1 is first quartile; 2 is second quartile; 3 is third quartile; 4 is fourth quartile. First quartile means that the fund outperformed 75 per cent of other similar funds after 12 months.

ROLLING 12-MONTH TOTAL RATE OF RETURN FOR THE MUTUAL FUND OVER TIME

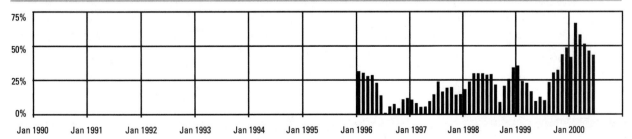

Jan 1990   Jan 1991   Jan 1992   Jan 1993   Jan 1994   Jan 1995   Jan 1996   Jan 1997   Jan 1998   Jan 1999   Jan 2000

SPECTRUM UNITED GLOBAL GROWTH FUND

Vos value rating		
Reward	**Risk**	**Best balance**
★★★★★	★	★★★★★

Fund profile

This is a global equity fund with a twist. It invests in global small- and medium-sized companies that exhibit excellent upside potential, aiming for superior long-term returns by identify emerging companies before other investors do. This strategy has worked during the last year as investors rekindled their love affair with small-cap stocks. This fund is suitable for more aggressive investors because of the inherent risk associated with investing in small-cap stocks, but it should also generate higher rates of return.

Managers Chip Skinner and Lawrence Kymisis of Mercury Asset Management, London, England, use a bottom-up investment style to select companies that sell for reasonable prices considering their growth potential. To reduce risk, the fund avoids large investments in one country.

Fund performance

This fund either outperforms or underperforms similar funds. In turn, it has been frequently either first or fourth quartile relative to similar funds. During the previous year it posted a return of 85.3 per cent. Its best 12-month rate of return was a gain of 147 per cent, and its average rate of return after 12 months was 12.8 per cent. During the previous 10 years, this fund has appreciated in value by an average of 15.1 per cent per year.

The fund manager has invested 49 per cent of its assets in the United States, with an additional 14 per cent in Japan, in companies like Macrovision, Emcore, Mercator Software, MMC Networks, and SBA Communications.

Fund risks

This fund has endured some excessive volatility and earned a one-star Vos Value Rating for risk. Its worst 12-month return was a decline of 34 per cent. It declined in value after 12 months 32 per cent of the time. During the bear market of 1998 the fund declined in value by 17.5 per cent, while the average global equity fund declined in value by 13.6 per cent. But this fund took only four months to recover.

Fund prospects

Small cap stocks have had a great run recently, but many investors believe there is more to come. Many of these companies are growing at a faster rate and with lower valuations than their large-cap counterparts, but investors are still ignoring them. This scenario cannot last forever. Eventually small-cap stocks should enjoy some additional price appreciation. Investors looking for an aggressive small-cap stock fund should consider Spectrum Global Growth. Considering the risk associated with such a fund, however, investors should limit their investment.

FUND DETAILS

Fund name	**Spectrum United Global Growth**	Fund size (in $ millions)	$76
Fund family	Spectrum Investment Management Limited	Percentage in foreign holdings	100.00%
Mutual fund investment category	Global Equity	RRSP eligible	20%
Start date for data shown	July 1982	Sales charge	Optional
Number of funds in investment category	281	Redemption charge	Optional
Dividend frequency	Annual	Management expense ratio	2.41%

FUND PERFORMANCE

	1 month	6 months	1 year	3 years	5 years	10 years
Returns ending June 2000	12.7%	20.8%	85.3%	36.5%	21.2%	15.1%
Best historical return	25.8%	90.4%	147.0%	44.0%	24.0%	15.7%
Average historical return	1.1%	7.1%	12.8%	8.2%	6.5%	6.3%
Worst historical return	-26.5%	-32.3%	-34.0%	-12.5%	-5.7%	0.8%
Value at risk of $1,000	$948	$824	$798	$857	$794	$1,241

RETURNS GREATER THAN

	1 month	6 months	1 year	3 years	5 years	10 years
10 per cent	3%	52%	51%	39%	19%	7%
Zero	60%	71%	68%	67%	82%	100%
Percentage of time fund lost $	40%	29%	32%	33%	18%	0%
Number of periods evaluated	216	211	205	181	157	97

DOWNSIDE RISK

	Worst setback since start date	In bear 1987	In bear 1990	In bear 1994	In bear 1998
Setback for mutual fund	-40.4%	-34.1%	-36.4%	-11.6%	-17.5%
Setback for peer group	-12.7%	-24.2%	-14.6%	-5.9%	-13.6%
Setback ended in	Oct. 1990	Nov. 1987	Oct. 1990	Feb. 1995	Sept. 1998
Months to recover from loss	32	67	32	14	4

ROLLING 12-MONTH QUARTILE RANKING OF MUTUAL FUND PERFORMANCE OVER TIME

Global equity

1 is first quartile; 2 is second quartile; 3 is third quartile; 4 is fourth quartile. First quartile means that the fund outperformed 75 per cent of other similar funds after 12 months.

ROLLING 12-MONTH TOTAL RATE OF RETURN FOR THE MUTUAL FUND OVER TIME

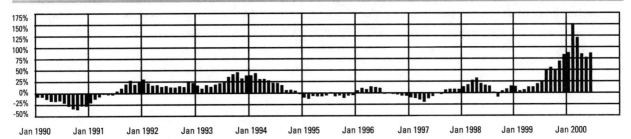

TALVEST GLOBAL SMALL CAP FUND

Vos value rating		
Reward	**Risk**	**Best balance**

Fund profile

A mutual fund that focuses on global small companies provides investors with a whole new range of opportunities. Small-cap funds invest in small companies, whose total market capitalization ranges between $50 million and $1 billion. Few investors have enjoyed the benefits of investing in small companies that operate throughout the globe, yet this fund, managed by Catherine Somhegyi of Nicholas Applegate Capital Management, has displayed excellent returns for its investors. Canada has some great small-cap stocks, too, but investing in a global small-cap fund allows you to benefit from great companies in other countries.

The economic environment is favourable for small-cap stocks. Technology allows small companies to develop more innovative products and services and to grow faster than they did in the past, certainly faster than most larger companies. Over the long term, small-cap stocks have outperformed large-cap stocks. The benefits of investing in global small companies include higher performance, more diversification, and additional opportunities outside our country. Cisco Systems, Intel, Microsoft, and Dell are several examples of companies that were once small-cap stocks, but that rapidly grew. In turn, their investors have reaped some very impressive gains.

Fund performance

The fund is still young, but already it has more than doubled in value. During the previous year alone, it posted a gain of 108 per cent. Its best 12-month rate of return was a gain of 210 per cent, and the average rate of return after 12 months was 93 per cent. However, investors shouldn't expect this to be the norm. The fund has invested in companies like Tollgrade Communications, Three-Five Systems, and Zygo. To reduce some of the risk, the fund is well diversified by security and country.

Fund risks

This fund will decline in value, and investors shouldn't ignore the risk. Its worst setback ever was a loss of 25 per cent. During the same period, the average global equity fund declined in value by 5.1 per cent. Unfortunately, the fund hasn't recovered its loss.

Fund prospects

Small-cap stocks have had a great run recently, and many investors believe there's more to come, because small-cap stocks still trade at very reasonable valuations. Small companies are attracting capital, people, and resources to compete effectively within a global economy. Investors in this fund will also achieve a higher level of diversification from its global scope. Investors looking for an aggressive small-cap stock should consider the Talvest Global Small Cap Fund. Considering the risk associated with such a fund, however, they should limit their investment to a small portion of their portfolio.

FUND DETAILS

Fund name	**Talvest Global Small Cap**	Fund size (in $ millions)	$152
Fund family	Talvest Fund Management Inc.	Percentage in foreign holdings	90.93%
Mutual fund investment category	Global Equity	RRSP eligible	20%
Start date for data shown	February 1998	Sales charge	Optional
Number of funds in investment category	281	Redemption charge	Optional
Dividend frequency	Semi-Annually	Management expense ratio	2.90%

FUND PERFORMANCE

	1 month	6 months	1 year	3 years	5 years	10 years
Returns ending June 2000	14.9%	16.3%	108.5%			
Best historical return	31.4%	121.5%	210.0%			
Average historical return	4.9%	38.4%	93.5%			
Worst historical return	-12.6%	-3.4%	33.6%			
Value at risk of $1,000	$898	$989	$1,368			

RETURNS GREATER THAN

	1 month	6 months	1 year	3 years	5 years	10 years
10 per cent	31%	88%	100%			
Zero	72%	92%	100%			
Percentage of time fund lost $	28%	8%	0%			
Number of periods evaluated	29	24	18			

DOWNSIDE RISK

	Worst setback since start date	In bear 1987	In bear 1990	In bear 1994	In bear 1998
Setback for mutual fund	-25.0%				-13.9%
Setback for peer group	-5.1%				-13.6%
Setback ended in	May 2000				Sept. 1998
Months to recover from loss	?				3

ROLLING 12-MONTH QUARTILE RANKING OF MUTUAL FUND PERFORMANCE OVER TIME

Global equity

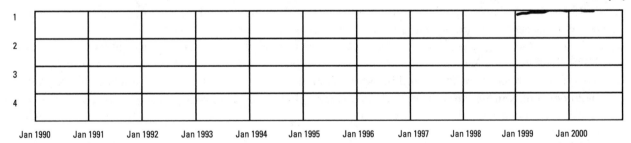

1 is first quartile; 2 is second quartile; 3 is third quartile; 4 is fourth quartile. First quartile means that the fund outperformed 75 per cent of other similar funds after 12 months.

ROLLING 12-MONTH TOTAL RATE OF RETURN FOR THE MUTUAL FUND OVER TIME

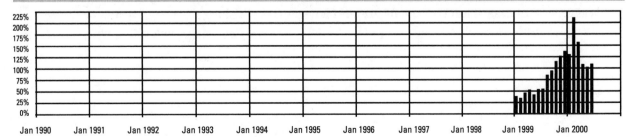

UNIVERSAL SELECT MANAGERS FUND

Vos value rating		
Reward	Risk	Best balance

Fund profile

This is a very unique global equity fund. It's run by five top investment management teams, who select 10 investments apiece, so it focuses on a concentrated portfolio of investments. After all, with more than 10,000 companies around the world to invest in, you incur a lot of risk when you restrict yourself to only 50. On the other hand, if these managers all identify good investments, the fund could appreciate significantly in value.

This fund is ideal for investors who want some rock 'n' roll in their fund. With five investment teams managing their money, led by Brian Ashfor-Russell, Paul Baran, Stephen Peak, James Broadfoot, and Peter Cundill, investors can achieve a certain level of diversification between manager, style, country, and securities.

Fund performance

This fund has had a great start, doubling in value in its short history. During the previous year, the fund posted a gain of 33.3 per cent. Its best 12-month rate of return was a gain of 72.9 per cent, and the average rate of return after 12 months was 53.8 per cent. In the past, the fund has done nothing but impress, but investors should still have realistic expectations for the future.

The managers have invested 44 per cent of the fund in the United States and another 21 per cent in Europe, focusing heavily on technology and telecommunications and on companies like DeBeers, Scottish & Newcastle, STMicroelectronics, Epcos, Intel, and Vodafone Airtouch.

Fund risks

Investors should not ignore the risk. This fund's worst setback was a loss of 10.5 per cent. During the same period, the average global equity fund declined in value by 5.1 per cent. Unfortunately, the fund has not recovered its loss. Thus, investors should either be willing to accept this level of risk or diversify some of the risk away by investing in a combination of investments. After all, the fund has invested 50 per cent of its assets in two sectors, which may not always work to its advantage.

Fund prospects

This fund is unique and cannot be compared to other funds in judging its future potential. If everything goes well, the fund will generate some exceptional returns. If everything doesn't go so well, then things could get nasty. However, considering the investment process and the people involved, it will not likely tank. Investors looking for a unique global equity fund with five great managers making prudent investment decisions should consider the Universal Select Managers Fund.

FUND DETAILS

Fund name	**Universal Select Managers**	Fund size (in $ millions)	$6,168
Fund family	Mackenzie Financial Corporation	Percentage in foreign holdings	73.09%
Mutual fund investment category	Global Equity	RRSP eligible	20%
Start date for data shown	October 1998	Sales charge	Optional
Number of funds in investment category	281	Redemption charge	Optional
Dividend frequency	Annual	Management expense ratio	2.29%

FUND PERFORMANCE

	1 month	6 months	1 year	3 years	5 years	10 years
Returns ending June 2000	3.4%	1.6%	33.3%			
Best historical return	12.5%	46.6%	72.9%			
Average historical return	4.0%	25.2%	53.8%			
Worst historical return	-7.0%	1.6%	33.3%			
Value at risk of $1,000	$948	$1,081	$1,354			

RETURNS GREATER THAN

	1 month	6 months	1 year	3 years	5 years	10 years
10 per cent	19%	94%	100%			
Zero	67%	100%	100%			
Percentage of time fund lost $	33%	0%	0%			
Number of periods evaluated	21	16	10			

DOWNSIDE RISK

	Worst setback since start date	In bear 1987	In bear 1990	In bear 1994	In bear 1998
Setback for mutual fund	-10.5%				
Setback for peer group	-5.1%				
Setback ended in	May 2000				
Months to recover from loss	?				

ROLLING 12-MONTH QUARTILE RANKING OF MUTUAL FUND PERFORMANCE OVER TIME

Global equity

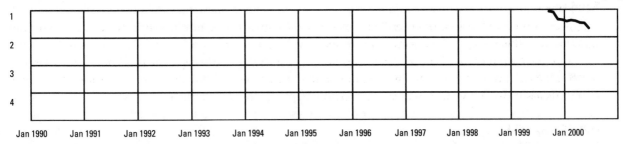

1 is first quartile; 2 is second quartile; 3 is third quartile; 4 is fourth quartile. First quartile means that the fund outperformed 75 per cent of other similar funds after 12 months.

ROLLING 12-MONTH TOTAL RATE OF RETURN FOR THE MUTUAL FUND OVER TIME

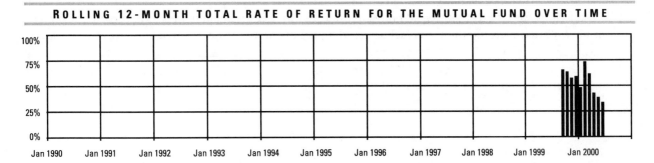

AIM AMERICAN BLUE CHIP GROWTH

Vos value rating		
Reward	**Risk**	**Best balance**
★★★★★	★★★	★★★★★

Fund profile

U.S. equity markets regularly used to trounce Canada's, but during the previous year even a good U.S. equity fund had a hard time keeping Canadian equity funds in sight. However, that doesn't mean investors should ignore the U.S., the largest capital market in the world. Over the long term, this market provides excellent growth opportunities for investors while reducing the risk associated with investing, and investors shouldn't base their investment decisions on one or two years. Over the last 15 years, good U.S. equity funds have appreciated in value by 15 per cent a year. A $1,000 investment in 1985 would be worth more than $8,137 today, not bad considering most investors still have 15 years until retirement, or until they need their money.

U.S. equity funds are ideal for Canadian investors looking to participate in the growth of the U.S. equity market and its wealth of technology and biotechnology companies of all sizes. Investors wanting to participate in the success of these companies could consider the AIM American Blue Chip Growth Fund, an aggressive fund with an excellent long-term track record. Trent May and Doug McEldowney of Invesco in Houston manage the fund.

Fund performance

During the previous year the fund has prudently invested in technology and telecommunications and generated a return of 31.2 per cent. The best three-year rate of return for this fund was a gain of 37.6 per cent annualized, and the average annualized three-year rate of return was 16 per cent. During the previous five years this fund has appreciated in value by an average of 22.3 per cent per year. Such great performance has earned the fund a five-star Vos Value Rating for reward and the best balance between risk and reward. The fund has made large investments in both technology and telecommunications. It has invested in companies like America Online, Pfizer, Charles Schwab, Cisco, Redback Networks, and Genentech.

Fund risks

Active funds take active risks, and this fund is no exception. As a result, the fund has been fourth quartile when compared to other funds after 12 months. The worst setback that this fund has ever incurred was a loss of 14.2 per cent. During the same period, the average U.S. diversified equity fund did not decline in value at all. The fund took nine months to recover its loss.

Fund prospects

U.S. equity funds will continue to face downward pressure as inflation re-emerges and corporate profits remain volatile. Over the long term, investors should prepare for some downside risk. But if they're looking for a fund with above-average performance to include in their mutual fund portfolio, they should seriously consider the merits of the AIM American Blue Chip Growth Fund. A growth bias with superior management will generate superior results over the long term.

FUND DETAILS

Fund name	**AIM American Blue Chip Growth**	Fund size (in $ millions)	$214
Fund family	AIM Funds Management Inc.	Percentage in foreign holdings	0.00%
Mutual fund investment category	U.S. Diversified Equity	RRSP eligible	20%
Start date for data shown	November 1991	Sales charge	Optional
Number of funds in investment category	286	Redemption charge	Optional
Dividend frequency	Annual	Management expense ratio	2.85%

FUND PERFORMANCE

	1 month	6 months	1 year	3 years	5 years	10 years
Returns ending June 2000	16.9%	9.3%	31.2%	32.2%	22.3%	
Best historical return	16.9%	33.9%	50.7%	37.6%	24.4%	
Average historical return	1.4%	8.0%	16.6%	16.0%	15.1%	
Worst historical return	-6.9%	-13.4%	-10.6%	3.6%	6.4%	
Value at risk of $1,000	$943	$968	$996	$1,142	$1,377	

RETURNS GREATER THAN

	1 month	6 months	1 year	3 years	5 years	10 years
10 per cent	3%	57%	56%	58%	73%	
Zero	62%	85%	94%	100%	100%	
Percentage of time fund lost $	38%	15%	6%	0%	0%	
Number of periods evaluated	104	99	93	69	45	

DOWNSIDE RISK

	Worst setback since start date	In bear 1987	In bear 1990	In bear 1994	In bear 1998
Setback for mutual fund	-14.2%			-1.7%	-6.6%
Setback for peer group	0.0%			-4.9%	-12.0%
Setback ended in	Feb. 1996			April 1994	Aug. 1998
Months to recover from loss	9			6	2

ROLLING 12-MONTH QUARTILE RANKING OF MUTUAL FUND PERFORMANCE OVER TIME

U.S. diversified equity

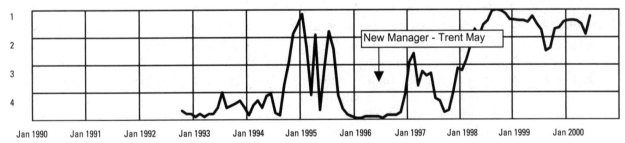

1 is first quartile; 2 is second quartile; 3 is third quartile; 4 is fourth quartile. First quartile means that the fund outperformed 75 per cent of other similar funds after 12 months.

ROLLING 12-MONTH TOTAL RATE OF RETURN FOR THE MUTUAL FUND OVER TIME

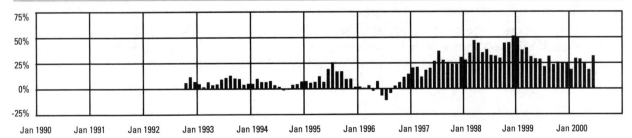

CIBC U.S. INDEX RRSP FUND

Vos value rating		
Reward	**Risk**	**Best balance**
★★★★	★★★★★	★★★★★

Fund profile

This fund aims to provide long-term growth of capital by investing in securities to match the performance of the Standard & Poor's (S&P) 500 Total Return Index. For tax reasons, it can be held only within your RRSP. The fund doesn't aim to outperform the U.S. market, but simply to duplicate its performance. It adds value relative to similar funds by not losing value through erroneous stock picking, aggressive sector rotation, or market timing. However, this fund still incurs some currency risk. If the Canadian dollar appreciates in value, the fund will decline in value unless the decline is offset by a gain in the S&P 500 Index. Index investing has grown in popularity, especially in the United States, since many active investment managers can't outperform their indexing counterparts. This fund is ideal for investors who want to invest in the U.S. in their Registered Retirement Savings Plan (RRSP) without using their foreign content.

Fund performance

The U.S. stock market is well known for its market efficiency, making it difficult—but not impossible—to beat. Active managers who invested aggressively in technology and telecommunications outperformed the market, but without such an aggressive approach many mutual funds underperformed the S&P 500 Index. To replicate the index, this highly diversified fund invests in the biggest publicly traded companies in America. It earned a four-star Vos Value Rating for reward but a five-star Vos Value Rating for the best balance between risk and reward. To duplicate the performance of the market benchmark, the fund has invested in such companies as Microsoft, General Electric, IBM, Wal-Mart, Cisco Systems, Lucent Technologies, Intel, Merck & Co., and Exxon.

Fund risks

Index funds usually score average to below-average on risk but this fund bucked the trend, earning a five-star Vos Value Rating for risk. During the bear market of 1998 the fund declined in value by 9.8 per cent versus the average U.S. equity fund, which declined by 12 per cent. The fund took two months to recover from the loss. Investors can't participate in the growth of companies that aren't included in the index and must be content with the index's rate of return. Nor can index investors participate in the value-added benefits of active fund management. On the other hand, these benefits come with risk that index investors don't have to endure.

Fund prospects

Investors should be aware that U.S. equities are currently trading at higher stock multiples than equities in Europe or Asia. This is one of the reasons U.S. markets have been so volatile recently. Many analysts still warn of a stock-market correction in the short term. But stock-market correction or not, aggressive investors should still allocate a portion of their investments to U.S. equities, as well as those from other geographic regions. Over the long term, the U.S. economy should continue to appreciate in value, and an excellent way to participate in this opportunity is to invest in the CIBC U.S. Index RRSP Fund.

FUND DETAILS

Fund name	**CIBC U.S. Index RRSP**	Fund size (in $ millions)	$761
Fund family	CIBC Securities Inc.	Percentage in foreign holdings	0.00%
Mutual fund investment category	U.S. Diversified Equity	RRSP eligible	100%
Start date for data shown	August 1996	Sales charge	None
Number of funds in investment category	286	Redemption charge	None
Dividend frequency	Annual	Management expense ratio	0.90%

FUND PERFORMANCE

	1 month	6 months	1 year	3 years	5 years	10 years
Returns ending June 2000	1.0%	1.3%	7.6%	20.9%		
Best historical return	9.7%	26.3%	50.5%	31.4%		
Average historical return	2.0%	12.3%	26.5%	26.0%		
Worst historical return	-9.8%	-3.1%	4.4%	20.9%		
Value at risk of $1,000	$949	$1,005	$1,073	$1,795		

RETURNS GREATER THAN

	1 month	6 months	1 year	3 years	5 years	10 years
10 per cent	0%	79%	92%	100%		
Zero	70%	95%	100%	100%		
Percentage of time fund lost $	30%	5%	0%	0%		
Number of periods evaluated	47	42	36	12		

DOWNSIDE RISK

	Worst setback since start date	In bear 1987	In bear 1990	In bear 1994	In bear 1998
Setback for mutual fund	-9.8%				-9.8%
Setback for peer group	-12.0%				-12.0%
Setback ended in	Aug. 1998				Aug. 1998
Months to recover from loss	2				2

ROLLING 12-MONTH QUARTILE RANKING OF MUTUAL FUND PERFORMANCE OVER TIME

U.S. diversified equity

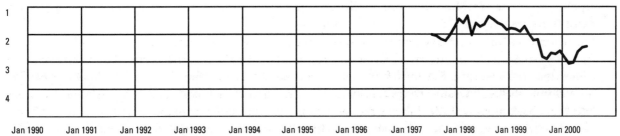

1 is first quartile; 2 is second quartile; 3 is third quartile; 4 is fourth quartile. First quartile means that the fund outperformed 75 per cent of other similar funds after 12 months.

ROLLING 12-MONTH TOTAL RATE OF RETURN FOR THE MUTUAL FUND OVER TIME

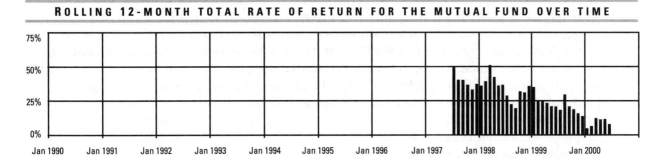

ETHICAL NORTH AMERICAN EQUITY FUND

Vos value rating		
Reward	**Risk**	**Best balance**
★★★★★	★	★★★★

Fund profile

Ethical funds aim to invest within an ethical and moral framework. Through a well-diversified portfolio of common stocks, this fund invests in premier American companies with strong management, financial strength, and a strong comparative and competitive advantage. Cynthia Frick of Alliance Capital Management, a sub-advisor to the fund, is the manager. Her firm's investment strategy emphasizes stock selection, portfolio concentration, and opportunistic trading to add value for shareholders. This strategy has worked very well, to the benefit of investors.

U.S. equities provided investors with below-average results during the previous year but, during the previous 10 years, they generated exceptional returns. Investors can still capitalize on growth opportunities, but they should expect periods of higher volatility.

Fund performance

Since new management took over the fund, its performance has improved, and it has earned a five-star Vos Value Rating for reward. The fund's best 12-month rate of return was a gain of 67.6 per cent. It has earned an average 12-month rate of return of 16.2 per cent. This performance has frequently allowed the fund to post first-quartile performance compared to similar funds.

The fund manager aims to identify and invest in companies with strong earnings-growth potential before the investment community recognizes their intrinsic value. She has made investments in communications, consumer products, technology, and financial services companies, including Dell, Home Depot, MBNA, and AT&T Corporation—all of these companies meet the fund's ethical and moral framework. Investors should be prepared from time to time for some short-term underperformance customarily associated with active investment management.

Fund risks

The worst setback incurred by the fund was a loss of 24.9 per cent posted during the bear market of 1987, a period where the fund displayed above-average risk when compared to similar mutual funds. Bottom-up stock selection could also result in an unfavourable portfolio, and it could underperform similar funds. To avoid this situation the portfolio managers establish parameters for industries and stocks to control the risk associated with bottom-up stock selection. This fund is aggressive and has underperformed during bear markets, but investors can minimize this risk with a well-diversified portfolio of mutual funds.

Fund prospects

Over the long term, U.S. equity markets offer excellent value. In the short term anything can happen in this uncertain economic environment. This shouldn't deter investors from establishing and implementing an appropriate investment plan that includes U.S. equities and top-performing mutual funds like the Ethical North American Equity Fund. Investors should feel cautiously optimistic about the prospects available in the U.S. The American economy should continue to grow at a reasonable rate, the direct result of stable interest rates, reasonable inflation levels, and an increasing amount of consumer disposable income. Growth investors should build a well-diversified portfolio of mutual funds that includes U.S. equity funds, but they should have realistic expectations about the future.

FUND DETAILS

Fund name	**Ethical North American Equity**	Fund size (in $ millions)	$397
Fund family	Ethical Funds Inc.	Percentage in foreign holdings	98.97%
Mutual fund investment category	U.S. Diversified Equity	RRSP eligible	20%
Start date for data shown	July 1982	Sales charge	None
Number of funds in investment category	286	Redemption charge	None
Dividend frequency	Annual	Management expense ratio	2.52%

FUND PERFORMANCE

	1 month	6 months	1 year	3 years	5 years	10 years
Returns ending June 2000	4.4%	4.7%	16.9%	32.0%	30.1%	19.5%
Best historical return	14.4%	42.6%	67.6%	42.8%	33.5%	20.3%
Average historical return	1.4%	8.2%	16.2%	14.6%	12.5%	11.0%
Worst historical return	-22.8%	-24.5%	-19.8%	-6.1%	-0.6%	6.6%
Value at risk of $1,000	$947	$910	$867	$1,008	$1,097	$1,952

RETURNS GREATER THAN

	1 month	6 months	1 year	3 years	5 years	10 years
10 per cent	3%	59%	63%	56%	49%	38%
Zero	65%	77%	83%	95%	99%	100%
Percentage of time fund lost $	35%	23%	17%	5%	1%	0%
Number of periods evaluated	216	211	205	181	157	97

DOWNSIDE RISK

	Worst setback since start date	In bear 1987	In bear 1990	In bear 1994	In bear 1998
Setback for mutual fund	-25.0%	-25.0%	-18.4%	-10.2%	-13.9%
Setback for peer group	-24.1%	-28.6%	-15.3%	-4.9%	-12.0%
Setback ended in	Oct. 1987	Oct. 1987	Oct. 1990	June 1994	Aug. 1998
Months to recover from loss	63	63	27	11	3

ROLLING 12-MONTH QUARTILE RANKING OF MUTUAL FUND PERFORMANCE OVER TIME

U.S. diversified equity

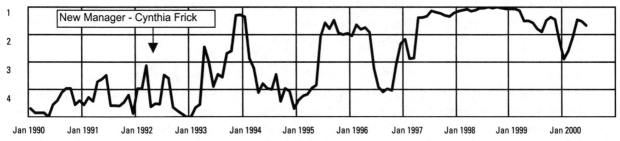

1 is first quartile; 2 is second quartile; 3 is third quartile; 4 is fourth quartile. First quartile means that the fund outperformed 75 per cent of other similar funds after 12 months.

ROLLING 12-MONTH TOTAL RATE OF RETURN FOR THE MUTUAL FUND OVER TIME

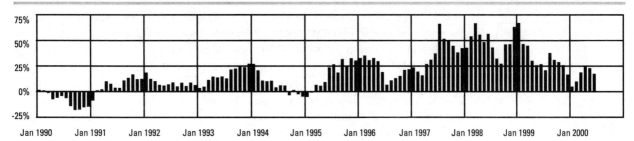

JANUS AMERICAN EQUITY FUND

Vos value rating		
Reward	**Risk**	**Best balance**
★★★★★	★★	★★★★★

Fund profile

This fund aims to provide investors with an above-average rate of return over the long term by investing in leading American companies. Its aggressive strategy has generated above-average performance. The fund is managed by Warren Lambert of Janus Capital Corporation, a sub-advisor to the fund, which has managed money since 1970 and now manages more than $450 billion—more than the entire Canadian mutual fund industry. The manager has positioned it to capitalize on changes taking place in the technology and telecommunications industries. He uses a team of analysts and portfolio managers to identify companies with superior competitive and comparative advantages. The fund can also invest up to 30 per cent of its assets in non-U.S. companies, which can increase returns and reduce risk for investors.

This U.S. equity fund has generated some very impressive results over the short term. Although it's more risky, it's a good example of how active managers can add value when they make prudent investment decisions. Investors should have realistic expectations, however, since a combination of a volatile capital market and more money invested with Janus will make it difficult to keep up the current pace. But Janus loves to prove its critics wrong so don't underestimate this fund.

Fund performance

During the previous year the fund posted a gain of 39.1 per cent and earned a five-star Vos Value Rating for reward and the best balance between reward and risk. It has been frequently first quartile after 12 months, especially when new management took over day-to-day responsibility. Currently the fund is heavily invested in technology and communication companies such as Amazon.com, an online book retailer, Nokia, a telecommunications company, and Cisco, a technology company. If the performance of these high-flying technology stocks reverses, this fund will suffer. However, these sectors can provide above-average growth and above-average rates of return.

Fund risks

With a large percentage of the fund's holdings invested in several sectors and companies, this mutual fund could incur above-average risk, although it has successfully managed this risk in the past. During the bear of 1998, the fund declined by 12.6 per cent, the same as the average U.S. equity fund, although all the risk has been trivial. In fact, the fund's worst 12-month return was actually a gain of 13.4 per cent. Astute investors will use periods of economic weakness as buying opportunities.

Fund prospects

Investors shouldn't ignore the above-average risk associated with this highly concentrated portfolio. But with above-average risk comes the ability to generate above-average rates of return. Continued growth in technology and communications should continue to fuel excellent returns, although there's no assurance that this will happen indefinitely. Investors looking for an aggressive U.S. equity fund should consider the Janus American Equity Fund as a valuable component of a well-diversified portfolio of mutual funds.

FUND DETAILS

Fund name	**Janus American Equity**	Fund size (in $ millions)	$355
Fund family	Scudder Maxxum Co.	Percentage in foreign holdings	75.22%
Mutual fund investment category	U.S. Diversified Equity	RRSP eligible	20%
Start date for data shown	February 1995	Sales charge	Optional
Number of funds in investment category	286	Redemption charge	Optional
Dividend frequency	Annual	Management expense ratio	2.90%

FUND PERFORMANCE

	1 month	6 months	1 year	3 years	5 years	10 years
Returns ending June 2000	1.5%	-2.0%	39.1%	45.3%	38.4%	
Best historical return	17.9%	59.7%	84.3%	59.7%	48.6%	
Average historical return	3.1%	20.9%	42.6%	39.6%	44.1%	
Worst historical return	-12.6%	-2.0%	13.4%	24.1%	38.4%	
Value at risk of $1,000	$939	$1,038	$1,174	$2,093	$5,156	

RETURNS GREATER THAN

	1 month	6 months	1 year	3 years	5 years	10 years
10 per cent	11%	92%	100%	100%	100%	
Zero	69%	98%	100%	100%	100%	
Percentage of time fund lost $	31%	2%	0%	0%	0%	
Number of periods evaluated	65	60	54	30	6	

DOWNSIDE RISK

	Worst setback since start date	In bear 1987	In bear 1990	In bear 1994	In bear 1998
Setback for mutual fund	-14.1%				-12.6%
Setback for peer group	-3.1%				-12.0%
Setback ended in	May 2000				Aug. 1998
Months to recover from loss	?				3

ROLLING 12-MONTH QUARTILE RANKING OF MUTUAL FUND PERFORMANCE OVER TIME

U.S. diversified equity

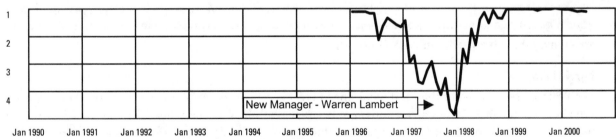

1 is first quartile; 2 is second quartile; 3 is third quartile; 4 is fourth quartile. First quartile means that the fund outperformed 75 per cent of other similar funds after 12 months.

ROLLING 12-MONTH TOTAL RATE OF RETURN FOR THE MUTUAL FUND OVER TIME

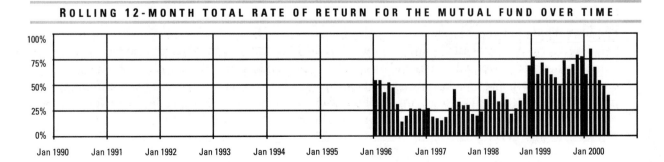

AGF AGGRESSIVE GROWTH FUND

Vos value rating		
Reward	**Risk**	**Best balance**
★★★★★	★	★★★★★

Fund profile

There are aggressive mutual funds, and then there's the AGF Aggressive Growth Fund, which has redefined the meaning of higher returns for higher risk. This fund aims to achieve maximum growth by investing in small- and medium-sized U.S. companies with superior growth potential. Richard Driehaus of Driehaus Capital Management, a sub-advisor, manages the fund using a bottom-up growth investment style to achieve the fund's investment goals.

The stories for U.S. and Canadian small- to mid-cap equities are very similar. Over the long term, small caps are supposed to outperform their large-cap counterparts. During the previous year, they did. Driehaus has capitalized on the opportunities even while general market appreciation was below average, but when general markets appreciate Driehaus redefines the meaning of upside potential. During the 12-month period ending February 2000, this fund posted a gain of 285 per cent. Needless to say, this fund is very risky and should be considered only by investors who can withstand almost any level of risk.

Fund performance

By adding value for investors, the fund earned a five-star Vos Value Rating for reward. The fund frequently outperforms similar funds because of the manager's aggressive investment style, and it has frequently posted first-quartile performance after 12 months. However, because of its aggressive investment style, the fund has also underperformed similar funds, as it did in 1997. The fund has made large investments in technology, consumer cyclical companies, and, to a lesser extent, energy, investing in such companies as Power-One, ADC Telecommunications, CDW Computer Centers, and Mercury Interactive. It will actively buy and sell companies when prudent. The fund will also allow a small-cap stock to remain in the fund even after it becomes a large-cap stock, as long as the stock remains a desirable investment. This strategy of holding the winners has added value for investors.

Fund risks

Historically, the biggest risk for investors was underperforming similar funds. The fund declined in value during the bear market of 1998 by 19.5 per cent—less than the average fund, although it earned only a one-star Vos Value Rating for risk, indicating its sporadic performance. In the spring of 2000, the fund encountered a large setback. But it has done an excellent job in managing risk over the longer term. The worst 12-month rate of return was a loss of 10.9 per cent. Therefore, even when the fund underperforms it has typically earned positive returns.

Fund prospects

Small-cap stocks have generated some very impressive results, and they could have some more upside left. They are trading at lower valuations and displaying improved fundamentals, and investor confidence is on the rise as people seek better investments in a robust U.S. economy. The fund is not immune to a market-wide correction, and it could also decline in value significantly during volatile economic conditions. Those who want to invest in an aggressive top-performing U.S. equity fund should consider the AGF Aggressive Growth Fund in their mutual fund portfolios over the long term.

FUND DETAILS

Fund name	**AGF Aggressive Growth**	Fund size (in $ millions)	$1,345
Fund family	AGF Funds Inc.	Percentage in foreign holdings	97.40%
Mutual fund investment category	U.S. Small/Mid-Cap Equity	RRSP eligible	20%
Start date for data shown	July 1993	Sales charge	Optional
Number of funds in investment category	43	Redemption charge	Optional
Dividend frequency	Annual	Management expense ratio	2.55%

FUND PERFORMANCE

	1 month	6 months	1 year	3 years	5 years	10 years
Returns ending June 2000	13.9%	18.1%	121.8%	72.8%	45.3%	
Best historical return	40.7%	149.2%	285.0%	87.1%	55.3%	
Average historical return	3.0%	20.3%	41.7%	27.4%	29.2%	
Worst historical return	-17.9%	-14.5%	-10.9%	6.2%	10.2%	
Value at risk of $1,000	$911	$902	$942	$1,290	$1,675	

RETURNS GREATER THAN

	1 month	6 months	1 year	3 years	5 years	10 years
10 per cent	18%	66%	66%	90%	100%	
Zero	63%	80%	84%	100%	100%	
Percentage of time fund lost $	37%	20%	16%	0%	0%	
Number of periods evaluated	84	79	73	49	25	

DOWNSIDE RISK

	Worst setback since start date	In bear 1987	In bear 1990	In bear 1994	In bear 1998
Setback for mutual fund	-26.1%			-11.3%	-19.5%
Setback for peer group	-9.8%			-8.9%	-21.1%
Setback ended in	May 2000			June 1994	Aug. 1998
Months to recover from loss	?			10	4

ROLLING 12-MONTH QUARTILE RANKING OF MUTUAL FUND PERFORMANCE OVER TIME

U.S. small/mid-cap equity

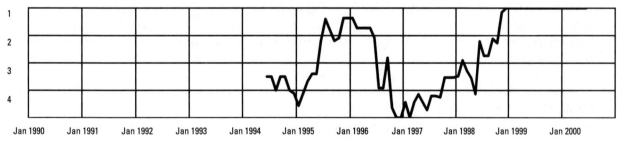

1 is first quartile; 2 is second quartile; 3 is third quartile; 4 is fourth quartile. First quartile means that the fund outperformed 75 per cent of other similar funds after 12 months.

ROLLING 12-MONTH TOTAL RATE OF RETURN FOR THE MUTUAL FUND OVER TIME

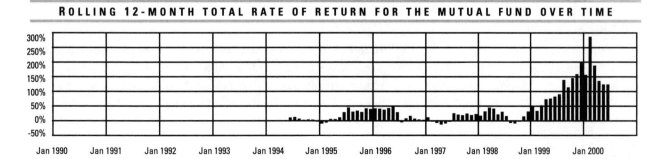

AGF INTERNATIONAL STOCK CLASS FUND

Vos value rating		
Reward	**Risk**	**Best balance**
★★★★★	★★	★★★★★

Fund profile

This international equity fund invests in undervalued stocks from around the world, excluding the United States. It's managed by Charles Brandes and Jeff Busby of Brandes Investment Partners; they are consistently listed by Nelson's World Best Money Managers among the top 10 international equity fund managers in the world. This fund has performed so well because of the managers' proven investment philosophy, which is modeled after legendary value investor Benjamin Graham. They rely on bottom-up value investing to identify companies that trade below their true intrinsic value. This investment strategy has worked very well, and investors have been handsomely rewarded.

International equity funds, which invest outside of North America, have always taken a back seat to U.S. and global equity funds. But over the last year, these funds outperformed. This trend could continue as investors realize the benefits of international investing, which include good rates of return and excellent diversification. If the AGF International Group International Stock Class Fund continues its performance, it will be hard to ignore the benefits of international investing.

Fund performance

The fund has earned a five-star Vos Value Rating for reward and the best balance between risk and reward. With astute stock picking and country allocation, the fund has generated above-average returns for investors. During the previous year the fund posted a gain of 26.4 per cent, almost 10 per cent higher than the average fund. Its best 12-month rate of return was a gain of 42.7 per cent, and the average rate of return after 12-months was a gain of 22.9 per cent.

The fund has made significant investments in Japan and the United Kingdom and also holds 14 per cent of its assets in Latin America. The best-performing industries for this fund were telecommunications, electrical & electronics, and industrials. It recently purchased shares in British Aerospace, the firth-largest aerospace and defence company in the world and in companies like Hitachi in Japan, HSBC Holdings in Hong Kong, Telefonos De Mexico, and Korea Electric Power.

Fund risks

International investing allows investors to better diversify their portfolios, because international stock markets tend to go up when domestic stocks go down and vice versa. In addition, this fund invests in a variety of countries and industries, so the fund itself is also highly diversified. During the bear market of 1998, it declined in value by 14.7 per cent, less than the average international equity fund.

Fund prospects

With value-added management and improved prospects for the non-North American equity markets, investors should consider the AGF International Stock Class Fund for their portfolios. With its value style, investors won't double their money overnight, but this fund will likely exhibit a lot less downside risk than similar funds. And unlike some other value funds, this one actually makes money because Brandes knows the difference between junk and a good investment.

FUND DETAILS

Fund name	**AGF International Stock Class**	Fund size (in $ millions)	$696
Fund family	AGF Funds Inc.	Percentage in foreign holdings	97.06%
Mutual fund investment category	International Equity	RRSP eligible	20%
Start date for data shown	July 1997	Sales charge	Optional
Number of funds in investment category	110	Redemption charge	Optional
Dividend frequency	Annual	Management expense ratio	2.71%

FUND PERFORMANCE

	1 month	6 months	1 year	3 years	5 years	10 years
Returns ending June 2000	5.8%	3.4%	26.4%	21.8%		
Best historical return	13.2%	26.9%	42.7%	21.8%		
Average historical return	1.8%	10.7%	22.9%	21.8%		
Worst historical return	-12.9%	-11.3%	-0.5%	21.8%		
Value at risk of $1,000	$930	$985	$1,098	$1,807		

RETURNS GREATER THAN

	1 month	6 months	1 year	3 years	5 years	10 years
10 per cent	6%	74%	92%	100%		
Zero	67%	90%	96%	100%		
Percentage of time fund lost $	33%	10%	4%	0%		
Number of periods evaluated	36	31	25	1		

DOWNSIDE RISK

	Worst setback since start date	In bear 1987	In bear 1990	In bear 1994	In bear 1998
Setback for mutual fund	-14.7%				-14.7%
Setback for peer group	-16.1%				-16.1%
Setback ended in	Sept. 1998				Sept. 1998
Months to recover from loss	2				2

ROLLING 12-MONTH QUARTILE RANKING OF MUTUAL FUND PERFORMANCE OVER TIME

International equity

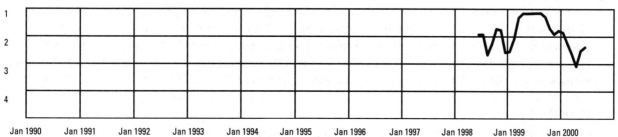

1 is first quartile; 2 is second quartile; 3 is third quartile; 4 is fourth quartile. First quartile means that the fund outperformed 75 per cent of other similar funds after 12 months.

ROLLING 12-MONTH TOTAL RATE OF RETURN FOR THE MUTUAL FUND OVER TIME

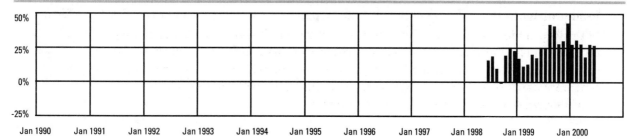

CIBC INTERNATIONAL SMALL COMPANIES FUND

Vos value rating		
Reward	Risk	Best balance

Fund profile

Last year, small companies had their heyday, and the CIBC International Small Companies Fund doubled its value within the period. This fund invests in smaller, high-growth companies outside of North America. This has some enormous advantages, because smaller companies have historically provided investors with better growth opportunities over the long-term. Managed by Robert Treich of Pictet International Management, this fund is in fact the only international small-cap fund available to investors in Canada. Considering its results, investors should make the extra effort to get informed and get invested. This fund will exhibit more risk than most funds, but investors can eliminate the bulk of the risk with a well-diversified portfolio of mutual funds.

Fund performance

This young fund will become a major contender over the long term, and most investors shouldn't consider if they should invest but when they should invest. During the past year, the fund appreciated in value by 104 per cent. Its best 12-month rate of return was a gain of 146.1 per cent, and the average rate of return after 12 months was 46.6 per cent.

The fund has invested extensively in Europe and to a lesser extent in other countries around the world. It has invested in numerous successful little companies including A Nova, Solving, Marionnaud Parfume, Joint Corp, Sumitomo Real Estate, and Honda Tsushin.

Fund risks

Higher returns are associated with higher risk. The worst 12-month return posted by this fund was a decline of 7.1 per cent, and it declined in value after 12 months 14 per cent of the time. During the bear market of 1998 the fund declined in value by 22.2 per cent. During the same period the average international equity fund declined by 16.1 per cent. But the fund took only 10 months to recover its loss. Investors should keep in mind, though, that this fund doesn't enjoy good times without fail. In 1998, for example, it underperformed similar funds and generated fourth-quartile performance.

Fund prospects

During the previous year, international small companies earned a new respect with investors, and investors should reevaluate the opportunities provided by international small companies. These companies should generate above-average rates of return. Many are aggressively using technology to build better products and services for export around the world. In short, international small companies will provide opportunities for the astute investors. There will be risk, but if you manage it prudently and have realistic expectations, you will be rewarded.

FUND DETAILS

Fund name	**CIBC International Small Companies**	Fund size (in $ millions)	$75
Fund family	CIBC Securities Inc.	Percentage in foreign holdings	94.97%
Mutual fund investment category	International Equity	RRSP eligible	20%
Start date for data shown	October 1997	Sales charge	None
Number of funds in investment category	110	Redemption charge	None
Dividend frequency	Annual	Management expense ratio	2.50%

FUND PERFORMANCE

	1 month	6 months	1 year	3 years	5 years	10 years
Returns ending June 2000	4.3%	22.1%	104.0%			
Best historical return	27.3%	105.8%	146.1%			
Average historical return	3.0%	25.5%	46.6%			
Worst historical return	-13.0%	-16.6%	-7.1%			
Value at risk of $1,000	$911	$855	$933			

RETURNS GREATER THAN

	1 month	6 months	1 year	3 years	5 years	10 years
10 per cent	9%	79%	59%			
Zero	70%	79%	86%			
Percentage of time fund lost $	30%	21%	14%			
Number of periods evaluated	33	28	22			

DOWNSIDE RISK

	Worst setback since start date	In bear 1987	In bear 1990	In bear 1994	In bear 1998
Setback for mutual fund	-22.2%				-22.2%
Setback for peer group	-16.1%				-16.1%
Setback ended in	Sept. 1998				Sept. 1998
Months to recover from loss	10				10

ROLLING 12-MONTH QUARTILE RANKING OF MUTUAL FUND PERFORMANCE OVER TIME

International equity

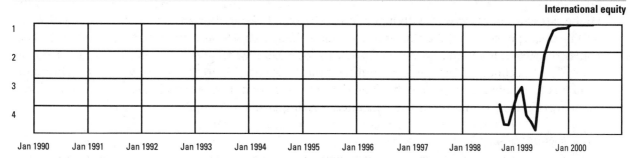

1 is first quartile; 2 is second quartile; 3 is third quartile; 4 is fourth quartile. First quartile means that the fund outperformed 75 per cent of other similar funds after 12 months.

ROLLING 12-MONTH TOTAL RATE OF RETURN FOR THE MUTUAL FUND OVER TIME

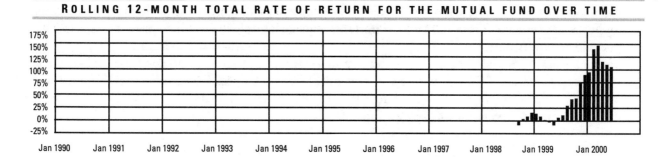

GREAT WEST LIFE INTERNATIONAL EQUITY FUND

Vos value rating		
Reward	**Risk**	**Best balance**
★★★★★	★★★★	★★★★★

Fund profile

This fund aims for an above-average, risk-adjusted rate of return by investing in a well-diversified portfolio of international companies. International equity mutual funds invest outside of North America and so do not participate in the growth of the North American stock market—global equity funds invest all over the world. Studies indicate that, over the longer term, international equities reduce risk without sacrificing return. Although U.S. and global equity funds have outperformed during the previous 10 years, international equity funds outperformed during the previous year. Several factors contributed to the difference in returns. The U.S. Federal Reserve Board has increased interest rates to combat inflation, which has been unfavourable to North American stock markets. Meanwhile, Asian and Pacific Rim stock markets have resolved some of their problems and exhibited signs of new life. The only bad thing for international equities during the previous year was a decline in the value of the Euro currency.

The Great West Life International Equity Fund is managed by Anthony Regan of Putnam Investment Management, a sub-advisor to the fund. Putnam has built an excellent reputation. This fund is ideally suited for investors looking to diversify their investments outside of North America.

Fund performance

During the previous year the fund posted a gain of 39.4 per cent, a very respectable result in the midst of a difficult economic environment. The fund's best 12-month rate of return was a gain of 53.1 per cent, and its average 12-month rate of return was a gain of 19.2 per cent. The fund has frequently been first quartile after 12 months, and has never been fourth quartile after 12 months. It has earned a five-star Vos Value Rating for reward and for the best balance between risk and reward.

The fund has invested 21 per cent of its portfolio in Japan, 18.8 per cent in the United Kingdom, and 14 per cent in France; the fund has invested in companies like Vodaphone, Nokia, Sony, and China Telecom.

Fund risks

International equity funds can diversify a lot of the risk associated with investing in equities. They also reduce the risk of a mutual-fund portfolio. The fund's worst 12-month rate of return was a loss of 2.1 per cent. During the bear market of 1998, it declined by 18.3 per cent more than the average fund.

Future prospects

The Euro has declined significantly, so international equities may exhibit a better risk-and-reward profile than North American stock markets as European stock markets reestablish themselves for future growth. Japan has endured bank reform and is on track for additional growth, and the regions of Asia and the Pacific Rim have improved their economic activity by revising their fiscal and monetary policies. International equities could offer investors excellent value for their dollar for an additional year. International stock markets will still fluctuate in the short term, but at different times of the economic cycle than other, developed stock markets. Investors looking for an excellent international equity fund should consider the Great West Life International Equity Fund.

FUND DETAILS

Fund name	**GWL International Equity (P) Opt A**	Fund size (in $ millions)	$157
Fund family	The Great-West Life Assurance Company	Percentage in foreign holdings	100.00%
Mutual fund investment category	International Equity	RRSP eligible	20%
Start date for data shown	December 1994	Sales charge	None
Number of funds in investment category	110	Redemption charge	None
Dividend frequency	N	Management expense ratio	2.84%

FUND PERFORMANCE

	1 month	6 months	1 year	3 years	5 years	10 years
Returns ending June 2000	4.6%	1.0%	39.4%	21.3%	19.7%	
Best historical return	13.0%	38.9%	53.1%	27.3%	21.5%	
Average historical return	1.5%	9.7%	19.2%	17.8%	19.6%	
Worst historical return	-12.4%	-10.6%	-2.1%	10.9%	16.9%	
Value at risk of $1,000	$938	$976	$1,059	$1,389	$2,241	

RETURNS GREATER THAN

	1 month	6 months	1 year	3 years	5 years	10 years
10 per cent	3%	68%	79%	100%	100%	
Zero	73%	89%	98%	100%	100%	
Percentage of time fund lost $	27%	11%	2%	0%	0%	
Number of periods evaluated	67	62	56	32	8	

DOWNSIDE RISK

	Worst setback since start date	In bear 1987	In bear 1990	In bear 1994	In bear 1998
Setback for mutual fund	-18.3%			-5.8%	-18.3%
Setback for peer group	-16.1%			-5.3%	-16.1%
Setback ended in	Sept. 1998			Feb. 1995	Sept. 1998
Months to recover from loss	9			5	9

ROLLING 12-MONTH Quartile RANKING OF MUTUAL FUND PERFORMANCE OVER TIME

International equity

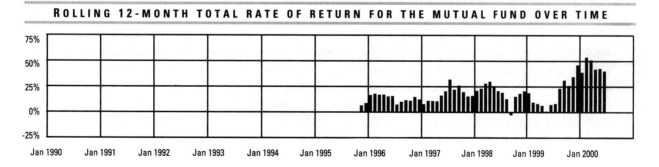

1 is first quartile; 2 is second quartile; 3 is third quartile; 4 is fourth quartile. First quartile means that the fund outperformed 75 per cent of other similar funds after 12 months.

ROLLING 12-MONTH TOTAL RATE OF RETURN FOR THE MUTUAL FUND OVER TIME

AIM EUROPEAN GROWTH FUND

Vos value rating		
Reward	**Risk**	**Best balance**
★★★★★	★	★★★★

Fund profile

This fund aims to provide investors with an above-average rate of return by investing in equity securities of companies based in Europe and, to a lesser degree, emerging Europe, Africa, and the Middle East. The fund invests in companies that can deliver strong earnings growth and emphasizes company fundamentals. Steven Chamberlain of Invesco, AIM's parent company, manages the fund.

European equities have generated above-average rates of return during the previous year and they could easily repeat during the next year. This fund is suitable for investors who are looking for a more aggressive mutual fund that invests in Europe. Considering the fund is managed from London, England, the manager should have home-field advantage.

Fund performance

This is an aggressive European equity fund that generated a return of 53.4 per cent during the previous year. Its performance has been volatile relative to similar funds, and it has frequently been first or fourth quartile after 12 months. Recent performance has improved, and the fund has earned a five-star Vos Value Rating for reward. The best 12-month rate of return for the fund was a gain of 72.3 per cent. The average 12-month rate of return was a gain of 19.9 per cent.

The fund maintains approximately 80 holdings in a variety of companies and industry sectors. It has made large investments in the United Kingdom and Germany, while emphasizing telecommunications and financial services companies. It holds investments in companies like Nokia, Vodafone Group, Ericsson, and Telelogic.

Fund risks

With a new money manager handling day-to-day operations, the fund has not posted any fourth-quartile returns. However, it is still risky and may post fourth-quartile performance in the future. During the bear market of 1998, the fund declined in value by 20 per cent, more than the average European equity fund. Thus, the fund scored only a one-star Vos Value Rating for risk, indicating that it takes a lot of risk in the short term.

The fund has displayed more downside risk than similar mutual funds, but it has recovered from its setbacks very quickly. During the bear of 1998 the fund took only four months to recover.

Fund prospects

European countries are experiencing better capital-market returns than other countries around the world. However, there are still positive growth opportunities within these regions, especially over the longer term, and it's not too late for investors to participate. Investors should note that, to obtain long-term, above-average performance, they often have to endure some short-term risk. This fund will continue to search for attractive growth opportunities regardless of Europe's economic situation. The fund currently focuses on companies with strong management, sound corporate strategy, and a solid commitment to shareholder value. Investors looking for an excellent mutual fund that invests in Europe have found the perfect fund with the AIM European Growth Fund.

FUND DETAILS

Fund name	**AIM European Growth**	Fund size (in $ millions)	$531
Fund family	AIM Funds Management Inc.	Percentage in foreign holdings	100.00%
Mutual fund investment category	European Equity	RRSP eligible	20%
Start date for data shown	August 1992	Sales charge	Optional
Number of funds in investment category	89	Redemption charge	Optional
Dividend frequency	Annual	Management expense ratio	2.96%

FUND PERFORMANCE

	1 month	6 months	1 year	3 years	5 years	10 years
Returns ending June 2000	-1.3%	5.0%	53.4%	34.5%	27.2%	
Best historical return	18.9%	71.1%	72.3%	46.2%	33.3%	
Average historical return	1.5%	10.4%	19.9%	19.2%	18.7%	
Worst historical return	-10.7%	-5.6%	-5.0%	1.7%	7.6%	
Value at risk of $1,000	$946	$966	$976	$1,073	$1,528	

RETURNS GREATER THAN

	1 month	6 months	1 year	3 years	5 years	10 years
10 per cent	3%	51%	50%	65%	86%	
Zero	62%	77%	88%	100%	100%	
Percentage of time fund lost $	38%	23%	12%	0%	0%	
Number of periods evaluated	95	90	84	60	36	

DOWNSIDE RISK

	Worst setback since start date	In bear 1987	In bear 1990	In bear 1994	In bear 1998
Setback for mutual fund	-20.0%			-6.1%	-20.0%
Setback for peer group	-18.5%			-6.0%	-18.5%
Setback ended in	Sept. 1998			Jan. 1995	Sept. 1998
Months to recover from loss	4			4	4

ROLLING 12-MONTH QUARTILE RANKING OF MUTUAL FUND PERFORMANCE OVER TIME

European equity

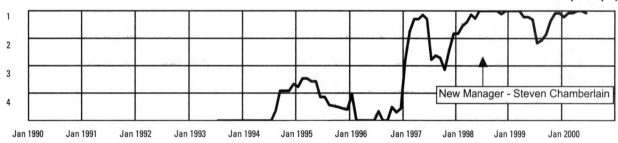

1 is first quartile; 2 is second quartile; 3 is third quartile; 4 is fourth quartile. First quartile means that the fund outperformed 75 per cent of other similar funds after 12 months.

ROLLING 12-MONTH TOTAL RATE OF RETURN FOR THE MUTUAL FUND OVER TIME

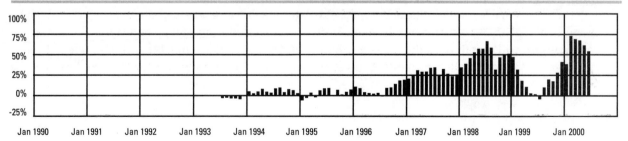

UNIVERSAL EUROPEAN OPPORTUNITIES FUND

Vos value rating		
Reward	**Risk**	**Best balance**
★★★★★	★	★★★★

Fund Profile

Stephen Peak of Henderson Investors manages the Universal European Opportunities Fund. It invests in small companies within the emerging markets of southern European countries that are modernizing their infrastructure. In addition, the fund invests in Eastern European countries that are trading freely for the first time.

Investors in small European companies have experienced above-average rates of return for the last 3 years. Exports of major European countries have increased as their exchange rates have fallen. The business climate has improved, investor confidence has risen, and stock markets have prospered.

This fund is ideally suited for investors seeking higher returns from an aggressive small company fund with the potential to incur more risk.

Fund performance

During the previous year the fund generated a return of 42.6 per cent. Its best 12-month rate of return was a gain of 87.5 per cent, and its average rate of return after 12 months was 30.5 per cent. In turn, the fund has earned a five-star Vos Value Rating for reward.

The fund has invested heavily in the Netherlands, France, and the United Kingdom, focusing on companies within the technology, telecommunications, and consumer cyclical sectors. The fund has invested in companies like Sagem, an electronics company, Buhrmann, a consumer distributing company, Versa Telecom, a telecommunications company, and Telepizza, a pizzeria in Spain.

Fund risks

Inherently there is more risk in investing in small companies. However, the manager of the fund has done an excellent job of managing this increased risk during the short and long term. Still, the fund may underperform and display more downside risk than other European funds that invest in large-cap stocks. Stock markets have achieved recent highs, and investors may experience some short-term setbacks before making any large gains.

The worst setback that this fund has ever incurred was a loss of 17.5 per cent. During the same period, the average European equity fund declined in value by 18.5 per cent. The fund took 10 months to recover its loss.

Future prospects

European stock markets have forged ahead, but this trend cannot last forever. Investors can still find value and reasonable rates of return, but market volatility will increase as global capital markets feel the pressure of higher interest rates and the fear of inflation. Aggressive investors who want European small-cap exposure will benefit from the Universal European Opportunities Fund, but will also face increased risk associated with small-cap investing. Investors who invest prudently and for the long term will be richly rewarded.

FUND DETAILS

Fund name	**Universal European Opportunities**	Fund size (in $ millions)	$1,919
Fund family	Mackenzie Financial Corporation	Percentage in foreign holdings	95.52%
Mutual fund investment category	European Equity	RRSP eligible	20%
Start date for data shown	October 1994	Sales charge	Optional
Number of funds in investment category	89	Redemption charge	Optional
Dividend frequency	Annual	Management expense ratio	2.40%

FUND PERFORMANCE

	1 month	6 months	1 year	3 years	5 years	10 years
Returns ending June 2000	1.0%	5.5%	42.6%	26.5%	28.8%	
Best historical return	21.8%	61.5%	87.5%	38.3%	36.2%	
Average historical return	2.2%	15.3%	30.5%	28.4%	30.2%	
Worst historical return	-11.4%	-11.9%	-7.3%	20.7%	24.4%	
Value at risk of $1,000	$944	$925	$1,014	$1,821	$3,047	

RETURNS GREATER THAN

	1 month	6 months	1 year	3 years	5 years	10 years
10 per cent	4%	91%	90%	100%	100%	
Zero	78%	92%	95%	100%	100%	
Percentage of time fund lost $	22%	8%	5%	0%	0%	
Number of periods evaluated	69	64	58	34	10	

DOWNSIDE RISK

	Worst setback since start date	In bear 1987	In bear 1990	In bear 1994	In bear 1998
Setback for mutual fund	-17.5%			-0.1%	-17.5%
Setback for peer group	-18.5%			-1.9%	-18.5%
Setback ended in	Sept. 1998			Oct. 1994	Sept. 1998
Months to recover from loss	10			1	10

ROLLING 12-MONTH QUARTILE RANKING OF MUTUAL FUND PERFORMANCE OVER TIME

European equity

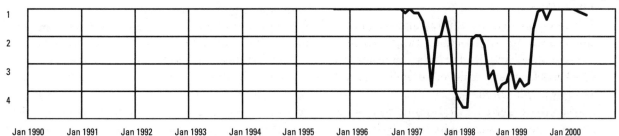

1 is first quartile; 2 is second quartile; 3 is third quartile; 4 is fourth quartile. First quartile means that the fund outperformed 75 per cent of other similar funds after 12 months.

ROLLING 12-MONTH TOTAL RATE OF RETURN FOR THE MUTUAL FUND OVER TIME

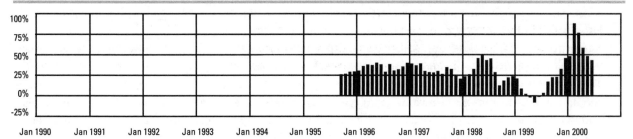

FIDELITY JAPANESE GROWTH FUND

Vos value rating		
Reward	**Risk**	**Best balance**
★★★★★	★★	★★★★★

Fund profile

The Fidelity Japanese Growth Fund aims for an above-average, risk-adjusted rate of return by investing in securities issued by Japanese companies. Japan's stock market was out of favour during the mid- to late-1990s, but investors have fared very well recently. Japan has outperformed other major international capital markets, and foreign investors have rekindled their love affair with Japanese stocks, purchasing shares of Japanese companies and driving up prices. However, the Japanese economy remains fragile, with high unemployment rates, low interest rates, weak consumer demand, and low industrial output. In addition, fears of inflation in the Unites States could wreck havoc on global capital markets.

Manager Jay Talbot uses Fidelity's bottom-up stock-picking approach, selecting companies with strong balance sheets, good management, and strong upside potential. He typically invests in companies that have a strong competitive position in a strong and growing industry, as well as companies with attractive valuations.

Fund performance

This fund has earned investors an above-average rate of return and in turn a five-star Vos Value Rating for reward and the best balance between risk and reward. The fund has frequently been first quartile after 12 months, but has displayed some short-term inconsistency. During the previous year the fund earned a rate of return of 61.7 per cent. Its best 12-month rate of return was a gain of 127.2 per cent, and its average rate of return after 12 months was 14.3 per cent.

The fund has invested 25 per cent of its assets in electrical machinery, with smaller investments in communications, banks, retail, and chemical companies. Altogether it has invested in 119 companies including Tokyo Seimitsu, a precision instruments company, NTT Docomo, a communications company, and Toyota, the motor vehicle company.

Fund risks

The fund incurred below-average risk but has displayed some exceptional performance, which indicates that the fund is willing to take risk. In turn, the fund earned a two-star Vos Value Rating for risk. It has displayed some above-average downside risk compared to more conservative mutual funds. Its worst 12-month rate of return was a loss of 24.4 per cent. During the bear market of 1998, the fund declined by 28.1 per cent, less than the average fund in this category. Investors should realize that investing in a specific region could increase their risk. They should therefore invest in Japan within the context of a well-diversified portfolio.

Fund prospects

Investors should not expect significant changes in the underlying fundamentals of the Japanese economy. Weak economic conditions and corporate restructuring mean that Japan's sustainable growth is low. These short-term problems generate short-term volatility, but when they are rectified, capital markets should continue to appreciate in value. Japanese mutual funds have definitely incurred some downside risk, and investors should be rewarded for enduring it. But a change in investor sentiment has recently begun to fuel market performance, and investors looking for an above-average Japanese fund should consider the Fidelity Japanese Growth Fund.

FUND DETAILS

Fund name	**Fidelity Japanese Growth**	Fund size (in $ millions)	$472
Fund family	Fidelity Investments Canada Limited	Percentage in foreign holdings	96.58%
Mutual fund investment category	Japanese Equity	RRSP eligible	20%
Start date for data shown	August 1993	Sales charge	Optional
Number of funds in investment category	27	Redemption charge	Optional
Dividend frequency	Quarterly	Management expense ratio	2.92%

FUND PERFORMANCE

	1 month	6 months	1 year	3 years	5 years	10 years
Returns ending June 2000	8.0%	-10.6%	61.7%	23.5%	15.4%	
Best historical return	16.4%	85.9%	127.2%	35.1%	16.8%	
Average historical return	0.9%	7.2%	14.3%	3.1%	4.3%	
Worst historical return	-11.6%	-19.8%	-24.4%	-10.5%	-6.8%	
Value at risk of $1,000	$919	$835	$802	$743	$752	

RETURNS GREATER THAN

	1 month	6 months	1 year	3 years	5 years	10 years
10 per cent	10%	40%	33%	25%	33%	
Zero	52%	54%	49%	35%	54%	
Percentage of time fund lost $	48%	46%	51%	65%	46%	
Number of periods evaluated	83	78	72	48	24	

DOWNSIDE RISK

	Worst setback since start date	In bear 1987	In bear 1990	In bear 1994	In bear 1998
Setback for mutual fund	-38.9%			-23.9%	-28.1%
Setback for peer group	-43.4%			-20.5%	-43.4%
Setback ended in	Sept. 1998			Feb. 1995	Sept. 1998
Months to recover from loss	10			60	10

ROLLING 12-MONTH QUARTILE RANKING OF MUTUAL FUND PERFORMANCE OVER TIME

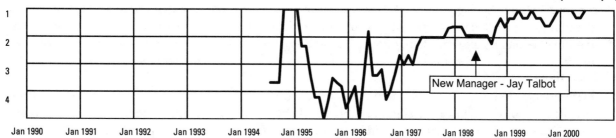

Japanese equity

1 is first quartile; 2 is second quartile; 3 is third quartile; 4 is fourth quartile. First quartile means that the fund outperformed 75 per cent of other similar funds after 12 months.

ROLLING 12-MONTH TOTAL RATE OF RETURN FOR THE MUTUAL FUND OVER TIME

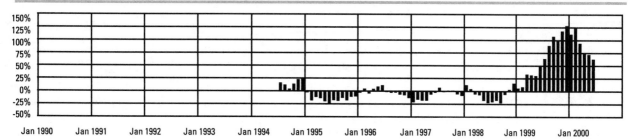

FIDELITY FAR EAST FUND

Vos value rating		
Reward	**Risk**	**Best balance**
★★★★★	★	★★★★

Fund profile

This fund generates capital appreciation by investing in companies that conduct a large portion of their business in the Asian and Pacific Rim region. The fund is managed by K.C. Lee of Fidelity Management and Research, who utilizes Fidelity's traditional bottom-up approach to selecting investments. Lee prefers to visit the companies that the fund invests in, and they all show consistent earnings growth and good management. They also trade at very reasonable prices. This fund is ideally suited for more aggressive investors who want to invest in a top-performing regional fund with a concentrated portfolio. It exhibits more risk than a more conservative fund, but it also provides additional opportunities.

Fund performance

During the previous year the fund generated a return of 13.7 per cent. The best three-year rate of return for this fund was a gain of 33.8 per cent annualized, and the average annualized three-year rate of return was 10.8 per cent. During the previous five years, the fund has appreciated in value by an average of 9.2 per cent per year. This performance earned it a five-star Vos Value Rating for reward, indicating the fund generated some very good returns considering the economic conditions of the region.

The fund has invested 57 per cent of its assets in Hong Kong and in three companies in particular: Hutchison Whampoa, Cheung Kong Holdings, and HSBC Holdings, which comprise 45 per cent of the fund. The fund has invested in a total of 157 different stocks.

Fund risks

This region has been plagued with a lot of volatility during the previous 10 years. The worst 12-month return posted by this fund was a decline of 48.3 per cent, and it declined in value after 12 months 20 per cent of the time. During the bear market of 1998 the fund declined in value by 54.6 per cent, while similar funds declined in value by 52 per cent. But the fund took only 15 months to recover its loss.

Fund prospects

Investors should remain cautious in the short term, but the long-term opportunities for this region are solid. During the previous two years these markets rebounded significantly, and company valuations are becoming stretched at the high end. This factor, in conjunction with higher volatility in capital markets, could unnerve some investors. However, if they want to participate in the success in this region by investing in a top-performing Asian fund that doesn't invest in Japan, they should consider the Fidelity Far East Fund for their portfolio. It is truly unique and has the distinct ability to add value for investors.

FUND DETAILS

Fund name	**Fidelity Far East**	Fund size (in $ millions)	$903
Fund family	Fidelity Investments Canada Limited	Percentage in foreign holdings	94.72%
Mutual fund investment category	Asia Ex-Japan Equity	RRSP eligible	20%
Start date for data shown	October 1991	Sales charge	Optional
Number of funds in investment category	13	Redemption charge	Optional
Dividend frequency	Annual	Management expense ratio	2.86%

FUND PERFORMANCE

	1 month	6 months	1 year	3 years	5 years	10 years
Returns ending June 2000	8.9%	-10.3%	13.7%	3.1%	9.2%	
Best historical return	36.0%	53.4%	99.9%	33.8%	25.3%	
Average historical return	1.5%	9.5%	19.1%	10.8%	11.3%	
Worst historical return	-26.9%	-38.2%	-48.3%	-10.7%	-2.7%	
Value at risk of $1,000	$897	$789	$704	$873	$993	

RETURNS GREATER THAN

	1 month	6 months	1 year	3 years	5 years	10 years
10 per cent	10%	67%	65%	47%	52%	
Zero	61%	77%	80%	90%	93%	
Percentage of time fund lost $	39%	23%	20%	10%	7%	
Number of periods evaluated	105	100	94	70	46	

DOWNSIDE RISK

	Worst setback since start date	In bear 1987	In bear 1990	In bear 1994	In bear 1998
Setback for mutual fund	-54.6%			-23.3%	-54.6%
Setback for peer group	-52.0%			-18.6%	-52.0%
Setback ended in	Aug. 1998			Jan. 1995	Aug. 1998
Months to recover from loss	15			12	15

ROLLING 12-MONTH QUARTILE RANKING OF MUTUAL FUND PERFORMANCE OVER TIME

Asia ex-Japan equity

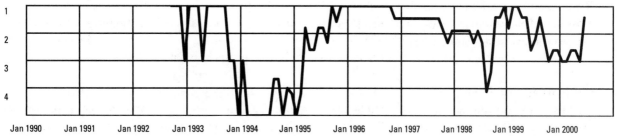

1 is first quartile; 2 is second quartile; 3 is third quartile; 4 is fourth quartile. First quartile means that the fund outperformed 75 per cent of other similar funds after 12 months.

ROLLING 12-MONTH TOTAL RATE OF RETURN FOR THE MUTUAL FUND OVER TIME

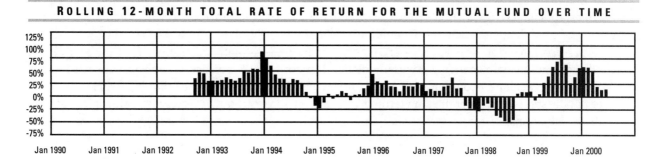

SCUDDER PACIFIC FUND

Vos value rating		
Reward	**Risk**	**Best balance**
★★★★★	★★★★★	★★★★★

Fund profile

The Scudder Pacific Fund aims to provide a superior long-term return by investing in companies within Asia and the Pacific Rim. The portfolio managers for the Scudder Pacific Fund, Elizabeth Allan, Theresa Gusman, and Nicholas Bratt, use a bottom-up investment strategy to select stocks. Relying on fundamental research, the managers identify companies that generate above-average growth opportunities and whose shares trade at a realistic price.

Capital markets within this region have recently rebounded, although the economy remains weak and fragile due to higher unemployment rates in the region than in North America, low interest rates, weak consumer demand, and low industrial output. However, stock markets appreciate and depreciate in value based on future expectations, which remain robust. Investors shouldn't ignore investment opportunities in Asia and the Pacific Rim, and the fact that this fund is aggressive.

Fund performance

This fund has posted first-quartile performance frequently after 12 months, earning a triple five-star Vos Value Rating for reward, risk, and the best balance between risk and reward. During the previous year the fund posted a gain of 29.7 per cent. Its best 12-month rate of return was a gain of 123.5 per cent, and its average rate of return after 12 months was 19.8 per cent. Unfortunately the fund hasn't earned money frequently, because of poor economic conditions in the Pacific Rim region, and it posted gains after 12 months only 64 per cent of the time.

The fund has made investments in a blend of large companies, some exhibiting value characteristics and some exhibiting growth characteristics, including Samsung Electronic, China Telecom, and Sony. It has invested 22 per cent of its holdings in each of Hong Kong and Japan, focusing on technology, manufacturing, and communications companies.

Fund risks

Asia and the Pacific Rim have exhibited above-average risk in the past. However, relative to similar mutual funds, this one actually exhibited less risk. During the bear market of 1998, for example, it declined in value by 39.2 per cent less than the average fund.

Fund prospects

The fund diversifies by investing in several countries, including Japan, China, India, Thailand, Singapore, Indonesia, Malaysia, South Korea, Taiwan, Hong Kong, the Philippines, Australia, and New Zealand. With increased diversification, it can generate excellent returns.

Aggressive investors should consider investing in this region opportunistically. This fund's value will continue to gyrate with changing government, fiscal, and monetary policies, as well as corporate reform. Although this region's economic outlook is improving, there's no assurance that investors will earn a profit in the short term. Over the long term, this region offers very attractive growth opportunities at very realistic valuations.

FUND DETAILS

Fund name	**Scudder Pacific**	Fund size (in $ millions)	$29
Fund family	Scudder Maxxum Co.	Percentage in foreign holdings	100.00%
Mutual fund investment category	Asia-Pacific Rim Equity	RRSP eligible	20%
Start date for data shown	November 1995	Sales charge	None
Number of funds in investment category	52	Redemption charge	None
Dividend frequency	Annual	Management expense ratio	2.00%

FUND PERFORMANCE

	1 month	6 months	1 year	3 years	5 years	10 years
Returns ending June 2000	3.0%	-11.3%	29.7%	12.5%		
Best historical return	18.2%	62.1%	123.5%	24.1%		
Average historical return	1.2%	9.1%	19.8%	8.9%		
Worst historical return	-13.6%	-26.5%	-33.7%	-6.3%		
Value at risk of $1,000	$898	$791	$706	$841		

RETURNS GREATER THAN

	1 month	6 months	1 year	3 years	5 years	10 years
10 per cent	11%	49%	38%	57%		
Zero	57%	61%	64%	71%		
Percentage of time fund lost $	43%	39%	36%	29%		
Number of periods evaluated	56	51	45	21		

DOWNSIDE RISK

	Worst setback since start date	In bear 1987	In bear 1990	In bear 1994	In bear 1998
Setback for mutual fund	-39.2%				-39.2%
Setback for peer group	-45.9%				-45.9%
Setback ended in	Aug. 1998				Aug. 1998
Months to recover from loss	10				10

ROLLING 12-MONTH QUARTILE RANKING OF MUTUAL FUND PERFORMANCE OVER TIME

Asia-Pacific Rim equity

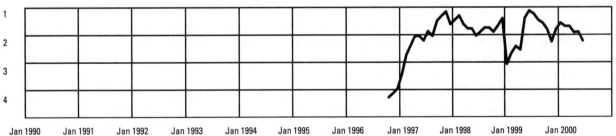

1 is first quartile; 2 is second quartile; 3 is third quartile; 4 is fourth quartile. First quartile means that the fund outperformed 75 per cent of other similar funds after 12 months.

ROLLING 12-MONTH TOTAL RATE OF RETURN FOR THE MUTUAL FUND OVER TIME

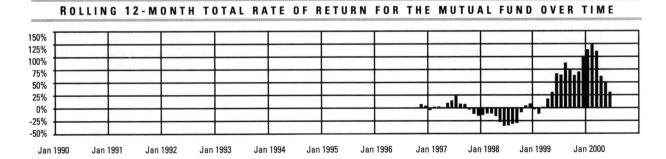

GREEN LINE LATIN AMERICAN GROWTH FUND

Vos value rating		
Reward	**Risk**	**Best balance**
★★★★★	★★★★	★★★★★

Fund profile

The Green Line Latin American Growth Fund aims for growth by investing in stocks of companies that conduct most of their business in Latin America. Latin American countries have fared better in the recent past than they have in previous years, although the region is still plagued with potential currency devaluation, heavy indebtedness, and a lot of volatility. In particular, Brazil has recovered since the devaluation of the real in January 1999.

The fund is managed by Andy Skov of Morgan Stanley Dean Witter. Morgan Stanley Dean Witter is a pioneer in emerging-market investing. The fund is ideally suited for more aggressive investors who want to participate in the growth exhibited by this region, but investors should be very aware of the risks.

Fund performance

During the previous year the fund has appreciated in value by 23.5 per cent. Its best three-year rate of return was a gain of 21.6 per cent annualized, and the average annualized three-year rate of return was 6.5 per cent. During the previous five years, this fund appreciated in value by an average of 11.1 per cent a year. It has generated good returns when compared to other Latin American funds and has earned a five-star Vos Value Rating for reward.

The fund has invested 52 per cent of its assets in South America and 43 per cent in Mexico, in companies like Telefonos de Mexico and Wal-Mart de Mexico.

Fund risks

Latin American funds are very risky. The worst 12-month return posted by this fund was a decline of 41.2 per cent, and it declined in value after 12 months 29 per cent of the time. During the bear market of 1998, this fund declined in value by 43.4 per cent, while the average Latin American equity fund declined by 46.6 per cent. But this fund took only 18 months to recover.

Fund prospects

Many investors in Brazil and Argentina took a wait-and-see approach during the previous year, when these countries devalued their currencies, and they missed out on some nice gains. But long-term investors who invested on weakness participated in the gains. Despite the unique risk and return characteristics associated with these funds, Latin American countries offer excellent upside potential for aggressive investors. Lower than expected inflation and improved fiscal and monetary policies should boost capital markets. The region should also be aided by the implementation of the International Monetary Fund Accord that was implemented in 1999. Higher commodity prices and improved investor sentiment shouldn't hurt either. Investors looking for the expertise of a global powerhouse should consider the Green Line Latin American Growth Fund.

FUND DETAILS

Fund name	Green Line Latin American Growth	Fund size (in $ millions)	$40
Fund family	TD Asset Management Inc.	Percentage in foreign holdings	100.00%
Mutual fund investment category	Latin American Equity	RRSP eligible	20%
Start date for data shown	December 1994	Sales charge	None
Number of funds in investment category	12	Redemption charge	None
Dividend frequency	Annual	Management expense ratio	2.80%

FUND PERFORMANCE

	1 month	6 months	1 year	3 years	5 years	10 years
Returns ending June 2000	11.0%	1.2%	23.5%	3.3%	11.1%	
Best historical return	24.2%	45.8%	78.9%	21.6%	15.1%	
Average historical return	0.7%	6.5%	11.6%	6.5%	9.6%	
Worst historical return	-33.2%	-39.6%	-41.2%	-6.2%	-0.3%	
Value at risk of $1,000	$873	$666	$658	$911	$1,132	

RETURNS GREATER THAN

	1 month	6 months	1 year	3 years	5 years	10 years
10 per cent	10%	50%	68%	31%	50%	
Zero	63%	63%	71%	88%	88%	
Percentage of time fund lost $	37%	37%	29%	13%	13%	
Number of periods evaluated	67	62	56	32	8	

DOWNSIDE RISK

	Worst setback since start date	In bear 1987	In bear 1990	In bear 1994	In bear 1998
Setback for mutual fund	-44.9%			-37.4%	-43.4%
Setback for peer group	-49.0%			-32.0%	-46.6%
Setback ended in	Jan. 1999			Feb. 1995	Aug. 1998
Months to recover from loss	13			27	18

ROLLING 12-MONTH QUARTILE RANKING OF MUTUAL FUND PERFORMANCE OVER TIME

Latin American equity

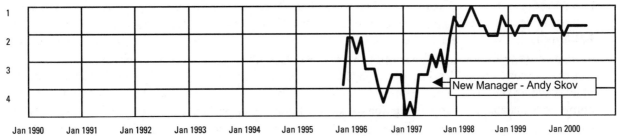

1 is first quartile; 2 is second quartile; 3 is third quartile; 4 is fourth quartile. First quartile means that the fund outperformed 75 per cent of other similar funds after 12 months.

ROLLING 12-MONTH TOTAL RATE OF RETURN FOR THE MUTUAL FUND OVER TIME

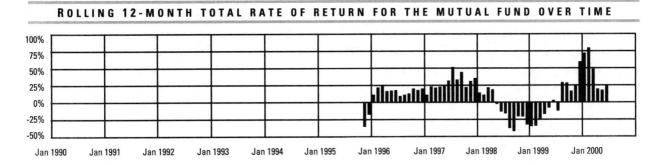

GREEN LINE EMERGING MARKETS FUND

Vos value rating		
Reward	**Risk**	**Best balance**
★★★★★	★★★	★★★★★

Fund profile

Emerging markets, defined by the World Bank as countries with a low per-capita income, generated some very acceptable rates of return during the previous year, attributable in part to a doubling in value of stock markets in Russia and Turkey. Emerging markets also include Brazil, Mexico, Portugal, Thailand, Turkey, and Argentina, where economic uncertainty prevails amidst high capital-market volatility, currency devaluation, and indebtedness. The risks of investing in these countries should not be ignored, but they can grow very rapidly, if not predictably. So prudent investors can add value to their portfolios by investing in emerging markets.

The fund is managed by Andy Skov of Morgan Stanley Dean Witter, a highly respected global investment manager who pioneered emerging-market investing. The fund is ideally suited for more aggressive investors who want to participate in these countries' growth but who also want prudent diversification among countries, industries, and companies.

Fund performance

During the previous year the fund posted a very respectable rate of return of 35.2 per cent. Its best three-year return was a gain of 12.5 per cent annualized, and the average annualized three-year rate of return was 1 per cent. During the previous five years the fund appreciated by an average of 6.9 per cent per year. This fund has generated some very impressive returns when compared to other emerging-market mutual funds. In turn, the fund earned a five-star Vos Value Rating for reward and the best balance between risk and reward. It has invested heavily in Pacific Rim companies like Far East Textile and Tong Yang Confectionery.

Fund risks

The rewards can sometimes be great, but the risks are high if you invest in emerging-market mutual funds. The worst 12-month return posted by this fund was a decline of 46.4 per cent, and it declined in value after 12 months 40 per cent of the time. During the bear market of 1998, it declined in value by 50.5 per cent, compared to a 45.3-per-cent decline for the average emerging-markets equity fund. But it took only 15 months to recover.

Fund prospects

Emerging market mutual funds offer a unique risk and reward profile. They tend to go up or down consistently, but rarely sideways. With improved government, fiscal, and monetary policies, and with deregulation in these regions, the future could be bright for emerging markets. Investor sentiment has recently increased with positive changes, so these markets could offer some upside potential for the aggressive investor. Two volatile years have passed, interest rates are lower, and currencies are firmer. All these factors should bode well for investors in the Green Line Emerging Markets Fund.

FUND DETAILS

Fund name	**Green Line Emerging Markets**	Fund size (in $ millions)	$115
Fund family	TD Asset Management Inc.	Percentage in foreign holdings	100.00%
Mutual fund investment category	Emerging Markets Equity	RRSP eligible	20%
Start date for data shown	December 1992	Sales charge	None
Number of funds in investment category	42	Redemption charge	None
Dividend frequency	Annual	Management expense ratio	2.83%

FUND PERFORMANCE

	1 month	6 months	1 year	3 years	5 years	10 years
Returns ending June 2000	5.3%	-3.6%	35.2%	3.5%	6.9%	
Best historical return	21.8%	59.1%	101.8%	12.5%	11.1%	
Average historical return	1.0%	6.7%	11.4%	1.0%	0.6%	
Worst historical return	-25.5%	-38.0%	-46.4%	-13.1%	-9.5%	
Value at risk of $1,000	$894	$729	$699	$715	$635	

RETURNS GREATER THAN

	1 month	6 months	1 year	3 years	5 years	10 years
10 per cent	9%	56%	44%	18%	6%	
Zero	56%	64%	60%	52%	50%	
Percentage of time fund lost $	44%	36%	40%	48%	50%	
Number of periods evaluated	91	86	80	56	32	

DOWNSIDE RISK

	Worst setback since start date	In bear 1987	In bear 1990	In bear 1994	In bear 1998
Setback for mutual fund	-50.5%			-28.3%	-50.5%
Setback for peer group	-45.1%			-22.7%	-45.3%
Setback ended in	Sept. 1998			Feb. 1995	Sept. 1998
Months to recover from loss	15			29	15

ROLLING 12-MONTH QUARTILE RANKING OF MUTUAL FUND PERFORMANCE OVER TIME

Emerging markets equity

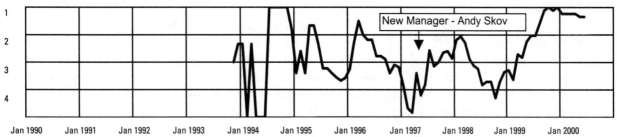

1 is first quartile; 2 is second quartile; 3 is third quartile; 4 is fourth quartile. First quartile means that the fund outperformed 75 per cent of other similar funds after 12 months.

ROLLING 12-MONTH TOTAL RATE OF RETURN FOR THE MUTUAL FUND OVER TIME

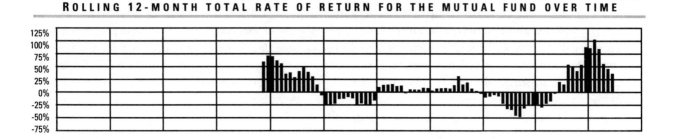

ROYAL ENERGY FUND

Vos value rating		
Reward	**Risk**	**Best balance**
★★★★★	★★	★★★★★

Fund profile

Unlike natural resource funds, this one focuses primarily on the energy sector. It aims to invest in the best companies engaged directly or indirectly in the exploration, development, production, or distribution of oil and gas products or other activities related to the energy sector.

Several variables have contributed to a recent upswing in prices for oil, gas, and several base metals. Oil prices have increased as oil-producing nations cut back their production. Rising natural gas prices south of the border have had a positive impact on prices in Canada. The key to successful investing in this sector is the ability to find companies that have good-quality assets and can generate strong cash flow independent of the commodity price. Gordon Zive of Royal Bank Investment Management has managed this fund since 1994.

Fund performance

During the previous three years, oil and gas stocks have been strong relative to other resource stocks, and the fund has earned a five-star Vos Value Rating for reward. The fund has been first quartile frequently compared to similar funds after 12 months, especially when oil companies are doing well. The best 12-month rate of return for the fund was a gain of 115.6 per cent during the summer of 1993. Its performance will depend in future on the strength of Canada's oil patch. The fund has made large investments in the Canadian oil and gas industry in companies such as Penn West Petroleum, Alberta Energy, Suncor Energy, Talisman Energy, and Petro-Canada.

Fund risks

Investing in one sector of the Canadian economy—and especially the resource sector—increases risk. The fund has declined in value frequently and significantly during the previous five years, as this sector was plagued by poor economic conditions caused by excess capacity and weak demand from Asian countries. The worst 12-month return posted by this fund was a decline of 40.4 per cent. It declined in value after 12 months 40 per cent of the time. During the bear market of 1998, the fund declined in value by 45.7 per cent, while the average natural resources fund declined in value by 55.1 per cent. The fund still hasn't recovered from the 1998 decline.

Fund prospects

Resource stocks could be a good investment for investors because they are currently exhibiting real value. Their stock price is very low compared to the underlying assets, and several factors are working in their favour. When a global crisis occurs, for example, resource stocks usually go down in value, providing a buying opportunity. When signs appear of a good and sustainable economic recovery, as in Japan, resource stocks begin to outperform. Resource companies are earning bigger profits and producing excellent cash-flow growth. Most resource stocks are conservatively valued, and some are selling at their lowest valuations in history. However, investors should also be aware that the Organization of Petroleum Exporting Countries (OPEC) is aiming to increase production, which will effect supply and price.

FUND DETAILS

Fund name	**Royal Energy**	Fund size (in $ millions)	$261
Fund family	Royal Mutual Funds Inc.	Percentage in foreign holdings	6.66%
Mutual fund investment category	Specialty—Natural Resources	RRSP eligible	100%
Start date for data shown	July 1982	Sales charge	None
Number of funds in investment category	46	Redemption charge	None
Dividend frequency	N	Management expense ratio	2.44%

FUND PERFORMANCE

	1 month	6 months	1 year	3 years	5 years	10 years
Returns ending June 2000	-3.1%	26.5%	24.2%	1.1%	9.2%	10.2%
Best historical return	24.8%	75.3%	115.6%	28.7%	25.5%	14.0%
Average historical return	0.9%	5.1%	10.3%	7.6%	8.5%	9.1%
Worst historical return	-22.8%	-33.1%	-40.4%	-14.9%	-4.9%	3.9%
Value at risk of $1,000	$908	$780	$742	$804	$939	$1,599

RETURNS GREATER THAN

	1 month	6 months	1 year	3 years	5 years	10 years
10 per cent	6%	45%	40%	36%	36%	31%
Zero	56%	56%	60%	81%	89%	100%
Percentage of time fund lost $	44%	44%	40%	19%	11%	0%
Number of periods evaluated	216	211	205	181	157	97

DOWNSIDE RISK

	Worst setback since start date	In bear 1987	In bear 1990	In bear 1994	In bear 1998
Setback for mutual fund	-51.6%	-30.5%	-19.2%	-29.3%	-45.7%
Setback for peer group	-50.6%	-27.1%	-35.9%	-17.2%	-55.1%
Setback ended in	Feb. 1999	Nov. 1987	Jan. 1991	Jan. 1995	Aug. 1998
Months to recover from loss	?	27	22	20	?

ROLLING 12-MONTH QUARTILE RANKING OF MUTUAL FUND PERFORMANCE OVER TIME

Specialty—natural resources

1 is first quartile; 2 is second quartile; 3 is third quartile; 4 is fourth quartile. First quartile means that the fund outperformed 75 per cent of other similar funds after 12 months.

ROLLING 12-MONTH TOTAL RATE OF RETURN FOR THE MUTUAL FUND OVER TIME

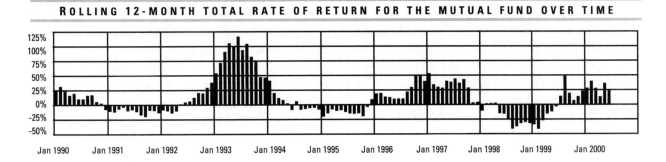

GREEN LINE PRECIOUS METALS

Vos value rating		
Reward	**Risk**	**Best balance**
★★★★★	★★★★★	★★★★★

Fund profile

This fund aims to generate long-term capital growth by investing in Canadian companies engaged in exploration, mining, and production of precious metals. Gold has displayed significant upside potential in the past, but has stagnated lately as nations sold off their gold reserves, glutting the market and pushing prices down. Gold prices will remain at historic lows as supply exceeds demand, which will reduce gold companies' profitability and shareholder value.

Gold has traditionally provided investors with excellent value and a hedge against inflation. It'll regain its glory, although nobody knows when. Any company is worth owning at the right price, and this applies to gold as well. Investors who can buy low and sell high will make a profit. The worst is likely over, but the path back to profitability will be long and plagued with difficulties. Margot Naudie of TD Asset Management manages the Green Line Precious Metals Fund.

Fund performance

The fund hasn't made money over the longer term, but in the short term it has added value during a volatile market. The fund frequently outperformed similar funds after 12 months and has earned a triple five-star Vos Value Rating, indicating that it has added value for investors in a very tough investment category. During the previous year the fund generated a return of 0.1 per cent. The best 12-month rate of return for this fund was a gain of 91.1 per cent, and the average rate of return after 12 months was 6.7 per cent.

The fund has invested in companies such as Placer Dome, Barrick Gold, Glodcorp, Platexco, and Franco-Nevada. Some of its competitors made a little more money during the previous year, because they invested in shell companies that turned into Internet companies. However, this hasn't turned into a viable strategy.

Fund risks

Investors have endured downside risk during the life of this fund. It declined in value during the bear market of 1998 by 65.5 per cent, more than the average mutual fund. The fund's worst 12-month rate of return was a gain of 49.6 per cent, and it has posted a negative return after 12 months 52 per cent of the time. In the past, this sector has displayed above-average downside risk and remains volatile.

Fund prospects

The fund's recent results should not discourage investors. Gold still has investment potential and merit, and gold prices should not remain at this level forever. The question is, how much bleeding will investors still have to endure? Eventually demand will have to fall in line with supply. Then mining companies should increase profitability and shareholder value. Aggressive investors could consider putting a portion of their portfolios in this sector. If and when performance in this sector reverses, these funds will likely appreciate very quickly.

FUND DETAILS

Fund name	**Green Line Precious Metals**	Fund size (in $ millions)	$67
Fund family	TD Asset Management Inc.	Percentage in foreign holdings	15.59%
Mutual fund investment category	Specialty—Precious Metals	RRSP eligible	100%
Start date for data shown	December 1994	Sales charge	None
Number of funds in investment category	17	Redemption charge	None
Dividend frequency	Annual	Management expense ratio	2.29%

FUND PERFORMANCE

	1 month	6 months	1 year	3 years	5 years	10 years
Returns ending June 2000	4.3%	-0.6%	0.1%	-11.6%	-1.8%	
Best historical return	39.2%	88.6%	91.1%	12.5%	3.2%	
Average historical return	0.7%	3.0%	6.7%	-9.3%	0.3%	
Worst historical return	-22.2%	-38.2%	-49.6%	-22.8%	-2.6%	
Value at risk of $1,000	$859	$756	$585	$476	$879	

RETURNS GREATER THAN

	1 month	6 months	1 year	3 years	5 years	10 years
10 per cent	13%	31%	32%	3%	0%	
Zero	54%	47%	48%	19%	50%	
Percentage of time fund lost $	46%	53%	52%	81%	50%	
Number of periods evaluated	67	62	56	32	8	

DOWNSIDE RISK

	Worst setback since start date	In bear 1987	In bear 1990	In bear 1994	In bear 1998
Setback for mutual fund	-65.5%			-10.4%	-65.5%
Setback for peer group	-37.6%			-6.9%	-37.6%
Setback ended in	Aug. 1998			Jan. 1995	Aug. 1998
Months to recover from loss	?			2	?

ROLLING 12-MONTH QUARTILE RANKING OF MUTUAL FUND PERFORMANCE OVER TIME

Specialty—Precious metals

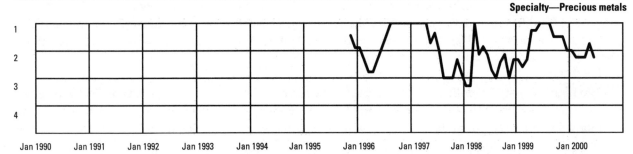

1 is first quartile; 2 is second quartile; 3 is third quartile; 4 is fourth quartile. First quartile means that the fund outperformed 75 per cent of other similar funds after 12 months.

ROLLING 12-MONTH TOTAL RATE OF RETURN FOR THE MUTUAL FUND OVER TIME

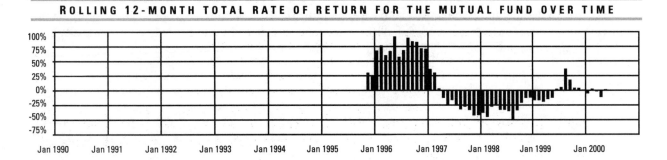

TALVEST GLOBAL HEALTH CARE FUND

Vos value rating		
Reward	**Risk**	**Best balance**
★★★★★	★★★★★	★★★★★

Fund profile

The health field is hot for several reasons. Life expectancy in developed countries is 78 years; it's 43 years in the least developed countries. Higher life expectancy means higher demand for the products and services that increase life expectancy. The World Health Organization expects the population aged 65 and over in developed countries to increase by at least 200 per cent in the next 30 years.

According to the Health Care Financing Administration, health care spending increases with age. When baby boomers age, they will spend more on health care than ever before. People over the age of 65 spend 10 times more on health care than any other group.

Health care companies spend big money on research and development, which will further advance the industry as they introduce new products and services.

Investors who want to participate in the growth of this industry should consider the Talvest Health Care Fund, managed by Ed Owens of Wellington Management. Owens has earned an excellent reputation around the world as an excellent manager in health care. He uses a bottom-up process to identify companies trading at very reasonable valuations.

Fund performance

During the previous year the fund posted a gain of 71.1 per cent, the fund's best 12-month rate of return. Its average rate of return after 12 months was 30 per cent. During the previous three years, the fund generated a return of 39.7 per cent per year. Based on these excellent results, the fund earned a triple five-star Vos Value Rating for reward, risk, and the best balance between risk and reward.

The fund has invested in companies like Amerisource Health, The Healthcare Company, and IMS Health. You don't usually see these companies in a health care fund, and that's why this fund is unique.

Fund risks

The fund's worst 12-month return was a gain of 5.6 per cent. During the bear market of 1998, it declined in value by 11 cent, while the average health care fund declined by 48.4 per cent, and it took only two months to recover. This is the biggest benefit of this fund—its ability to manage risk in a very volatile sector of the economy.

Fund prospects

This fund makes an ideal complement to your portfolio even if you have already invested in a health care fund. With a demographic shift and health care spending on the rise, the future looks good for this fund. Investors who want to allocate a portion of their portfolio to a specialty fund should consider the Talvest Health Care fund. It will certainly make your portfolio healthier.

FUND DETAILS

Fund name	**Talvest Global Health Care**	Fund size (in $ millions)	$194
Fund family	Talvest Fund Management Inc.	Percentage in foreign holdings	93.28%
Mutual fund investment category	Specialty—Health Care	RRSP eligible	20%
Start date for data shown	December 1996	Sales charge	Optional
Number of funds in investment category	26	Redemption charge	Optional
Dividend frequency	Semi-Annually	Management expense ratio	2.90%

FUND PERFORMANCE

	1 month	6 months	1 year	3 years	5 years	10 years
Returns ending June 2000	11.3%	61.3%	71.1%	39.7%		
Best historical return	19.4%	61.3%	71.1%	39.7%		
Average historical return	2.7%	16.3%	30.0%	31.2%		
Worst historical return	-11.0%	-6.3%	5.6%	21.2%		
Value at risk of $1,000	$937	$1,014	$1,103	$1,802		

RETURNS GREATER THAN

	1 month	6 months	1 year	3 years	5 years	10 years
10 per cent	12%	84%	94%	100%		
Zero	77%	95%	100%	100%		
Percentage of time fund lost $	23%	5%	0%	0%		
Number of periods evaluated	43	38	32	8		

DOWNSIDE RISK

	Worst setback since start date	In bear 1987	In bear 1990	In bear 1994	In bear 1998
Setback for mutual fund	-11.0%				-11.0%
Setback for peer group	-48.4%				-48.4%
Setback ended in	Aug. 1998				Aug. 1998
Months to recover from loss	2				2

ROLLING 12-MONTH QUARTILE RANKING OF MUTUAL FUND PERFORMANCE OVER TIME

Specialty—Health care

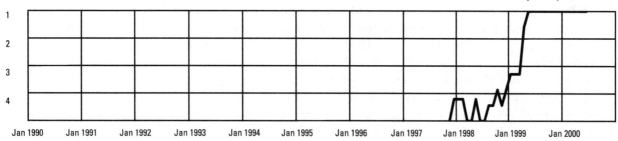

1 is first quartile; 2 is second quartile; 3 is third quartile; 4 is fourth quartile. First quartile means that the fund outperformed 75 per cent of other similar funds after 12 months.

ROLLING 12-MONTH TOTAL RATE OF RETURN FOR THE MUTUAL FUND OVER TIME

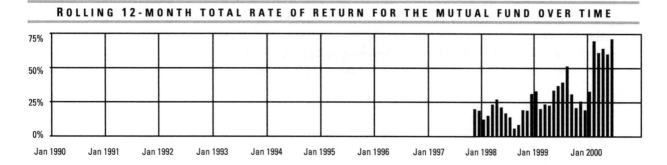

AIM GLOBAL TECHNOLOGY FUND

Vos value rating		
Reward	**Risk**	**Best balance**
★★★★★	★★★	★★★★★

Fund profile

Technology is the latest rage, and it has attracted a lot of investors. The reason for all the excitement is simple: growth. Telecommunications is growing explosively, especially in developing nations, and demand for Internet access exceeds supply. By the year 2003, according to forecasters, Internet-generated revenues will soar to more than $1.3 trillion, and personal computer demand is expected to grow exponentially worldwide. Computer expenditures as a percentage of Gross Domestic Product (GDP) will increase to 8.5 per cent, and wireless communications spending could reach $80 billion. In the previous four years alone the number of Internet users has risen from 3 million to 100 million. The AIM Global Technology Fund aims to invest and profit from all this growth.

Bill Keithler of AIM Capital Management in Houston manages the fund. It is ideal for very aggressive investors who can handle an above-average amount of risk.

Fund performance

During the previous year the fund generated a return of 124.5 per cent. Its best 12-month rate of return was a gain of 276.1 per cent, and the average rate of return after 12 months was 80.6 per cent. Such superior performance has allowed the fund to earn a five-star Vos Value Rating for reward and the best balance between risk and reward.

The fund invests mainly in the technology, Internet, and electronics industries, in companies like SDL, Cisco, Ciena, Nokia, and Corning, and it has avoided the majority of the dot.com companies.

Fund risks

The worst 12-month return posted by this fund was a decline of 8.1 per cent, and it has declined in value after 12 months 6 per cent of the time. During the bear market of 1998, it declined in value by 20.1 per cent, while the average science and technology fund declined in value by 15.5 per cent. However, the fund took only four months to recover its loss.

Fund prospects

Long-term investors will be well served in a mutual fund that invests in this high-growth, high-risk sector, although they should diversify and avoid investing more than 5 per cent of their portfolio in this area. Some of these mutual funds have appreciated in value by more than 250 per cent within one year, but investors obviously should not expect the same return every year. Over the long term this sector will continue to outpace the rest of the economy, but the share prices of a lot of companies in this sector already reflect this growth, so future stock prices may not increase so dramatically, and investors should expect the same downside risk as upside potential. Nevertheless, investors looking for a mutual fund that opportunistically invests in this sector should consider the AIM Global Technology Fund.

FUND DETAILS

Fund name	**AIM Global Technology**	Fund size (in $ millions)	$1,096
Fund family	AIM Funds Management Inc.	Percentage in foreign holdings	100.00%
Mutual fund investment category	Specialty—Science & Technology	RRSP eligible	20%
Start date for data shown	December 1996	Sales charge	Optional
Number of funds in investment category	74	Redemption charge	Optional
Dividend frequency	Annual	Management expense ratio	2.85%

FUND PERFORMANCE

	1 month	6 months	1 year	3 years	5 years	10 years
Returns ending June 2000	17.7%	12.4%	124.5%	70.5%		
Best historical return	33.3%	130.8%	276.1%	92.0%		
Average historical return	4.8%	36.3%	80.6%	75.7%		
Worst historical return	-16.5%	-12.8%	-8.1%	64.3%		
Value at risk of $1,000	$892	$920	$989	$4,461		

RETURNS GREATER THAN

	1 month	6 months	1 year	3 years	5 years	10 years
10 per cent	23%	84%	91%	100%		
Zero	70%	92%	94%	100%		
Percentage of time fund lost $	30%	8%	6%	0%		
Number of periods evaluated	43	38	32	8		

DOWNSIDE RISK

	Worst setback since start date	In bear 1987	In bear 1990	In bear 1994	In bear 1998
Setback for mutual fund	-27.4%				-20.1%
Setback for peer group	-21.2%				-15.5%
Setback ended in	May 2000				Aug. 1998
Months to recover from loss	?				4

ROLLING 12-MONTH QUARTILE RANKING OF MUTUAL FUND PERFORMANCE OVER TIME

Specialty—Science and technology

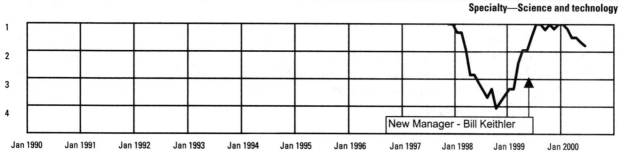

1 is first quartile; 2 is second quartile; 3 is third quartile; 4 is fourth quartile. First quartile means that the fund outperformed 75 per cent of other similar funds after 12 months.

ROLLING 12-MONTH TOTAL RATE OF RETURN FOR THE MUTUAL FUND OVER TIME

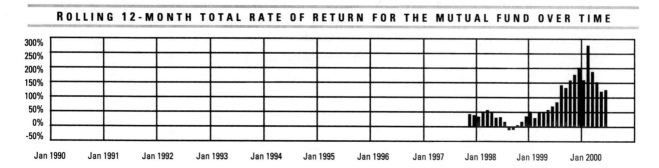

TALVEST GLOBAL SCIENCE AND TECHNOLOGY FUND

Vos value rating		
Reward	**Risk**	**Best balance**
★★★★★	★★★★★	★★★★★

Fund profile

This fund aims to earn money by investing in science and technology companies around the world. To the benefit of many investors, it has achieved its objective and more. The technology sector continues to grow for a number of reasons. With globalization, for example, larger, new-economy companies can identify and capitalize on opportunities throughout the world. In addition, governments have deregulated, and are privatizing their utilities to allow them to better compete in a global environment. Meanwhile, advances in technology allow companies to compete through the development of new products. Companies can also use technology to increase productivity and reduce costs, while offering services that increase sales. The Internet can also enhance a company's competitive and comparative advantage.

Managed by Stephan Kahn of TAL Global Asset Management, this fund has clearly led all science and technology funds in Canada and should be considered by aggressive investors who can withstand the risk associated with such a volatile sector.

Fund performance

During the previous year the fund generated a return of 160.7 per cent—not bad for a year's work. Its best 12-month rate of return was a gain of 258.8 per cent, and its average rate of return after 12 months was 84 per cent. The value at risk (VAR) of $1,000 invested for three years was $4,026. This means that an investment of $1,000 grew to at least $4,026 after three years 95 per cent of the time.

The fund invests in a combination of sectors associated with technology through companies like Entrust Technologies, Ariba, Ciena, and Juniper Networks. The fund has avoided business-to-consumer companies like Amazon.com, which are a little riskier than the B2B companies.

Fund risks

This fund's worst 12-month return was a decline of 2.2 per cent. It declined in value after 12 months 6 per cent of the time. During the bear market of 1998, it declined in value by 19.9 per cent, while the average science and technology fund declined by 15.5 per cent. But this fund took only three months to recover.

Fund prospects

The biggest risk associated with this fund is investors' unrealistic expectations. The value of an investment doesn't double or triple every year. The long-term economic trend for this industry is very favourable, but investors have to realize that sometimes these funds can decline in value by up to 15 per cent in a day. In addition, many of these companies are richly valued, although many also offer excellent investment opportunities. Still, aggressive investors who want a dedicated and very capable money manager handling their investments in this sector should consider the Talvest Global Science and Technology Fund.

FUND DETAILS

Fund name	**Talvest Global Science & Technology**	Fund size (in $ millions)	$403
Fund family	Talvest Fund Management Inc.	Percentage in foreign holdings	85.02%
Mutual fund investment category	Specialty—Science & Technology	RRSP eligible	20%
Start date for data shown	November 1996	Sales charge	Optional
Number of funds in investment category	74	Redemption charge	Optional
Dividend frequency	Annual	Management expense ratio	2.53%

FUND PERFORMANCE

	1 month	6 months	1 year	3 years	5 years	10 years
Returns ending June 2000	20.2%	37.6%	160.7%	85.9%		
Best historical return	38.2%	130.8%	258.8%	97.6%		
Average historical return	5.2%	37.1%	84.0%	78.4%		
Worst historical return	-19.9%	-7.4%	-2.2%	56.9%		
Value at risk of $1,000	$903	$966	$1,066	$4,026		

RETURNS GREATER THAN

	1 month	6 months	1 year	3 years	5 years	10 years
10 per cent	27%	87%	94%	100%		
Zero	73%	90%	94%	100%		
Percentage of time fund lost $	27%	10%	6%	0%		
Number of periods evaluated	44	39	33	9		

DOWNSIDE RISK

	Worst setback since start date	In bear 1987	In bear 1990	In bear 1994	In bear 1998
Setback for mutual fund	-19.9%				-19.9%
Setback for peer group	-15.5%				-15.5%
Setback ended in	Aug. 1998				Aug. 1998
Months to recover from loss	3				3

ROLLING 12-MONTH QUARTILE RANKING OF MUTUAL FUND PERFORMANCE OVER TIME

Specialty—Science and technology

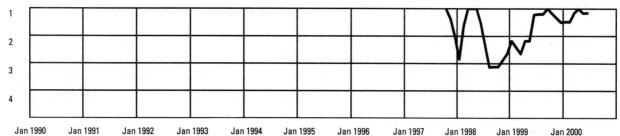

1 is first quartile; 2 is second quartile; 3 is third quartile; 4 is fourth quartile. First quartile means that the fund outperformed 75 per cent of other similar funds after 12 months.

ROLLING 12-MONTH TOTAL RATE OF RETURN FOR THE MUTUAL FUND OVER TIME

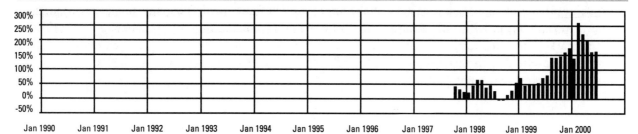

SPECTRUM UNITED GLOBAL TELECOMMUNICATIONS

Vos value rating		
Reward	**Risk**	**Best balance**
★★★★	★★★★★	★★★★★

Fund profile

This sector fund aims for a superior rate of return by investing in telecommunications companies around the world that have a significant competitive and comparative advantage within their marketplaces. Manager John Lathrop of MFS Institutional Advisors, a sub-advisor to the fund, relies on fundamental research to identify the best investment opportunities, maintains a strict valuation discipline, and maximizes industry and geographic diversification to reduce risk.

Telecommunications is a dynamic and growing industry, which could provide excellent upside potential for the aggressive investor. The demand for telecommunications services in developing nations is growing rapidly. Demand for phone service, cellular phone service, and the Internet is higher than the near-term supply. In the United States, the telecom industry is estimated to be worth $2 trillion. Telephone lines alone have increased tenfold during the previous 40 years. In the previous four years, the number of Internet users rose to 100 million from 3 million.

Fund performance

The industry has benefited from deregulation, technological innovation, and consolidation. During the previous year, this fund posted a gain of 51.1 per cent. Its best 12-month period was a gain of 112.5 per cent. Sector funds are notorious for generating superior performance in the short term, and this fund is no exception. Unfortunately, some sector funds also underperform during an economic cycle. Thus, investors should diversify their portfolios. The fund has invested in such multinational companies such as Corning, Nortel Networks, EMC, Ciena, China Telecom, and ADC Telecommunications.

Fund risks

During the bear market of 1998, the fund declined in value by 18.1 per cent—less than the average fund—and took four months to recover. The fund's worst 12-month rate of return was a loss of 8.6 per cent during the winter of 1997. Its value at risk of $1,000 after five years was $2,714. This means that, after five years, an investment of $1,000 was worth more than $2,714 at least 95 per cent of the time. Investors should consider this sector within the context of a diversified portfolio. Historically it has displayed very little downside risk, but things will likely change in the near future.

Fund prospects

Over the long term, the telecommunications industry will become a large part of the modern economy. Each year consumers are bombarded with new products and services that are smaller, faster, and apparently invaluable to our lifestyles. Investors in the Spectrum United Global Telecommunications Fund can participate in this growth, although the industry will remain volatile as companies begin to cut prices to gain market share, reducing profitability in the short term. Over the long term, winning companies should reward shareholders through higher profits and a larger market share. But investors will have to learn to deal with above-average volatility.

FUND DETAILS

Fund name	**Spectrum United Global Telecom**	Fund size (in $ millions)	$335
Fund family	Spectrum Investment Management Limited	Percentage in foreign holdings	91.20%
Mutual fund investment category	Specialty—Telecommuncations	RRSP eligible	20%
Start date for data shown	May 1994	Sales charge	Optional
Number of funds in investment category	12	Redemption charge	Optional
Dividend frequency	Annual	Management expense ratio	2.60%

FUND PERFORMANCE

	1 month	6 months	1 year	3 years	5 years	10 years
Returns ending June 2000	9.9%	-0.8%	51.1%	44.5%	29.7%	
Best historical return	20.8%	80.6%	112.5%	58.7%	37.7%	
Average historical return	2.2%	15.3%	31.3%	24.8%	28.3%	
Worst historical return	-18.1%	-7.5%	-8.6%	8.4%	22.1%	
Value at risk of $1,000	$925	$932	$990	$1,304	$2,714	

RETURNS GREATER THAN

	1 month	6 months	1 year	3 years	5 years	10 years
10 per cent	9%	62%	73%	92%	100%	
Zero	69%	84%	94%	100%	100%	
Percentage of time fund lost $	31%	16%	6%	0%	0%	
Number of periods evaluated	74	69	63	39	15	

DOWNSIDE RISK

	Worst setback since start date	In bear 1987	In bear 1990	In bear 1994	In bear 1998
Setback for mutual fund	-22.4%			-3.8%	-18.1%
Setback for peer group	-21.4%			-4.3%	-18.3%
Setback ended in	May 2000			Jan. 1995	Aug. 1998
Months to recover from loss	?			2	4

ROLLING 12-MONTH QUARTILE RANKING OF MUTUAL FUND PERFORMANCE OVER TIME

Specialty—Telecommunications

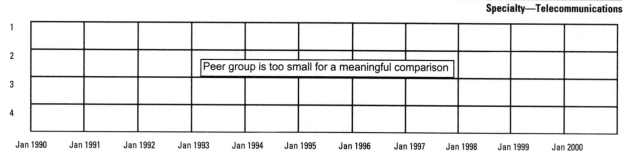

1 is first quartile; 2 is second quartile; 3 is third quartile; 4 is fourth quartile. First quartile means that the fund outperformed 75 per cent of other similar funds after 12 months.

ROLLING 12-MONTH TOTAL RATE OF RETURN FOR THE MUTUAL FUND OVER TIME

Part B

Stocks

Introduction to Stocks

Investing in stocks

This chapter is an introductory guide to investing in stocks. Investors frequently feel confused about investing in stocks and bewildered by the abundance of rational yet sometimes contradictory advice from professionals, who have spent their careers evaluating the merits of equities. There are some basic concepts, however, that all investors should understand as they analyze their investment objectives and try to select stocks to further them. This section discusses some of these basic concepts and demonstrates how an investor can use stocks to make money. Let's start by defining what a stock is and why a stock has value.

Common stock represents ownership in a company. As with ownership of other types of property, stock ownership carries risks and privileges. A shareholder has a right to vote for the company's directors and to participate in the company's annual meeting. A shareholder also shares in the earnings of the corporation. In addition, a shareholder receives a copy of the company's annual report disclosing details of its financial affairs every year. All publicly listed companies that sell shares to investors are required by law to issue an annual report. This document is an excellent source of information for investors—don't invest in a company without at least reading this report.

Along with the rights of ownership, a shareholder also incurs some risk and uncertainty. The returns on the shareholder's investment are based on the success of the firm or the perception thereof. The rate of return received by an investor who purchases common stock is equal to the dividends paid by the company plus any capital gain (or capital loss) generated. For example, if Allan bought stock in Ma Bell Inc. for $10 per share on January 1, 2000, received $1 in dividends on December 1, 2000, and then sold the stock for $12 on December 31, 2000, his rate of return would be:

(Ending price – Beginning price + Dividend) ÷ Beginning price
= (12 – 10 + 1) ÷ 10 = 3/10 (or 30 per cent)

When he first bought his shares in Ma Bell Inc., Allan did not know that he would be able to sell the stock at the end of 1998 for $12. He knew that the stock might rise in value. In fact, that's one of the reasons he bought it. But he also knew that it could lose value. If Allan had wanted more certainty, he could have invested in a savings account generating a return of 5 per cent. The difference between investing in a savings account and in Ma Bell Inc. is the amount of risk incurred by Allan. As a stockholder, he could not know with absolute certainty that his shares would generate a predictable rate of return. In turn, investors like Allan demand a higher rate of return to compensate them for the risk.

Savings accounts are considered risk-free, or at least extremely safe investments. Stocks come with higher risk, because the outcome of investing in stocks is never certain. A good return in one year may be followed by a disappointment in the next year.

As we discussed briefly in our introduction to mutual funds, investment risk can be reduced through diversification. Whether you're buying individual stocks or mutual funds, you can reduce risk by combining investments in a way that minimizes risk and maximizes return. For example, Allan is considering investing in a ski resort in northern British Columbia. He anticipates a 40 per cent return on his investment if B.C. gets more than four feet of snow this winter. If it receives less than this, the value of his investment will decline by 20 per cent. To hedge his investment Allan could invest in a California vacation property, where skiers go if it doesn't snow in B.C. If B.C. receives less than four feet of snow this winter, Allan's investment in California will increase in value by 40 per cent. However, if B.C. receives more than four feet of snow, Allan's investment in California will decline in value by 20 per cent. By investing half his money in each property, Allan's portfolio will increase in value by 20 per cent regardless of how much snow falls in B.C. This is called diversification.

Following a strategy of diversification, investors acquire a number of stocks within their portfolios that come with different risks and rewards. As the number of stocks in a portfolio grows, the overall risk declines. Diversification reduces the risk of loss associated with the performance of one particular stock. This risk is referred to as unsystematic risk.

Unsystematic risk is the risk attributable to a specific company. For example, the risk associated with ski resorts is the risk of unfavourable weather. However, this risk can be diversified away if an investor invests in a company that creates snowmaking machines or provides a product or service that will be in demand when there is no snow.

Not all risk can be eliminated through diversification. The risk that remains after diversification is called market or systematic risk. The total risk of investing in stocks consists of unsystematic (or diversifiable) risk plus systematic (or non-diversifiable) risk.

The table below illustrates that the more securities an investor owns the further the volatility (measured by standard deviation) declines.

REDUCING RISK: DIVERSIFIABLE AND NON-DIVERSIFIABLE RISK

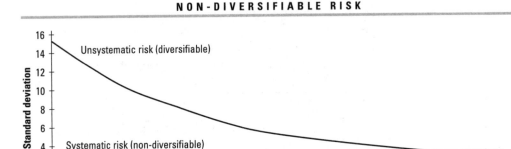

Why invest in stocks?

As the first part of this book demonstrated, many investors have successfully made money by investing in Canadian equity mutual funds. These mutual funds, in turn, invest in some of the very same companies we'll discuss in this section. If these funds earn money by investing in Canadian stocks, why can't you?

This section will show you how to create your own mutual fund by investing in a variety of stocks yourself, or how to complement your mutual fund holdings by investing in one or several stocks. Even if you decide not to invest in stocks at all, you'll gain a better understanding of common stock investing and the performance of individual stocks.

If the likelihood of a significant decline in the value of a mutual fund investment is low, the likelihood of incurring a large loss by investing in a common stock is much higher. Some of the largest Canadian companies have experienced setbacks in the price of their stock of up to 50 per cent, although the value of stock in these same companies may have also doubled or tripled within the same year. In any case, investors who buy common stock incur potentially more risks and returns than do mutual fund investors.

Based on past performance, it has been shown that an investment in stocks will outperform other investments over the long term. For reasons that we discussed earlier, such as management fees and diversification strategies of mutual funds, a direct investment in a single successful company will usually outperform the average mutual fund. However, an investment in an unsuccessful company will compare poorly with the average mutual fund. The critical factor is selecting a good sector; the right company will become the icing on the cake.

Which company is a good investment?

You've decided to invest in the stock market. You've also decided to invest most of your money in Canadian equity mutual funds, while directing a small portion of your money toward the common stock of some Canadian corporations.

Your first step is to identify an industry that you believe will outperform the overall economy in the long term. After all, a company's long-term growth prospects will depend on the growth of the industry in which it operates. A well-run company that manufactures and distributes record players won't grow at the same rate as a company that produces CD players.

Comparing industries

Investing in the right industry is just as important as investing in the right company. The performance of 14 industries in Canada during a period of 10 years has been widely divergent. The table below indicates the historical rates of return for these industries, compared with the TSE 300 and two BARRA-style indices. This table illustrates the importance of investing in the right industry. Remember that this period includes some of the worst bear markets that investors have experienced.

COMPARING INDUSTRY RETURNS

Index name	3 months %	1 year %	3 years %	5 years %	10 years %
TSE 300	8.1	47.4	18.3	19.7	13.8
TSE 35	3.7	33.4	17.8	17.7	13.7
TSE Communications and media	1.5	22.7	24.1	22.6	14.4
TSE Conglomerates	14.8	10.3	6.5	15.3	10.4
TSE Consumer products	18.7	21.3	20.9	19.1	15.9
TSE Financial services	11.5	15.4	9.2	23.3	16.9
TSE Gold and silver	12.8	-14.6	-18.0	-15.1	-2.2
TSE Industrial products	9.1	124.6	43.9	35.9	22.8
TSE Merchandising	16.9	-3.8	-1.8	6.4	4.4
TSE Metals and minerals	-5.7	-11.0	-11.8	-4.0	2.8
TSE Oil and gas	20.6	26.5	4.0	11.9	7.7
TSE Paper and forest products	-5.6	3.7	0.3	1.8	4.8

continued

COMPARING INDUSTRY RETURNS (CONTINUED)

Index name	3 months %	1 year %	3 years %	5 years %	10 years %
TSE Pipelines	4.6	-26.3	-4.9	6.6	7.1
TSE Real estate	19.4	4.2	1.2	7.3	-13.4
TSE Transport and environment	8.9	-15.7	-10.6	1.3	-5.3
TSE Utilities	-13.7	77.3	42.7	37.9	23.1
BARRA Growth index	0.8	56.4	21.8	19.1	12.7
BARRA Value index	10.3	10.8	7.8	16.0	12.7

Source: Toronto Stock Exchange and Barra

Industry characteristics

All the stocks listed on the TSE can be broken down into two categories—those that are and aren't sensitive to changes in interest rates. Companies that are sensitive to changes in interest rates include companies in the following industries:

- banks
- utilities
- insurance companies
- construction companies

When interest rates fall, these interest-sensitive stocks tend to do well.

The following companies are sensitive to changes in the economy in general. As inflation comes alive, the new market leaders are companies involved in:

- steel
- gold mining
- forestry and lumber

Lower interest rates encourage people to spend money, so when interest rates have been low and are starting to rise, good companies in the following sectors perform well:

- retail stores
- cosmetics
- restaurants
- tobacco

Near the end of a cycle of interest-rate levels, when interest rates have peaked and are starting back down, companies perform well in sectors like:

- pharmaceuticals
- chemicals

Promising companies

Once you have identified the right industry, you then have to identify and assess the most promising companies within the industry and evaluate the prices of their common stock.

You can approach this evaluation much as you would evaluate the price of a house. For example, suppose that a new bungalow at 425 Main Street in London, Ontario, costs $150,000, while the new bungalow at 426 Main Street is priced at $100,000. These two homes have similar qualities, and their prices should be similar. If they're not, purchasers will always buy the cheaper home until demand causes its price to increase to a more realistic level or the price of the more expensive home declines in value.

When buying stocks, investors can identify ones that are trading below their actual value. When other investors also see this value, the price of the stock will increase as investors acknowledge the actual value of the firm by buying shares in it. The value of the stock is generated by the value of the dividends. Corporations pay dividends to shareholders to compensate them for taking the additional risk of investing in the common stock of the company. The company that is able to pay the largest dividend will be worth the most—companies that are able to increase their dividend the fastest will also have their stock appreciate the fastest.

Investing in common stocks is more risky than other investments, because common stock investors have the least protection in the case of bankruptcy. If a firm goes bankrupt, first the lawyers and accountants appointed to handle the receivership will be paid; then suppliers, employees, banks, and bond holders, in that order. The last individuals who receive payments are the common shareholders. If the firm doesn't raise enough money through the sale of all its assets, the common shareholders are out of luck and will receive no payment. The other side of the coin is that if the company is prosperous and the firm generates large profits, those profits are returned to the shareholders only.

The firm returns money to shareholders in the form of a dividend. Investors who invest in a savings account at the bank receive interest payments. Investors who invest in common shares receive dividend payments. A dividend is a payment made to investors in the common stock of a company from the company's earnings or profits. Some companies pay large dividends; other companies don't pay dividends at all and instead reinvest profits back in the company. This may allow the company to grow faster and pay a larger dividend in the future. The value of a common stock is derived from the assets the company owns and future dividend payments. The higher these values, the higher the price of the stock.

Investors must realize that there is a difference between investing in the common stock of a great company and investing in a great common stock. Great companies are not always great investments, but not-so-great companies that are attractively priced can be great investments.

Understanding stock tables

You can find everything you need to know about a company's day-to-day financial performance in the stock tables in newspapers and financial journals, but you have to know how to read these tables. There are minor variations from one newspaper to another, but they're all similar to the following table:

52 weeks					Yld		Vol				
Hi	Lo	Stock	Sym	Div	%	100s	Hi	Lo	Net close	Chg
50-3/8	42	BCE Inc.	B	2.68	5.4	21680	5-3/8	49-1/8	50-1/8	+1-1/8

A STOCK TABLE

52 weeks, Hi and Lo: These figures show the highest price and the lowest price (in dollars) that the stock traded at over the previous 52 weeks.

Stock: This is the name of the company whose stock information you're looking at.

Sym: This is the symbol that represents the stock on the ticker. (You can see the ticker in action in brokerage offices.)

Yld, Div: This is the company's estimated annual dividend per share.

Yld, %: This is the stock's dividend yield.

Vol, 100s: This is the number of shares that have been traded throughout the day, in 100s.

Hi and Lo: These figures represent the highest price throughout the day and the lowest price throughout the day.

Net close: This gives the closing price at the end of the day.

Chg: This is the percentage change from the previous day.

To find further information on a particular company, you can look at a series of its annual reports. You can also find useful information on a particular company's financial performance in the chapter of this book entitled, Best of the Best Blue-Chip Stocks for Canadians on page 189.

Value outperforms growth

Companies whose stock price is high relative to the company's underlying assets are considered growth companies. Companies with strong financial statements and a reasonable stock price are considered value companies. Value companies have low price-to-book (P/B) ratios and low price-to-earnings (P/E) ratios. Growth companies have high price-to-book (P/B) ratios and high price-to-earnings (P/E) ratios.

Value investors look at balance sheets and income statements to find companies that have either fallen out of favour with other investors or are undervalued and whose stock price is low given the company's fundamentals. Value investors are searching for companies that have intrinsic value that other investors are currently overlooking by focusing on companies with high P/B and P/E ratios. Growth investors prefer stocks with earnings that are accelerating faster than the economy. The growth investor is less concerned with the company's intrinsic evaluations as long as earnings continue to grow.

A company called BARRA collects and analyzes data related to financial markets and has created indices to measure the performance of companies that exhibited desirable characteristics for growth and value investors. BARRA divides the 200 largest companies on the Toronto Stock Exchange (TSE) into two separate groups: value companies and growth companies.

The following graph illustrates the pattern of the BARRA indices since January 1982.

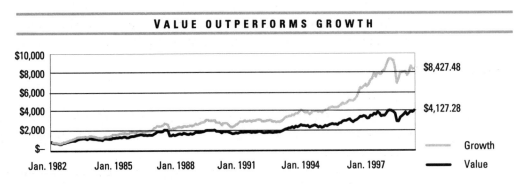

VALUE OUTPERFORMS GROWTH

Source: *Barra*

This graph illustrates that value companies have outperformed during this period. Investors in the TSE 300 would have finished in the middle, but still earned a very respectable rate of return. (The TSE 300 is an index of 300 large companies traded on the Toronto Stock Exchange.) However, investors should realize that, in the short term, either value or growth stocks could outperform. During 1998 and 2000, because of companies like Nortel, growth stocks have outperformed value by a larger margin than ever before.

Volatility: The bear market of 1998 is normal stock market behaviour

Investors are cautious about investing in stocks or equity mutual funds during volatile market periods. The most recent volatile period endured by investors was the stock market correction of 1998. The Toronto Stock Exchange 300 Index declined by 29.3 per cent from April 22, 1998, to August 31, 1998. Investors who invested a large portion of their investments in Canadian equities have incurred large setbacks. With such a large setback, many investors were left questioning their future investment strategies. Should I sell; should I hold; should I buy; what should I do?

Each investor will have a different answer. However, investors should remember some of the following facts.

- Equities have and will continue to provide a higher rate of return than other investments over the long term, but with more risk.

- Without risk, investors would not earn higher rates of return.

- Long-term investors will incur setbacks, and they should not despair when risk comes to fruition. It's a natural and essential part of investing in equities.

The table below illustrates the risk of investing in equities. Since January 1956 there have been 25 different stock market corrections greater than 5 per cent affecting the companies included in the TSE 300. In each case, investors regained their investment. During this period investors experienced a lot of volatility. Drastic setbacks were very infrequent, but small setbacks weren't.

DISPERSIONS IN EQUITY MARKET RETURNS		
Stock market corrections from January 1956 to June 2000	Number of corrections	Average setback
Corrections > 30 per cent	2	-37.05%
Corrections between 20 and 30 per cent	5	-25.06%
Corrections between 10 and 20 per cent	7	-14.56%
Corrections between 5 and 10 per cent	11	-7.14%
Total	25	-15.19%

The time taken to recover the loss varied over different periods. But in each case investors were better off staying invested in equities after a market correction.

Purchasing stocks

Bid and ask

As with most things in life, the people who want to sell stock usually want more than anyone else will pay for it, and the people who want to buy stock usually want to pay less than anyone wants to sell it for.

Buyers bid; sellers ask. A stock may have an asking price of $10 and a bid of $9.75. If you wanted to sell the stock right away, you would have to accept the bid price of $9.75.

If you wanted to buy the stock right away, you would have to pay the ask price of $10. You can also place an order to buy or sell a stock at a price between the bid and ask, for instance, at $9.85, but if you do there's no guarantee that your order will be filled.

Bid and ask prices are constantly changing in relation to supply and demand.

Board lots

When you go to the supermarket to buy eggs, you see a price listed for one dozen. When it comes to eggs, one dozen is the standard unit.

When it comes to stocks, the standard unit is 100 shares. Just as 12 eggs are called a dozen, 100 shares are called a board lot. For stocks trading over $1, the bid and ask prices are quoted per board lot. A purchase of fewer than 100 shares is known as an odd lot.

Placing an order

All investors should know how to place an order properly with a stockbroker to buy or sell stocks. There are three basic types of orders:

1. **Market order:** You want to buy a particular stock at the current market price. For example, let's say you want to buy 100 shares of BCE Inc. You would call your stockbroker and ask what BCE is trading at. The broker may say, "50 bid, $50.25 ask." If you find this range attractive, you say, "Buy 100 shares of BCE at the market." Your broker will repeat the order to you and then place it. You now own 100 shares of BCE purchased at market, which may be $50.25 or higher or lower depending on how fast the market is moving.

2. **Limit order:** You want to buy or sell a stock only if it trades at a specified price. You also have to set a time limit for your order. You could set the time limit for one day, one month, or any duration in between. Or you could place an order good until cancelled, in which case the order stays in effect until it's either executed or cancelled by you.

   For example, if BCE is trading at $50, but you don't want to pay more than $48 for it, you would tell your broker to buy BCE at $48, good for a week. At the end of one week, if the trade hasn't been executed, it's automatically cancelled.

3. **Stop order:** You want to sell a stock whose price has gone up and is now starting to fall, so you instruct your broker to place a stop order.

   For example, if you bought a stock at $20, it rose to $40, and it's now starting to head lower, you don't want to lose your profits. So you phone your broker and say, place a stop order to sell 100 shares at $35. Now, if the stock drops to $35, your shares will automatically be sold at the best price available.

IUnits

A large portion of a Canadian equity mutual fund's return is derived from blue-chip stocks. Historically, during a bull market led by blue-chip stocks, the S&P/TSE 60 index (a blue-chip index) may increase in value by 20 per cent, outperforming three-quarters of Canadian mutual funds.

As a result, some people have given up trying to beat the market, preferring simply to settle for the same return as the market index itself. To accomplish this you can invest in an index fund linked to the return of a particular group of stocks such as the S&P/TSE 60 or some other index. These funds are passively managed, and their holdings match the assets in a particular index such as the S&P/TSE 60 or the S&P 500. An index fund that matches the S&P 500 index holds exactly the same 500 stocks as the S&P 500 charts, in exactly the same quantity. Index funds will never win first prize for their performance, but nor will they win the booby prize.

Alternatively, you can buy index participation units directly from the TSE, saving the administration and management fees charged by most mutual fund operators. S&P/TSE 60 Index Participation units (IUnits) allow you to buy a single security, through your broker, that represents the diversified portfolio of Canadian companies comprising the S&P/TSE 60 Index. IUnits pay dividends, and you can hold them within your RRSP, but you forgo the advantages offered by mutual fund companies that offer index products, such as reporting, consolidation, and access to a larger selection of index products. Some of these index mutual funds effectively replicate the performance of a foreign equity market while remaining RSP-eligible.

How to Read the Stock Charts in This Book

The following chapter contains a description of each company listed on pages 189 and 190. A one-page stock chart accompanies each description. The stock chart combines six tables that illustrate the historical performance of a stock. An explanation of how to read a stock chart follows.

COMPANY DETAILS

Company name	Bombardier	Industry classification	Industrial products
Recent price	$40.20	Market capitalization (in $ millions)	$27,622
52-week price range from low to high	$18.95–$43.10	Ticker symbol	BBD.b
Overall assessment of potential risk (one is most risky)	20/30	Phone number for annual report	514-861-9481 ext. 390
Number of mutual funds that hold this stock as a top 15 holding	403	Stock analysis start date	July 1982

Company name: This gives the name of the company that is being analyzed.

Recent price: This discloses the price per share for the stock that is being analyzed. The price given is the price of the stock at the end of June 2000.

52-week price range from low to high: This discloses the price range for the stock during the previous year. Investors who bought at the bottom would have invested at the yearly low. Investors who bought at the top would have invested at the yearly high.

Overall assessment of potential risk (One is most risky): This indicates the company's downside risk. Companies with good valuations score higher than companies with higher valuations.

Number of mutual funds that hold this stock in their top 15 holdings: Canadian equity, dividend, and balanced funds all invest in a variety of Canadian companies. (Information provided by MorningStar Canada.)

Industry classification: This indicates the industry in which the company operates.

Market capitalization (in $ millions): The market capitalization is the total value of the company's stock. An investor who wanted to buy all the shares of Bombardier based on a price of $40.20 would have to pay $27.6 billion for the entire firm.

Ticker symbol: The Toronto Stock Exchange provides information on the performance of a company based on its ticker symbol.

Phone number for annual report: The company publishes an annual report for investors or other individuals. The annual report describes the company's business and its current and future activities, and highlights its financial performance. Investors who want to order an annual report can call this number and request a copy.

Stock analysis start date: This is the date of the earliest data on the company's historical performance analyzed for its stock chart. Many companies in this book have a history longer than the start date, but using more recent data (the last 20 years or so) provides a reasonable assessment of the company's performance.

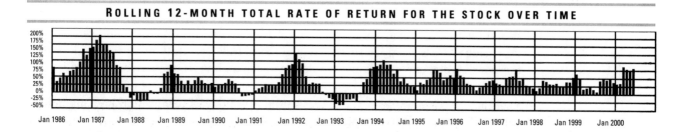

ROLLING 12-MONTH TOTAL RATE OF RETURN FOR THE STOCK OVER TIME

The first bar in this graph indicates the stock's performance for the period February 1, 1985 to January 31, 1986. The next bar illustrates the performance for the period March 1, 1985 to February 28, 1986. As we move to the right, the bars illustrate the performance of the stock closer to the current date. Thus, the return for the Bombardier stock for the one-year period ending June 30, 2000 is 80.2 per cent, as indicated by the last bar at the right. Investors should note that some investments have large swings in performance from one period to the next.

STOCK PERFORMANCE

	1 month	1 year	3 years	5 years	10 years	15 years
Returns ending June 2000	2.7%	80.2%	38.2%	38.3%	34.6%	38.0%
Best historical return	37.8%	177.5%	90.2%	63.3%	41.4%	39.4%
Average historical return	3.2%	41.4%	37.5%	35.8%	33.5%	36.7%
Worst historical return	-25.0%	-34.5%	6.6%	17.2%	24.5%	34.4%
Value at risk of $1,000	$900	$840	$1,502	$2,626	$11,554	$85,891

Returns ending June 2000: These are the returns earned by the stock for the various periods (that is, one month, one year, and so on) ending June 2000. For example, the one-month rate of return for Bombardier stock was a gain of 2.7 per cent. The one-year rate of return from July 1, 1999, to June 30, 2000, was 80.2 per cent; the three-year rate of return from July 1, 1997, to June 30, 2000, was 38.2 per cent annualized; and the five-year rate of return from July 1, 1995, to June 30, 2000, was 38.3 per cent annualized. The 10-year rate of return for the stock from July 1, 1990, to June 30, 2000, was 34.6 per cent annualized.

Best historical return: This figure summarizes the stock's historical range of rates of return. The best historical return discloses the very best performance the stock has achieved since the start date of our analysis. The best one-month return for Bombardier stock was a gain of 37.8 per cent. Thus, an investor who had invested in Bombardier prior to its best one-month rate of return would have gained 37.8 per cent in that month. The best one-year rate of return was a gain of 177.5 per cent; an investor who held Bombardier stock throughout this stock's best one-year period would have gained 177.5 per cent, and so on. With this information, investors can compare the performance of the stock ending June 2000 with the stock's best performance. Note: All numbers are calculated using average annual compounded rates of return.

Average historical return: The average historical rate of return shows how the stock has performed historically on average. Investors in Bombardier stock on average earned 3.2 per cent per month. After one year, investors on average earned 41.4 per cent; the average three-year rate of return for the stock was 37.5 per cent; the average five-year rate of return for the stock was 35.8 per cent; and the average 10-year rate of return was 33.5 per cent.

Worst historical return: The worst historical return gives investors an indication of the downside risk associated with a particular stock. Investors in Bombardier stock prior to the stock's worst one-month loss would have seen their investment decline in value by 25 per cent. The worst one-year loss posted by the stock was a decline of 34.5 per cent. The worst rate of return posted by the stock during a period of three years was an annualized gain of 6.6 per cent. Thus, investors who invested in this stock for a minimum of three years could still have made money historically, although very little. The worst five-year rate of return for the stock was a gain of 17.2 per cent, and the worst 10-year rate of return was a gain of 24.5 per cent.

Value at risk: The last line in this section is something new. Value at risk (VAR) of $1,000 shows investors the minimum value that their $1,000 investment would have reached after each period, with 95 per cent certainty. For example, $1,000 would have been worth more than $900 after the following month, 95 per cent of the time. After 12 months a $1,000 investment would have been worth $840 after 12 months at least 95 per cent of the time. After five years the $1,000 investment would have been worth at least $2,626. The higher the number, the better the downside protection for investors. The 10-year VAR is greater than $11,000, indicating that, 95 per cent of the time, an investment of $1,000 held for 10 years would grow to more than $11,000. The lower the VAR, the higher the implied risk for a particular investment. Investments with a high VAR over the short term have done an excellent job of preserving investors' wealth.

RETURNS GREATER THAN						
	1 month	1 year	3 years	5 years	10 years	15 years
10 per cent	20%	82%	98%	100%	100%	100%
Zero	63%	86%	100%	100%	100%	100%
Percentage of time stock lost $	37%	14%	0%	0%	0%	0%
Number of periods evaluated	216	205	181	157	97	37

This table illustrates the frequency with which a particular stock achieves or fails to meet an investor's goals. The table is divided into three achievement levels:

1. The frequency with which the stock achieved a return greater than 10 per cent over different periods.

2. The frequency with which the stock achieved a return greater than zero.

3. The frequency with which the stock achieved a return less than zero (or lost money) over different periods.

In this example, Bombardier stock achieved a return greater than zero after one month 63 per cent of the time and a return greater than zero after one year 86 per cent of the time. After five years the stock has always posted a return greater than zero historically.

The last line in the table entitled "Number of periods evaluated" indicates the number of periods included in this analysis.

DOWNSIDE RISK

	Worst setback since start date	In bear 1987	In bear 1990	In bear 1994	In bear 1998
Setback for stock	-45.5%	-45.5%	-28.0%	-8.3%	-19.7%
Setback for stock market	-19.2%	-23.2%	-16.3%	-9.7%	-24.6%
Setback ended in	Dec. 1987	Dec. 1987	Nov. 1990	Jan. 1995	Aug. 1998
Months to recover from loss	10	10	6	1	4

The downside risk table evaluates the performance of the stock during different periods when capital markets have displayed significant declines in value, referred to as bear markets. It's useful for investors to evaluate the performance of their investments during more difficult economic environments. Some investments will decline significantly during bear markets; some will not decline in value. In addition, companies that operate in different industries will have very different performances. Investors can read the downside risk table and get a good approximation of how different investments react during these difficult times.

The table is divided into five setback periods: the worst setback since the stock analysis date and the four recent bear periods (in the 1980s and 1990s).

The worst setback since start date measures the worst decline an investor could have experienced with this stock in the period analyzed. Many stocks fluctuate over time; this figure discloses the largest drop from high to low that the stock has ever posted. Bombardier stock declined in value by 45.5 per cent, and the setback ended in December 1987. During the same period, the average Canadian equity fund declined in value by 19.2 per cent. However, after incurring this loss Bombardier stock regained its former value within 10 months. Investors should note that this column discloses the worst setback for the stock since the start date. The columns that disclose the stock's performance during the four bear markets evaluate the performance of the stock only during those periods, although these bears sometimes capture the stock's worst setback.

STOCK FINANCIAL FUNDAMENTAL INFORMATION

	1990	1991	1992	1993	1994	1995	1996	1997	1998	1999	Change
Average share price	$1.02	$1.33	$1.76	$1.70	$2.65	$3.83	$5.06	$7.06	$9.14	$11.71	28.1%
Earnings per share	$0.09	$0.09	$0.11	$0.14	$0.18	$0.11	$0.29	$0.29	$0.38	$0.51	34.2%
Book value per share	$0.58	$0.71	$0.77	$1.02	$1.21	$1.24	$1.62	$1.78	$2.20	$2.43	10.5%
Price-to-earnings ratio	11.3	14.8	16.0	12.1	14.7	34.8	17.4	24.3	24.1	23.0	-4.5%
Price-to-book ratio	1.8	1.9	2.3	1.7	2.2	3.1	3.1	4.0	4.2	4.8	16.0%
Profit margin	3.4%	3.4%	3.0%	3.6%	4.0%	2.1%	4.9%	4.6%	4.5%	5.1%	14.0%
Asset turnover	1.30	1.00	1.00	1.10	1.10	1.10	1.00	0.80	0.80	0.80	-0.7%
Leverage	3.4	3.8	4.5	3.5	3.4	3.9	3.7	4.4	4.8	5.1	7.4%
Return on equity	15.5%	12.7%	14.3%	13.7%	14.9%	8.9%	17.9%	16.3%	17.3%	21.0%	21.5%
Dividend per share	$0.02	$0.02	$0.03	$0.03	$0.04	$0.05	$0.05	$0.08	$0.09	$0.11	22.0%
Dividend yield	2.0%	1.5%	1.7%	1.8%	1.5%	1.3%	1.0%	1.1%	1.0%	1.0%	0.9%

This table provides investors with a summary of some key financial information reported by the company during the previous 10 years (if applicable). The rows in the table indicate the different variables used in our analysis. The columns provide data based on the company's annual or fiscal period (the period over which they report their financial information) ending in the stated year. The first data column provides financial information for 1990, and the second-last column, at the right, provides information for the company in 1999. The last column at the right side of the table, headed Change, provides the annualized change that the company reported for the previous year. The change is reported only if the company provided complete information for the previous two years and did not post negative variables. The underlying companies' annual reports or Datastream provided all stock financial fundamental information.

Average share price: The average share price is the average price for the calendar year, adjusted for stock splits.

Earnings per share: A company that generates larger profits is more valuable than a company that generates smaller profits. The value of a stock includes the current value of all the dividend payments. Dividend payments are made to investors by the company from profits to compensate investors for holding the stock. The larger the profits, the better the probability that companies will pay higher dividends. A company's earnings per share equals the company's total earnings divided by the number of shares outstanding. In 1990 earnings per share for Bombardier was $0.09. Therefore, each share of the company generated $0.09 of earnings. Investors like to see an upward trend in profits, but the most important factor is that investors pay a reasonable price for each share of common stock.

Book value per share: The book value per share is equal to the value of the company's assets after paying all creditors. The creditors are the banks and the company's suppliers as well as the company's bond holders. Therefore, the book value is the value of the company if it sold all its assets for a price equal to that reported in the financial statements and paid off all its debts. What's left over is the book value of the firm. Dividing this book value by the number of shares outstanding gives the book value per share. In 1990 the book value per share for Bombardier was $0.58, which is less than the average price for the stock of $1.02 per share. Here the company's stock was trading at more than book value per share. So, if you had bought all the shares in the company at the current (1990) price and sold all the assets for a price equal to their book value, you would have suffered a loss. Many companies trade at a price higher than their book value per share, but some mismanaged companies trade at less than book value per share. Book value per share isn't always the best estimate of the actual value of the stock. Investors like companies whose book value per share increases over time, but the stock price is still a reasonable proxy for the book value per share.

Price-to-earnings ratio: The price-to-earnings ratio is equal to the company's stock price divided by the company's earnings per share. The price-to-earnings ratio, or P/E ratio, gives investors a good indication of how much they're paying for the company's historical earnings. The P/E ratio for Bombardier in 1990 was 11.3, which is the company's stock price of $1.02 divided by earnings per share of $0.09. Therefore, investors paid $11.30 for every $1 in historical earnings. If the company's earnings didn't grow, and the company paid all its earnings in the form of a dividend, investors would receive their money back in 11.3 years. It's important for investors that companies grow, since earnings increase and investors get their money back faster. Earnings growth can also be accomplished through cost reductions and other means. In general, lower P/E multiples with strong earnings growth is better than higher P/E multiples with low earnings growth.

Price-to-book ratio: The price-to-book ratio is equal to the company's average share price divided by its book value per share. In 1990 Bombardier's price-to-book ratio or P/B ratio was equal to 1.8. The company's average stock price was $1.02 divided by $0.58, which is equal to 1.8 or the P/B ratio. Thus, investors are paying $1.80 for every $1 of equity the company reported. Lower P/B ratios with high earnings growth are better than higher P/B ratios with low earnings growth.

Profit margin: The profit margin is equal to the company's net income divided by its sales. Higher profit margins are better than lower profit margins. Higher profit margins will increase the company's net income faster with each $1 increase in its sales. A profit margin of 3.4 per cent indicates that the company would earn $.034 more for every $1 increase in sales. Thus, companies with high profit margins can increase net income faster than companies with lower profit margins, because companies with lower profit margins have to sell more.

Asset turnover: Asset turnover measures how efficiently the senior management of the company manages the company's assets. The asset turnover ratio is equal to the company's sales divided by the assets the company utilizes. If a company has assets of $5 and sales of $10, its asset turnover ratio would equal $10 divided by $5, or 2. This means the company can generate $2 worth of sales for every $1 of assets employed. Therefore, higher asset turnover ratios are better. Investors prefer companies that have an increasing asset turnover ratio because senior management is utilizing the assets of the company more efficiently and effectively to generate additional sales, and in turn, more profits.

Leverage: When a company borrows money to invest, it's leveraging. Therefore, when a company borrows more money to invest in buildings or equipment it's increasing its leverage. Leverage is equal to the assets of the firm divided by the value of the firm owned by the shareholders. For example, a firm has assets worth $10. It borrows $5 from the bank and receives $5 from the owners. The leverage ratio would equal $10 (assets) divided by $5 (shareholders), or 2. The higher the leverage the better for investors, if the company is making money. But the reverse is true if the company is losing money.

Return on equity: Return on equity is one of the key ratios that investors use to gauge the financial health of a company. The higher the return on equity the better. The return on equity measures how fast the company's earnings will grow. Investors like fast earnings growth because it leads to higher dividends, which generate a larger return. The return on equity is equal to the firm's net income divided by shareholder equity (the value of the firm to investors). A good approximation of the shareholders' equity is the book value of the firm (although this isn't true in all cases). Bombardier Inc.'s 1990 earnings per share were $0.09, and divided by the book value per share of $0.58 this gives a 15.5 per cent return on equity.

However, there is a second method for calculating earnings per share. Multiplying the profit margin (3.4 per cent), asset turnover (1.34), and leverage (3.4) ratios for Bombardier together will also generate a return on equity of 15.5 per cent (sometimes there could be a difference due to rounding). Thus, it's essential for investors to monitor the trend of earnings. The earnings trend can be explained by the firm's trend in profit margin, asset turnover, and leverage.

In turn, we can relate return on equity to earnings per share. If you multiply return on equity (15.5 per cent) by book value per share ($0.58) you get earnings per share of $0.09. The higher the return on equity, the faster the growth of earnings per share. Ultimately, this will lead to higher shareholder value.

Dividend per share: The dividend per share is equal to the amount of income that the investor receives from holding a share of the company's stock. Companies pay dividends from earnings. Thus, higher earnings can sustain higher dividends. Higher dividends provide investors with more income. Companies' dividend policies vary depending on their ability to pay and their growth prospects.

Dividend yield: The dividend yield is equal to the dividend per share divided by the stock price for the company. In 1990 Bombardier paid a dividend of $.02. Dividing this dividend by the share price of $1.02 generates a dividend yield of 2 per cent. A higher yield is better for investors, but higher dividend payments will also deplete the company's cash, which it could reinvest in the company and ensure future sustained growth.

Best of the Best Blue-Chip Stocks for Canadians

The Toronto Stock Exchange has created several indices for use in analyzing various groups of stocks. These indices cover all major sectors of the Canadian economy. The TSE monitors and adjusts these indices to take into consideration current information.

The 30 companies described and analyzed in this chapter are all included in the TSE 300 Index, and they have proven their ability to add shareholder value. Some of these companies have generated better returns than others, but each company is considered a leader within its industry. Each company has reasonable prospects for the future, is reasonably priced, and should offer investors future growth potential. Each sector within the TSE 300 is represented at least once, with two exceptions—pipelines and paper and forest products. Investors should remember that the risk associated with investing in equities is very high. Therefore you should build a portfolio of stocks to diversify your risk.

BLUE-CHIP STOCKS FOR THE NEW MILLENNIUM

Company name	Ticker symbol	Style	Page number
Alcan Aluminum	AL	Value	192
Aliant	AIT	Value	194
Bank of Montreal	BMO	Value	196
Barrick Gold	ABX	Growth	198
BCE	BCE	Value	200
Bell Canada International	BI	Growth	202
Biovail	BVF	Growth	204
Bombardier	BBD.b	Value	206
Canadian National Railways	CNR	Value	208
Canadian Natural Resources	CNQ	Value	210
Canadian Pacific	CP	Value	212
Celestica	CLS	Growth	214
C-MAC Industries	CMS	Growth	216
Cognos	CSN	Growth	218
Four Seasons Hotels	FSH	Value	220
Loblaw Companies	L	Growth	222
Magna International	MG.a	Value	224
Manulife Financial	MFC	Value	226
Nortel Networks	NT	Growth	228
Onex	OCX	Growth	230

continued

Company name	Ticker symbol	Style	Page number
Petro-Canada	PCA	Growth	232
Power Corporation of Canada	POW	Value	234
Research in Motion	RIM	Growth	236
Rogers Communications	RCI.b	Growth	238
Royal Bank of Canada	RY	Value	240
Sears Canada	SC	Value	242
Sun Life	SLC	Value	244
Suncor Energy	SU	Growth	246
Thomson Corporation	TOC	Growth	248
Toronto-Dominion Bank	TD	Value	250
TrizecHahn	TZH	Growth	252

ALCAN ALUMINUM LIMITED

Company profile

A Canadian company that is one of the world's leading integrated aluminum companies, Alcan operates in over 30 countries and is involved in bauxite mining, power generation, and aluminum refining, smelting, manufacturing, recycling, and research. Alcan has its own electrical generating facilities in Canada and has developed proprietary process technology. The company began operations in 1902 as the Northern Aluminum Company.

Alcan's strategic priorities include strengthening the position of aluminum as the material of choice in the marketplace while aggressively seeking opportunities to maximize shareholder value. The company has established and implemented aggressive new targets for 2000 and beyond. The company is committed to completing the proposed merger of Alcan, Pechiney of France (but not Algroup of Switzerland as initially anticipated) to form a new global leader in the industry. It has encountered some difficulties receiving approval from the European Commission's Merger Task Force (MTF). The two-way merger should significantly improve the operating results of the combined company.

Alcan generated $7.32 billion in sales during 1999 with net income of $460 million—$61 million higher than the net income reported in 1998.

Stock performance

The stock's performance should improve once the merger is complete. Management can then achieve efficiencies, improving the overall firm's profit. The best 12-month rate of return for the stock was a gain of 95.2 per cent, and the average return after 12 months was 12.8 per cent. During the previous 15 years the stock has appreciated in value by an average of 10.5 per cent per year.

Stock risks

Cyclical stocks are riskier than other stocks. The worst 12-month rate of return for Alcan's common stock was a loss of 37.8 per cent. During the bear market of 1994 the stock declined by 10.1 per cent, but regained its losses within three months. Management has done an excellent job negating some of the risk associated with the metals and minerals industry but management has not eliminated the risk—so be careful.

Stock financial fundamentals

Alcan's return on equity has decreased during the previous 10 years due to a decline in leverage and asset turnover. Return on equity can increase significantly from one year to the next if the company can increase its profit margin, improve its asset turnover, and manage its debt prudently.

Future prospects

A cyclical stock can be very rewarding during good times and very painful during bad times. There should be more good times than bad times ahead. Although Alcan is not immune to a global recession, the demand for aluminum should increase, to the benefit of the company and its shareholders. This stock is suitable only for speculative investors who are aware of the above-average risks associated with investing in this industry. Over the long term, Alcan should continue to make impressive gains within a turbulent sector, but it is an old-economy company, which will limit both risk and reward.

COMPANY DETAILS

Company name	**Alcan Aluminum**	Industry classification	Metals and Minerals
Recent price	$46.00	Market capitalization (in $ millions)	$10,068
52-week price range from low to high	$42.90–$67.25	Ticker symbol	AL
Overall assessment of potential risk (one is more risky)	19/30	Phone number for annual report	514-848-8000
Number of mutual funds that hold this stock as a top 15 holding	186	Stock analysis start date	July 1982

ROLLING 12-MONTH TOTAL RATE OF RETURN FOR THE STOCK OVER TIME

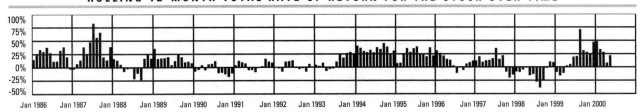

STOCK PERFORMANCE*

	1 month	1 year	3 years	5 years	10 years	15 years
Returns ending June 2000	-8.5%	0.1%	1.2%	4.0%	8.2%	10.5%
Best historical return	22.3%	95.2%	33.3%	28.8%	14.8%	14.8%
Average historical return	1.2%	12.8%	10.2%	10.6%	9.7%	9.9%
Worst historical return	-29.0%	-37.8%	-10.7%	-3.4%	4.5%	5.0%
Value at risk of $1,000	$908	$816	$943	$1,212	$1,793	$2,851

RETURNS GREATER THAN*

	1 month	1 year	3 years	5 years	10 years	15 years
10 per cent	13%	51%	49%	52%	45%	57%
Zero	54%	69%	89%	98%	100%	100%
Percentage of time stock lost $	46%	31%	11%	2%	0%	0%
Number of periods evaluated	216	205	181	157	97	37

DOWNSIDE RISK*

	Worst setback since start date	In bear 1987	In bear 1990	In bear 1994	In bear 1998
Setback for stock	-43.9%	-34.2%	-25.0%	-10.1%	-43.9%
Setback for stock market	-24.6%	-23.2%	-16.3%	-9.7%	-24.6%
Setback ended in	Aug. 1998	Nov. 1987	Nov. 1990	April 1994	Aug. 1998
Months to recover from loss	16	69	33	3	16

STOCK FINANCIAL FUNDAMENTAL INFORMATION

	1990	1991	1992	1993	1994	1995	1996	1997	1998	1999	Change
Average share price	$24.42	$23.69	$23.27	$25.02	$32.80	$40.91	$43.53	$46.74	$41.14	$45.72	11.1%
Earnings per share	$2.70	($0.29)	($0.76)	($0.71)	$0.48	$3.14	$2.37	$2.90	$2.54	$3.09	21.7%
Book value per share	$25.75	$24.47	$24.23	$24.20	$26.90	$27.06	$28.20	$30.64	$36.28	$37.55	3.5%
Price-to-earnings ratio	9.0	-81.7	-30.6	-35.2	68.3	13.0	18.4	16.1	16.2	14.8	-8.6%
Price-to-book ratio	0.9	1.0	1.0	1.0	1.2	1.5	1.5	1.5	1.1	1.2	7.4%
Profit margin	5.8%	-0.7%	-1.8%	-1.7%	0.9%	5.6%	5.2%	6.1%	5.0%	6.2%	24.9%
Asset turnover	.84	.72	.75	.74	.82	.96	.81	0.8	.76	.74	-2.8%
Leverage	2.1	2.3	2.4	2.4	2.3	2.2	2.0	1.9	1.8	1.8	-3.2%
Return on equity	10.5%	-1.2%	-3.1%	-2.9%	1.8%	11.6%	8.4%	9.5%	7.0%	8.2%	17.5%
Dividend per share	$1.31	$0.99	$0.54	$0.41	$0.62	$0.82	$0.83	$0.89	$0.89	$0.90	.2%
Dividend yield	5.3%	4.2%	2.3%	1.5%	1.2%	1.5%	1.9%	1.8%	2.2%	1.9%	-9.8%

*Source: The raw data used in developing this table was provided by Datastream.

ALIANT INC.

Company profile

Bruncor, Island Telecom Inc., Maritime Telegraph and Telephone Company, and NewTel Enterprises Limited combined to form Aliant in July 1999. The company is now a growing communications company that is aggressively pursuing new opportunities. The company is divided into four parts: telecommunications, mobile communications, information technology, and emerging business.

Emerging business is likely Aliant's most exciting division. This area focuses on capitalizing on new, technology-based products and services, including computer telephony integration, TV over copper, high-speed e-commerce, and new media. However, Aliant also focuses on its core stable of products and services. The company's philosophy is to meet and exceed its clients' communications needs. To achieve this goal it continues to add new services to its product line-up. The company plans to continue its aggressive growth strategy by expanding its current client base and by acquiring other companies.

Aliant encompasses four regional telecommunications companies: NBTel, MTT, IslandTel, and NewTel. The companies will operate under their brand names, but will share their back-office operations. This synergy should enhance their operating income and improve their competitive and comparative advantage. Thus far the strategy has paid off, and the proof is in their market share: Aliant holds 86 per cent of the long-distance market, 78 per cent of the mobility market, and a 71 per cent share of the Internet market in Atlantic Canada.

Stock performance

This is a very impressive debut for this newly merged company. During the previous year the company's stock appreciated in value by 66.2 per cent, out-performing a lot of other Canadian investments. If management can build on this great momentum, investors will continue to enjoy similarly great returns. This is not an easy objective to achieve but, considering the company's strengths and unique market position, it is very plausible.

Stock risks

Recently the company's stock encountered a small setback, but over the long term its stock should appreciate in value. The worst one-month rate of return posted by Aliant's stock was a decline of 6.4 per cent; the stock has posted a positive rate of return after one month 75 per cent of the time.

Stock financial fundamentals

The stock is trading at a price-to-earnings ratio of 15.6. This means that it would take investors 15 years to recover their investment if earnings did not grow. Fortunately, Aliant's earnings per share increased by 15.9 per cent during the previous year. This is good for investors.

Future prospects

This telecommunications company operates in one of the fasting-growing and most dynamic industries in the world. It has a strong brand in the markets where it competes and has the backing of BCE, Canada's largest telecommunications company. Aliant also has strong revenue growth, good profit margins, a prudent level of debt, and reasonable valuations. In turn, investors should expect good things from this company, but the future is never certain. Investors should still invest carefully and diversify their portfolio, but this new-economy company should meet their investment expectations.

COMPANY DETAILS

Company name	**Aliant**	Industry classification	Utilities
Recent price	$36.15	Market capitalization (in $ millions)	$4,815
52-week price range from low to high	$21.50–$41.75	Ticker symbol	AIT
Overall assessment of potential risk (one is more risky)	18/30	Phone number for annual report	1-877-248-3113
Number of mutual funds that hold this stock as a top 15 holding	28	Stock analysis start date	July 1999

ROLLING 12-MONTH TOTAL RATE OF RETURN FOR THE STOCK OVER TIME

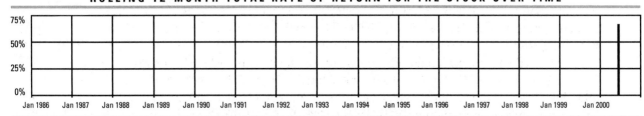

STOCK PERFORMANCE*

	1 month	1 year	3 years	5 years	10 years	15 years
Returns ending June 2000	3.9%	66.2%				
Best historical return	23.9	66.2%				
Average historical return	4.6%	66.2%				
Worst historical return	-6.4%	66.2%				
Value at risk of $1,000	$949	$1,662				

RETURNS GREATER THAN*

	1 month	1 year	3 years	5 years	10 years	15 years
10 per cent	25%	100%				
Zero	75%	100%				
Percentage of time stock lost $	25%	0%				
Number of periods evaluated	12	1				

DOWNSIDE RISK*

	Worst setback since start date	In bear 1987	In bear 1990	In bear 1994	In bear 1998
Setback for stock	-10.3%				
Setback for stock market	0.0%				
Setback ended in	May 2000				
Months to recover from loss	?				

STOCK FINANCIAL FUNDAMENTAL INFORMATION

	1990	1991	1992	1993	1994	1995	1996	1997	1998	1999	Change
Average share price										$ 22.81	
Earnings per share									$ 1.26	$ 1.46	15.9%
Book value per share									$ 8.30	$ 8.74	5.3%
Price-to-earnings ratio										15.6	
Price-to-book ratio										2.6	
Profit margin									9.2%	9.1%	-0.6%
Asset turnover									0.64	0.70	9.4%
Leverage									2.6	2.6	1.2%
Return on equity									15.2%	16.7%	10.1%
Dividend per share									$ 0.76	$ 0.84	10.8%
Dividend yield										3.7%	

*Source: The raw data used in developing this table was provided by Datastream.

BANK OF MONTREAL

Company profile

The Bank of Montreal is a major Canadian chartered bank that operates more than 1,000 branches in all the provinces and territories of Canada and around the world. BMO offers a full range of commercial, corporate, government, international, investment, and retail banking products and services. A wholly-owned subsidiary, Nesbitt Burns, provides brokerage, underwriting, and investment management services. BMO also offers financial services across the U.S. through wholly-owned Harris Bankcorp and has interests in other financial service companies.

The bank can trace its history to the early 1800s, when it opened its first branch in the heart of the business district in Montreal. From the early days of lending to fur traders, the bank has established a dynamic global network that includes 32 lines of business. It introduced the first virtual bank in North America, mbanx, which provides clients with full-service banking over the Internet.

In 1999 the bank generated sales of over $7.9 billion and achieved a net income of more than $1.3 billion. The bank currently derives more than 50 per cent of its earnings from operations outside of Canada and is aggressively pursuing offshore growth.

Stock performance

The banks are back! Since Paul Martin disallowed the merger between BMO and the Royal Bank, both have struggled to add shareholder value. However, after a year of restructuring, they once again earned record-breaking profits. During the previous year BMO's stock appreciated in value by 21.2 per cent. The best 12-month rate of return for the stock was a gain of 83.0 percent, and the average rate of return after 12 months was 17.6 per cent. During the previous 15 years the stock has appreciated in value by an average of 15.7 per cent per year.

Stock risks

Since achieving its all-time high in 1998, BMO stock consistently declined in value until February of 2000. From peak to trough the stock declined in value by 42.6 per cent, while the stock market in general appreciated in value. But the worst is likely over. Expect a sharp comeback.

Stock financial fundamentals

With profit margins of 16 per cent and a return on equity of 13.7 per cent, this bank can generate large amounts of cash flow and profits. With a very low price-to-earnings multiple, this stock looks very cheap from a historical perspective.

Future prospects

This stock is very reasonably valued. With a new president and an unclear strategy, many investors decided to take their money elsewhere during the last year. However, things are back on track with a prudent Internet strategy, expansion into the United States, and a very profitable branch network. Conservative and aggressive investors alike could consider this stock for a portion of their investment portfolio. With a dividend yield of 3.3 per cent and positive earnings-per-share growth, the stock should appreciate in value.

COMPANY DETAILS

Company name	Bank of Montreal	Industry classification	Financial Services
Recent price	$62.50	Market capitalization (in $ millions)	$16,752
52-week price range from low to high	$42.00–$65.80	Ticker symbol	BMO
Overall assessment of potential risk (one is more risky)	31/30	Phone number for annual report	416-867-6785
Number of mutual funds that hold this stock as a top 15 holding	483	Stock analysis start date	July 1982

ROLLING 12-MONTH TOTAL RATE OF RETURN FOR THE STOCK OVER TIME

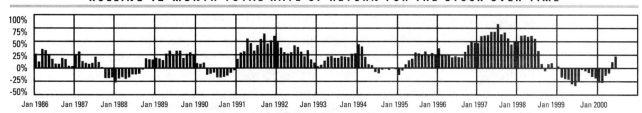

STOCK PERFORMANCE*

	1 month	1 year	3 years	5 years	10 years	15 years
Returns ending June 2000	3.3%	21.2%	8.3%	20.9%	21.2%	15.7%
Best historical return	15.8%	83.0%	47.3%	33.4%	26.5%	19.8%
Average historical return	1.6%	17.6%	17.5%	16.6%	16.8%	17.0%
Worst historical return	-24.7%	-32.1%	-3.4%	1.7%	11.0%	14.0%
Value at risk of $1,000	$929	$813	$1,017	$1,264	$3,241	$8,193

RETURNS GREATER THAN*

	1 month	1 year	3 years	5 years	10 years	15 years
10 per cent	7%	60%	73%	77%	100%	100%
Zero	61%	73%	95%	100%	100%	100%
Percentage of time stock lost $	39%	27%	5%	0%	0%	0%
Number of periods evaluated	216	205	181	157	97	37

DOWNSIDE RISK*

	Worst setback since start date	In bear 1987	In bear 1990	In bear 1994	In bear 1998
Setback for stock	-42.6%	-30.2%	-23.7%	-20.9%	-32.4%
Setback for stock market	0.0%	-23.2%	-16.3%	-9.7%	-24.6%
Setback ended in	Feb. 2000	Nov. 1987	April 1990	June 1994	Sept. 1998
Months to recover from loss	?	20	9	11	?

STOCK FINANCIAL FUNDAMENTAL INFORMATION

	1990	1991	1992	1993	1994	1995	1996	1997	1998	1999	Change
Average share price	$13.89	$18.18	$22.50	$25.20	$25.73	$28.58	$35.02	$54.77	$70.13	$57.16	-18.5%
Earnings per share	$2.10	$2.31	$2.38	$2.59	$3.01	$3.45	$4.21	$4.69	$4.72	$4.76	$ 0.8
Book value per share	$15	$16.05	$17.69	$19.41	$21.39	$23.41	$25.89	$29.18	$32.71	$34.87	$ 6.6
Price-to-earnings ratio	6.6	7.9	9.5	9.7	8.5	8.3	8.3	11.7	14.9	12.0	-19.2%
Price-to-book ratio	0.9	1.1	1.3	1.3	1.2	1.2	1.4	1.9	2.1	1.6	-23.5%
Profit margin	13.0%	13.8%	13.0%	13.2%	14.6%	16.2%	17.7%	17.0%	17.0%	16.0%	-6.3%
Asset turnover	0.4	0.4	0.4	0.4	0.4	0.4	0.4	0.3	0.3	0.3	5.1%
Leverage	25.8	26.2	25.5	24.3	25.6	24.4	25.1	27.3	25.9	24.9	-3.9%
Return on equity	14.0%	14.4%	13.5%	13.3%	14.1%	14.7%	16.3%	16.1%	14.4%	13.7%	-5.4%
Dividend per share	$ 1.06	$ 1.06	$ 1.06	$ 1.12	$ 1.20	$ 1.32	$ 1.48	$ 1.64	$ 1.76	$ 1.88	6.8%
Dividend yield	7.6%	5.8%	4.7%	4.4%	4.7%	4.6%	4.2%	3.0%	2.5%	3.3%	31.1%

*Source: The raw data used in developing this table was provided by Datastream.

BARRICK GOLD CORPORATION

Company profile

Barrick Gold Corporation is a major gold producer with extensive interests in North and South America, including mines in the U.S., Canada, Peru, and Chile. It was formed through a merger of CamFlo Mines Ltd., Bob-Claire Investments, and the former Barrick Resources. The company generates revenue by exploring for and producing gold, which they sell in the market. It earns a profit if it can sell gold at a price higher than the cost of producing it. When gold prices were high, a gold company could spend a lot of money producing gold and still generate a profit. But gold prices have declined for years as the fundamentals for the industry deteriorated, partly because of central banks selling their inventory. Barrick Gold, however, has generated significant profits with its aggressive cost controls and hedging programs. Barrick is also a low-cost producer, with cash operating costs per ounce of $195.

In 1999 Barrick generated more than $2 billion from the sale of gold, posted a profit of $483 million and produced more than 3.66 million ounces of gold.

Stock performance

Depending on your timing, you could have either made or lost a fortune in the short term on Barrick stock. Its best three-year rate of return was a gain of 104.9 per cent annualized, and the average annualized three-year rate of return was 29.1 per cent. During the previous 10 years, the stock has appreciated in value by an average of 9.7 per cent per year. This is a cyclical stock in the resource sector, which is ignored by most growth investors, who prefer technology over resources. This is currently putting a lot of downward pressure on resource stocks.

Stock risk

This stock has exhibited a lot of upside and downside volatility, so don't ignore the risk or the opportunity. During the bear market of 1998, Barrick stock declined in value by 49.1 per cent and it still hasn't recovered, while the average Canadian equity investment declined in value by 24.6 per cent.

Stock financial fundamentals

Profits go up but the price of the stock keeps going down. In turn, the price-to-earnings multiple of the stock has declined to 22.6, less than the market as a whole and a lot less than richly valued technology stocks. The profit margins for this company are high, at 22.6 per cent, but asset turnover is low. During 9 out of the previous 10 years the company reported a profit and management is committed to generating profits in the future.

Future prospects

If the price of gold appreciates in value this stock will soar. Unfortunately, the likelihood of gold appreciating in value is very low. There is an oversupply of gold, which depresses the price along with investors' appetite for gold stocks. But Barrick can generate good profits, and eventually this will be reflected in the price of the stock.

COMPANY DETAILS

Company name	**Barrick Gold**	Industry classification	Gold & Silver
Recent price	$26.75	Market capitalization (in $ millions)	$10,583
52-week price range from low to high	$22.50–$38.20	Ticker symbol	ABX
Overall assessment of potential risk (one is more risky)	9/30	Phone number for annual report	1-800-720-7415
Number of mutual funds that hold this stock as a top 15 holding	91	Stock analysis start date	June 1983

ROLLING 12-MONTH TOTAL RATE OF RETURN FOR THE STOCK OVER TIME

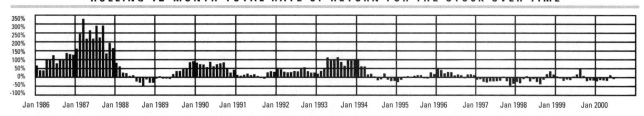

STOCK PERFORMANCE*

	1 month	1 year	3 years	5 years	10 years	15 years
Returns ending June 2000	-2.4%	-4.7%	-2.8%	-4.3%	9.7%	26.7%
Best historical return	50.9%	326.2%	104.9%	69.1%	45.9%	26.8%
Average historical return	2.1%	32.6%	29.1%	28.0%	28.4%	24.6%
Worst historical return	-38.9%	-45.3%	-16.0%	-9.1%	8.5%	21.4%
Value at risk of $1,000	$857	$731	$713	$808	$2,706	$22,966

RETURNS GREATER THAN*

	1 month	1 year	3 years	5 years	10 years	15 years
10 per cent	21%	54%	71%	78%	95%	100%
Zero	54%	65%	79%	83%	100%	100%
Percentage of time stock lost $	46%	35%	21%	17%	0%	0%
Number of periods evaluated	205	194	170	146	86	26

DOWNSIDE RISK*

	Worst setback since start date	In bear 1987	In bear 1990	In bear 1994	In bear 1998
Setback for stock	-52.3%	-38.9%	-15.3%	-24.9%	-49.1%
Setback for stock market	-24.6%	-23.2%	-16.3%	-9.7%	-24.6%
Setback ended in	Aug. 1998	Oct. 1987	April 1990	Jan. 1995	Aug. 1998
Months to recover from loss	?	27	2	12	?

STOCK FINANCIAL FUNDAMENTAL INFORMATION

	1990	1991	1992	1993	1994	1995	1996	1997	1998	1999	Change
Average share price	$11.19	$12.64	$16.79	$28.78	$32.86	$33.70	$39.11	$31.92	$28.68	$27.86	-2.9%
Earnings per share	$0.26	$0.39	$0.79	$0.99	$1.07	$1.13	$0.82	($0.46)	$1.19	$1.23	3.6%
Book value per share	$2.79	$3.45	$4.45	$5.50	$9.81	$11.26	$12.87	$12.74	$14.58	$15.82	8.5%
Price-to-earnings ratio	43.0	32.4	21.3	29.1	30.7	29.8	47.7	-69.4	24.1	22.6	-6.2%
Price-to-book ratio	4.0	3.7	3.8	5.2	3.3	3.0	3.0	2.5	2.0	1.8	-10.5%
Profit margin	23.2%	26.7%	32.5%	31.9%	26.7%	22.9%	16.8%	-9.6%	23.4%	22.6%	-3.3%
Asset turnover	.22	.26	.36	.41	.27	.36	.29	.29	.27	.27	-0.5%
Leverage	1.8	1.6	1.5	1.4	1.5	1.2	1.3	1.3	1.3	1.3	-0.8%
Return on equity	9.3%	11.3%	17.8%	18.0%	10.9%	10.0%	6.4%	-3.6%	8.2%	7.8%	-4.5%
Dividend per share	$ 0.05	$ 0.06	$ 0.19	$ 0.11	$ 0.13	$ 0.12	$ 0.19	$ 0.22	$ 0.27	$ 0.30	10.0%
Dividend yield	0.4%	0.5%	1.1%	0.4%	0.4%	0.4%	0.5%	0.7%	0.9%	1.1%	13.2%

*Source: The raw data used in developing this table was provided by Datastream.

BCE INCORPORATED

Company profile

More than 500,000 investors and 350 mutual funds own this stock. As Canada's largest telecommunications company, BCE Inc. is the parent of Bell Canada, Bell Canada International, Teleglobe, CGI, and other subsidiaries. Through them, BCE designs, manufactures, and markets telecommunications equipment, including cellular phones and paging equipment, and provides telecommunications and directory services. Nortel Networks was one of BCE's most successful subsidiaries, and its value distorted BCE's financial profile. To realize the true value of the whole firm, its executives decided during the previous year to offer investors 1.58 shares of Nortel Networks for each BCE share they owned. This butterfly restructuring allowed BCE investors to own an investment in Nortel Networks directly instead of an investment in Nortel through BCE shares. In turn, BCE's share price appreciated because of the restructuring.

Alexander Graham Bell's initial experiments led to the formation of Bell Telephone in 1880. Since then the company has diversified and grown into one of Canada's largest and most successful companies. During 1999 BCE generated more than $14.2 billion in sales and a profit of $1.9 billion. The company recently acquired CTV, a broadcasting company, which will complement their media division. With additional investments in telephone services, satellite television, and Internet services, BCE is determined to meet its growth objectives.

Stock performance

Recently this stock has soared to new heights. Its best 12-month rate of return was a gain of 175.1 per cent, and the average rate of return after 12 months was 24 per cent. During the previous 15 years the stock has appreciated in value by an average of 18.7 per cent per year. BCE has historically posted above-average gains, and it continues to pursue new growth strategies. If these strategies work, investors will be rewarded.

Stock risks

During the bear market of 1998 the stock declined in value by 35.9 per cent. During the same period, the average Canadian equity investment declined in value by 24.6 per cent. The stock took four months to recover its loss. In general, BCE has experienced less downside risk than the average stock.

Stock financial fundamentals

The stock's fundamentals do not include any of the results generated by BCE's former subsidiary Nortel Networks. However, investors should treat the fundamentals section with some caution since the average price is very different than the current price, which will distort the ratios. BCE is trading at a very reasonable price, likely because investors are concerned about the future.

Future prospects

BCE Inc. is not immune to a Canadian or global recession, but top management has proven it can add value for shareholders in both the short and long term. However, it's the future that counts. BCE has some great assets and management has to use them prudently as a foundation to add shareholder value.

COMPANY DETAILS

Company name	**BCE**	Industry classification	Utilities
Recent price	$35.10	Market capitalization (in $ millions)	$22,608
52-week price range from low to high	$31.80–$38.00	Ticker symbol	BCE
Overall assessment of potential risk (one is more risky)	17/30	Phone number for annual report	1-800-339-6353
Number of mutual funds that hold this stock as a top 15 holding	15	Stock analysis start date	July 1982

ROLLING 12-MONTH TOTAL RATE OF RETURN FOR THE STOCK OVER TIME

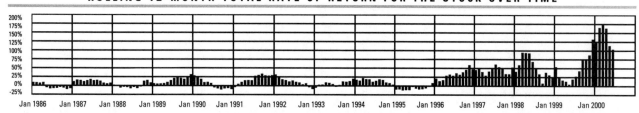

STOCK PERFORMANCE*

	1 month	1 year	3 years	5 years	10 years	15 years
Returns ending June 2000	1.1%	102.2%	58.4%	49.8%	26.9%	18.7%
Best historical return	32.9%	175.1%	82.6%	57.4%	29.7%	21.5%
Average historical return	1.9%	24.0%	18.0%	14.9%	13.6%	16.9%
Worst historical return	-17.1%	-10.8%	0.4%	3.0%	5.6%	13.2%
Value at risk of $1,000	$936	$930	$1,079	$1,287	$1,867	$7,450

RETURNS GREATER THAN*

	1 month	1 year	3 years	5 years	10 years	15 years
10 per cent	8%	63%	61%	59%	72%	100%
Zero	63%	81%	100%	100%	100%	100%
Percentage of time stock lost $	37%	19%	0%	0%	0%	0%
Number of periods evaluated	216	205	181	157	97	37

DOWNSIDE RISK*

	Worst setback since start date	In bear 1987	In bear 1990	In bear 1994	In bear 1998
Setback for stock	-35.9%	-12.9%	-18.7%	-12.6%	-35.9%
Setback for stock market	-23.0%	-23.2%	-16.3%	-9.7%	-24.6%
Setback ended in	Sept. 1998	Nov. 1987	Sept. 1990	Jan. 1995	Sept. 1998
Months to recover from loss	4	18	8	12	4

STOCK FINANCIAL FUNDAMENTAL INFORMATION

	1990	1991	1992	1993	1994	1995	1996	1997	1998	1999	Change
Average share price	$4.89	$5.33	$5.57	$5.50	$5.85	$5.39	$6.77	$9.47	$13.63	$18.85	38.3%
Earnings per share					$1.76	$1.12	$1.70	$2.11	$1.60	$1.75	9.4%
Book value per share					$16.41	$16.18	$16.62	$12.74	$18.75	$25.20	34.4%
Price-to-earnings ratio					3.3	4.8	4.0	4.5	8.5	10.8	26.4%
Price-to-book ratio					0.4	0.3	0.4	0.7	0.7	0.7	2.9%
Profit margin					5.0%	2.8%	3.8%	3.9%	3.7%	7.9%	111.1%
Asset turnover					0.57	0.63	0.68	0.85	8.46	3.85	-54.5%
Leverage					3.8	3.9	3.9	5.0	0.3	0.2	-15.2%
Return on equity					10.7%	6.9%	10.2%	-16.6%	8.5%	6.9%	-18.6%
Dividend per share					$1.34	$1.36	$1.36	$1.36	$1.36	$1.36	0.0%
Dividend yield					22.9%	25.2%	20.1%	14.4%	10.0%	7.2%	-27.7%

*Source: The raw data used in developing this table was provided by Datastream.

BELL CANADA INTERNATIONAL

Company profile

This company's objective is to develop leading-edge communication companies in markets outside of Canada. It focuses primarily on Latin America and the Asia Pacific. BCE is a major shareholder, and as a major Canadian communications company, BCE sees a strategic fit for Bell Canada International within the BCE family of companies.

Bell Canada International (BCI) operates in the telecommunications sector. The trend in this sector is toward consolidation as companies strive to meet the enormous and growing demand for voice and broadband data communications in Asia and Latin America. BCI will focus on four key strategies: First, it will provide broadband access and services to business and residential customers. Second, it will attempt to meet the demand for alternative voice services. Third, it will align itself with competent partners to maximize economies and improve its understanding of local markets. Fourth, it will become a self-financed organization.

In 1999, BCI changed leadership from Derek Burney to Michael Sabia, who joined BCI from a major North American transportation company. In 1999 it increased its total number of subscribers to 5.5 million, a significant jump from 1998, but still lost a lot of money in the short term.

Stock performance

Investors like BCI's business model, because, when a business model works, a company can make a lot of money for shareholders. During the previous year, BCI's stock appreciated in value by 129.9 per cent, although its average 12-month rate of return was a gain of 15.7 per cent. The environment in which this company operates holds potential for both failure and success. But with the backing of BCE, Canada's largest telecommunications company, success is certainly a likely possibility.

Stock risks

During the bear market of 1998, BCI's stock declined in value by 62.5 per cent. During the same time period, the average Canadian equity investment declined in value by 24.6 per cent. BCI stock took 17 months to recover its loss. This stock is highly risky, but highly risky stocks also have the potential to generate higher returns.

Stock financial fundamentals

The recent price appreciation in this stock has increased the stock's valuation. Its overall assessment of potential risk is very high. In addition, the company has been incurring some large losses. This could hamper future growth and the ultimate rate of return earned by investors.

Future prospects

Operating in Latin American countries introduces political, economic, and business risks, which all have to be managed. However, considering the populations of those regions who still need to acquire phones and telecommunications equipment, the future potential is huge. Aggressive investors should invest cautiously and be prepared for some volatility along the way. The fundamentals are good; make sure the price is right.

COMPANY DETAILS

Company name	**Bell Canada International**	Industry classification	Utilities
Recent price	$43.00	Market capitalization (in $ millions)	$3,391
52-week price range from low to high	$14.50–$48.75	Ticker symbol	BI
Overall assessment of potential risk (one is more risky)	3/30	Phone number for annual report	514-392-2323
Number of mutual funds that hold this stock as a top 15 holding	5	Stock analysis start date	October 1997

ROLLING 12-MONTH TOTAL RATE OF RETURN FOR THE STOCK OVER TIME

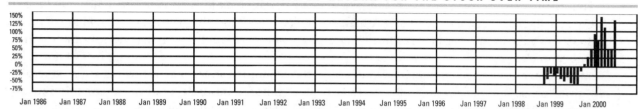

Jan 1986 Jan 1987 Jan 1988 Jan 1989 Jan 1990 Jan 1991 Jan 1992 Jan 1993 Jan 1994 Jan 1995 Jan 1996 Jan 1997 Jan 1998 Jan 1999 Jan 2000

STOCK PERFORMANCE*

	1 month	1 year	3 years	5 years	10 years	15 years
Returns ending June 2000	36.3%	129.9%				
Best historical return	36.3%	139.2%				
Average historical return	3.1%	15.7%				
Worst historical return	-42.6%	-46.8%				
Value at risk of $1,000	$821	$538				

RETURNS GREATER THAN*

	1 month	1 year	3 years	5 years	10 years	15 years
10 per cent	36%	41%				
Zero	48%	45%				
Percentage of time stock lost $	52%	55%				
Number of periods evaluated	33	22				

DOWNSIDE RISK*

	Worst setback since start date	In bear 1987	In bear 1990	In bear 1994	In bear 1998
Setback for stock	-62.5%				-62.5%
Setback for stock market	-23.0%				-24.6%
Setback ended in	Sept. 1998				Sept. 1998
Months to recover from loss	17				17

STOCK FINANCIAL FUNDAMENTAL INFORMATION

	1990	1991	1992	1993	1994	1995	1996	1997	1998	1999	Change
Average share price								$23.60	$24.96	$20.15	-19.3%
Earnings per share							($0.57)	($0.92)	($0.83)	($6.10)	634.9%
Book value per share							$3.33	$7.80	$6.83	$4.61	-32.5%
Price-to-earnings ratio								(25.7)	(30.1)	(3.3)	-89.0%
Price-to-book ratio								3.0	3.7	4.4	19.6%
Profit margin							-11.8%	-13.9%	-8.5%	-59.6%	602.6%
Asset turnover							.28	.26	.26	.22	-16.6%
Leverage							5.1	3.2	5.5	10.1	85.9%
Return on equity							-17.1%	-11.8%	-12.2%	-132.3%	988.9%
Dividend per share							$ –	$ –	$–	$ –	0.0%
Dividend yield								0.0%	0.0%	0.0%	0.0%

*Source: The raw data used in developing this table was provided by Datastream.

BIOVAIL CORPORATION

Company profile

Biovail Corporation International is a unique Canadian company that creates generic formulations of medications. This company offers investors an interesting opportunity to participate in the pharmaceutical sector of the economy. Biovail is a full-service pharmaceutical company. It applies proprietary drug delivery technologies in developing oral controlled-release products. Biovail applies its technology to patent-free drugs, improving branded versions, and created generic oral controlled-release products.

In Canada, Biovail sells its products directly through its Canadian sales and marketing division. In the rest of North America, Europe, and more than 50 other countries, it sells through partnerships and licensing agreements with some of the world's largest pharmaceutical companies. Thus far, Biovail has developed 17 different drug products and is currently working on 16 new ones. In 1999, the company generated more than $250 million in revenue and posted a profit of more than $42 million—a direct result of a great profit margin.

Stock performance

Wow! When things go right investors certainly prosper, although investors should remember that the record reflects only the past. Investors should maintain a realistic outlook on the future, which means they shouldn't expect the same rates of return as in the past. Nevertheless, the best 12-month rate of return for the stock was a gain of 874.5 per cent, and the average rate of return after 12 months was 151.5 per cent. During the previous year the stock appreciated in value by 121.9 per cent.

Stock risks

The worst 12-month return posted by this stock was a decline of 17.5 per cent, and the stock declined in value after 12 months 17.5 per cent of the time. During the bear market of 1998, the stock declined in value by 38.7 per cent. During the same time period, the average Canadian equity investment declined in value by 24.6 per cent. Biovail stock took nine months to recover its loss.

Stock financial fundamentals

High profit margins lead to big profits, and this company has generated both. The company generated earnings per share of $1.81 during 1999, an increase of 43.7 per cent over 1998. The stock's price-to-earnings ratio is 20.6, a reasonable valuation considering the company's historical growth and great profit margins.

Future prospects

The company's core strengths are innovation and creativity, which enable it to develop new products for future growth. The company also employs a unique business model, which has generated above-average profit margins, although they have declined recently. In the future, the changing demographics of the baby boomers should ensure lots of demand for this company's products. The biggest risk to its stock is changes in technology. Biovail must ensure it remains on the leading edge, but not on the bleeding edge.

COMPANY DETAILS

Company name	**Biovail**	Industry classification	Consumer Products
Recent price	$82.65	Market capitalization (in $ millions)	$5,050
52-week price range from low to high	$34.52–$104.00	Ticker symbol	BVF
Overall assessment of potential risk (one is more risky)	15/30	Phone number for annual report	416-285-6000
Number of mutual funds that hold this stock as a top 15 holding	57	Stock analysis start date	May 1994

ROLLING 12-MONTH TOTAL RATE OF RETURN FOR THE STOCK OVER TIME

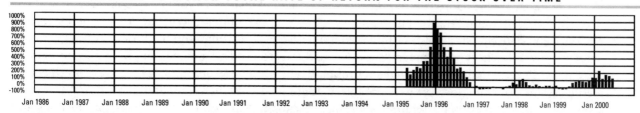

Jan 1986 Jan 1987 Jan 1988 Jan 1989 Jan 1990 Jan 1991 Jan 1992 Jan 1993 Jan 1994 Jan 1995 Jan 1996 Jan 1997 Jan 1998 Jan 1999 Jan 2000

STOCK PERFORMANCE*

	1 month	1 year	3 years	5 years	10 years	15 years
Returns ending June 2000	16.0%	121.9%	58.2%	81.0%		
Best historical return	47.5%	874.5%	151.8%	108.7%		
Average historical return	7.1%	151.5%	71.7%	91.0%		
Worst historical return	-33.0%	-17.5%	6.2%	79.1%		
Value at risk of $1,000	$856	$855	$1,432	$19,136		

RETURNS GREATER THAN*

	1 month	1 year	3 years	5 years	10 years	15 years
10 per cent	41%	76%	97%	100%		
Zero	69%	83%	100%	100%		
Percentage of time stock lost $	31%	17%	0%	0%		
Number of periods evaluated	74	63	39	15		

DOWNSIDE RISK*

	Worst setback since start date	In bear 1987	In bear 1990	In bear 1994	In bear 1998
Setback for stock	-38.7%			-7.5%	-38.7%
Setback for stock market	-23.0%			-5.9%	-24.6%
Setback ended in	Sept. 1998			Dec. 1994	Sept. 1998
Months to recover from loss	9			1	9

STOCK FINANCIAL FUNDAMENTAL INFORMATION

	1990	1991	1992	1993	1994	1995	1996	1997	1998	1999	Change
Average share price					$1.55	$5.61	$19.93	$19.63	$25.58	$37.23	45.5%
Earnings per share						$0.05	$0.63	$0.96	$1.26	$1.81	43.7%
Book value per share						$0.13	$1.00	$2.02	$1.58	$12.62	698.7%
Price-to-earnings ratio						112.2	31.6	20.4	20.3	20.6	1.3%
Price-to-book ratio						43.2	19.9	9.7	16.2	3.0	-81.8%
Profit margin						27.8%	35.4%	43.0%	40.0%	35.4%	-11.4%
Asset turnover						0.33	1.12	0.85	0.55	0.28	-48.3%
Leverage						4.3	1.6	1.3	3.6	1.4	-60.7%
Return on equity						38.5%	63.0%	47.5%	79.7%	14.3%	-82.0%
Dividend per share						$–	$–	$–	$–	$–	0.0%
Dividend yield						0.0%	0.0%	0.0%	0.0%	0.0%	0.0%

*Source: The raw data used in developing this table was provided by Datastream.

BOMBARDIER INCORPORATED

Company profile

As a Canadian and as an investor you have to love this all-Canadian company. Bombardier is one of Canada's biggest and most impressive success stories. In 1937, Joseph-Armand Bombardier, a Quebec inventor and entrepreneur, produced a snowmobile to make it easier to travel during the harsh Quebec winters. Five years later, he founded l'Auto-Neige Bombardier to manufacture the vehicles.

Currently the company has five main groups: Transportation Equipment manufactures rail transit vehicles and diesel engine components for customers such as GO Transit and the Toronto Transit Commission. Aerospace manufactures surveillance systems and aircraft. (This group is going gangbusters.) Motorized Consumer Products manufactures snowmobiles, recreational watercraft, and small gasoline engines. Bombardier Services provides technical support services for aviation customers and for snow-grooming equipment. Bombardier Capital provides financial and real estate services.

Bombardier generates 90 per cent of its sales outside Canada, primarily in the U.S. and Europe. 1999 was a record year for this company. Net income was up 30 per cent, to $718 million, revenue was up 18 per cent, to $13.6 billion, and the backlog of orders was up 7 per cent, to $27.2 billion. The company benefited from increased profit margins and a large turnaround in the recreational products division.

Stock performance

Investors in the common stock of Bombardier have been richly rewarded, and that includes employees. There are more millionaire employees working at Bombardier than at any other company in Canada.

The best three-year rate of return for the stock was a gain of 90.2 percent annualized, and the average annualized three-year rate of return was 37.5 per cent. During the previous 10 years the stock has appreciated in value by an average of 34.6 per cent. Historically, Bombardier has set the standards to which its competitors aspire.

Stock risks

The road to success for Bombardier has included several setbacks. The worst 12-month return posted by this stock was a decline of 34.5 per cent. The stock declined in value after 12 months 14 per cent of the time.

Stock financial fundamentals

Bombardier has had a phenomenal run, and it shows no signs of letting up. However, with success the common stock has become increasingly more expensive. This growth has increased the price-to-earnings (P/E) ratio for the company from 11.3 in 1990 to 23 in 1999. Thus investors are currently paying $23 for every $1 of historical earnings. This growth can be attributed to Bombardier's high return on equity, its large increase in sales, and a decline in interest rates.

Future prospects

Bombardier will continue to be a great Canadian success story. Almost weekly, it announces one achievement after another. However, Bombardier will have to continue to find and exploit significant avenues of growth to fuel its upward momentum. If it doesn't, investors may experience new levels of downside risk. In the new global economy, Bombardier must continue to generate the growth required to justify a stock price of $40.20, a task that Bombardier is more than capable of achieving.

COMPANY DETAILS

Company name	**Bombardier**	Industry classification	Industrial Products
Recent price	$40.20	Market capitalization (in $ millions)	$27,622
52-week price range from low to high	$18.95–$43.10	Ticker symbol	BBD.b
Overall assessment of potential risk (one is more risky)	20/30	Phone number for annual report	514-861-9481 ext. 390
Number of mutual funds that hold this stock as a top 15 holding	403	Stock analysis start date	July 1982

ROLLING 12-MONTH TOTAL RATE OF RETURN FOR THE STOCK OVER TIME

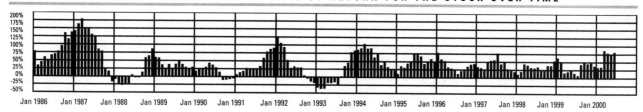

STOCK PERFORMANCE*

	1 month	1 year	3 years	5 years	10 years	15 years
Returns ending June 2000	2.7%	80.2%	38.2%	38.3%	34.6%	38.0%
Best historical return	37.8%	177.5%	90.2%	63.3%	41.4%	39.4%
Average historical return	3.2%	41.4%	37.5%	35.8%	33.5%	36.7%
Worst historical return	-25.0%	-34.5%	6.6%	17.2%	24.5%	34.4%
Value at risk of $1,000	$900	$840	$1,502	$2,626	$11,554	$85,891

RETURNS GREATER THAN*

	1 month	1 year	3 years	5 years	10 years	15 years
10 per cent	20%	82%	98%	100%	100%	100%
Zero	63%	86%	100%	100%	100%	100%
Percentage of time stock lost $	37%	14%	0%	0%	0%	0%
Number of periods evaluated	216	205	181	157	97	37

DOWNSIDE RISK*

	Worst setback since start date	In bear 1987	In bear 1990	In bear 1994	In bear 1998
Setback for stock	-45.5%	-45.5%	-28.0%	-8.3%	-19.7%
Setback for stock market	-19.2%	-23.2%	-16.3%	-9.7%	-24.6%
Setback ended in	Dec. 1987	Dec. 1987	Nov. 1990	Jan. 1995	Aug. 1998
Months to recover from loss	10	10	6	1	4

STOCK FINANCIAL FUNDAMENTAL INFORMATION

	1990	1991	1992	1993	1994	1995	1996	1997	1998	1999	Change
Average share price	$1.02	$1.33	$1.76	$1.70	$2.65	$3.83	$5.06	$7.06	$9.14	$11.71	28.1%
Earnings per share	$0.09	$0.09	$0.11	$0.14	$0.18	$0.11	$0.29	$0.29	$0.38	$0.51	34.2%
Book value per share	$0.58	$0.71	$0.77	$1.02	$1.21	$1.24	$1.62	$1.78	$2.20	$2.43	10.5%
Price-to-earnings ratio	11.3	14.8	16.0	12.1	14.7	34.8	17.4	24.3	24.1	23.0	-4.5%
Price-to-book ratio	1.8	1.9	2.3	1.7	2.2	3.1	3.1	4.0	4.2	4.8	16.0%
Profit margin	3.4%	3.4%	3.0%	3.6%	4.0%	2.1%	4.9%	4.6%	4.5%	5.1%	14.0%
Asset turnover	1.34	1.00	1.04	1.07	1.08	1.11	1.00	0.81	0.81	0.80	-0.7%
Leverage	3.4	3.8	4.5	3.5	3.4	3.9	3.7	4.4	4.8	5.1	7.4%
Return on equity	15.5%	12.7%	14.3%	13.7%	14.9%	8.9%	17.9%	16.3%	17.3%	21.0%	21.5%
Dividend per share	$0.02	$0.02	$0.03	$0.03	$0.04	$0.05	$0.05	$0.08	$0.09	$0.11	22.0%
Dividend yield	2.0%	1.5%	1.7%	1.8%	1.5%	1.3%	1.0%	1.1%	1.0%	0.9%	-4.6%

*Source: The raw data used in developing this table was provided by Datastream.

CANADIAN NATIONAL RAILWAYS

Company profile

Canadian National Railways operates Canada's largest railway system, with more than 15,777 miles of track through out North America. CN's rail network serves all five of Canada's major ports: Halifax, Montreal, Thunder Bay, Prince Rupert, and Vancouver. Its three major businesses are Merchandise, Bulk, and Intermodal & Automotive. CN moves forest products, grain and grain products, coal, sulphur, and fertilizers over 143, 613 miles for over 5,000 customers across North America.

The company was incorporated in 1919, but its history goes back to the first railways in Canada. Formerly a Crown corporation, CN went public through an initial public offering in December 1995 that generated proceeds of over $2.2 billion for the Canadian government. The company's merger with Illinois Central was approved and completed in 1999 and the company is currently attempting to receive approval from the U.S. Surface Transportation Board to merge with Burlington Northern Santa Fe.

In 1999, CN generated revenue of more than $5.2 billion and a profit of $746 million. The company employs 23,493 people.

Stock performance

During 1999 this stock has generated better results than most investments, but recently the stock has disappointed in the short term. During the previous year the stock declined in value by 11.4 per cent. However, the common stock hasn't been tested over a long period, and investors shouldn't regard such a loss as the norm. Even though the stock declined in value during the previous year, CN has generated better results than the average stock in the transportation and environment sector. The best 12-month rate of return for the stock was a gain of 189.4 percent, and the average rate of return after 12 months was 50.9 per cent.

Stock risks

The stock has posted a loss after 12 months 23 per cent of the time, but has currently displayed very little downside risk. During the bear market of 1998 the stock declined in value by 25.6 per cent but took only seven months to recover its loss.

Stock financial fundamentals

CN had difficult financial times while the Canadian government owned the firm. However, during the last three years it has made impressive strides to become a viable and sustainable public company. Its earnings per share have improved to $3.71 per share in 1999, an impressive gain from 1995, when the firm made $2.48 per share. The improvement in earnings can be attributed to higher profit margins for the company.

Future prospects

CN is attempting to complete some mergers in the U.S., knowing it will have to build new strategic relationships to compete effectively in the U.S. market. To this end, in July 1998, CN acquired Illinois Central Corporation (IC). CN has also established a marketing alliance with Kansas City Southern Railway to operate an efficient Chicago–Kansas City service made possible by the IC acquisition. Those who want to invest in a transportation company should consider CN. At a price of $43.10, it is reasonably priced but the company has a lot of fixed costs and it needs to operate efficiently to add shareholder value. Investors should expect some short-term volatility, which should provide a buying opportunity.

COMPANY DETAILS

Company name	**Canadian National Railway**	Industry classification	Transportation & Environment
Recent price	$43.10	Market capitalization (in $ millions)	$8,411
52-week price range from low to high	$33.25–$54.57	Ticker symbol	CNR
Overall assessment of potential risk (one is more risky)	28/30	Phone number for annual report	1-888-888-5909
Number of mutual funds that hold this stock as a top 15 holding	124	Stock analysis start date	December 1995

ROLLING 12-MONTH TOTAL RATE OF RETURN FOR THE STOCK OVER TIME

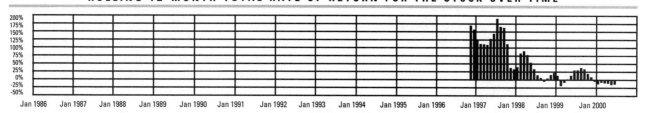

Jan 1986 Jan 1987 Jan 1988 Jan 1989 Jan 1990 Jan 1991 Jan 1992 Jan 1993 Jan 1994 Jan 1995 Jan 1996 Jan 1997 Jan 1998 Jan 1999 Jan 2000

STOCK PERFORMANCE*

	1 month	1 year	3 years	5 years	10 years	15 years
Returns ending June 2000	6.2%	-11.4%	14.3%			
Best historical return	50.2%	189.4%	61.4%			
Average historical return	3.2%	50.9%	38.2%			
Worst historical return	-12.1%	-16.5%	11.1%			
Value at risk of $1,000	$910	$886	$1,424			

RETURNS GREATER THAN*

	1 month	1 year	3 years	5 years	10 years	15 years
10 per cent	16%	68%	100%			
Zero	56%	77%	100%			
Percentage of time stock lost $	44%	23%	0%			
Number of periods evaluated	55	44	20			

DOWNSIDE RISK*

	Worst setback since start date	In bear 1987	In bear 1990	In bear 1994	In bear 1998
Setback for stock	-32.7%				-25.6%
Setback for stock market	0.0%				-24.6%
Setback ended in	Feb. 2000				Sept. 1998
Months to recover from loss	?				7

STOCK FINANCIAL FUNDAMENTAL INFORMATION

	1990	1991	1992	1993	1994	1995	1996	1997	1998	1999	Change
Average share price						$10.39	$14.63	$31.09	$40.22	$44.54	10.7%
Earnings per share						$2.48	$6.14	$2.72	$3.08	$3.71	20.5%
Book value per share						$14.34	$18.19	$20.09	$23.42	$30.24	29.1%
Price-to-earnings ratio						4.2	2.4	11.4	13.1	12.0	-8.1%
Price-to-book ratio						0.7	0.8	1.5	1.7	1.5	-14.2%
Profit margin						10.3%	27.0%	11.0%	14.0%	14.2%	2.1%
Asset turnover						0.67	0.58	0.54	0.36	0.32	-9.5%
Leverage						2.5	2.2	2.3	2.6	2.7	0.9%
Return on equity						17.3%	33.8%	13.5%	13.2%	12.3%	-6.7%
Dividend per share							$0.40	$0.46	$0.53	$0.60	13.0%
Dividend yield							2.7%	1.5%	1.3%	1.3%	2.2%

*Source: The raw data used in developing this table was provided by Datastream.

CANADIAN NATURAL RESOURCES

Company profile

Canadian Natural Resources is a senior oil and natural gas exploration, development, and production company based in Calgary, Alberta. The company's assets are based exclusively in Western Canada, and it recently increased its asset base with the acquisition of BP Amoco's oil assets in Alberta for $1 billion. CNR has effected a consistent growth strategy while adhering to effective cost controls, achieving excellent yearly growth in its operating and financial results. The company increased its revenue by 47 per cent during the previous year to $1.28 billion and increased its net earnings by more than 239 per cent to $200.2 million. Its financial results improved considerably in that period due to the increase in price of oil.

The company has attracted strong leadership, which has allowed it consistently to deliver results that exceed its peers'. During the previous 10 years CNR has generated a proven track record of increasing earnings and assets. This should provide an excellent foundation for Canadian Natural Resources to continue this trend into the twenty-first century.

Stock performance

The best 12-month rate of return for the stock was a gain of 1,071.8 per cent, and the average rate of return after 12 months was 68.1 per cent. During the previous 15 years the stock has appreciated in value by an average of 46.5 per cent per year. Over the long term the stock has been very successful. The value at risk of $1,000 for 15 years for CNR is $23,106; this means that 95 per cent of the time, your investment would have appreciated in value to at least $23,106, 95 per cent of the time.

Stock risks

During the bear market of 1998, the stock declined in value by 54.9 per cent. During the same period the average Canadian equity investment declined in value by 24.6 per cent. The stock took 21 months to recover its loss. The oil and gas industry will continue to be very risky, but it is likely going to be less risky than other resource sectors.

Stock financial fundamentals

Have you seen the price of gas lately at your local gas station and wondered who is making all the money you're spending? Gas companies vow they aren't benefiting, but this oil and gas company increased its earnings per share by 227.1 per cent during the previous year. This increase can be attributed to higher profit margins and better asset turnover. The company's return on equity also increased in 1999 to 11.4 per cent.

Future prospects

The price for a barrel of oil will likely decline in the short term but remain a lot higher than last year. This environment should bode well for oil and gas companies. They will be able to generate good profits and shareholder value without causing a riot at the local gas station. With a good balance sheet and a more robust business environment, CNR's future looks better each day. However, it is still a cyclical industry, and this stock will still incur risk.

COMPANY DETAILS

Company name	**Canadian Natural Resources**	Industry classification	Oil & Gas
Recent price	$43.00	Market capitalization (in $ millions)	$4,832
52-week price range from low to high	$29.50–$49.45	Ticker symbol	CNQ
Overall assessment of potential risk (one is more risky)	27/30	Phone number for annual report	403-517-6700
Number of mutual funds that hold this stock as a top 15 holding	138	Stock analysis start date	July 1982

ROLLING 12-MONTH TOTAL RATE OF RETURN FOR THE STOCK OVER TIME

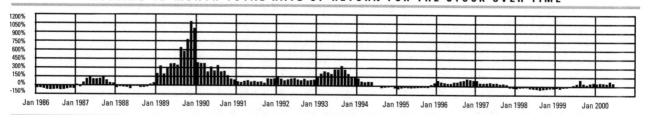

STOCK PERFORMANCE*

	1 month	1 year	3 years	5 years	10 years	15 years
Returns ending June 2000	-9.5%	48.3%	6.3%	21.7%	39.9%	46.5%
Best historical return	161.1%	1071.8%	264.5%	212.2%	93.6%	48.4%
Average historical return	3.5%	68.1%	53.0%	57.9%	59.5%	34.0%
Worst historical return	-42.9%	-87.8%	-64.7%	-43.0%	16.8%	21.6%
Value at risk of $1,000	$774	$277	$85	$89	$6,646	$23,106

RETURNS GREATER THAN*

	1 month	1 year	3 years	5 years	10 years	15 years
10 per cent	24%	57%	63%	78%	100%	100%
Zero	53%	58%	73%	87%	100%	100%
Percentage of time stock lost $	47%	42%	27%	13%	0%	0%
Number of periods evaluated	216	205	181	157	97	37

DOWNSIDE RISK*

	Worst setback since start date	In bear 1987	In bear 1990	In bear 1994	In bear 1998
Setback for stock	-95.8%	-53.8%	-16.5%	-52.6%	-54.9%
Setback for stock market	-0.2%	-23.2%	-16.3%	-9.7%	-24.6%
Setback ended in	June 1986	Feb. 1988	Jan. 1991	Jan. 1995	Aug. 1998
Months to recover from loss	44	24	4	17	21

STOCK FINANCIAL FUNDAMENTAL INFORMATION

	1990	1991	1992	1993	1994	1995	1996	1997	1998	1999	Change
Average share price	$1.56	$2.66	$5.17	$15.88	$18.91	$15.96	$27.11	$36.19	$25.75	$30.23	17.4%
Earnings per share	$0.07	$0.09	$0.13	$0.60	$0.85	$0.61	$1.14	$1.14	$0.59	$1.93	227.1%
Book value per share	$0.24	$0.46	$0.75	$2.86	$5.34	$6.70	$11.03	$12.19	$12.80	$16.98	32.7%
Price-to-earnings ratio	22.3	29.6	39.8	26.5	22.2	26.2	23.8	31.7	43.6	15.7	-64.1%
Price-to-book ratio	6.5	5.8	6.9	5.6	3.5	2.4	2.5	3.0	2.0	1.8	-11.5%
Profit margin	29.2%	22.0%	17.3%	25.5%	24.6%	17.2%	17.8%	14.5%	7.7%	18.6%	140.9%
Asset turnover	0.38	0.35	0.45	0.31	0.30	0.27	0.26	0.26	0.23	0.24	2.2%
Leverage	2.7	2.5	2.2	2.7	2.2	1.9	2.2	2.5	2.6	2.6	0.2%
Return on equity	29.2%	19.6%	17.3%	21.0%	15.9%	9.1%	10.3%	9.4%	4.6%	11.4%	146.6%
Dividend per share	$—	$—	$—	$—	$—	$—	$—	$—	$—	$—	$—
Dividend yield	0.0%	0.0%	0.0%	0.0%	0.0%	0.0%	0.0%	0.0%	0.0%	0.0%	0.0%

*Source: The raw data used in developing this table was provided by Datastream.

CANADIAN PACIFIC

Company profile

The company's history can be traced back to February 15, 1881, when the Canadian government approved the contract to build a national rail line. Currently, the company is directly involved in rail and ship transportation, energy development and exploration, and hotel operations in North America and various locations throughout the world.

The company owns the Canadian Pacific Railway, Soo Line Railroad, and the Delaware and Hudson Railway Company. It is involved in the energy business through various holdings including PanCanadian Petroleum and Fording. Through its affiliated companies, CP explores for, develops and markets hydrocarbons, coal and other metallurgical resources. Through CP Ships, it owns or leases and operates ships to provide container and bulk services between the Montreal and the U.S., Northern Europe, and various Mediterranean and African countries. Canadian Pacific Hotels and Resorts is Canadian Pacific's best household name, famous around the world with both business and recreational travelers, and CP is Canada's largest operator of full-service hotels. It manages more than 70 properties in various locations around the world including Canada, the U.S., Mexico, and Bermuda with more than 29,000 rooms. CP's best-known properties are the Banff Springs Hotel in Alberta and Le Chateau Frontenac in Quebec City.

1999 was a good year for this company. Revenue was up 12 per cent and operating income was up 20 per cent.

Stock performance

Investors looking at the future not at the past should like what they see in a company like Canadian Pacific. The best 12-month rate of return for the stock was a gain of 103.1 per cent, and the average rate of return after 12 months was 11.6 per cent. During the previous 15 years, the stock has appreciated in value by an average of 7 per cent per year, not very good, but the following 15 years should be a lot better.

Stock risks

During the bear market of 1998 the stock declined in value by 29.3 per cent. During the same time period the average Canadian equity investment declined in value by 24.6 per cent. The stock still hasn't recovered its loss.

Stock financial fundamentals

During the previous year Canadian Pacific posted earnings per share of $2.67, up 11.7 per cent from the previous year. The price-to-earnings (P/E) ratio declined by 20.6 per cent, to 12.4. This means that investors are paying $12.40 for each $1 of historical earnings. Based on these valuations the company is cheap.

Future prospects

Conservative investors should consider accumulating some shares in this company. The fundamentals are good. The outlook for rail and ship transportation, energy development and exploration, and hotel operations is very favourable. The company's stock is trading at a reasonable price. CP has to focus on its profit margins to ensure it can add shareholder value. However, if the company cannot maintain these profit margins, the stock could decline in value.

COMPANY DETAILS

Company name	**Canadian Pacific**	Industry classification	Conglomerates
Recent price	$38.40	Market capitalization (in $ millions)	$12,221
52-week price range from low to high	$26.80–$40.65	Ticker symbol	CP
Overall assessment of potential risk (one is more risky)	25/30	Phone number for annual report	403-218-8000
Number of mutual funds that hold this stock as a top 15 holding	137	Stock analysis start date	July 1982

ROLLING 12-MONTH TOTAL RATE OF RETURN FOR THE STOCK OVER TIME

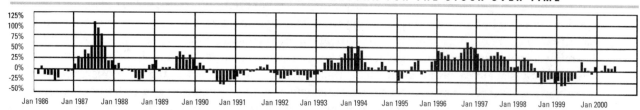

STOCK PERFORMANCE*

	1 month	1 year	3 years	5 years	10 years	15 years
Returns ending June 2000	8.6%	11.6%	0.9%	12.0%	8.6%	7.0%
Best historical return	22.2%	103.1%	37.3%	30.7%	11.5%	14.0%
Average historical return	1.2%	11.6%	9.1%	8.6%	6.7%	8.7%
Worst historical return	-17.6%	-31.3%	-13.7%	-7.5%	2.4%	4.6%
Value at risk of $1,000	$900	$790	$754	$867	$1,441	$2,334

RETURNS GREATER THAN*

	1 month	1 year	3 years	5 years	10 years	15 years
10 per cent	11%	43%	43%	43%	7%	24%
Zero	51%	63%	82%	86%	100%	100%
Percentage of time stock lost $	49%	37%	18%	14%	0%	0%
Number of periods evaluated	216	205	181	157	97	37

DOWNSIDE RISK*

	Worst setback since start date	In bear 1987	In bear 1990	In bear 1994	In bear 1998
Setback for stock	-41.0%	-32.8%	-32.5%	-20.6%	-29.3%
Setback for stock market	-2.9%	-23.2%	-16.3%	-9.7%	-24.6%
Setback ended in	Nov. 1992	Nov. 1987	Sept. 1990	Jan. 1995	Aug. 1998
Months to recover from loss	32	20	58	6	?

STOCK FINANCIAL FUNDAMENTAL INFORMATION

	1990	1991	1992	1993	1994	1995	1996	1997	1998	1999	Change
Average share price	$21.33	$19.51	$16.89	$19.95	$21.98	$22.23	$29.90	$38.23	$37.45	$33.20	-11.3%
Earnings per share	$1.11	($2.87)	($1.50)	($0.09)	$1.21	($1.82)	$2.41	$2.74	$2.39	$2.67	11.7%
Book value per share	$24.55	$21.02	$19.66	$18.84	$19.89	$17.04	$18.46	$22.23	$24.04	$24.67	2.6%
Price-to-earnings ratio	19.2	(6.8)	(11.3)	(221.7)	18.2	(12.2)	12.4	14.0	15.7	12.4	-20.6%
Price-to-book ratio	0.9	0.9	0.9	1.1	1.1	1.3	1.6	1.7	1.6	1.3	-13.6%
Profit margin	3.4%	-9.1%	-5.3%	-0.4%	5.8%	-7.8%	9.6%	9.9%	7.9%	7.8%	-1.4%
Asset turnover	0.52	0.49	0.44	0.38	0.42	0.50	0.57	0.55	0.52	0.55	6.7%
Leverage	2.6	3.1	3.2	2.8	2.5	2.8	2.4	2.3	2.4	2.5	3.5%
Return on equity	4.5%	-13.7%	-7.6%	-0.5%	6.1%	-10.7%	13.1%	12.3%	9.9%	10.8%	8.9%
Dividend per share	$0.92	$0.63	$0.32	$0.32	$0.32	$0.36	$0.48	$0.48	$0.54	$0.56	4.0%
Dividend yield	4.3%	3.2%	1.9%	1.6%	1.5%	1.6%	1.6%	1.3%	1.4%	1.7%	17.0%

*Source: The raw data used in developing this table was provided by Datastream.

CELESTICA

Company profile

Wow! What a success story for this company. Since its initial public offering (IPO) in 1998, the company has done nothing but impress. As part of the new economy, Celestica is a global leader in the electronics manufacturing services industry. It provides a range of products and services including design, prototyping, assembly, testing, product assurance, supply chain management, worldwide distribution, and sales service. The company's goal is to be its customers' supplier of choice within the electronics industry. To achieve this objective Celestica focuses on customer satisfaction, value, leadership, and technology. Celestica's major clients are leading original equipment manufacturers that operate in the computer and communications sectors such as Cisco Systems, Dell Computer, Hewlett-Packard, IBM, Lucent Technologies, and Sun Microsystems. Celestica has grown quickly in the previous three years. In 1997 it had sales of more than $2.9 billion. With 18 acquisitions in the last 18 months, this has grown to more than $7.7 billion in 1999. Celestica also posted a profit of $123 million in 1999, not bad for a fast-growing technology company. Celestica has more than 21,000 employees worldwide and operates 32 manufacturing and design facilities around the world.

Stock performance

Celestica is defining the new economy, and investors love it. The best 12-month rate of return for the stock was a gain of 327.6 per cent, and the average rate of return after 12 months was 188.7 per cent. Since the company's initial public offering the stock has gone up—almost in a straight line.

Stock risks

Currently, after 12 months, the stock has always posted a gain, but it still hasn't been tested over the long term. During the bear market of 1998, the stock declined in value by 41.4 per cent. During the same period the average Canadian equity investment declined in value by 21.8 per cent. But Celestica stock took only three months to recover its loss. In the short term, the stock's worst one-month decline was a loss of 35.1 per cent. Investors should expect this volatility to continue as they attempt to value this firm's future potential correctly.

Stock financial fundamentals

The company posted a profit of 61 cents per share in 1999, up from a loss of 70 cents in 1998. The company has made large improvements in its profit margin, asset turnover, and leverage ratios thereby improving its return on equity and profits. However, investors expect big things in the future and have bid the stock price up to $72.10, increasing the price-to-earnings (P/E) ratio to nosebleed levels. However, these levels could be justified considering the company's growth rate.

Future prospects

Celestica is a global leader in the white-hot electronics manufacturing services industry. Investors who want to participate should consider this company. Investors should remember, though, that there is a lot of upside and downside potential to this stock. Therefore, invest prudently and diversify.

COMPANY DETAILS

Company name	**Celestrica**	Industry classification	Industrial Products
Recent price	$72.10	Market capitalization (in $ millions)	$11,743
52-week price range from low to high	$30.25–$91.80	Ticker symbol	CLS
Overall assessment of potential risk (one is more risky)	3/30	Phone number for annual report	416-448-2211
Number of mutual funds that hold this stock as a top 15 holding	97	Stock analysis start date	July 1998

ROLLING 12-MONTH TOTAL RATE OF RETURN FOR THE STOCK OVER TIME

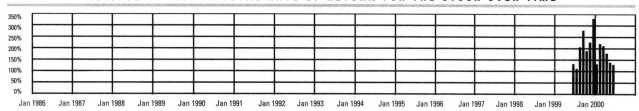

STOCK PERFORMANCE*

	1 month	1 year	3 years	5 years	10 years	15 years
Returns ending June 2000	3.3%	126.4%				
Best historical return	58.4%	327.6%				
Average historical return	9.2%	188.7%				
Worst historical return	-35.1%	108.7%				
Value at risk of $1,000	$739	$2,193				

RETURNS GREATER THAN*

	1 month	1 year	3 years	5 years	10 years	15 years
10 per cent	54%	100%				
Zero	75%	100%				
Percentage of time stock lost $	25%	0%				
Number of periods evaluated	24	13				

DOWNSIDE RISK*

	Worst setback since start date	In bear 1987	In bear 1990	In bear 1994	In bear 1998
Setback for stock	-41.4%				-41.4%
Setback for stock market	-20.0%				-21.8%
Setback ended in	Sept. 1998				Sept. 1998
Months to recover from loss	3				3

STOCK FINANCIAL FUNDAMENTAL INFORMATION

	1990	1991	1992	1993	1994	1995	1996	1997	1998	1999	Change
Average share price									$14.04	$34.22	143.7%
Earnings per share								($0.14)	($0.70)	$0.61	+187.1%
Book value per share								$5.57	$8.82	$14.70	66.7%
Price-to-earnings ratio									(20.1)	56.1	-379.7%
Price-to-book ratio									1.6	2.3	46.2%
Profit margin								-0.3%	-1.5%	1.3%	+187.0%
Asset turnover								1.45	1.97	2.96	50.3%
Leverage								5.0	2.7	1.1	-60.0%
Return on equity								-2.5%	-7.9%	4.1%	+152.3%
Dividend per share								$–	$–	$–	0.0%
Dividend yield									0.0%	0.0%	0.0%

*Source: The raw data used in developing this table was provided by Datastream.

C-MAC INDUSTRIES INC.

Company profile

This company competes globally in the electronics industry and has become a leading diversified designer and manufacturer of integrated electronic manufacturing solutions. From components to full systems, C-MAC has the expertise to be a one-stop-shop for its customers. The company services the communications, automotive, instrumentation, defence, and aerospace equipment markets worldwide. C-MAC also offers additional services, which include product design, supply chain management, and assembly and testing. In addition to its manufacturing capabilities the company also offers design services throughout North America and Europe.

C-MAC has had a sensational 1999. Revenues are at record highs, and the balance sheet is strong. This has allowed the company to position itself to pursue aggressive growth and improve profitability, ensuring a successful year in 2000 as it continues to increase its client business while strengthening relationships with current clients. During the previous year the company's sales grew by 85 per cent, to $1.2 billion, and net earnings by 78 per cent, to $45.2 million. During this time the company also made eight strategic acquisitions, improving its facilities and manufacturing capabilities.

Stock performance

There are good times and there are bad times. But the good times are here now for C-MAC. During the previous year, the stock was up 354.5 per cent, catapulting it into blue-chip status. The best 12-month rate of return for the stock was a gain of 491.5 per cent, and the average rate of return after 12 months was 67.3 per cent. However, prior to the previous year, the stock's performance was good but not this exceptional.

Stock risks

What goes up usually comes down, and this stock has declined in value. The worst 12-month return posted by this stock was a decline of 75 per cent, and the stock declined in value after 12 months 29 per cent of the time. The worst setback that this stock has ever incurred was a loss of 83.3 per cent. During the same period, the average Canadian equity investment declined in value by 6.2 per cent. In turn, the stock took thirty-one months to recover this loss, but it did recover.

Stock financial fundamental

The stock price increased significantly because of the company's ability to generate excellent profit growth. During the previous year, earnings per share increased by 71.2 per cent to 82 cents per share. The company has increased its earnings per share by increasing sales while maintaining good profit margins, asset turnover, and leverage.

Future prospects

Technology changes quickly. To continue this impressive momentum, C-MAC will have to continue its leadership as a diversified designer and manufacturer of integrated electronic manufacturing solutions. This is a tough task in the global electronics industry, but management is committed to achieving that goal. Aggressive investors could consider this stock for a portion of their portfolio, but it's a risky stock that will incur volatility.

COMPANY DETAILS

Company name	**C-MAC Industries**	Industry classification	Industrial Products
Recent price	$70.00	Market capitalization (in $ millions)	$4,997
52-week price range from low to high	$15.88–$80.25	Ticker symbol	CMS
Overall assessment of potential risk (one is more risky)	7/30	Phone number for annual report	514-282-7629
Number of mutual funds that hold this stock as a top 15 holding	108	Stock analysis start date	January 1993

ROLLING 12-MONTH TOTAL RATE OF RETURN FOR THE STOCK OVER TIME

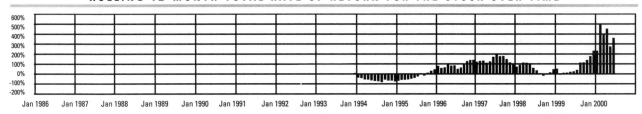

STOCK PERFORMANCE*

	1 month	1 year	3 years	5 years	10 years	15 years
Returns ending June 2000	22.4%	354.5%	101.9%	107.9%		
Best historical return	49.1%	491.5%	127.4%	114.5%		
Average historical return	4.2%	67.3%	52.3%	44.6%		
Worst historical return	-45.1%	-75.0%	-27.5%	1.6%		
Value at risk of $1,000	$816	$386	$419	$1,525		

RETURNS GREATER THAN*

	1 month	1 year	3 years	5 years	10 years	15 years
10 per cent	32%	62%	76%	94%		
Zero	60%	71%	80%	100%		
Percentage of time stock lost $	40%	29%	20%	0%		
Number of periods evaluated	90	79	55	31		

DOWNSIDE RISK*

	Worst setback since start date	In bear 1987	In bear 1990	In bear 1994	In bear 1998
Setback for stock	-83.3%			-83.3%	-33.7%
Setback for stock market	-6.2%			-9.7%	-24.6%
Setback ended in	Dec. 1994			Dec. 1994	Aug. 1998
Months to recover from loss	31			31	5

STOCK FINANCIAL FUNDAMENTAL INFORMATION

	1990	1991	1992	1993	1994	1995	1996	1997	1998	1999	Change
Average share price			$4.96	$6.28	$2.86	$1.89	$3.40	$8.12	$11.47	$18.33	59.8%
Earnings per share			$0.24	$0.21	$0.09	$0.15	$0.28	$0.39	$0.48	$0.82	71.2%
Book value per share			$0.95	$1.80	$2.01	$2.07	$2.57	$2.87	$4.29	$7.67	78.8%
Price-to-earnings ratio			20.5	29.7	32.1	12.6	12.0	20.9	23.9	22.3	-6.6%
Price-to-book ratio			5.2	3.5	1.4	0.9	1.3	2.8	2.7	2.4	-10.6%
Profit margin			8.3%	5.4%	2.3%	3.1%	4.5%	5.0%	4.0%	4.2%	3.4%
Asset turnover			0.49	0.62	0.49	0.69	0.83	0.84	0.67	0.79	16.8%
Leverage			6.2	3.5	4.0	3.4	2.9	3.2	4.1	3.3	-20.7%
Return on equity			25.5%	11.7%	4.4%	7.3%	11.0%	13.5%	11.2%	10.7%	-4.3%
Dividend per share			$–	$–	$–	$–	$–	$–	$–	$–	$–
Dividend yield			0.0%	0.0%	0.0%	0.0%	0.0%	0.0%	0.0%	0.0%	0.0%

*Source: The raw data used in developing this table was provided by Datastream.

COGNOS INC.

Company profile

Cognos develops, markets, and supports complementary lines of software tools for customers' mission-critical software. The company operates in traditional and e-business markets. It is a major world vendor of business intelligence solutions for e-business. Its products enable users to explore, gather, analyze, and report data more productively. This allows Cognos to be an important contributor to its customers' success. One of its most successful products is a Web-based technology that provides the foundation of an e-business infrastructure.

Cognos is one of the world's largest and most successful business intelligence companies. Founded in 1969 in Ottawa, it has its U.S. sales headquarters in Massachusetts. Cognos has done business with more than 14,000 customers located in more than 60 countries around the globe. It employs more than 2,100 people, and its software is available from more than 2,800 global partners and resellers.

The company generates revenue by licensing its software and providing related services such as support. Using this strategy the company generated more than $385.6 million in sales and posted a profit of $58.4 million. Considering the demand for this company's products and services the next year should also be very impressive.

Stock performance

This stock's performance has been exceptional. The best three-year rate of return for the stock was a gain of 134.9 per cent annualized, and the average annualized three-year rate of return was 32.1 per cent. During the previous 10 years the stock has appreciated in value by an average of 43.9 per cent per year. Over 95 per cent of the time, investors who invested $1,000 for 10 years saw their investment grow in value to at least $6,017. Investors should not expect these types of returns again, but the company still has the potential to generate abnormal rates of return for shareholders.

Stock risks

The risk is very high. The worst setback that this stock has ever incurred was a loss of 78.4 per cent. During the same period, the average Canadian equity investment declined in value by 1.4 per cent. The stock took over five years to recover the loss but it did.

Stock financial fundamentals

With profit margins in the mid-teens, good asset turnover, and a prudent level of leverage, the company has generated a return on equity of 27.8 per cent in 1999 and posted a profit of 50 cents per share. The price-to-earnings ratio has increased to 37.6 in 1999. This means investors are paying $37.60 for $1 of historical earnings, and is justifiable considering the company's excellent growth potential and growth rate.

Future prospects

This company is a true visionary. As mentioned, one of its most successful products, its Web-based technology, provides the foundation of an e-business infrastructure. This should ensure the company's future growth potential. But with success comes competition, and changes in technology could render its products obsolete. This factor in conjunction with high valuation will likely increase the volatility associated with this growth stock, which is exhibiting a lot of momentum.

COMPANY DETAILS

Company name	**Cognos Industry**	Industry classification	Industrial Products
Recent price	$61.20	Market capitalization (in $ millions)	$5,351
52-week price range from low to high	$14.30–$66.25	Ticker symbol	CSN
Overall assessment of potential risk (one is more risky)	12/30	Phone number for annual report	613-738-1440
Number of mutual funds that hold this stock as a top 15 holding	60	Stock analysis start date	September 1986

ROLLING 12-MONTH TOTAL RATE OF RETURN FOR THE STOCK OVER TIME

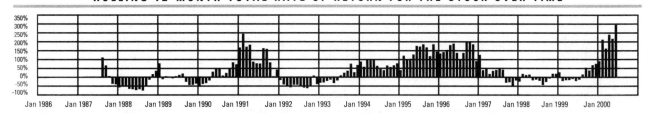

STOCK PERFORMANCE*

	1 month	1 year	3 years	5 years	10 years	15 years
Returns ending June 2000	13.3%	291.6%	43.5%	56.9%	43.9%	
Best historical return	50.0%	291.6%	134.9%	76.1%	48.6%	
Average historical return	3.5%	43.1%	32.1%	33.3%	30.2%	
Worst historical return	-38.3%	-71.3%	-31.3%	-16.4%	16.6%	
Value at risk of $1,000	$774	$464	$468	$560	$6,017	

RETURNS GREATER THAN*

	1 month	1 year	3 years	5 years	10 years	15 years
10 per cent	31%	57%	65%	78%	100%	
Zero	49%	63%	78%	86%	100%	
Percentage of time stock lost $	51%	37%	22%	14%	0%	
Number of periods evaluated	166	155	131	107	47	

DOWNSIDE RISK*

	Worst setback since start date	In bear 1987	In bear 1990	In bear 1994	In bear 1998
Setback for stock	-78.4%	-73.6%	-47.6%	-21.2%	-49.8%
Setback for stock market	-1.4%	-23.2%	-16.3%	-9.7%	-24.6%
Setback ended in	Nov. 1989	Jan. 1988	Jan. 1990	Feb. 1994	Sept. 1998
Months to recover from loss	61	83	59	10	15

STOCK FINANCIAL FUNDAMENTAL INFORMATION

	1990	1991	1992	1993	1994	1995	1996	1997	1998	1999	Change
Average share price	$1.31	$2.74	$1.67	$1.68	$2.82	$6.32	$15.90	$18.62	$16.97	$18.78	10.7%
Earnings per share	$0.03	$0.02	($0.03)	$0.02	$0.05	$0.10	$0.55	$0.50	$0.97	$0.50	-48.5%
Book value per share	$0.27	$0.28	$0.24	$0.26	$0.32	$0.42	$1.82	$2.11	$2.86	$1.80	-37.1%
Price-to-earnings ratio	43.7	137.0	(55.7)	84.0	56.4	63.2	28.9	37.2	17.5	37.6	114.7%
Price-to-book ratio	4.9	9.8	7.0	6.5	8.8	15.0	8.7	8.8	5.9	10.4	75.8%
Profit margin	4.1%	3.0%	-4.7%	3.1%	7.0%	11.9%	18.8%	13.3%	19.2%	15.5%	-19.6%
Asset turnover	1.68	1.21	1.29	1.19	1.12	1.08	1.04	1.10	1.01	1.03	2.0%
Leverage	1.6	2.0	2.1	2.1	2.0	1.8	1.5	1.6	1.7	1.7	-0.1%
Return on equity	11.1%	7.1%	-12.5%	7.7%	15.6%	23.8%	30.2%	23.7%	33.9%	27.8%	-18.1%
Dividend per share	$–	$–	$–	$–	$–	$–	$–	$–	$–	$–	0.0%
Dividend yield	0.0%	0.0%	0.0%	0.0%	0.0%	0.0%	0.0%	0.0%	0.0%	0.0%	0.0%

*Source: The raw data used in developing this table was provided by Datastream.

FOUR SEASONS HOTELS

Company profile

If you have ever had the luxury of staying at a Four Seasons hotel, you will understand why this is one the world's premier luxury hospitality companies. The company's objective is to manage the finest hotels, resorts, residence clubs, and other residential projects. Four Seasons identifies attractive properties and refurbishes them using superior designs, then supports them with the highest level of integrity and service. This strategy allows the company to meet and exceed the expectations of its discerning client.

Four Seasons was established in 1978 in Toronto. The company now operates 47 luxury hotel and resort properties located in 19 major countries, with approximately 13,780 guestrooms. It currently has an additional 21 hotels and resorts under construction or development. Four Seasons generates the majority of its earnings by managing but not owning the properties. This allows the company to avoid the risk associated with the volatile real estate market, yet to benefit from the management fees associated with operating the hotels. This strategy has allowed the company to generate more than $2.4 billion in sales and earnings of more than $86 million.

Four Seasons targets the affluent customer who is willing to pay a large premium for service. In turn, the Four Seasons should be able to generate good profit margins and good value for investors.

Stock performance

During the previous year the stock appreciated in value by 44.4 per cent. The best three-year rate of return for the stock was a gain of 56.2 per cent annualized, and the average annualized three-year rate of return was 18.6 per cent. During the previous 10 years, the stock has appreciated in value by an average of 17.7 per cent per year.

Stock risks

A poor economic outlook could send this stock downhill very quickly as guests stop coming, which occurred in 1998. During the bear market of 1998, the stock declined in value by 45.1 per cent. During the same period, the average Canadian equity investment declined in value by 24.6 per cent. But the stock took only six months to recover from its loss.

Stock financial fundamentals

Profit margins in excess of 30 per cent and a prudent level of leverage have both contributed to a return on equity of 21.3 per cent. Such a high return on equity contributed to the company's earnings per share growth. During the previous year, the company increased its earnings per share by 22.3 per cent to $2.52.

Future prospects

The business model for the luxury hotel business is simple: let somebody else build it and you manage it, while providing exceptional service and charging clients a premium for the privilege. Okay, this may be a little simplistic, but Four Seasons makes a lot of money on this simple formula. With additional expansion planned and a robust economy, things should continue to bode well for this company. The major risk is an economic slowdown, which would slow sales considerably as guests revisit their accommodation expenditures.

COMPANY DETAILS

Company name	**Four Seasons Hotels**	Industry classification	Merchandising
Recent price	$92.70	Market capitalization (in $ millions)	$2,801
52-week price range from low to high	$50.50–$94.15	Ticker symbol	FSH
Overall assessment of potential risk (one is more risky)	16/30	Phone number for annual report	416-441-4329
Number of mutual funds that hold this stock as a top 15 holding	15	Stock analysis start date	March 1986

ROLLING 12-MONTH TOTAL RATE OF RETURN FOR THE STOCK OVER TIME

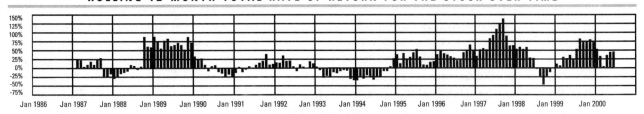

STOCK PERFORMANCE*

	1 month	1 year	3 years	5 years	10 years	15 years
Returns ending June 2000	4.3%	44.4%	31.5%	40.8%	17.7%	
Best historical return	25.8%	137.3%	56.2%	42.9%	22.6%	
Average historical return	2.0%	22.2%	18.6%	14.8%	14.9%	
Worst historical return	-38.1%	-45.1%	-14.5%	-7.6%	7.8%	
Value at risk of $1,000	$868	$754	$785	$812	$2,485	

RETURNS GREATER THAN*

	1 month	1 year	3 years	5 years	10 years	15 years
10 per cent	23%	57%	63%	65%	89%	
Zero	54%	71%	78%	85%	100%	
Percentage of time stock lost $	46%	29%	22%	15%	0%	
Number of periods evaluated	172	161	137	113	53	

DOWNSIDE RISK*

	Worst setback since start date	In bear 1987	In bear 1990	In bear 1994	In bear 1998
Setback for stock	-47.2%	-40.2%	-35.9%	-39.3%	-45.1%
Setback for stock market	-3.8%	-23.2%	-16.3%	-9.7%	-24.6%
Setback ended in	Mar. 1994	Oct. 1987	Oct. 1990	Mar. 1994	Sept. 1998
Months to recover from loss	22	8	63	22	6

STOCK FINANCIAL FUNDAMENTAL INFORMATION

	1990	1991	1992	1993	1994	1995	1996	1997	1998	1999	Change
Average share price	$16.58	$17.30	$18.95	$16.46	$13.22	$16.44	$22.40	$40.29	$43.23	$61.66	42.6%
Earnings per share	$0.86	$0.13	$0.32	($4.30)	$0.29	($2.62)	$1.04	$1.24	$2.06	$2.52	22.3%
Book value per share	$5.50	$6.23	$8.89	$4.52	$4.91	$1.98	$3.07	$7.55	$9.74	$11.85	21.7%
Price-to-earnings ratio	19.3	133.1	59.2	(3.8)	45.6	(6.3)	21.5	32.5	21.0	24.5	16.6%
Price-to-book ratio	3.0	2.8	2.1	3.6	2.7	8.3	7.3	5.3	4.4	5.2	17.2%
Profit margin	8.9%	1.7%	6.5%	-120.1%	6.7%	-57.1%	26.5%	16.8%	27.5%	30.5%	11.1%
Asset turnover	0.81	0.49	0.22	0.19	0.25	0.34	0.29	0.53	0.47	0.35	-26.2%
Leverage	2.2	2.4	2.5	4.2	3.6	6.9	4.4	1.8	1.6	2.0	22.7%
Return on equity	15.6%	2.1%	3.6%	-95.1%	5.9%	-132.3%	33.9%	16.4%	21.1%	21.3%	0.5%
Dividend per share	$0.22	$0.11	$0.11	$0.11	$0.11	$0.11	$0.11	$0.11	$0.11	$0.11	$–
Dividend yield	1.3%	0.6%	0.6%	0.7%	0.8%	0.7%	0.5%	0.3%	0.3%	0.2%	-29.9%

*Source: The raw data used in developing this table was provided by Datastream.

LOBLAW COMPANIES LIMITED

Company profile

A truly national food retailer, Loblaw aims to provide the best in one-stop shopping for consumer households. The company has aggressively reinvested its earnings to establish its national presence. Although the company is very selective about its acquisitions and growth strategy, Loblaw continues to invest in new products and technology. It now operates grocery stores under various banners, including Loblaws, Provigo, SuperCentre, Zehrs, Save-Easy, Atlantic SuperCentre, Lucky Dollar Foods, Extra Foods, SuperValue, Loeb, Fortinos, NoFrills, Dominion, The Real Canadian Superstore and others. The company has successfully introduced President's Choice Financial, with more than 100 bank machines and in-store pavilions.

Loblaw is one of the largest private-sector employers in Canada. It employed a staff of more than 108,000 and generated sales of $18.7 billion in 1999, an increase of more than $6.3 billion over 1998. The company reported a profit in 1999 of $379 million. Loblaw has generated such favourable operating results because it adheres to the fundamental principles of unique products, convenient services, and innovative shopping experiences for their customers. The food industry is competitive, but by occupying the number-one market position in Canada Loblaw can certainly offset this disadvantage.

Stock performance

During the previous 10 years Loblaw has generated some very impressive results. The Canadian market is becoming saturated, and investors shouldn't anticipate the same kind of results, although above-average results are still achievable. During the previous year the company generated a return of 14.3 per cent, outperforming other merchandising stocks by a large margin. The best 12-month rate of return for the stock was a gain of 94.5 per cent, and the average rate of return after 12 months was 24.2 per cent. During the previous 15 years the stock has appreciated in value by an average of 20 per cent per year.

Stock risks

Loblaw's common stock does incur risk from time to time, but it hasn't incurred the same level of downside risk as similar companies or other Canadian companies.

Stock financial fundamentals

The company's fundamentals have improved during the previous year because its earnings and balance sheet improved at a faster rate than the company's common stock. The increase in asset turnover from 1.94 to 2.34 helped increase the return on equity to 13 per cent. This factor increased earnings per share by 29.2 per cent to $1.37.

Future prospects

Loblaw has capitalized on growth opportunities in the past, which benefited shareholders, and growth should continue. Good locations, recognized brand names, and good service have attracted a loyal base of consumers. The company has an excellent portfolio of stores strategically located across Canada and a proven management team that is results-oriented. Loblaw should continue to generate above-average risk-adjusted performance. Investors should not expect 40 per cent returns, but low double-digit returns should be achievable. People need to eat, and Loblaw will be there to serve them. This should provide some downside protection. Low profit margins require large volumes to generate higher profits, which could limit the upside.

COMPANY DETAILS

Company name	**Loblaw Companies**	Industry classification	Merchandising
Recent price	$42.40	Market capitalization (in $ millions)	$11,685
52-week price range from low to high	$29.80–$44.95	Ticker symbol	L
Overall assessment of potential risk (one is more risky)	14/30	Phone number for annual report	416-922-8500
Number of mutual funds that hold this stock as a top 15 holding	44	Stock analysis start date	July 1982

ROLLING 12-MONTH TOTAL RATE OF RETURN FOR THE STOCK OVER TIME

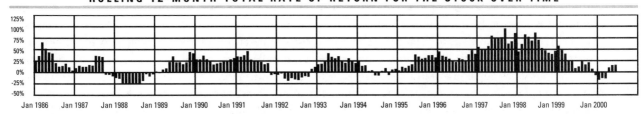

STOCK PERFORMANCE*

	1 month	1 year	3 years	5 years	10 years	15 years
Returns ending June 2000	-3.5%	14.3%	31.5%	36.6%	23.7%	20.0%
Best historical return	22.3%	94.5%	57.1%	41.7%	28.1%	23.0%
Average historical return	2.0%	24.2%	22.1%	19.1%	17.6%	21.0%
Worst historical return	-18.6%	-25.2%	-2.9%	2.7%	10.2%	18.0%
Value at risk of $1,000	$929	$861	$1,056	$1,459	$2,857	$13,236

RETURNS GREATER THAN*

	1 month	1 year	3 years	5 years	10 years	15 years
10 per cent	10%	74%	73%	90%	100%	100%
Zero	59%	83%	97%	100%	100%	100%
Percentage of time stock lost $	41%	17%	3%	0%	0%	0%
Number of periods evaluated	216	205	181	157	97	37

DOWNSIDE RISK*

	Worst setback since start date	In bear 1987	In bear 1990	In bear 1994	In bear 1998
Setback for stock	-35.4%	-30.7%	-6.2%	-15.2%	-17.7%
Setback for stock market	-13.1%	-23.2%	-16.3%	-9.7%	-24.6%
Setback ended in	Nov. 1988	Dec. 1987	Jan. 1990	June 1994	Oct. 1998
Months to recover from loss	16	27	2	8	2

STOCK FINANCIAL FUNDAMENTAL INFORMATION

	1990	1991	1992	1993	1994	1995	1996	1997	1998	1999	Change
Average share price	$5.39	$6.47	$5.91	$7.30	$7.43	$8.98	$11.79	$19.62	$31.20	$37.02	18.7%
Earnings per share	$0.37	$0.39	$0.29	$0.36	$0.50	$0.60	$0.72	$0.88	$1.06	$1.37	29.2%
Book value per share	$2.70	$3.22	$3.56	$3.83	$4.31	$4.74	$5.35	$6.08	$9.46	$10.56	11.6%
Price-to-earnings ratio	14.6	16.6	20.4	20.3	14.9	15.0	16.4	22.3	29.4	27.0	-8.2%
Price-to-book ratio	2.0	2.0	1.7	1.9	1.7	1.9	2.2	3.2	3.3	3.5	6.3%
Profit margin	1.0%	1.1%	0.7%	0.9%	1.2%	1.5%	1.8%	1.9%	2.1%	2.0%	-4.5%
Asset turnover	3.98	3.66	3.73	3.40	3.39	3.07	2.79	2.74	1.94	2.34	20.7%
Leverage	3.6	3.1	2.9	3.0	2.9	2.8	2.7	2.7	2.7	2.8	0.4%
Return on equity	13.7%	12.1%	8.1%	9.4%	11.6%	12.7%	13.5%	14.5%	11.2%	13.0%	15.8%
Dividend per share	$0.07	$0.08	$0.08	$0.08	$0.09	$0.11	$0.12	$0.15	$0.20	$0.22	10.0%
Dividend yield	1.3%	1.2%	1.4%	1.1%	1.2%	1.2%	1.0%	0.8%	0.6%	0.6%	-7.3%

*Source: The raw data used in developing this table was provided by Datastream.

MAGNA INTERNATIONAL

Company profile

In 1957, Frank Stronach set up his own tool-and-die company (originally called Multimatic Investments Limited), which evolved into a multi-million dollar automotive parts supplier. Magna International now designs, develops, and manufactures technologically advanced automotive systems, components, and complete modules for installation in cars and trucks built by Ford, Chrysler, GM, Volkswagen, and others. The company has become a leading global supplier in the automotive industry. Magna is now one of the most diversified automotive suppliers in the world and even assembles some niche vehicles for selected customers.

Several years ago Magna began investing in horse-racing tracks and other entertainment businesses. Then, in March 2000, the company successfully spun out Magna Entertainment Corp (MEC) through a special 20 per-cent stock dividend. MEC will now focus on racetracks, while Magna will focus on its core business.

Magna has experienced phenomenal growth during its 40-year history, but has also incurred the occasional severe setback. In 1999 the company employed more than 59,000 people in 174 manufacturing divisions and 33 product development and engineering centres in 19 countries. It generated sales in excess of $13.5 billion and a profit of $627 million, while expanding through acquisitions.

Stock performance

Investors could have made or lost a bundle in this stock. The stock has exhibited both above-average upside potential and downside risk. The best three-year rate of return for the stock was a gain of 203.6 per cent annualized, and the average annualized three-year rate of return was 21.6 per cent. During the previous 10 years the stock has appreciated in value by an average of 37.4 per cent per year. However, during the previous year, value stocks underperformed, and this stock declined in value by 14 per cent.

Stock risks

Ouch! Investors in Magna stock have experienced above-average risk. The worst 12-month rate of return for the common stock was a decline of 75.5 per cent. The stock's worst setback since the start date was a decline of 93 per cent. Amazingly, it recovered in 18 months. During the stock-market correction of 1987, Magna stock declined by 71.8 per cent and took 54 months to recover.

Stock financial fundamentals

During the past 10 years, earnings per share have grown as Magna recovered from a financial nightmare. The price-to-earnings (P/E) ratio has declined by 34 per cent during the previous year to 10.7 as the stock price declined in value and earnings improved. In turn, the company has improved its balance sheet and is now trading at a very realistic valuation.

Future prospects

During 1998 the company made material investments outside the automotive industry. This caused the stock price to decline. Investors who want exposure to a growing company in the automotive industry could consider Magna International. The company does offer some upside potential, but the stock will still exhibit risk. If the auto industry continues to surge forward, this stock could participate handsomely. However, investors shouldn't expect triple-digit returns, just good absolute returns.

COMPANY DETAILS

Company name	**Magna International**	Industry classification	Industrial Products
Recent price	$69.55	Market capitalization (in $ millions)	$5,462
52-week price range from low to high	$55.10–$90.00	Ticker symbol	MG.a
Overall assessment of potential risk (one is more risky)	29/30	Phone number for annual report	905-726-2462
Number of mutual funds that hold this stock as a top 15 holding	120	Stock analysis start date	July 1982

ROLLING 12-MONTH TOTAL RATE OF RETURN FOR THE STOCK OVER TIME

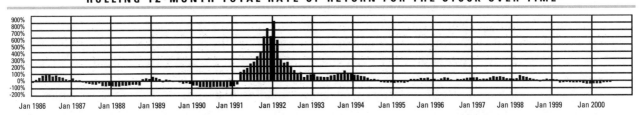

STOCK PERFORMANCE*

	1 month	1 year	3 years	5 years	10 years	15 years
Returns ending June 2000	-3.7%	-14.0%	-3.9%	4.6%	37.4%	11.5%
Best historical return	80.5%	817.1%	203.6%	94.5%	37.4%	20.3%
Average historical return	2.1%	38.7%	21.6%	16.7%	17.7%	14.3%
Worst historical return	-48.2%	-75.5%	-50.2%	-34.4%	8.0%	8.0%
Value at risk of $1,000	$877	$365	$253	$191	$2,393	$3,506

RETURNS GREATER THAN*

	1 month	1 year	3 years	5 years	10 years	15 years
10 per cent	19%	59%	61%	51%	93%	92%
Zero	50%	65%	71%	74%	100%	100%
Percentage of time stock lost $	50%	35%	29%	26%	0%	0%
Number of periods evaluated	216	205	181	157	97	37

DOWNSIDE RISK*

	Worst setback since start date	In bear 1987	In bear 1990	In bear 1994	In bear 1998
Setback for stock	-93.0%	-71.8%	-84.6%	-29.9%	-19.6%
Setback for stock market	-14.4%	-23.2%`	-16.3%	-9.7%	-24.6%
Setback ended in	Nov. 1990	Nov. 1987	Nov. 1990	Nov. 1994	Sept. 1998
Months to recover from loss	18	54	18	18	?

STOCK FINANCIAL FUNDAMENTAL INFORMATION

	1990	1991	1992	1993	1994	1995	1996	1997	1998	1999	Change
Average share price	$3.91	$11.21	$28.73	$48.20	$56.74	$55.89	$63.48	$82.49	$97.13	$79.98	-17.7%
Earnings per share	($7.98)	$0.58	$2.88	$3.06	$4.14	$5.15	$4.92	$8.22	$5.98	$7.46	24.7%
Book value per share	$8.22	$9.53	$14.59	$16.74	$21.50	$25.65	$33.16	$45.42	$65.94	$68.63	4.1%
Price-to-earnings ratio	(0.5)	19.3	10.0	15.8	13.7	10.9	12.9	10.0	16.2	10.7	-34.0%
Price-to-book ratio	0.5	1.2	2.0	2.9	2.6	2.2	1.9	1.8	1.5	1.2	-20.9%
Profit margin	-11.6%	0.8%	4.1%	5.4%	6.6%	7.0%	5.3%	7.6%	4.7%	4.3%	-9.4%
Asset turnover	1.10	1.37	1.68	1.68	1.54	1.49	1.34	1.44	1.07	1.35	26.0%
Leverage	7.6	5.5	2.8	2.0	1.9	1.9	2.1	1.7	1.8	1.9	5.0%
Return on equity	-97.1%	6.1%	19.7%	18.3%	19.3%	20.1%	14.8%	18.1%	9.1%	10.9%	19.9%
Dividend per share	$0.12	$ -	$0.20	$0.50	$0.80	$1.07	$1.07	$1.13	$1.31	$1.32	1.0%
Dividend yield	3.1%	0.0%	0.7%	1.0%	1.4%	1.9%	1.7%	1.4%	1.3%	1.7%	22.4%

*Source: The raw data used in developing this table was provided by Datastream.

MANULIFE FINANCIAL CORP

Company profile

Within the last year the insurance industry has undergone major changes as many insurance companies, including Manulife, have demutualized. This means the company is no longer owned by participating policyholders, but by shareholders. In light of this change, Manulife completed an initial public offering (IPO) in 1999. This should allow the company to better position itself within a highly competitive marketplace.

Manulife Financial is one of the leading global providers of insurance and wealth-management products such as life insurance, pensions, annuities, and group benefits. The company operates in Canada, the U.S., and Asia. Canada's largest life insurance company, Manulife also has the largest market capitalization of any publicly traded life-insurance company in Canada. The company's world headquarters are in Toronto, and it employs more than 28,000 people in 15 countries and territories worldwide. In 1999 Manulife generated total revenue of $14 billion and a profit of $866 million.

Stock performance

This stock hasn't been publicly traded for a year yet, but it has provided some excitement thus far. The 52-week range is between $15.25 and $28.25, providing opportunistic investors with some handsome profits. However, the stock isn't very consistent, posting positive rates of return after one month 67 per cent of the time.

Stock risks

This stock hasn't been tested over time, so it will display a lot more volatility in the future than in the past. The worst setback that this stock has ever incurred was a loss of 7.4 per cent. During the same period the average Canadian equity investment declined in value by 1 per cent, but Manulife stock only took two months to recover.

Stock financial fundamentals

The stock is currently trading at a price-to-earnings (P/E) ratio of 10.6. This means that investors are paying $10.60 for each $1 of historical earnings. This is a relatively low P/E ratio, but investors are currently unwilling to pay a higher price for the stock considering the prospects for the company and its track record of growth. During the previous year Manulife increased its return on equity by 13.5 per cent to 13.7 per cent.

Future prospects

Manulife Financial has a strong balance sheet, is competitive in the financial services industry, and is very dedicated to increasing shareholder value. The company has established operations throughout the world to help it achieve this objective. It has generated good earnings growth and continues to invest in new projects to fuel its growth. This is a value stock and it trades at a very reasonable valuation. However, the financial services industry is consolidating as companies acquire other companies, and this could provide both opportunities and threats for Manulife and its shareholders. Nevertheless, investors can expect reasonable rates of return from this company. It has the right business model and fundamentals, so if investors get the stock price right they can make money.

COMPANY DETAILS

Company name	**Manulife Financial**	Industry classification	Financial Services
Recent price	$26.10	Market capitalization (in $ millions)	$12,583
52-week price range from low to high	$15.25–$28.25	Ticker symbol	MFC
Overall assessment of potential risk (one is more risky)	23/30	Phone number for annual report	1-800-795-9767
Number of mutual funds that hold this stock as a top 15 holding	76	Stock analysis start date	October 1999

ROLLING 12-MONTH TOTAL RATE OF RETURN FOR THE STOCK OVER TIME

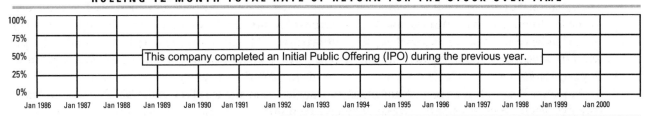

This company completed an Initial Public Offering (IPO) during the previous year.

Jan 1986 Jan 1987 Jan 1988 Jan 1989 Jan 1990 Jan 1991 Jan 1992 Jan 1993 Jan 1994 Jan 1995 Jan 1996 Jan 1997 Jan 1998 Jan 1999 Jan 2000

STOCK PERFORMANCE*

	1 month	1 year	3 years	5 years	10 years	15 years
Returns ending June 2000	-3.0%					
Best historical return	19.6%					
Average historical return	5.0%					
Worst historical return	-5.2%					
Value at risk of $1,000	$957					

RETURNS GREATER THAN*

	1 month	1 year	3 years	5 years	10 years	15 years
10 per cent	22%					
Zero	67%					
Percentage of time stock lost $	33%					
Number of periods evaluated	9					

DOWNSIDE RISK*

	Worst setback since start date	In bear 1987	In bear 1990	In bear 1994	In bear 1998
Setback for stock	-7.4%				
Setback for stock market	-1.0%				
Setback ended in	Jan. 2000				
Months to recover from loss	2				

STOCK FINANCIAL FUNDAMENTAL INFORMATION

	1990	1991	1992	1993	1994	1995	1996	1997	1998	1999	Change
Average share price										$18.31	
Earnings per share							$1.38	$1.70	$1.98	$1.73	-12.5%
Book value per share							$11.75	$13.87	$16.43	$12.67	-22.9%
Price-to-earnings ratio										10.6	
Price-to-book ratio										1.4	
Profit margin							5.1%	6.1%	6.8%	6.2%	-8.9%
Asset turnover							0.21	0.20	0.20	0.25	24.2%
Leverage							11.1	10.1	8.9	9.0	0.3%
Return on equity							11.7%	12.3%	12.0%	13.7%	13.5%
Dividend per share							$—	$—	$—	$—	0.0%
Dividend yield										0.0%	0.0%

*Source: The raw data used in developing this table was provided by Datastream.

NORTEL NETWORKS

Company profile

The stock market darling of 1999, Nortel Networks almost single-handedly propelled the Toronto Stock Exchange to a 30 per cent annual gain. Established when Northern Telecom merged with Bay Networks in 1998, the company designs, develops, manufactures, markets, installs, and services fully digital telecommunications and e-commerce systems. It also provides support and financing for all its products. Bay Networks, a leader in the worldwide data-networking market, is now a subsidiary and has become a major player in the global telecommunications industry, second only to AT&T in the U.S. Nortel Networks' major competitors are CISCO Systems and Lucent Technology.

Nortel began as a department within Bell Canada that developed telephone equipment. In 1985 it became a separate company. In 2000, BCE Inc. sold the majority of its investment in Nortel through a butterfly restructuring (see BCE Inc.)

In 1999 the company generated sales of over $32 billion. Its client list includes the corporate elite around the world, including Qwest in the U.S., JazzTel in Spain, Telstra in Australia, and Federa in the Netherlands, and the company adds new clients on a daily basis.

Stock performance

In one word—superior! Nortel Networks has rewarded investors exceptionally well for accepting above-average risk. During the last year the stock appreciated in value by more than 200 per cent. The best 12-month period for the common stock was a gain of 288.4 per cent, and the average 12-month return was 34.5 per cent. Nortel Networks' common stock has posted positive rates of return after 12 months 71 per cent of the time, displaying significant periods of upside potential.

Stock risks

In return for above-average performance investors have incurred above-average risk. The worst 12-month period for the stock was a decline of 31.5 per cent. The stock has underperformed during bear markets, declining by 47.2 per cent in 1998, when the average Canadian investment declined in value by 24.6 per cent. But Nortel took only four months to recover its loss.

Stock financial fundamentals

Nortel Networks has grown quickly during the past 10 years, and the company's stock multiples have increased as well, assisted by a decline in interest rates and investor anticipation of continued growth. The company posted a profit during the previous year but continues to trade at nosebleed valuation as investors bid up the price of the stock.

Future prospects

Last year we said that investors should have realistic expectations for the future. This year we will say it again, because Nortel Networks defied expectations during the previous year. Investors should remember that a company that is worth $304 billion dollars eventually has to make big profits or the stock price will decline. Yet rarely a month goes by without an announcement from Nortel of a major new customer. Short-term volatility provides good buying opportunities, but don't underestimate the risk or reward associated with this stock.

COMPANY DETAILS

Company name	**Nortel Networks**	Industry classification	Industrial Products
Recent price	$102.70	Market capitalization (in $ millions)	$304,226
52-week price range from low to high	$29.80–$105.67	Ticker symbol	NT
Overall assessment of potential risk (one is more risky)	2/30	Phone number for annual report	1-800-466-7835
Number of mutual funds that hold this stock as a top 15 holding	850	Stock analysis start date	July 1982

ROLLING 12-MONTH TOTAL RATE OF RETURN FOR THE STOCK OVER TIME

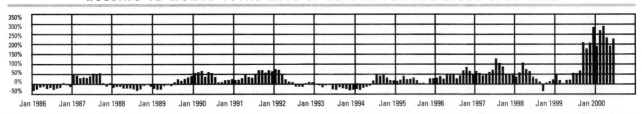

STOCK PERFORMANCE*

	1 month	1 year	3 years	5 years	10 years	15 years
Returns ending June 2000	28.8%	224.5%	88.4%	76.2%	39.3%	27.6%
Best historical return	34.7%	288.4%	101.5%	76.2%	39.3%	27.6%
Average historical return	2.8%	34.5%	21.0%	18.2%	17.0%	19.0%
Worst historical return	-34.7%	-31.5%	-10.1%	-6.3%	2.9%	10.0%
Value at risk of $1,000	$881	$773	$883	$953	$1,635	$5,995

RETURNS GREATER THAN*

	1 month	1 year	3 years	5 years	10 years	15 years
10 per cent	20%	60%	52%	71%	69%	100%
Zero	58%	71%	85%	94%	100%	100%
Percentage of time stock lost $	42%	29%	15%	6%	0%	0%
Number of periods evaluated	216	205	181	157	97	37

DOWNSIDE RISK*

	Worst setback since start date	In bear 1987	In bear 1990	In bear 1994	In bear 1998
Setback for stock	-47.2%	-34.4%	-16.5%	-28.9%	-47.2%
Setback for stock market	-23.0%	-23.2%	-16.3%	-9.7%	-24.6%
Setback ended in	Sept. 1998	Nov. 1987	Sept. 1990	March 1994	Sept. 1998
Months to recover from loss	4	30	3	20	4

STOCK FINANCIAL FUNDAMENTAL INFORMATION

	1990	1991	1992	1993	1994	1995	1996	1997	1998	1999	Change
Average share price	$3.71	$5.24	$6.08	$5.26	$5.45	$6.31	$9.08	$14.95	$19.11	$34.44	80.2%
Earnings per share	$0.26	$0.29	$0.34	($0.44)	$0.28	$0.29	$0.41	$0.54	($0.37)	$0.95	+356.8%
Book value per share	$1.92	$2.16	$2.54	$1.99	$2.32	$2.55	$2.97	$3.31	$6.32	$6.85	8.4%
Price-to-earnings ratio	14.3	18.1	17.9	(12.0)	19.5	21.8	22.1	27.7	(51.6)	36.3	+170.2%
Price-to-book ratio	1.9	2.4	2.4	2.6	2.3	2.5	3.1	4.5	3.0	5.0	66.3%
Profit margin	6.4%	6.0%	6.3%	-8.2%	4.5%	4.1%	4.8%	5.3%	-3.2%	7.6%	+335.7%
Asset turnover	0.99	0.86	0.90	0.86	1.01	1.13	1.18	1.19	0.87	1.03	19.4%
Leverage	2.1	2.6	2.4	3.2	2.6	2.5	2.4	2.6	2.1	1.8	-15.8%
Return on equity	13.5%	13.4%	13.4%	-22.1%	12.1%	11.4%	13.8%	16.3%	-5.9%	13.9%	+336.9%
Dividend per share	$0.04	$0.05	$0.05	$0.06	$0.06	$0.07	$0.09	$0.10	$0.11	$0.11	$–
Dividend yield	1.1%	1.0%	0.8%	1.1%	1.1%	1.1%	1.0%	0.7%	0.6%	0.3%	-44.5%

*Source: The raw data used in developing this table was provided by Datastream.

ONEX CORPORATION

Company profile

Onex is a Canadian conglomerate with investments in a variety of companies. The company generated revenues of almost $15 billion in 1999 and posted a profit of $293 million. Through Celestica, the company invests in electronic manufacturing services. It has an interest in ClientLogic, a provider of integrated customer relationship services with an e-bias. Onex has interests in the telecommunications industry through Gramercy Communications partners and Crest Communications and has invested in business-to-business e-commerce with @Onex and insLogic.com. Onex controls the world's largest in-flight caterers through Sky Chefs and, with Dura Automotive, the company is the world's largest manufacturer of driver-control systems for small vehicles. In J.L. French Automotive Castings, Onex has an investment in a leading supplier of aluminum die-cast components. With Magnatrax, Onex is a leading manufacturing of engineered building systems and components. Onex also has made investments in other attractive companies.

Gerald Schwartz began the company 20 years ago with $2 million and became a household name during 1999, when he attempted to buy both Air Canada and Canadian Airlines and merge the two. Even though he failed to consolidate the airline industry, he has been able to create shareholder value, a fact that many investors soon realized as they bid up the price of the stock regardless of the outcome of the airline bid.

Stock performance

A good conglomerate will provide diversification and the potential for higher rates of return. Investors in Onex have received above-average rates of return, but they have also incurred more risk. The best three-year rate of return for the stock was a gain of 77.4 per cent annualized, and the average annualized three-year rate of return was 22.7 per cent. During the previous 10 years the stock has appreciated in value by a whopping 29 per cent per year.

Stock risks

This company has experienced both good times and bad times, and its stock has experienced bad times as well, just like many other companies. Its worst setback was a loss of 69.5 per cent. During the same period, the average Canadian equity investment declined in value by 16.3 per cent, unfortunately, the stock took 31 months to recover its loss.

Stock financial fundamentals

Investors rekindled their love affair with this company during the previous year. In turn, the price-to-earnings (P/E) ratio has increased by 78.5 per cent to 30.3, a P/E multiple that's usually reserved for growth stocks. The company pays a nominal dividend but prefers to reinvest profits back into high-growth ventures that will increase its earning potential in the future.

Future prospects

Onex has a great foundation of companies that it can use to add shareholder value but investors have already factored that into the price of the stock. In short, the company has great management, good assets, great momentum, and a good balance sheet. The stock will exhibit a lot of volatility as investors further evaluate the company's assets and, if they continue to like what they see, the stock will continue to appreciate.

COMPANY DETAILS

Company name	**Onex**	Industry classification	Conglomerates
Recent price	$21.90	Market capitalization (in $ millions)	$3,591
52-week price range from low to high	$11.75–$29.72	Ticker symbol	OCX
Overall assessment of potential risk (one is more risky)	6/30	Phone number for annual report	416-643-5500
Number of mutual funds that hold this stock as a top 15 holding	93	Stock analysis start date	May 1987

ROLLING 12-MONTH TOTAL RATE OF RETURN FOR THE STOCK OVER TIME

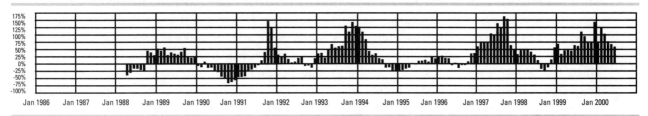

STOCK PERFORMANCE*

	1 month	1 year	3 years	5 years	10 years	15 years
Returns ending June 2000	2.3%	57.5%	48.8%	45.8%	29.0%	
Best historical return	72.7%	161.7%	77.4%	55.8%	30.8%	
Average historical return	2.1%	31.1%	22.7%	22.0%	20.4%	
Worst historical return	-38.2%	-64.5%	-15.2%	-8.4%	9.1%	
Value at risk of $1,000	$853	$603	$700	$939	$3,404	

RETURNS GREATER THAN*

	1 month	1 year	3 years	5 years	10 years	15 years
10 per cent	21%	65%	65%	77%	97%	
Zero	56%	71%	73%	94%	100%	
Percentage of time stock lost $	44%	29%	27%	6%	0%	
Number of periods evaluated	158	147	123	99	39	

DOWNSIDE RISK*

	Worst setback since start date	In bear 1987	In bear 1990	In bear 1994	In bear 1998
Setback for stock	-69.5%	-51.6%	-67.6%	-26.5%	-28.1%
Setback for stock market	-16.3%	-23.2%	-16.3%	-9.7%	-24.6%
Setback ended in	Oct. 1990	Jan. 1988	Oct. 1990	Feb. 1995	Aug 1998
Months to recover from loss	31	64	31	21	4

STOCK FINANCIAL FUNDAMENTAL INFORMATION

	1990	1991	1992	1993	1994	1995	1996	1997	1998	1999	Change
Average share price	$2.60	$2.31	$1.85	$3.03	$3.67	$3.51	$3.76	$7.11	$8.31	$13.62	63.9%
Earnings per share	$0.22	$0.07	$0.07	$0.22	$0.22	$0.31	$0.39	$0.26	$0.49	$0.45	-8.2%
Book value per share	$3.77	$3.17	$2.88	$3.20	$4.25	$4.56	$5.13	$5.55	$6.45	$7.78	20.7%
Price-to-earnings ratio	11.8	33.0	26.5	13.8	16.7	11.3	9.6	27.4	17.0	30.3	78.5%
Price-to-book ratio	0.7	0.7	0.6	0.9	0.9	0.8	0.7	1.3	1.3	1.7	35.7%
Profit margin	1.0%	0.4%	0.2%	0.6%	0.9%	0.7%	1.8%	0.9%	1.0%	0.5%	-45.8%
Asset turnover	1.28	1.31	1.77	3.43	2.09	2.24	0.84	0.91	1.17	1.09	-6.8%
Leverage	4.8	4.5	5.7	3.3	2.7	4.3	5.1	6.1	6.5	9.7	50.7%
Return on equity	5.8%	2.2%	2.4%	6.9%	5.2%	6.8%	7.6%	4.7%	7.6%	5.8%	-23.9%
Dividend per share	$0.08	$0.09	$0.10	$0.10	$0.10	$0.11	$0.11	$0.11	$0.11	$0.11	0.0%
Dividend yield	3.1%	3.9%	5.4%	3.3%	2.7%	3.1%	2.9%	1.5%	1.3%	0.8%	-39.0%

*Source: The raw data used in developing this table was provided by Datastream.

PETRO-CANADA

Company profile

Many investors will recognize the Petro-Canada brand name from its downstream gas stations. The company is Canada's second-largest gas marketer, with a 17 per cent market share, and it averaged throughput per gas station of 3.6 million litres, the highest among the national gas stations. In fact, Petro-Canada is the largest integrated oil-and-gas company within Canada. It explores for, develops, produces, and markets crude oil and natural gas. It also transports, refines, distributes, and markets crude oil into a full range of petroleum products and services.

Petro-Canada was formed in 1975, when the Canadian Government transferred many of its energy assets into a newly formed crown corporation. Petro-Canada then bought Atlantic Richfield Canada, Pacific Petroleum, Petrofina Canada, and the refining and marketing assets of BP Canada.

When the government privatized its assets, Petro-Canada completed an initial public offering (IPO) in July 1991. After becoming a publicly traded company, Petro-Canada restructured to improve profitability and earn investor confidence. The company worked with Chevron Canada and Mobil Oil Canada to construct an oil transshipment terminal to accommodate crude oil from Hibernia, an offshore oil well near Newfoundland. Petro-Canada hopes to soon increase production in this facility to 27,000 barrels per day.

Stock performance

Finally a good year for the oil-and-gas sector. During the previous year, the company's stock appreciated in value by 39.9 per cent. The best 12-month rate of return for the stock was a gain of 84.4 per cent, and the average rate of return after 12 months was 15.6 per cent. Investors should expect realistic returns with some volatility going forward.

Stock risks

The bad times of 1997 and 1998 are likely over, but investors shouldn't forget the lessons. The worst setback that this stock has ever incurred was a loss of 47.8 per cent. During the same period, the average Canadian equity investment declined in value by 24.6 per cent. The stock took 21 months to recover the loss.

Stock financial fundamentals

The price-to-earnings (P/E) ratio for this company decreased by 63.1 per cent during the previous year as profits soared. The company has substantially improved its balance sheet, still has a prudent level of debt and has improved its asset turnover and profit margins.

Future prospects

With its strength in natural gas, refining, marketing, and lubricants, Petro-Canada is very well positioned for growth throughout the next decade. The company is increasing its exposure to Grand Banks oil and other oil-sands opportunities. Investors who like the oil-and-gas sector could consider this brand-name company within their portfolio. Oil prices will likely decline but still remain high enough to allow Petro-Canada to generate good profits for investors.

COMPANY DETAILS

Company name	**Petro-Canada**	Industry classification	Oil & Gas
Recent price	$27.65	Market capitalization (in $ millions)	$7,516
52-week price range from low to high	$19.00–$31.15	Ticker symbol	PCA
Overall assessment of potential risk (one is more risky)	11/30	Phone number for annual report	403-296-4040
Number of mutual funds that hold this stock as a top 15 holding	124	Stock analysis start date	July 1991

ROLLING 12-MONTH TOTAL RATE OF RETURN FOR THE STOCK OVER TIME

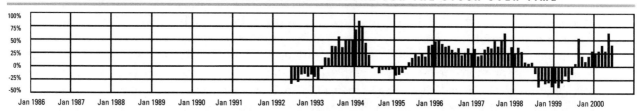

STOCK PERFORMANCE*

	1 month	1 year	3 years	5 years	10 years	15 years
Returns ending June 2000	-3.3%	39.9%	9.0%	17.8%		
Best historical return	28.4%	84.4%	33.7%	30.1%		
Average historical return	1.2%	15.6%	14.9%	16.1%		
Worst historical return	-30.7%	-37.8%	-2.8%	4.0%		
Value at risk of $1,000	$901	$703	$1,046	$1,379		

RETURNS GREATER THAN*

	1 month	1 year	3 years	5 years	10 years	15 years
10 per cent	16%	60%	62%	73%		
Zero	52%	66%	96%	100%		
Percentage of time stock lost $	48%	34%	4%	0%		
Number of periods evaluated	108	97	73	49		

DOWNSIDE RISK*

	Worst setback since start date	In bear 1987	In bear 1990	In bear 1994	In bear 1998
Setback for stock	-47.8%			-16.5%	-47.8%
Setback for stock market	-24.6%			-9.7%	-24.6%
Setback ended in	Aug. 1998			Jan. 1995	Aug. 1998
Months to recover from loss	21			6	21

STOCK FINANCIAL FUNDAMENTAL INFORMATION

	1990	1991	1992	1993	1994	1995	1996	1997	1998	1999	Change
Average share price		$11.10	$8.93	$10.64	$12.43	$13.24	$17.65	$23.65	$22.10	$20.04	-9.3%
Earnings per share			$0.04	$0.66	$1.06	$0.79	$0.94	$1.13	$0.35	$0.86	145.7%
Book value per share			$10.72	$11.25	$11.94	$12.53	$13.64	$14.47	$14.51	$15.02	3.5%
Price-to-earnings ratio			223.3	16.1	11.7	16.8	18.8	20.9	63.1	23.3	-63.1%
Price-to-book ratio			0.8	0.9	1.0	1.1	1.3	1.6	1.5	1.3	-12.4%
Profit margin			0.2%	3.6%	5.7%	4.1%	4.5%	5.1%	1.9%	3.8%	99.7%
Asset turnover			0.88	0.81	0.77	0.73	0.71	0.72	0.59	0.70	19.3%
Leverage			2.3	2.0	2.0	2.1	2.2	2.1	2.1	2.1	-0.4%
Return on equity			0.4%	5.9%	8.9%	6.3%	6.9%	7.8%	2.4%	5.7%	137.4%
Dividend per share			$0.13	$0.13	$0.16	$0.20	$0.20	$0.29	$0.32	$0.34	6.0%
Dividend yield			1.5%	1.2%	1.3%	1.5%	1.1%	1.2%	1.4%	1.7%	17.2%

*Source: The raw data used in developing this table was provided by Datastream.

POWER CORPORATION OF CANADA

Company profile

Power Corporation of Canada, established in Montreal in 1925, has become a diversified management and holding company with a variety of direct and indirect interests. It holds 67.4 per cent of Power Financial Corporation, which controls 76.6 per cent of Great West Lifeco Inc. and 67.7 per cent of Investors Group Inc. Great West Lifeco owns and operates various businesses, including life and annuity insurance operations and London Life Insurance Company. Investors Group provides personal financial planning services in Canada with a dedicated sales force of 3,626. Power Financial Corporation also owns Pargesa Holding S.A., with large holdings in France, Belgium, Luxembourg, and Switzerland involved in broadcasting, utilities, specialty minerals, and energy. In addition, it owns Gesca Ltée, which owns the Montreal daily newspaper La Presse, three other dailies, and several weekly newspapers in Quebec. The company also owns Power Broadcasting Inc., which operates 17 radio stations and four television stations in Quebec and Ontario as well as two programming services in the U.S.

In 1999 Power Corporation incurred a small setback when total revenue declined to $14.7 billion. However, net income increased to $533 million during the year.

Stock performance

During the previous year this stock posted below-average performance but still managed to squeak out a gain of 10.1 per cent. The best 12-month rate of return for the stock was a gain of 131.9 per cent, and the average rate of return after 12 months was 26.8 per cent. During the previous 15 years the stock has appreciated in value by an average of 17.8 per cent per year.

Stock risks

Even with various interests, Power Corp. does not offer perfect diversification. During the crash of 1987, the stock declined in value by 34 per cent and took 21 months to recover. The worst 12-month rate of return was a loss of 33.1 per cent, and the common stock generated negative rates of return after 12 months 22 per cent of the time. This stock has exhibited above-average volatility, which can be minimized within a well-diversified portfolio.

Stock financial fundamentals

The company has consistently generated above-average results by effectively utilizing assets to generate shareholder value. Power Corp. increased its return on equity by 17.5 per cent, from 10.1 per cent in 1998 to 11.9 per cent in 1999. This made a significant contribution to the company's ability to increase its earnings per share to $1.76. The common stock is currently trading at a price-to-earnings ratio of 15.5, which is very reasonable for a company focused largely on financial services.

Future outlook

The company is committed to creating shareholder value. It's investing heavily in the financial services industry and is committed to making these investments grow. Well positioned for the short- to mid-term, the company should benefit from a robust business and economic environment. Investors who are looking for a more conservative investment with good upside potential could consider this stock for their portfolio.

COMPANY DETAILS

Company name	**Power Corporation of Canada**	Industry classification	Conglomerates
Recent price	$30.40	Market capitalization (in $ millions)	$5,943
52-week price range from low to high	$19.10–$31.80	Ticker symbol	POW
Overall assessment of potential risk (one is more risky)	21/30	Phone number for annual report	514-286-7456
Number of mutual funds that hold this stock as a top 15 holding	45	Stock analysis start date	July 1982

ROLLING 12-MONTH TOTAL RATE OF RETURN FOR THE STOCK OVER TIME

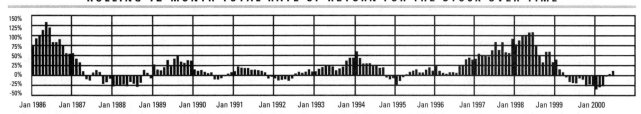

STOCK PERFORMANCE*

	1 month	1 year	3 years	5 years	10 years	15 years
Returns ending June 2000	13.1%	10.1%	23.7%	26.6%	18.6%	17.8%
Best historical return	28.6%	131.9%	70.2%	56.9%	27.5%	26.3%
Average historical return	2.1%	26.8%	23.8%	19.0%	16.9%	22.3%
Worst historical return	-24.2%	-33.1%	-2.7%	0.2%	5.7%	16.3%
Value at risk of $1,000	$929	$781	$1,057	$1,161	$2,205	$10,774

RETURNS GREATER THAN*

	1 month	1 year	3 years	5 years	10 years	15 years
10 per cent	13%	62%	77%	75%	88%	100%
Zero	58%	78%	97%	100%	100%	100%
Percentage of time stock lost $	42%	22%	3%	0%	0%	0%
Number of periods evaluated	216	205	181	157	97	37

DOWNSIDE RISK*

	Worst setback since start date	In bear 1987	In bear 1990	In bear 1994	In bear 1998
Setback for stock	-37.6%	-34.0%	-11.2%	-22.1%	-20.4%
Setback for stock market	0.0%	-23.2%	-16.3%	-9.7%	-24.6%
Setback ended in	Feb. 2000	Oct. 1987	Sept. 1990	Jan. 1995	Sept. 1998
Months to recover from loss	?	21	3	16	?

STOCK FINANCIAL FUNDAMENTAL INFORMATION

	1990	1991	1992	1993	1994	1995	1996	1997	1998	1999	Change
Average share price	$7.61	$8.01	$7.48	$8.74	$10.19	$10.04	$11.36	$17.89	$29.72	$27.22	-8.4%
Earnings per share	$0.84	$0.70	$0.51	$1.08	$0.58	$0.81	$0.95	$1.15	$1.42	$1.76	23.9%
Book value per share	$7.99	$8.06	$8.52	$8.96	$9.79	$10.20	$10.29	$11.96	$14.08	$14.85	5.5%
Price-to-earnings ratio	9.1	11.4	14.7	8.1	17.6	12.4	12.0	15.6	20.9	15.5	-26.1%
Price-to-book ratio	1.0	1.0	0.9	1.0	1.0	1.0	1.1	1.5	2.1	1.8	-13.2%
Profit margin	3.1%	2.7%	2.1%	4.4%	2.1%	2.8%	3.2%	2.6%	2.1%	2.7%	27.0%
Asset turnover	15.1	14.1	0.23	0.21	0.22	0.23	0.17	0.26	0.25	0.30	-0.9%
Leverage	0.22	0.22	12.8	13.2	12.8	12.3	14.2	21.2	18.8	17.6	-6.7%
Return on equity	10.5%	8.7%	6.0%	12.1%	5.9%	7.9%	9.2%	9.6%	10.1%	11.9%	17.5%
Dividend per share	$0.34	$0.35	$0.35	$0.35	$0.35	$0.35	$0.39	$0.40	$0.44	$0.49	11.0%
Dividend yield	4.5%	4.4%	4.7%	4.0%	3.4%	3.5%	3.4%	2.2%	1.5%	1.8%	21.6%

*Source: The raw data used in developing this table was provided by Datastream.

RESEARCH IN MOTION LTD.

Company profile

Situated close to the University of Waterloo, Research in Motion (RIM) has attracted a lot of young, talented individuals to work for the company. A leading designer, manufacturer, and marketer of wireless solutions, RIM delivers seamless access to time-sensitive information including e-mail, paging, Internet, and Intranet applications. RIM has a portfolio of award-winning products in the family, many of which can interact with and enhance third-party products. The most famous of the products in its portfolio is the BlackBerry, a pager with a mini-keyboard that allows users to send and receive wireless e-mail.

The company was founded in 1984 and initiated an initial public offering (IPO) in 1997, but it took until 1999 for the stock to soar to new heights. Considering how quickly technology changes, RIM has to become the industry leader within two years or else major competitors like telecommunications giant Nokia will squash the company. RIM's products have been described as engineering marvels, but its marketing efforts have been low-key. This makes the company super risky, because sales growth could subside and costs could increase, squeezing profit margins and the stock's upside potential.

Stock performance

If Santa came to my house at Christmas, I would like 100 shares of RIM. This is the kind of stock that makes millionaires of investors in short order. It also has the volatility to wipe out day traders, but that's another story. The stock's best 12-month rate of return was a gain of 1,407.3 per cent, and the average rate of return after 12 months was 405.6 per cent.

Stock risks

One of two scenarios will occur: you will either make or lose an insane amount of money. The stock has frequently increased or decreased in value by 75 per cent within days. During the bear market of 1998, it declined in value by 41.2 per cent, when the average Canadian equity investment declined in value by 24.6 per cent. On the other hand, RIM took just two months to recover its loss.

Stock financial fundamentals

There are no fundamentals. This stock is priced at or close to perfection. Any mistake and you should be prepared for the carnage. However, if the company incurs no mistakes, it will be a very jolly Christmas at your house!

Future prospects

This stock is very richly valued and volatile. The company has made investors both very rich and very poor, depending on when they bought or sold. This is not a stock that you want to buy and forget about. You should buy and sell opportunistically, when the price is right. This stock will decline in value by 30 per cent in a day based on a whisper that its costs are accelerating or sales are declining. If management can implement with success, you'll be able to count your fortunes. Assess the current situation and invest prudently.

COMPANY DETAILS

Company name	**Research in Motion**	Industry classification	Industrial Products
Recent price	$66.70	Market capitalization (in $ millions)	$4,756
52-week price range from low to high	$26.25–$260.00	Ticker symbol	RIM
Overall assessment of potential risk (one is more risky)	1/30	Phone number for annual report	519-888-7465
Number of mutual funds that hold this stock as a top 15 holding	14	Stock analysis start date	November 1997

ROLLING 12-MONTH TOTAL RATE OF RETURN FOR THE STOCK OVER TIME

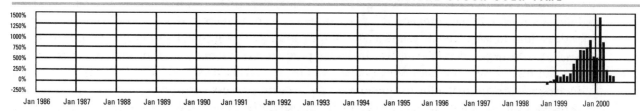

STOCK PERFORMANCE*

	1 month	1 year	3 years	5 years	10 years	15 years
Returns ending June 2000	38.4%	125.7%				
Best historical return	112.0%	1407.4%				
Average historical return	11.0%	405.6%				
Worst historical return	-58.6%	-41.2%				
Value at risk of $1,000	$740	$1,136				

RETURNS GREATER THAN*

	1 month	1 year	3 years	5 years	10 years	15 years
10 per cent	44%	95%				
Zero	56%	95%				
Percentage of time stock lost $	44%	5%				
Number of periods evaluated	32	21				

DOWNSIDE RISK*

	Worst setback since start date	In bear 1987	In bear 1990	In bear 1994	In bear 1998
Setback for stock	-76.1%				-41.2%
Setback for stock market	0.0%				-24.6%
Setback ended in	May 2000				Oct. 1998
Months to recover from loss	?				2

STOCK FINANCIAL FUNDAMENTAL INFORMATION

	1990	1991	1992	1993	1994	1995	1996	1997	1998	1999	Change
Average share price								$7.66	$6.47	$34.14	427.7%
Earnings per share							$0.01	$0.01	$0.15	$0.24	60.0%
Book value per share							$0.10	$0.86	$2.35	$2.50	6.4%
Price-to-earnings ratio								766.0	43.1	142.3	229.8%
Price-to-book ratio								8.9	2.8	13.7	396.0%
Profit margin							4.0%	3.2%	26.8%	21.4%	-20.0%
Asset turnover							0.93	0.33	0.23	0.41	75.2%
Leverage							2.7	1.1	1.0	1.1	7.3%
Return on equity							10.0%	1.2%	6.4%	9.6%	50.4%
Dividend per share							$–	$–	$–	$–	0.0%
Dividend yield								0.0%	0.0%	0.0%	0.0%

*Source: The raw data used in developing this table was provided by Datastream.

ROGERS COMMUNICATIONS

Company profile

Rogers operates wireless communication, cable systems, and media. Rogers Cantel is Canada's largest national wireless communications service provider; Rogers Cable serves more than 2.2 million cable TV customers, and Rogers Media operates 30 radio stations, home shopping and multicultural television channels, 16 consumer magazines, 45 business periodicals, directories, and information products, and a new media division.

During the previous year Rogers announced a partnership with Microsoft and AT&T. Microsoft will invest $400 million in Rogers convertible debentures with a conversion price of $35, a huge vote of confidence. AT&T has invested in Rogers Cantel. Rogers has also established partnerships with other international companies including Ericsson, Excite@home, and British Telecom. Rogers' strategy is simple: convergence, clustering, and bundling. To become a major player you have to acquire other companies, hence the Groupe Videotron offer. To offer several alternatives in the same market, you have to cluster, hence the acquisition of additional radio stations in major urban markets. Bundling is the last strategic advantage. Rogers has a variety of products and services it can bundle into one offer at an excellent price for consumers. In turn, the company has been able to reinvent itself and improve its balance sheet and operating results while becoming a major player within the Canadian marketplace.

Stock performance

Wow! This company has been notorious for underperforming the stock market in the past, but has proven its critics wrong during the previous two years. The stock gained 77.4 per cent during the last year and continues to fuel its growth through acquisitions, joint ventures, and divestitures. The stock has generated an average annual rate of return of 22.6 per cent during the previous 15 years. The best 12-month return for the stock was 283.9 per cent in 1998, and the average 12-month return was 37.7 per cent. Although Rogers may not achieve another 77.4 per cent annual return, telecommunications media offer investors above-average opportunities.

Stock risks

Rogers has exhibited above-average risk because of its excessive use of debt and the inherent risk of the industry. The stock's worst setback ended in January 1998, when it declined in value by 76.9 per cent, but it took only 14 months to recover. Its worst 12-month return was a loss of 62.2 per cent, and it posted a loss after 12 months 38 per cent of the time. In addition, the stock has frequently underperformed others, but this risk can be diversified away.

Stock financial fundamentals

Historically this company's financial fundamentals have been poor because of its use of debt and due to prior losses. However, Rogers has made large investments in cable and telecommunications systems during the 1990s and is now harvesting large dividends. During the previous year, Rogers generated excellent earnings-per-share, which increased by 26.5 per cent to $4.29 per share.

Future outlook

Rogers completed a partnership with Microsoft and AT&T in 1999. Now Rogers is benefiting from these strategic initiatives and new relationships that they have established with companies like Excite@home. Investors should continue to expect good things from Rogers.

COMPANY DETAILS

Company name	Rogers Communications	Industry classification	Communications & Media
Recent price	$41.95	Market capitalization (in $ millions)	$8,494
52-week price range from low to high	$22.30–$49.80	Ticker symbol	RCI.b
Overall assessment of potential risk (one is more risky)	5/30	Phone number for annual report	416-935-3550
Number of mutual funds that hold this stock as a top 15 holding	57	Stock analysis start date	July 1982

ROLLING 12-MONTH TOTAL RATE OF RETURN FOR THE STOCK OVER TIME

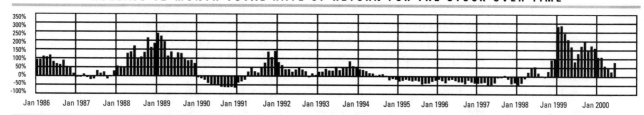

STOCK PERFORMANCE*

	1 month	1 year	3 years	5 years	10 years	15 years
Returns ending June 2000	7.2%	77.4%	69.3%	21.1%	17.8%	22.6%
Best historical return	55.7%	283.9%	81.7%	82.1%	36.8%	27.0%
Average historical return	2.7%	37.7%	22.2%	19.6%	18.2%	18.6%
Worst historical return	-32.3%	-62.2%	-30.9%	-19.4%	0.2%	9.4%
Value at risk of $1,000	$831	$563	$420	$509	$1,513	$4,270

RETURNS GREATER THAN*

	1 month	1 year	3 years	5 years	10 years	15 years
10 per cent	25%	58%	66%	64%	72%	97%
Zero	55%	62%	73%	81%	100%	100%
Percentage of time stock lost $	45%	38%	27%	19%	0%	0%
Number of periods evaluated	216	205	181	157	97	37

DOWNSIDE RISK*

	Worst setback since start date	In bear 1987	In bear 1990	In bear 1994	In bear 1998
Setback for stock	-76.9%	-34.7%	-65.7%	-29.9%	-48.2%
Setback for stock market	-5.5%	23.2%	-16.3%	-9.7%	-24.6%
Setback ended in	Jan. 1998	Oct. 1987	Oct. 1990	Jan. 1995	Jan. 1998
Months to recover from loss	14	4	30	?	14

STOCK FINANCIAL FUNDAMENTAL INFORMATION

	1990	1991	1992	1993	1994	1995	1996	1997	1998	1999	Change
Average share price	$8.60	$10.33	$13.59	$19.09	$20.49	$15.38	$12.09	$8.75	$9.85	$27.24	176.5%
Earnings per share	($1.13)	($0.76)	($1.30)	($1.89)	($1.16)	($1.78)	($1.60)	($3.17)	$3.39	$4.29	26.5%
Book value per share	$2.27	$1.71	$1.83	$0.90	$0.40	($1.31)	($3.00)	($6.14)	($2.73)	$4.45	-263.0%
Price-to-earnings ratio	(7.6)	(13.6)	(10.5)	(10.1)	(17.7)	(8.6)	(7.6)	(2.8)	2.9	6.3	118.5%
Price-to-book ratio	3.8	6.0	7.4	21.2	51.2	(11.7)	(4.0)	(1.4)	(3.6)	6.1	-269.7%
Profit margin	-18.0%	-9.9%	-17.3%	-22.7%	-8.9%	-11.7%	-11.5%	-21.0%	21.3%	26.2%	22.9%
Asset turnover	0.25	0.30	0.28	0.34	0.37	0.47	0.41	0.44	0.44	0.49	9.7%
Leverage	11.0	15.0	14.7	27.5	88.7	-24.9	-11.3	-5.6	-13.1	7.5	-157.6%
Return on equity	-49.8%	-44.4%	-71.0%	-210.0%	-290.0%	135.9%	53.3%	51.6%	-124.2%	96.4%	-177.6%
Dividend per share	$–	$–	$–	$–	$–	$–	$–	$–	$–	$–	$–
Dividend yield	0.0%	0.0%	0.0%	0.0%	0.0%	0.0%	0.0%	0.0%	0.0%	0.0%	0.0%

*Source: The raw data used in developing this table was provided by Datastream.

ROYAL BANK OF CANADA

Company profile

The Royal Bank of Canada is a major Canadian chartered bank. It serves almost 10 million customers globally from more than 1,410 branches and 4,585 bank machines in all provinces and territories of Canada. Founded in 1864 in Halifax, the bank now offers a full range of commercial, corporate, international, investment, and retail banking products and services. In addition, the bank provides brokerage, underwriting, and investment management services through wholly owned subsidiary RBC Dominion Securities and discount brokerage Royal Bank Action Direct. It also provides trust services, including pension and investment management, through Royal Trust. Finally, the bank offers creditor life, disability, individual life, and travel insurance and plans to offer home and auto insurance throughout Canada by the end of the year 2000. To achieve this objective the bank recently acquired two insurance companies in the U.S.

Royal Bank is committed to growing and diversifying its revenues, improving efficiency, managing risk, improving its balance sheet and financial strength, and attracting and retaining good employees. In 1999, Royal Bank generated gross revenues of more than $10.6 billion and profits of more than $1.7 billion.

Stock performance

Over the past 15 years, investors have not been disappointed with the performance of this stock. It has posted an average annual rate of return of 16.5 per cent. During the previous year it underperformed the Toronto Stock Exchange, but it still managed to post a gain of 20.3 per cent. The stock has generated lower rates of return from time to time, so investors should have a long-term investment horizon when buying it.

Stock risks

The stock price of Royal Bank has just endured its worst setback in over 20 years. During the bear market of 1998 its stock declined by 33.2 per cent while the average Canadian investment declined in value by 24.6 per cent. Unfortunately, the stock still hasn't recovered its loss.

Stock fundamentals

Companies that can earn a return on equity greater than 15 per cent over the long term make very attractive investments. Recently, Royal Bank has consistently achieved this benchmark. The bank has earned such an attractive return by improving its profit margin.

Future outlook

When interest rates go up, bank stocks tend to go down. However, investors must realize that this is a normal course of business. Over the long term, most banks have earned an excellent rate of return for their investors. Volatility occurs over the short term, but over the long term a good company adds value for investors. The bank will have to continue reducing costs and finding new sources of revenue such as the two U.S. insurance companies recently acquired by the bank. The company has a good business model and good fundamentals. At the right price this will be a good investment.

COMPANY DETAILS

Company name	**Royal Bank of Canada**	Industry classification	Financial Services
Recent price	$75.75	Market capitalization (in $ millions)	$22,928
52-week price range from low to high	$54.50–$82.25	Ticker symbol	RY
Overall assessment of potential risk (one is more risky)	30/30	Phone number for annual report	416-955-7806
Number of mutual funds that hold this stock as a top 15 holding	542	Stock analysis start date	July 1982

ROLLING 12-MONTH TOTAL RATE OF RETURN FOR THE STOCK OVER TIME

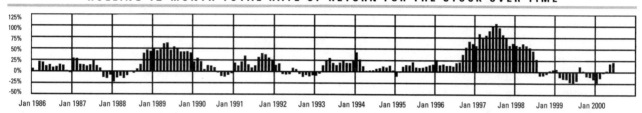

STOCK PERFORMANCE*

	1 month	1 year	3 years	5 years	10 years	15 years
Returns ending June 2000	-2.7%	20.3%	9.4%	23.4%	16.8%	16.5%
Best historical return	17.8%	104.6%	47.8%	31.9%	25.2%	19.6%
Average historical return	1.6%	17.9%	17.2%	16.2%	15.6%	16.7%
Worst historical return	-27.9%	-24.8%	1.9%	1.7%	10.8%	14.3%
Value at risk of $1,000	$918	$864	$1,135	$1,412	$2,936	$8,077

RETURNS GREATER THAN*

	1 month	1 year	3 years	5 years	10 years	15 years
10 per cent	8%	59%	69%	78%	100%	100%
Zero	62%	74%	100%	100%	100%	100%
Percentage of time stock lost $	38%	26%	0%	0%	0%	0%
Number of periods evaluated	216	205	181	157	97	37

DOWNSIDE RISK*

	Worst setback since start date	In bear 1987	In bear 1990	In bear 1994	In bear 1998
Setback for stock	-33.2%	-23.9%	-17.1%	-14.1%	-33.2%
Setback for stock market	-24.6%	-23.2%	-16.3%	-9.7%	-24.6%
Setback ended in	Aug. 1998	Nov. 1987	Sept. 1990	June 1994	Aug. 1998
Months to recover from loss	?	10	4	11	?

STOCK FINANCIAL FUNDAMENTAL INFORMATION

	1990	1991	1992	1993	1994	1995	1996	1997	1998	1999	Change
Average share price	$22.48	$25.75	$24.56	$26.75	$28.30	$29.70	$36.25	$63.20	$78.12	$68.79	-11.9%
Earnings per share	$3.00	$2.92	($0.05)	$0.46	$3.19	$3.49	$4.09	$5.01	$5.44	$5.11	-6.1%
Book value per share	$18.10	$19.40	$18.82	$18.09	$20.13	$22.42	$24.67	$27.91	$31.57	$34.34	8.8%
Price-to-earnings ratio	7.5	8.8	(491.2)	58.2	8.9	8.5	8.9	12.6	14.4	13.5	-6.3%
Price-to-book ratio	1.2	1.3	1.3	1.5	1.4	1.3	1.5	2.3	2.5	2.0	-19.0%
Profit margin	13.2%	14.3%	-0.3%	2.9%	17.4%	16.2%	18.9%	22.7%	22.1%	21.9%	-0.9%
Asset turnover	0.05	0.05	0.04	0.03	0.03	0.04	0.03	0.03	0.03	0.03	-2.6%
Leverage	24.0	22.6	23.7	28.7	27.1	25.9	28.0	28.3	28.1	25.1	-10.6%
Return on equity	16.6%	15.1%	-0.3%	2.5%	15.8%	15.6%	16.6%	18.0%	17.2%	14.9%	-13.6%
Dividend per share	$1.16	$1.16	$1.16	$1.16	$1.16	$1.18	$1.33	$1.52	$1.76	$1.88	7.0%
Dividend yield	5.2%	4.5%	4.7%	4.3%	4.1%	4.0%	3.7%	2.4%	2.3%	2.7%	21.3%

*Source: The raw data used in developing this table was provided by Datastream.

SEARS CANADA INC.

Company profile

If you're like 928,295 other Canadians, you opened a new Sears Credit Card account in 1999. Sears has utilized leading-edge technology to process credit-card applications within 20 seconds. As a reward for opening the account, Sears gives an applicant a $10 credit.

Canada's largest, single, full-line retailer of general merchandise and home-related services, Sears operates department and specialty stores nationwide including Sears Department Stores, Floor Covering Centres, Furniture & Appliances Stores, and Outlet Stores. In 1999, Sears also bought Eaton's for $60 million. Its other business endeavors include home repairs, travel services, and reselling long-distance service. Finally, the company still publishes a very successful catalogue and administers a state-of-the-art website.

Sears has built one of the strongest brand names in Canada, and more than 70 per cent of Canadian households are Sears Club members. In turn, from incurring major losses in 1992, the company posted record high earnings and profitability last year. Merchandising revenue grew by 12.5 per cent during 1999, twice the growth rate posted by the industry. Sears received the Innovative Retailer of the Year Award from the Retail Council of Canada, and the Canadian Marketing Association awarded Sears its Directors Choice Award for outstanding excellence in integrated marketing.

Stock performance

The biggest prize goes to the survivor, and Sears is a survivor in the merchandising industry. The best three-year rate of return for the stock was a gain of 67.8 per cent annualized, and the average annualized three-year rate of return was 12.6 per cent. During the previous 10 years the stock has appreciated in value by an average of 14.1 per cent per year.

Stock risks

Unfortunately, the merchandising industry is littered with bankruptcies and financially insecure companies. In fact, Sears at one time was one of these companies. When investors believe a company is heading downhill, they bail out and the wreckage is ugly. The worst setback that this stock has ever incurred was a loss of 60.9 per cent. During the same period the average Canadian equity investment declined in value by 2.9 per cent. It took an agonizing 51 months for the stock to recover from this loss.

Stock financial fundamentals

The company has made great improvements on its income statement and balance sheet. Earnings per share increased by 36.2 per cent during the previous year, attributable to higher profit margins.

Future prospects

If consumer spending continues to rise, this company will continue to make money for investors. If consumer spending decreases or if consumers go elsewhere, then watch out: this stock could again drop to a new low. Sears has the business model and fundamentals right, and at the right price the stock could make a significant contribution to your portfolio. In short, the future looks good, because Sears has managed to carve out a competitive position within the Canadian marketplace.

COMPANY DETAILS

Company name	**Sears Canada**	Industry classification	Merchandising
Recent price	$34.25	Market capitalization (in $ millions)	$3,643
52-week price range from low to high	$29.00–$42.50	Ticker symbol	SCC
Overall assessment of potential risk (one is more risky)	22/30	Phone number for annual report	416-941-4425
Number of mutual funds that hold this stock as a top 15 holding	43	Stock analysis start date	July 1982

ROLLING 12-MONTH TOTAL RATE OF RETURN FOR THE STOCK OVER TIME

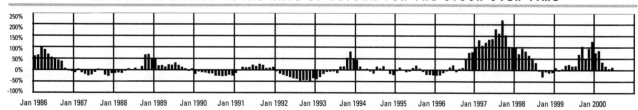

STOCK PERFORMANCE*

	1 month	1 year	3 years	5 years	10 years	15 years
Returns ending June 2000	0.7%	9.9%	23.9%	39.7%	14.1%	11.1%
Best historical return	28.9%	216.9%	67.8%	42.6%	15.9%	14.5%
Average historical return	1.5%	19.5%	12.6%	8.2%	4.6%	10.6%
Worst historical return	-26.9%	-46.6%	-22.9%	-11.2%	-5.0%	5.6%
Value at risk of $1,000	$893	$688	$633	$641	$671	$2,316

RETURNS GREATER THAN*

	1 month	1 year	3 years	5 years	10 years	15 years
10 per cent	16%	44%	40%	36%	25%	57%
Zero	52%	58%	69%	60%	76%	100%
Percentage of time stock lost $	48%	42%	31%	40%	24%	0%
Number of periods evaluated	216	205	181	157	97	37

DOWNSIDE RISK*

	Worst setback since start date	In bear 1987	In bear 1990	In bear 1994	In bear 1998
Setback for stock	-60.9%	-43.6%	-32.4%	-30.6%	-36.2%
Setback for stock market	-2.9%	-23.2%	-16.3%	-9.7%	-24.6%
Setback ended in	Nov. 1992	Nov. 1987	Dec. 1990	June 1994	Sept. 1998
Months to recover from loss	51	20	74	32	7

STOCK FINANCIAL FUNDAMENTAL INFORMATION

	1990	1991	1992	1993	1994	1995	1996	1997	1998	1999	Change
Average share price	$11.22	$11.81	$8.05	$7.71	$7.81	$7.32	$7.66	$17.98	$22.69	$30.50	34.4%
Earnings per share	$0.25	($0.34)	($1.04)	$0.05	$0.47	$0.13	$0.09	$1.10	$1.38	$1.88	36.2%
Book value per share	$11.25	$10.67	$9.10	$8.90	$9.13	$9.03	$9.00	$9.82	$10.96	$12.68	15.7%
Price-to-earnings ratio	44.9	(34.7)	(7.7)	154.2	16.6	56.3	85.1	16.3	16.4	16.2	-1.3%
Price-to-book ratio	1.0	1.1	0.9	0.9	0.9	0.8	0.9	1.8	2.1	2.4	16.2%
Profit margin	0.5%	-0.7%	-2.3%	0.1%	1.1%	0.3%	0.2%	2.5%	2.7%	3.3%	22.3%
Asset turnover	1.43	1.53	1.63	1.59	1.50	1.53	1.60	1.53	1.72	1.73	0.6%
Leverage	3.4	3.0	3.1	2.9	3.1	3.0	2.9	2.9	2.8	2.6	-4.3%
Return on equity	2.2%	-3.2%	-11.4%	0.6%	5.1%	1.4%	1.0%	11.2%	12.6%	14.8%	17.8%
Dividend per share	$0.24	$0.24	$0.24	$0.24	$0.24	$0.24	$0.24	$0.24	$0.24	$0.24	0.0%
Dividend yield	2.1%	2.0%	3.0%	3.1%	3.1%	3.3%	3.1%	1.3%	1.1%	0.8%	-25.6%

*Source: The raw data used in developing this table was provided by Datastream.

SUN LIFE

Company profile

Within the last year the insurance industry has undergone major changes as many insurance companies, including Sun Life, demutualized, transferring ownership from participating policyholders to shareholders. Sun Life completed its initial public offering (IPO) in 2000.

The company began operations in Canada in 1871 and, by 1999, had more than $300 billion of assets under administration. Sun Life Financial Services of Canada is a holding company for Sun Life Assurance Company of Canada. Sun Life and its group of companies provide individuals and corporations with a diversified range of products and services designed to meet their wealth management and insurance needs. The company has investments in companies like MFS, a well-regarded U.S. mutual fund company with $200 billion of assets, and in key markets around the globe, including the U.S., the UK, the Philippines, and Hong Kong. In addition, the company recently established a joint venture in India and is actively pursuing additional ventures in China.

Stock performance

The stock price doubled in the first three months after its IPO, not bad for an insurance company, and it makes a very compelling investment. But investors should have realistic expectations about the stock's performance. The best one-month rate of return was a gain of 33.7 per cent and the average one-month rate of return was a gain of 16.6 per cent.

Stock risks

The stock hasn't been tested over the long term, but its downside risk should be limited by its great valuation.

Stock financial fundamentals

Strong management, a strong balance sheet, a strong income statement, and a strong cash flow statement equal one strong company. However, much of this has already been factored into the price of the stock, which explains its rapid appreciation.

Future prospects

Sun Life has built a strong balance sheet, is competitive in the financial services industry, and has acquired some very interesting and profitable businesses. To help it grow globally, Sun Life has offices throughout the world. Its crown jewel is MFS, the U.S. mutual fund company, which operates some of the top-rated funds within their peer group.

This is a value stock trading at a very reasonable valuation. However, the financial services industry is consolidating as one company acquires another, and this could provide both opportunities and threats for Sun Life and its shareholders. Investors can still expect reasonable rates of return from this company. It has the right business model and fundamentals, so if investors get the stock price right they can make money.

COMPANY DETAILS

Company name	**Sun Life**	Industry classification	Financial Services
Recent price	$24.95	Market capitalization (in $ millions)	$10,521
52-week price range from low to high	$12.70–$25.25	Ticker symbol	SLC
Overall assessment of potential risk (one is more risky)	24/30	Phone number for annual report	1-800-786-5433
Number of mutual funds that hold this stock as a top 15 holding	60	Stock analysis start date	April 2000

ROLLING 12-MONTH TOTAL RATE OF RETURN FOR THE STOCK OVER TIME

This company completed an Initial Public Offering (IPO) during the previous year.

Jan 1986 Jan 1987 Jan 1988 Jan 1989 Jan 1990 Jan 1991 Jan 1992 Jan 1993 Jan 1994 Jan 1995 Jan 1996 Jan 1997 Jan 1998 Jan 1999 Jan 2000

STOCK PERFORMANCE*

	1 month	1 year	3 years	5 years	10 years	15 years
Returns ending June 2000	5.7%					
Best historical return	33.7%					
Average historical return	16.6%					
Worst historical return	5.7%					
Value at risk of $1,000	$1,062					

RETURNS GREATER THAN*

	1 month	1 year	3 years	5 years	10 years	15 years
10 per cent	67%					
Zero	100%					
Percentage of time stock lost $	0%					
Number of periods evaluated	3					

DOWNSIDE RISK*

	Worst setback since start date	In bear 1987	In bear 1990	In bear 1994	In bear 1998
Setback for stock	n/a				
Setback for stock market	n/a				
Setback ended in	n/a				
Months to recover from loss	n/a				

STOCK FINANCIAL FUNDAMENTAL INFORMATION

	1990	1991	1992	1993	1994	1995	1996	1997	1998	1999	Change
Average share price											
Earnings per share										$ 0.67	
Book value per share										$ 14.27	
Price-to-earnings ratio											
Price-to-book ratio											
Profit margin										1.8%	
Asset turnover										0.27	
Leverage										9.6	
Return on equity										4.7%	
Dividend per share										$–	
Dividend yield											

*Source: The raw data used in developing this table was provided by Datastream.

SUNCOR ENERGY INCORPORATED

Company profile

Suncor extracts crude oil from the oil-sands deposits of northern Canada, develops and markets conventional crude oil and natural gas in western Canada, and markets transportation fuels, petrochemicals, and heating oils under the Sunoco brand name in central Canada. In 1997 Sunoco began marketing natural gas directly to Ontario homeowners. And, in its first international venture, Suncor and partners have developed the Stuart Oil Shale Project near Gladstone in Queensland, Australia.

The company began in 1917 selling lubricating oils, kerosene, and spirits to Canadian war plants. In 1999 the company generated revenue of $2.3 billion, producing 142,800 barrels a day of crude oil, natural gas, and natural gas liquids and operating more than 500 Sunoco gasoline outlets throughout Ontario. Suncor generated net earnings of $200 million and is reinvesting in the company through such projects as the $2-billion Millennium oil sands expansion. The company is aiming to double its production in the next few years.

Suncor has improved its balance sheet and operating results as the price of oil has increased. However, the company realizes that it needs to balance economic growth, social responsibility, and environmental concerns to meet the needs of all the stakeholders. To achieve this objective, Suncor is constantly assessing possible improvements for the company.

Stock performance

Management aims to maximize the use of the company's assets. Suncor delivers solid results, record production, and higher cash flow year after year, even with low oil prices in the late 1990s. The stock price of Suncor increased by 14.6 per cent during the past year, not a very good result considering the performance generated by similar companies. The best 12-month rate of return for Suncor common stock was 111.2 per cent, and the average 12-month return was 30.6 per cent.

Stock risks

The worst 12-month rate of return for the stock was a loss of 16.3 per cent. During the market correction of 1994 the stock declined in value by 8.1 per cent and took seven months to recover its loss. During the market correction of 1998, the stock declined in value by 15.5 per cent and took eight months to recover. The stock will continue to display downside risk, but this can be diversified away in a portfolio of investments.

Stock financial fundamentals

This company has made big improvements over the past six years. Earnings per share increased to 80 cents in 1999 from 17 cents per share in 1993. The company's return on equity is still marginal, which could put downward pressure on the stock.

Future prospects

Investors looking for a conservative investment in the oil and gas industry, and who acquire Suncor stock at a reasonable price, should not be disappointed. Although the company is not immune to conditions that plague the industry historically, its stock has fared better than other resource companies in volatile markets. Investors will enjoy a big bounce in the company's stock if management can increase its asset turnover rate.

COMPANY DETAILS

Company name	Suncor Energy	Industry classification	Oil & Gas
Recent price	$34.20	Market capitalization (in $ millions)	$7,564
52-week price range from low to high	$26.00–$36.90	Ticker symbol	SU
Overall assessment of potential risk (one is more risky)	13/30	Phone number for annual report	403-269-8100
Number of mutual funds that hold this stock as a top 15 holding	120	Stock analysis start date	April 1993

ROLLING 12-MONTH TOTAL RATE OF RETURN FOR THE STOCK OVER TIME

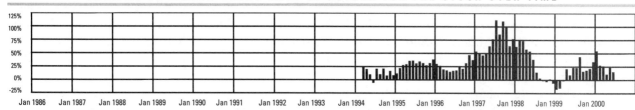

STOCK PERFORMANCE*

	1 month	1 year	3 years	5 years	10 years	15 years
Returns ending June 2000	2.3%	14.6%	24.3%	31.4%		
Best historical return	23.4%	111.2%	48.8%	36.2%		
Average historical return	2.4%	30.6%	33.7%	31.0%		
Worst historical return	-15.4%	-16.3%	14.3%	24.1%		
Value at risk of $1,000	$912	$973	$1,769	$3,375		

RETURNS GREATER THAN*

	1 month	1 year	3 years	5 years	10 years	15 years
10 per cent	11%	80%	100%	100%		
Zero	66%	91%	100%	100%		
Percentage of time stock lost $	34%	9%	0%	0%		
Number of periods evaluated	87	76	52	28		

DOWNSIDE RISK*

	Worst setback since start date	In bear 1987	In bear 1990	In bear 1994	In bear 1998
Setback for stock	-21.1%			-8.1%	-15.5%
Setback for stock market	-10.8%			-9.7%	-24.6%
Setback ended in	Jan. 1999			Feb. 1994	Aug. 1998
Months to recover from loss	3			7	8

STOCK FINANCIAL FUNDAMENTAL INFORMATION

	1990	1991	1992	1993	1994	1995	1996	1997	1998	1999	Change
Average share price				$7.21	$7.74	$9.60	$11.59	$19.67	$24.67	$27.43	11.2%
Earnings per share	$0.28	$0.18	($0.52)	$0.17	$0.28	$0.34	$0.43	$1.02	$0.85	$0.80	-5.9%
Book value per share	$2.76	$2.80	$2.15	$4.49	$4.79	$5.15	$5.70	$6.41	$6.87	$7.34	6.8%
Price-to-earnings ratio				42.4	27.6	28.2	27.0	19.3	29.0	34.3	18.1%
Price-to-book ratio				1.6	1.6	1.9	2.0	3.1	3.6	3.7	4.1%
Profit margin	6.9%	5.0%	-14.7%	2.5%	3.7%	3.9%	4.5%	10.8%	9.4%	7.7%	-17.9%
Asset turnover	0.39	0.35	0.39	0.74	0.74	0.78	0.74	0.60	0.49	0.44	-8.9%
Leverage	3.8	3.7	4.2	2.1	2.1	2.2	2.3	2.5	2.7	3.2	17.7%
Return on equity	10.1%	6.4%	-24.2%	3.8%	5.8%	6.6%	7.5%	15.9%	12.4%	10.9%	-11.9%
Dividend per share	$0.05	$0.13	$0.10	$0.10	$0.13	$0.14	$0.16	$0.34	$0.34	$0.34	0.0%
Dividend yield				1.4%	1.7%	1.5%	1.4%	1.7%	1.4%	1.2%	-10.1%

*Source: The raw data used in developing this table was provided by Datastream.

THOMSON CORPORATION

Company profile

The Thomson Corporation, one of the world's largest information and publishing businesses, has global interests in specialized information and publishing and owns newspapers throughout North America. The company continues to forge ahead and transform its business to take advantage of new Internet opportunities.

The company has five divisions:

Legal & Regulatory, with sales of $5.4 billion, is a leading provider of information and software-based solutions to legal, tax, accounting, trademark, corporate finance, and human resource professionals around the globe. In 1999 this division launched lawoffice.com

Thomson Financial provides comprehensive information and support to financial professionals. This market is expected to benefit from changes in technology including the Internet. Recently, Thomson offered to buy Primark, a leading information technology company in the U.S.

Reference, Scientific & Healthcare produces high-value information and services to researchers and other professionals in specific segments of the healthcare, academic, scientific, business, and government markets.

Thomson Learning provides books and teaching tools to individuals, schools, and corporations.

Thomson newspaper division provides a wide spectrum of information-based products and operates six daily newspapers, including the Globe and Mail in Toronto. Thomson is in the process of selling this division, with the exception of the Globe and Mail.

Stock performance

During the previous 12 months Thomson's stock has appreciated by 16.4 per cent, less than similar companies. But in the last three years, it has appreciated by an average of 19.6 per cent per year. The best 12-month rate of return was 91.5 per cent, and the average 12-month return was 19.9 per cent. In future, the company plans to focus more on Internet business and other high-growth initiatives. If it succeeds, the stock price should rise.

Stock risks

The worst 12-month return was a loss of 24 per cent. The stock has underperformed periodically, but has generally outperformed during stock market corrections. During the crash of 1998 it declined by 24.9 per cent, while the average Canadian investment declined by 24.6 per cent, but the stock took eight months to recover it loss.

Stock financial fundamentals

The company has sold businesses to improve its balance sheet. In 1998, for example, Thomson sold its travel business and recently it sold its newspapers. Thomson has generated good earnings-per-share growth and increased its book value by reinvesting the profits back into the company. The price-to-earnings (P/E) ratio decreased during the previous year from 34.5 in 1998 to 32.6 in 1999. These valuations are at a premium but still very reasonable considering the company's future prospects.

Future outlook

Thomson will have to continue to grow to maintain and increase its current stock price. Fortunately for investors Thomson can achieve this growth, since the divestiture of its newspaper division should provide the capital to fuel growth in other areas. The company has the fundamentals right. At a good price it should continue to generate impressive gains for investors.

COMPANY DETAILS

Company name	**Thomson Corporation**	Industry classification	Communications & Media
Recent price	$50.65	Market capitalization (in $ millions)	$31,530
52-week price range from low to high	$36.55–$55.50	Ticker symbol	TOC
Overall assessment of potential risk (one is more risky)	8/30	Phone number for annual report	1-800-663-9097
Number of mutual funds that hold this stock as a top 15 holding	114	Stock analysis start date	July 1982

ROLLING 12-MONTH TOTAL RATE OF RETURN FOR THE STOCK OVER TIME

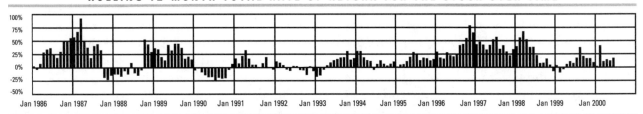

STOCK PERFORMANCE*

	1 month	1 year	3 years	5 years	10 years	15 years
Returns ending June 2000	5.3%	16.4%	19.6%	25.3%	16.4%	15.4%
Best historical return	35.7%	91.5%	40.3%	36.0%	17.7%	20.0%
Average historical return	1.7%	19.9%	17.0%	15.1%	12.8%	16.4%
Worst historical return	-29.0%	-24.0%	-7.5%	-0.8%	8.6%	13.6%
Value at risk of $1,000	$928	$863	$985	$1,107	$2,576	$7,574

RETURNS GREATER THAN*

	1 month	1 year	3 years	5 years	10 years	15 years
10 per cent	10%	66%	68%	64%	93%	100%
Zero	58%	81%	93%	98%	100%	100%
Percentage of time stock lost $	42%	19%	7%	2%	0%	0%
Number of periods evaluated	216	205	181	157	97	37

DOWNSIDE RISK*

	Worst setback since start date	In bear 1987	In bear 1990	In bear 1994	In bear 1998
Setback for stock	-37.3%	-37.3%	-29.3%	-13.3%	-24.9%
Setback for stock market	-23.2%	-23.2%	-16.3%	-9.7%	-24.6%
Setback ended in	Nov. 1987	Nov. 1987	April 1990	June 1994	Aug. 1998
Months to recover from loss	15	15	45	6	8

STOCK FINANCIAL FUNDAMENTAL INFORMATION

	1990	1991	1992	1993	1994	1995	1996	1997	1998	1999	Change
Average share price	$14.92	$15.81	$15.01	$15.44	$16.56	$18.15	$23.13	$32.11	$39.68	$41.76	5.2%
Earnings per share	$0.81	$0.61	$0.36	$0.62	$1.01	$1.84	$1.30	$1.26	$1.15	$1.28	11.3%
Book value per share	$6.08	$6.20	$6.29	$6.57	$7.56	$8.81	$9.54	$10.55	$15.66	$15.23	-2.7%
Price-to-earnings ratio	18.4	25.9	41.7	24.9	16.4	9.9	17.8	25.5	34.5	32.6	-5.4%
Price-to-book ratio	2.5	2.6	2.4	2.4	2.2	2.1	2.4	3.0	2.5	2.7	8.2%
Profit margin	7.2%	5.2%	2.8%	4.8%	6.7%	11.0%	7.4%	6.3%	7.6%	9.0%	19.0%
Asset turnover	0.68	0.68	0.71	0.69	0.66	0.72	0.59	0.64	0.49	0.53	8.9%
Leverage	2.7	2.7	2.9	2.9	3.0	2.6	3.2	3.0	2.0	1.8	-11.6%
Return on equity	13.3%	9.8%	5.7%	9.4%	13.4%	20.9%	13.6%	11.9%	7.3%	8.4%	14.4%
Dividend per share	$0.52	$0.51	$0.54	$0.58	$0.64	$0.70	$0.76	$0.82	$0.93	$0.96	3.0%
Dividend yield	3.5%	3.2%	3.6%	3.8%	3.9%	3.9%	3.3%	2.6%	2.3%	2.3%	-1.9%

*Source: The raw data used in developing this table was provided by Datastream.

TORONTO-DOMINION BANK

Company profile

Formed in 1955 through the amalgamation of the Bank of Toronto and the Dominion Bank, Toronto-Dominion operates more than 892 branches in all provinces and territories of Canada and has offices around the world. TD offers a full range of commercial, corporate, international, investment, and retail banking products and services in addition to brokerage, underwriting, and investment management services through wholly owned subsidiaries TD Securities and TD Evergreen. In the U.S., TD offers discount brokerage services through TD Waterhouse Group, the world's second largest discount broker with more than 3.1 million client accounts. This group continues to acquire similar companies in strategic countries around the world. TD recently merged with Canada Trust, which will allow TD to take the lead in personal and commercial banking, probably under the name TD Canada Trust. The company has gained a lot of momentum during the previous three years and is now Canada's largest bank by market capitalization. The company continues to pursue aggressive expansion plans and is attracting new clients on a regular basis.

In 1999 TD generated over $1.4 billion in profits, employed over 32,000 people, and operated 2,164 bank machines called Green Machines.

Stock performance

TD administers Green Line mutual funds, but its common stock proved to be a better investment (not adjusted for risk). This bank has done everything right. It invested in the Internet early, for example, and it bought Canada Trust. Investors have loved it, and the stock appreciated in value last year by 11.2 per cent. Its best 12-month rate of return was 139.5 per cent, and the average 12-month return was 22 per cent.

Stock risks

The stock has experienced above-average downside risk, underperforming during bear markets. During the market correction of 1998 the stock declined in value by 39.8 per cent, but recovered within seven months. During the market correction of 1987 the stock declined by 21.9 per cent, and took eight months to recover.

Stock financial fundamentals

TD's price-to-earnings (P/E) ratio decreased by 8.7 per cent during the previous year, as its earnings increased more than the price of its stock. The company now has a P/E ratio of 14 and a good track record of achieving earnings growth. In turn, TD could be considered a buy by some value investors.

Future prospects

The bank's profits depend heavily on the direction and level of interest rates and on capital-market activity. A little bad news could cause bank stocks to decline. However, banks have historically added a lot of value for shareholders over the long term. The worst 15-year rate of return posted by TD common stock was 10.1 per cent compounded annually. Patient investors who acquire the stock at attractive prices will benefit over the long term. In addition, TD is aggressively building its discount brokerage business, and this international growth strategy could generate more upside for investors. TD is a growth stock, and future volatility could increase as investors consider TD.com as more of an Internet investment.

COMPANY DETAILS

Company name	**Toronto-Dominion Bank**	Industry classification	Financial Services
Recent price	$36.00	Market capitalization (in $ millions)	$22,382
52-week price range from low to high	$24.40–$40.25	Ticker symbol	TD
Overall assessment of potential risk (one is more risky)	26/30	Phone number for annual report	1-800-463-9783
Number of mutual funds that hold this stock as a top 15 holding	515	Stock analysis start date	July 1982

ROLLING 12-MONTH TOTAL RATE OF RETURN FOR THE STOCK OVER TIME

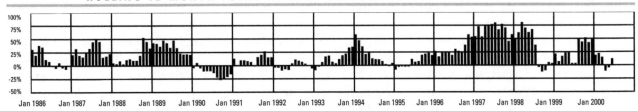

STOCK PERFORMANCE*

	1 month	1 year	3 years	5 years	10 years	15 years
Returns ending June 2000	-3.3%	11.2%	23.7%	31.5%	18.9%	17.1%
Best historical return	20.8%	139.5%	53.3%	37.3%	21.8%	22.0%
Average historical return	1.9%	22.0%	19.7%	17.5%	15.1%	18.9%
Worst historical return	-32.9%	-25.9%	-3.3%	1.9%	10.1%	14.8%
Value at risk of $1,000	$921	$902	$979	$1,300	$2,790	$9,330

RETURNS GREATER THAN*

	1 month	1 year	3 years	5 years	10 years	15 years
10 per cent	11%	62%	78%	69%	100%	100%
Zero	65%	79%	94%	100%	100%	100%
Percentage of time stock lost $	35%	21%	6%	0%	0%	0%
Number of periods evaluated	216	205	181	157	97	37

DOWNSIDE RISK*

	Worst setback since start date	In bear 1987	In bear 1990	In bear 1994	In bear 1998
Setback for stock	-39.8%	-21.9%	-31.0%	-13.4%	-39.8%
Setback for stock market	-24.6%	-23.2%	-16.3%	-9.7%	-24.6%
Setback ended in	Aug. 1998	Oct. 1987	Sept. 1990	June 1994	Aug. 1998
Months to recover from loss	7	8	35	15	7

STOCK FINANCIAL FUNDAMENTAL INFORMATION

	1990	1991	1992	1993	1994	1995	1996	1997	1998	1999	Change
Average share price	$8.75	$9.10	$8.75	$9.27	$10.53	$10.85	$13.45	$21.66	$27.84	$33.57	20.6%
Earnings per share	$0.90	$0.75	$0.63	$0.41	$1.07	$1.25	$1.47	$1.77	$1.81	$2.39	32.0%
Book value per share	$6.91	$7.28	$7.57	$7.65	$8.37	$9.15	$10.15	$11.38	$12.94	$17.25	33.3%
Price-to-earnings ratio	9.7	12.1	13.9	22.6	9.8	8.7	9.1	12.2	15.4	14.0	-8.7%
Price-to-book ratio	1.3	1.3	1.2	1.2	1.3	1.2	1.3	1.9	2.2	1.9	-9.5%
Profit margin	7.9%	7.1%	7.2%	4.6%	11.0%	10.2%	12.0%	13.5%	10.8%	13.2%	22.5%
Asset turnover	0.10	0.09	0.07	0.06	0.06	0.07	0.06	0.05	0.06	0.05	-4.7%
Leverage	16.1	15.7	16.2	18.4	19.7	19.7	20.7	24.1	23.6	20.0	-15.1%
Return on equity	13.0%	10.3%	8.3%	5.4%	12.8%	13.7%	14.5%	15.6%	14.0%	13.9%	-0.9%
Dividend per share	$0.38	$0.38	$0.38	$0.38	$0.41	$0.45	$0.51	$0.56	$0.66	$0.72	9.0%
Dividend yield	4.3%	4.2%	4.3%	4.1%	3.9%	4.1%	3.8%	2.6%	2.4%	2.1%	-9.5%

*Source: The raw data used in developing this table was provided by Datastream.

TRIZECHAHN CORPORATION

Company profile

TrizecHahn Corporation is one of the largest real-estate companies in North America and is currently expanding into global markets. It has more than US$7.9 billion in assets, an increase of more than 18 per cent since 1998, and a market capitalization of US$7.17 billion, an increase of 0.8 per cent over the previous year. The company has an innovative and opportunistic management group, who have a proven track record and extensive expertise in property development. Management is committed to building a company with sound financial strength and good cash-flow growth.

The company had a good year. Cash flow has grown consistently for the last four years. Its re-leasing rates grew by an average of 14 per cent, and it continues to provide value-added services for its tenants. TrizecHahn recently signed agreements, for example, to provide tenants with leading-edge technologies. The outlook for the real-estate industry remains favourable. The economy is growing, and companies need more space than ever.

TrizecHahn owns and manages 67 million square feet of office properties around the globe, including the 3.5-million-square-foot Sears Tower in Chicago. Its holdings include more than 117 office properties, and it has also developed retail, entertainment, and office projects.

Stock performance

Real estate comes with high risk but excellent opportunities for profit. TrizecHahn common stock generated above-average results for the sector, but did not outperform the Toronto Stock Exchange during the previous 12 months, when the stock posted a loss of 9.5 per cent. In the 1980s, when real estate was hot, the common stock of TrizecHahn posted a positive 12-month rate of return of 324 per cent.

Stock risks

Volatility and real-estate investing go hand in hand. The worst 12-month rate of return for the common stock of TrizecHahn was a decline of 80.5 per cent. The worst setback incurred by the stock was a loss of 92.6 per cent, and it took two years to recover. In short, investors can lose a lot of money if a real estate company's future prospects become too bleak.

Stock financial fundamentals

The company continues to generate record levels of earnings and cash flow, but investors fail to notice. During the previous year, management has increased earnings per share by 28.4 per cent to 95 cents per share.

Future outlook

The future for the real-estate sector has improved, but investors are still hesitant. They will not likely see a repeat of the glory days of the 1980s, but lower interest rates, higher corporate profits, and lease renegotiations should generate higher cash flow when tenants renew their leases.

TrizecHahn is committed to acquiring and developing real-estate property to improve cash flow. During the previous year this strategy may not have rewarded investors richly, but over the longer term it's a strategy worth considering. At a reasonable price and with a bullish real estate market, investors could gain from this stock.

COMPANY DETAILS

Company name	**Trizec Hahn**	Industry classification	Real Estate
Recent price	$26.50	Market capitalization (in $ millions)	$3,951
52-week price range from low to high	$18.50–$30.60	Ticker symbol	TZH
Overall assessment of potential risk (one is more risky)	10/30	Phone number for annual report	416-361-7200
Number of mutual funds that hold this stock as a top 15 holding	28	Stock analysis start date	July 1982

ROLLING 12-MONTH TOTAL RATE OF RETURN FOR THE STOCK OVER TIME

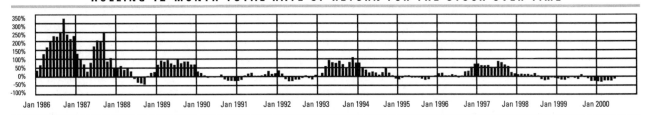

STOCK PERFORMANCE*

	1 month	1 year	3 years	5 years	10 years	15 years
Returns ending June 2000	12.8%	-9.5%	-0.5%	8.8%	10.3%	26.6%
Best historical return	125.8%	324.0%	107.0%	70.1%	39.5%	26.6%
Average historical return	2.1%	26.2%	19.0%	19.8%	18.3%	15.6%
Worst historical return	-42.1%	-80.5%	-49.2%	-10.1%	2.4%	9.0%
Value at risk of $1,000	$852	$287	$301	$898	$1,968	$4,000

RETURNS GREATER THAN*

	1 month	1 year	3 years	5 years	10 years	15 years
10 per cent	17%	48%	70%	75%	78%	89%
Zero	48%	61%	77%	93%	100%	100%
Percentage of time stock lost $	52%	39%	23%	7%	0%	0%
Number of periods evaluated	216	205	181	157	97	37

DOWNSIDE RISK*

	Worst setback since start date	In bear 1987	In bear 1990	In bear 1994	In bear 1998
Setback for stock	-92.6%	-47.4%	-29.0%	-21.8%	-22.4%
Setback for stock market	-5.5%	-23.2%	-16.3%	-9.7%	-24.6%
Setback ended in	Sept. 1985	Jan. 1988	Oct. 1990	Jan. 1995	Aug. 1998
Months to recover from loss	24	14	28	20	?

STOCK FINANCIAL FUNDAMENTAL INFORMATION

	1990	1991	1992	1993	1994	1995	1996	1997	1998	1999	Change
Average share price	$9.96	$10.39	$9.80	$15.31	$19.37	$18.35	$20.92	$32.02	$31.68	$28.71	-9.4%
Earnings per share	$0.80	$0.81	$0.52	$0.56	$2.48	$0.71	$0.16	$0.44	$0.74	$0.95	28.4%
Book value per share	$4.91	$5.69	$6.47	$7.73	$10.34	$11.02	$13.67	$15.47	$12.13	$12.86	6.0%
Price-to-earnings ratio	12.5	12.8	18.8	27.3	7.8	25.8	130.8	72.8	42.8	30.2	-29.4%
Price-to-book ratio	2.0	1.8	1.5	2.0	1.9	1.7	1.5	2.1	2.6	2.2	-14.5%
Profit margin	2.1%	2.5%	1.7%	1.8%	7.2%	12.9%	2.7%	6.4%	7.9%	8.4%	5.7%
Asset turnover	3.06	2.14	1.81	1.12	1.13	0.29	0.10	0.12	0.19	0.23	24.4%
Leverage	2.6	2.7	2.6	3.5	3.0	1.7	4.4	3.7	4.1	3.8	-7.9%
Return on equity	16.3%	14.2%	8.0%	7.2%	24.0%	6.4%	1.2%	2.8%	6.1%	7.4%	21.1%
Dividend per share	$ -	$ -	$ -	$0.07	$0.07	$0.09	$0.10	$0.35	$0.46	$0.52	13.0%
Dividend yield	0.0%	0.0%	0.0%	0.5%	0.4%	0.5%	0.5%	1.1%	1.5%	1.8%	24.7%

*Source: The raw data used in developing this table was provided by Datastream.

Appendix

Getting Free Money with Labour-Sponsored Funds[1]

A labour-sponsored venture capital corporation (LSVCC) is a mutual fund that invests in high-growth and high-risk early stage companies before they become publicly traded. They are called labour funds because they are sponsored by a labour union. As little as 10 years ago, small investors had very little opportunity to invest in these types of companies. The attraction here is the potential for higher rates of return. Morgan Stanley reports that the average annual rate of return on venture capital during the previous 20 years was 21.4 per cent, which was 3.9 per cent higher than for small-cap stocks.

Many of the world's biggest and best companies began with the backing of venture capital firms. Success in the technology industry, for example, has become legendary. Compaq, Netscape, Sun Microsystems, Apple Computers, Cisco, and Microsoft were all created in the previous 20 years from scratch. The benefits are great:

Increased opportunities. Venture capital firms invest in early- and late-stage entrepreneurial companies before they become publicly traded. By investing before others, they can participate in higher rates of return.

Reduced volatility. Venture capital funds are not susceptible to the short-term volatility of the stock market. Most of the companies owned by a venture capital firm are not traded on the stock exchange and do not encounter the daily gyrations of the market. So labour-sponsored funds reduce the volatility of an investor's portfolio. However, reduced overall portfolio volatility does not mean that there is little risk with these funds. The risk, like the opportunity, can be very large.

Government-sponsored financial incentives. Individuals who invest in a labour-sponsored fund receive a 15 per cent tax credit from the federal government, up to $750 annually. In addition, investors could receive an additional tax credit from their provincial government, which varies in amount by province. In return, investors have to invest in the fund for eight years. If they redeem the fund before this time, they have to repay the tax credit.

Increased foreign investments in an RRSP. For each $1 you invest in such a fund you can increase your foreign investments by $3, to a maximum of 45 per cent within your self-directed RRSP (50 per cent in 2001). Thus, if you have $50,000 in your RRSP and you have $12,500 invested outside of Canada, you can increase that amount to $27,500 by putting an additional $5,000 into a labour-sponsored fund in your RRSP.

The past five years have not generated eye-popping results for most of these funds. However, recently some of these funds have been able to exploit several successful investments, and some funds have doubled in value within a very short time. However, these funds do incur risk, in keeping with start-up companies in general. Long-term investors will be well served in a mutual fund that invests in this high-growth, high-risk, venture-capital market.

[1] The first section of this appendix is an excerpt from *101 Investment Tips* authored by Wilfred Vos and Jim Helik.

The key to selecting a good labour-sponsored mutual fund is the quality of the fund's management. Management must have the ability to find and invest in good-quality start-up businesses, with above-average growth prospects, at a reasonable price. Investors who want to participate in this sector could consider any of 17 different mutual funds (some of which are not available in every province) including the B.E.S.T. Discoveries Fund, Centerfire Growth Fund, the Canadian Science & Technology Fund, the Triax Growth Fund, or the Vengrowth Fund.

B.E.S.T. Discoveries Fund

To assess the merits of a labour-sponsored mutual fund, it is important to dig a little deeper into the fund's prospectus and other historical information. In the following section we will do just this with one of the funds mentioned above. The B.E.S.T. Discoveries Fund posted a return of 65.7 during the previous year and 15.4 during the previous three years. This fund is unique in three ways: It has displayed less downside risk than similar funds, especially during the spring of 2000—a period of above-average downside risk; the fund's portfolio is primarily comprised of private companies; and the fund has a limited but diversified number of investments. These three factors should contribute favourably to the fund's future performance.

The fund's primary objective is to achieve long-term capital appreciation for its unitholders. To achieve this objective, it invests in eligible businesses that have the greatest potential for long-term growth. The fund focuses primarily on niche businesses, but also on companies with a broader market focus that capitalize on innovative uses of engineering, science, and technology. To diversify the portfolio, the fund invests in companies that are in different stages of development, different industries, and that can take advantage of different business opportunities. Some of these companies operate in the telecommunications, information technology, computer, or life sciences industries. The following section is a quick synopsis of some of the companies that are part of the B.E.S.T. Discoveries Fund.

Apeks is an old-economy company with a great business model. It develops and manufactures rotary tri-cone drill bits for the open-pit mining industry. The advantage for shareholders is that Apeks is the only Canadian manufacturer of this product. Apeks also has a unique strategy of on-site consultation and customization, which enables mining companies to increase productivity and reduce production costs.

Bulldog is a leading provider of enterprise content management software and consulting services. By providing customers with flexible, best-of-breed enterprise content management solutions, it has developed partnerships with some major companies including Oracle and Sun Microsystems. Bulldog enables multinational companies such as Disney, Sony Pictures, and Microsoft to store media files (images, video, audio, text, and HTML) in a centralized digital library. The company can then provide access to the digital library to its employees and partners through a virtual private network or Intranet.

Channelware is a spin-off from Northern Telecom. It is a leading provider of alternative marketing and distribution in the software industry. The company's NetActive technology allows software products to become more accessible and affordable to the mass market. It distributes its product through licensing agreements with publishers, including Sega and Hasbro, two of the major players in the industry. Channelware's strategy is to open new markets for software products through rental, leasing, and promotional opportunities.

Chrysalis develops encryption technology for Internet and Intranet communications and electronic commerce companies. Chrysalis technology protects the integrity, confidentiality, and authenticity of electronic information, as well as enhancing the speed and reducing the cost for companies conducting business electronically. This has become a very robust industry since major Web sites like Yahoo and Amazon.com were shut down by computer hackers.

Eco Logic solves toxic chemical waste problems in a safe, permanent, and cost-effective manner. They convert on-site organic, hazardous materials into reusable or disposable products. This is a more competitive industry than some niche new-economy industries, but solving clients' waste problems is a value-added service that can be very profitable. (Some new-economy companies can't make such claims.) Applications for the services include PCBs, contaminated soils, chemical warfare agents, petrochemical wastes, and certain low-level radioactive wastes.

Indigo Books and Café is the second-largest bookstore business in Canada, where it operates 14 superstores that sell books, music, gifts and paper goods, videos, multimedia products, newspapers, and magazines. Its larger competitor, Chapters, is a publicly traded company that has encountered some setbacks recently. This should offer Indigo additional opportunities. Indigo also operates an online book retailing business through a Web site that is much more than an order form, a business model that has been very successful for Amazon.com. Indigo has designed its online business to give access to the same products as it sells in its stores. It also features a dedicated team of journalists and critics who provide original content and customer service support.

InternetSecure offers a secure, real-time credit-card processing system for Internet merchants and is currently the only non-financial institution in the world facilitating U.S. and Canadian dollar transactions. This company provides merchants with a bank-approved, real-time credit card processing system that can accommodate Visa, MasterCard, and American Express.

These are just some of the dynamic new- and old-economy companies included in the B.E.S.T Discoveries Fund, and it will derive its value from their high growth and high potential. Historically this fund has generated some very impressive returns and could be considered a great complement to another labour-sponsored fund or as an investment on its own. Investors looking to take advantage of an RSP eligible labour sponsored fund with a large tax credit should seriously consider the B.E.S.T. Discoveries Fund—a fund with excellent potential.

Glossary of Terms

Absorbed: An issue is absorbed when it has been entirely sold to the public.

Account Statement: A record that summarizes all transactions in an investor's account. Statements have to be provided to investors at least quarterly. However, some firms provide statements on a monthly basis.

Accrued Interest: Interest accumulated on a bond since the last interest payment.

Acquisition: When one corporation acquires a controlling interest in another corporation.

Across the Board: A movement—either up or down—in the stock market that affects almost all the stocks. For example, if almost all the stocks on a stock exchange appreciated in value then you would say "the movement was across the board."

Active Market: When a stock or a stock market experiences heavy trading volume.

ADR (American Depository Receipt): A receipt for shares of a foreign-based company. These receipts are traded on an American stock exchange.

Affiliated Company: A company that has less than 50 per cent of its shares owned by another company (*see* Subsidiary).

After Tax Real Rate of Return: The rate of return earned by an investor after deducting the tax expense and the rate of inflation. This number should be positive if you are making good investments.

All Time Periods (ATP) Chart: A combination of tables that illustrate the historical performance of a mutual fund.

Alternative Minimum Tax (AMT): A tax aimed at preventing affluent investors from using tax shelters to avoid paying income tax.

Analyst: An individual who researches corporations, industry groups, and the stock market to make buy and sell recommendations for investors.

Annual Meeting: A stockholder meeting that is held yearly. This meeting is held to allow corporate executives to report on the year's results, to elect the board of directors, and to transact any other business outstanding.

Annual Report: The formal financial statements issued by the company to shareholders after the company's year-end.

Annuity: A contract between a life insurance company and an investor that guarantees income for a predefined period.

Arrears: Dividends that weren't paid when due but are still owed to shareholders. This is a common feature of preferred shares.

Assets: All the valuables of a corporation or individuals.

Asset Allocation: The division of investment funds amongst various types of investment categories.

Average Cost: The average cost of acquiring an investment. For example, if an investor bought 100 shares at $50 each and 100 shares at $100 each, the average cost would be 100 x $50 plus 100 x $100 divided by 200, which is equal to $75 per share. The taxable capital gain for an investment is the selling price minus the average cost.

Averaging Down: Investing in additional securities of a particular investment when the price has declined to reduce your average cost.

Back Office: Those divisions at a broker-dealer that are not directly involved in sales or trading. These back office departments include accounting and record keeping.

Back-End Load: A fee that an investor pays when withdrawing money from an investment; this is also called "deferred sales charge."

Balance Sheet: A financial statement disclosing a corporation's assets, liabilities, and owners' equity as of a particular date.

Bankrupt: The legal status of a corporation (or an individual) that hasn't been able to pay its debts in an orderly fashion.

Basis Point: A financial industry term: 1/100th of 1 per cent is 1 basis point.

Bear: An investor who expects the market will decline.

Bear Market: A declining capital market.

Bell: A signal that indicates that trading on a major stock exchange has either opened or closed.

Bellwether Security: A stock that is perceived as an indicator of the overall stock market's direction. Bell Canada, for example, is considered a bellwether stock in Canada.

Beneficiary: A person who is, or will be, the recipient of the proceeds of assets (net of liabilities) held by an individual on the event of death.

Bid and Ask: A bid is the highest price a buyer is willing to pay for a security. An ask is the lowest price a seller is willing to accept for the security.

Big Board: Industry lingo for the New York Stock Exchange.

Black Monday: Monday, October 19, 1987. This was the day when the Dow Jones Industrial Average fell a record 508 points.

Block Trade: A large amount of a stock sold or bought as a single unit.

Blue Chip: A "brand name" leading company with an established record of earnings and dividend payments. The term blue chip is generated from the card game of poker, in which the blue chips are the most valuable. Blue-chip companies are the largest and most valuable companies.

Board Lot: A regular trading unit (number of shares) that has been uniformly established by stock exchanges.

Bond: A certificate proving a debt on which the issuer has a legal obligation to pay the debt holder an interest payment and repay the loan at maturity.

Book Value: The value of the assets belonging to the shareholders of a company after the creditors have been paid.

Bottom-Up Approach to Investing: An investment method where an investor will look for individual stocks that exhibit value. This approach assumes that an individual company's stock can do well, even though its industry group may not.

Broker: An individual who acts as an agent to facilitate the trade of securities for buyers and sellers. Brokers charge a fee for their services.

Bull: An investor who expects an increase in capital markets.

Bull Market: An increasing capital market.

Buying on Margin: Buying securities on credit after establishing a margin account at a brokerage firm.

Buy Order: An order placed with your broker to purchase a specified number of shares in a company at a particular price.

Call: An option that gives the holder the right, but not the obligation, to buy a specific number of shares or another commodity at a specified price within a specified time period.

Canadian Investor Protection Fund: A protection fund established by the stock exchanges and the Investment Dealers Association (IDA) to protect investors from losses resulting from the failure of a member firm.

Capital Gain or Loss: The profit or loss generated from the sale of an investment.

Capital Stock: All shares that represent ownership of a corporation, including preferred and common stock.

Closed-End Mutual Fund: A mutual fund with a limited number of shares issued. When these shares have been sold, the fund is closed.

Collateral: The assets of a company that are pledged for security against a loan or other liability.

Commission: The fee charged by an individual who sells investments in return for buying or selling the investments.

Common Stock: A security that represents ownership in a company.

Compounded Rates of Return: Interest and capital gains accumulated over a period of time, which are added to the original investment as a percentage of the original investment.

Conglomerate: A corporation that operates in a variety of different industries.

Consumer Price Index (CPI): A measure of price changes in consumer goods.

Correction: An upward movement in the price of an individual stock or the stock market after a downward movement.

Coupon: A certificate entitling the owner to an interest payment from the bond issuer.

Crash: A steep drop in stock prices.

Credit Rating: An assessment of a company's credit history and its future ability to pay its debt obligations.

Current Yield: The annual income (interest and dividends) received from a security throughout the year, divided by the current market value of the security.

Cyclical Stock: A stock that is very sensitive to changes in economic conditions.

Day Order: An order to buy or sell a stock that is valid only for the trading day the order is given.

Day Trade: To purchase and sell a stock within the same day.

Debenture: Similar to a bond, but the collateral behind the debenture is only the general earning power of the company.

Default: A bond is considered in default when the issuer is no longer able to make regular interest payments. Bankruptcy may result from a company defaulting on its bond obligations.

Defensive Stock: The stock of a corporation with an excellent record of stable profits and dividend payments. Defensive stocks tend to outperform during bear markets.

Derivative Instrument: A financial instrument whose price is based on the value of another security.

Disposable Income: Income that is left after paying taxes, food, clothing, transportation, and shelter. The remainder can be saved or spent.

Distributions: Money received from your investments. Stocks can provide either dividends or capital gains. Mutual funds can provide income, dividends, or capital gains.

Diversification: Investing in more than one security or asset class in order to reduce the overall risk associated with making an investment in one security or asset class.

Dividend: A payment made by a corporation to shareholders from the company's profits. There is no legal obligation to pay a dividend on common shares.

Dollar Cost Averaging: Investing a fixed dollar amount into an investment on a regular basis to take advantage of volatility.

DJIA (Dow Jones Industrial Average): Average of the prices of 30 well-known, predominantly blue-chip, industrial stocks.

Earnings Momentum: A corporation's earnings per share that is continuously increasing from one period to the next.

Earnings per Share: The portion of the company's profits that can be attributed to one common share. If the company earned $1,000 and had 1,000 shares outstanding, the earnings per share would be $1.

Economic Indicators: Key statistics indicating the direction of the overall economy.

Equity: An ownership interest in a business or corporation.

Expense Ratio: The total fees paid by mutual fund investors, stated as a percentage of the total investment.

Fiscal Year or Period: A corporation's accounting (tax) year. A corporation's fiscal year can end in any month; an individual's fiscal year for tax purposes ends on December 31.

Fixed Annuity: An annuity with a fixed value and pay out. Typically these policies pay a specific sum of money on a perpetual basis.

Fixed Income Securities: Investments that generate a predictable and consistent flow of income or returns for investors. Fixed income mutual fund investments include money market mutual funds, Canadian bond funds, and international bond funds.

Forecasting: Predicting future stock market trends using existing data.

Front-End Load: A sales charge charged at the time of purchase of an investment.

Front Office: A term used to identify personnel who deal directly with the public for a brokerage firm.

Fundamental Analysis: The evaluation of a common stock based on the attractiveness of the company's financial statements.

Futures Contract: An agreement to either take or make delivery of a standardized commodity on a particular date.

Glamour Stock: Stocks that achieve a wide following because they consistently produce higher sales and earnings over a long term.

GNP (Gross National Product): The total value of goods and services produced by the economy in a given period. GNP is closely related to Gross Domestic Product (GDP).

Going Public (IPO): An industry term used to describe the initial public offering (IPO) or sale of shares of a privately held corporation to the public.

Graham and Dodd Method of Investing: This is an investment theory established in the 1930s by Benjamin Graham and David Dodd that is summarized in their book *Security Analysis*. Graham and Dodd believed that investors should buy stocks in companies that have undervalued assets.

Guaranteed Investment Certificate (GIC): A deposit investment available at all major banks and trust companies. GICs are non-redeemable until maturity and offer a predetermined rate of interest.

Hedge Fund: A specialized open or closed investment company that has the ability to use leverage, options, short selling, or other investment techniques.

High Flyer: A very speculative and high-risk stock that moves up or down considerably in the short-term.

High Grade Bond: A bond that is rated "AAA" or "AA" by Moody's or Standard & Poor's rating services.

High Yield Bond: A bond that is rated "BB" or lower by Moody's or Standard & Poor's rating services. These bonds pay a higher yield to offset the greater risk.

Home Run: A large gain obtained by an investor in a short time period.

Income Statement: A financial statement that discloses the corporation's sales revenue, expenditures, and profits during the fiscal period.

Index: A measure that indicates the status of a group of companies or investments. For example, the TSE 300 measures the performance of 300 of Canada's largest publicly traded companies.

Index Fund: A mutual fund that buys securities to match the securities that comprise a broad-based index such as the S&P 500 Index.

Inflation: The rise in the prices of goods and services.

Interest: Fee (or rent) charged by a lender to a borrower for the use of the lender's money.

Investment: The use of money to generate more money, to receive income, dividends, or capital gains.

Investment Counselor: An individual who is qualified to give investment advice for a fee.

Leverage: The strategy of borrowing money to invest. Investors hope to earn more on the invested money than they had to pay to borrow it, thereby generating a profit for themselves.

Liabilities: The debts of a company.

Limit Order: An order to buy or sell a security at a particular price or better. If a limit order can't be executed at that price or better, the order won't be executed. A specific time limit may be applied to the order.

Load: The portion of the investment that is used to pay selling expenses. Loads are common in many mutual funds.

Macroeconomics: Analysis of the overall economy using information such as unemployment, inflation, production, and price levels.

Majority Shareholder: A shareholder who controls more than half of the outstanding voting shares of a company.

Management Fee: An expense paid by a mutual fund to the investment advisor for managing the portfolio investments.

Negative Cash Flow: An accounting period where a company spends more cash than it receives.

Net Asset Value (NAV): The net asset value of a mutual fund is the actual value of each share. This is calculated by dividing the total value of the fund by the number of shares outstanding.

New York Stock Exchange (NYSE): The oldest and largest stock exchange in the United States. This stock exchange is commonly referred to as the "Big Board" or "The Exchange."

No-Load Funds: Mutual funds that can be purchased, sold, and owned without any commission charges. The only charges involved are management fees. Shares are sold at the net asset value price, and no salesperson is paid to sell the shares.

No Transaction Fee (NTF) Program: A program that allows investors to buy hundreds of different no-load funds within the same account without paying any transaction fees. The program is so popular that even full-service brokerage firms are beginning to follow this practice.

Open-End Mutual Fund: A mutual fund that imposes no limit on the number of shares that can be issued, and thus will issue and redeem shares at an investor's request.

Overvalued: A security whose price is not justified by its future prospects and thus should eventually decline.

Penny Stock: A stock that is priced at less than $1 a share. Penny stocks are very volatile and speculative.

P/E Ratio: The price of a stock divided by the yearly earnings per share. It compares the price of a stock relative to its earnings, which is important to know when you compare one stock to another. It is also important in determining if a stock is under- or over-priced relative to other stocks.

Privately Held Company: A company whose shares are not publicly traded. Privately held stock is issued to a small number of shareholders, and the value or price of the stock is usually determined by comparisons with other similar companies, using factors such as earnings and gross income.

Pro-Forma Financial Statements: Financial statements that are used to project the estimated financial results of a new company. They consist of an income statement, balance sheet, and cash flow statement.

Prospectus: A document that details all material information about a mutual fund or security being issued. A prospectus must be given to all buyers and potential buyers of the new issue.

Qualified Plans: A plan that allows an individual to make a pre-tax deposit and have income tax deferred. A registered company pension plan allows employees to deposit part of their incomes in the plan with the tax-deferred privilege. A registered retirement savings plan (RRSP) is the only other type of qualified plan. An individual can select from a large number of different investments.

Quantitative Analysis: The study and analysis of numerical financial information for the basis of decision making. The principle of quantitative theory is that everything is expressed in measurable form and is therefore also predictable. Investors who use this theory believe that by studying specific market data they can accurately predict the market's movements.

Rally: A stock market rise that follows a period of stock market decline.

Relative Strength: A graphic illustration of the percentage (or fractional) difference between the price of a security and an index (or any other security). If the security and index rise and fall equally at the same time, the graph would be a straight line.

RESP (Registered Education Savings Plan): An investment vehicle for saving for your child's or grandchild's post-secondary education. Contributions made to RESPs aren't deductible for tax purposes, but the income earned in the plan grows tax-free.

Return on Investment (ROI): A company's ROI can be calculated by dividing the net income by the amount of capital invested in the company. There are two ways to increase ROI: reduce expenses or increase sales. An individual's ROI is equal to net proceeds of investment divided by initial investment.

Risk: A measurable possibility of losing money.

RRIF (Registered Retirement Income Fund): An income plan that can be purchased at any time and that provides a stream of income.

RRSP (Registered Retirement Savings Plan): A savings plan that allows individuals who have not reached age 69 to set aside money for retirement within certain limits.

Sales Charges: Several purchase options are available when you buy mutual funds. Back-end load (also referred to as deferred sales charge or redemption charge) means a charge may be applied when you sell mutual fund units, payable to the mutual fund company. Front-end load means the sales charge is applied at the time you purchase mutual fund units, payable to the mutual fund company. A no-load fund doesn't charge a sales fee for buying and selling your shares.

Secondary Market: Any market where previously issued securities are traded. The Toronto Stock Exchange (TSE) is the best-known example in Canada. Here investors can buy and sell stocks from each other through the Exchange.

Shareholders' Equity: The ownership interest in the firm by common shareholders. The shareholders' or owners' equity in the firm is equal to the firm's assets minus the firm's liabilities.

Stock: *See* Common Stock.

Specialty Fund: A mutual fund that invests in the stocks of a particular industry, such as the oil and gas, technology, or real estate industry.

Subsidiary: A company that is owned by another company through the ownership of 50 per cent or more of the common shares outstanding.

Take a Flier: Investing in a security with the full knowledge that the investment is highly risky.

Target Savings Goal (TSG): The amount of money required each year to build a portfolio large enough to support your preferred standard of living at retirement.

Technical Analysis: Using charts to read the price history and other statistical patterns of stocks or mutual funds. Many investors and most professionals use these charts to make investment decisions. A technical analyst is also known as a chartist.

Total Return: The percentage return of a portfolio, which includes dividends, interest, and capital gains. Total return is also known as portfolio performance.

Underwriter: A brokerage firm that handles the process of offering a company's stock to the public through an initial public offering.

Value Manager: A manager who searches for undervalued stocks that are priced below what the manager actually thinks they're worth. The goal of the value-oriented manager is to sell at a profit once the market realizes the stock's true value.

Variable Annuity: An annuity that works the same way a fixed annuity does except its value and paid-out amount vary according to the performance of a portfolio of mutual funds from which the contract holder can select.

Vos Value Rating (VVR): Measures a mutual fund's performance, underlying risk, and balance between risk and reward.

Withholding: The keeping back of either earned income, or interest or dividend payment by an employer or institution for remittance to Revenue Canada.

Yield: The percentage return on an investment.

Zero-Coupon Bond: A bond that provides no annual or semi-annual interest payments, and is issued at a fraction of its par value—just like a strip bond.

▮▮ Index